THE REAL
CUSTER

THE REAL

CUSTER

FROM BOY GENERAL
TO TRAGIC HERO

JAMES S. ROBBINS

REGNERY
HISTORY

ISBN 978-1-62157-209-1

Robbins, James S., 1962-
  The real Custer : from boy general to tragic hero / James S. Robbins.
     pages cm
  Includes bibliographical references.
  ISBN 978-1-62157-209-1
  1. Custer, George A. (George Armstrong), 1839-1876. 2. Generals--United States--Biography. 3. United States--History--Civil War, 1861-1865--Biography. 4. United States--History--Civil War, 1861-1865--Campaigns. 5. Indians of North America--Wars--1866-1895. 6. Indians of North America--Wars--Great Plains. 7. United States. Army--Biography. I. Title.
  E467.1.C99R67 2014
  973.8'2092--dc23
  [B]
                        2014006108

Published in the United States by
Regnery Publishing
A Salem Communications Company
300 New Jersey Avenue NW
Washington, DC 20001
www.Regnery.com

Manufactured in the United States of America

10 9 8 7 6 5 4 3 2 1

Books are available in quantity for promotional or premium use. For information on discounts and terms, please visit our website: www.Regnery.com.

Distributed to the trade by
Perseus Distribution
250 West 57th Street
New York, NY 10107

To E. L. R.

CONTENTS

LIST OF ILLUSTRATIONS

Mathew Brady, *George Armstrong Custer*.

I have so much to be thankful for in my life. God grant that I may always prove as deserving as I am grateful to Him for what He has given me. In years long numbered with the past, when I was merging upon manhood, my every thought was ambitious—not to be wealthy, not to be learned, but to be great. I desired to link my name with acts and men, and in such a manner as to be a mark of honor, not only to the present, but to future generations.

—GEORGE ARMSTRONG CUSTER

When you mention the name George Custer, most people first think of his Last Stand at the Little Bighorn. His was a tragic death, some even argue a foolish or needless one. Others see him as the Civil War–era "Boy General with the Golden Locks," at twenty-three the youngest general officer to that point in American history. From Gettysburg to Appomattox, Custer led every charge, as Abraham Lincoln said, "with a whoop and a shout." Or maybe Custer's fight with the Cheyenne on the Washita River comes to mind, which some called a significant battlefield victory, while others saw only a senseless massacre.

Custer is talked about, written about, debated, loved, and hated. His name has come to symbolize tragedy, recklessness, valor, and disaster. He has been lionized and demonized, admired and mocked. Much of his history has been denounced as myth, but his celebrity is rooted firmly

in reality. Custer became a legend for good reason. But whether elevated
to heroic perfection or denounced as a fiend, Custer the symbol has
overcome Custer the man.

The real Custer is more complex and interesting than the one-
dimensional caricatures he has often been reduced to in popular culture.
Custer was a polarizing figure even in his day, with strong supporters
and detractors. Biographers have grappled with this duality from the
start. Frederick Whittaker's influential though embellished account of
Custer's life came out the year George died, but even Whittaker felt it
necessary to address the Custer legend that had grown up during his
lifetime. "The popular idea of Custer as a soldier," Whittaker wrote, "is
that of a brave, reckless, dashing trooper, always ready to charge any
odds, without knowing or caring what was the strength of his enemy,
and trusting to luck to get out of his scrapes." But he argued that "the
real Custer" was "a remarkably quiet, thoughtful man, when any work
was on hand, one who never became flurried and excited in the hottest
battle." He also claimed Custer had never been caught by surprise, which
was not true, and was "equal to any emergency of whatever kind," which
may have been true until it wasn't.[1]

As for trusting to luck, throughout the Army the expression "Custer's
luck" meant having the good fortune to get out of trouble—until it came
to mean the opposite. "'Custer's luck' will no longer be so much envied
by his brother soldiers," journalist and Civil War veteran George Edward
Pound wrote four months after Little Bighorn. But Pound admired
Custer and said he "would not have so praised his luck had he not confided more in his courage," and that his fortune was not in the stars "but
in his own soul—the born spirit of the cavalryman that flowered into
exploits."[2]

What is it about Custer that makes him one of the most talked about
figures in American history?[3] Even in his day, Custer was a magnet for
attention. With his striking presence and unconventional uniforms, he

attracted comment wherever he went. But what he did once he had that attention is what made him memorable. He was talked about, but that was because he gave people something worth talking about. He cultivated an eccentric image, but he was more than simply the nineteenth-century equivalent of tabloid fodder.

At base, Custer was a hardened warrior. In the Vietnam War film *We Were Soldiers*, Lieutenant Colonel Hal Moore, portrayed by Mel Gibson, wonders aloud, "What was going through Custer's mind when he realized that he'd led his men into a slaughter?" Sergeant Major Basil Plumley, played by Sam Elliott, growls, "Sir, Custer was a pussy. You ain't." The expression soon appeared on bumper stickers and t-shirts. But even if Plumley said it, which is doubtful, it is far from the truth. Custer was physically brave and morally courageous. As his bugler Joseph Fought said, "He was always in the fight, no matter where it was." As a junior officer, he went out of his way to place himself in danger. As a commanding officer, he led from the front. To paraphrase the real Hal Moore, the only thing he had in the Ia Drang Valley that Custer didn't at Little Bighorn was air support.

Custer has been portrayed frequently in movies and television, in characters from the heroic to the absurd. He was a well-meaning fool in 2009's *Night at the Museum: Battle of the Smithsonian* who lamented, "I will always be famous for my biggest failure." Richard Mulligan played him as a volatile, arrogant clown in *Little Big Man* in 1970. Ronald Reagan, a self-described Custer buff, portrayed him in the historically challenged 1940 feature, *Santa Fe Trail*. "His image has been blurred and distorted over time," the Gipper wrote, "but in truth he was a brilliant officer and not at all the boastful show-off his detractors would have us believe."[4] Errol Flynn's interpretation of Custer in *They Died with Their Boots On* in 1941 also took some liberties with history but was a popular and critical success. Flynn best captured George's boyish spirit and charm, and the movie shaped perceptions of Custer for decades.

The continuing fascination with Custer stems partly from his contradictions. He was a good friend who inspired loyalty, but his outsized personality could provoke bitter rivalries. He was a devoted husband whose natural flirtatiousness opened him to rumors of infidelity. He didn't go to church, but he prayed before every battle. He was a lifelong Democrat who had to downplay his political views to placate radical Republicans. He was the scourge of the Confederacy but a close friend to many rebels. He was Sitting Bull's foe but said that if he had been born an Indian, he also would have abandoned the reservations to ride free on the Plains.

Custer lives strongest in the American memory as an Indian fighter, and while he criticized aspects of Native American culture, he also found much to admire. He took to the field against bands the government deemed hostile, but he said there was nothing better than living side by side with tribes at peace. He studied and attempted to understand the people of the Plains and was sometimes compared to them—the officer with the "heart of an Indian" who "charged like a Sioux chieftain." Custer was as willing to smoke the peace pipe as he was prepared to fight. But as a soldier, he followed orders, and his primary concern was achieving victory. He killed Indians in battle, just as he killed Confederates in the Civil War, and in greater numbers. He burned Native American lodges, just as he scoured the Shenandoah Valley. Whether in the West or the East, he said he preferred peace. But when the sword was drawn, he was determined to make war his way until the enemy was vanquished.

Custer did not do it all alone. His wife, Elizabeth, was his lifelong love and constant focus of his thoughts. He was very close to his family, and his brother Tom served by his side to the end. There were also the men he led into battle, his officers and staff who helped translate his orders into action, and especially his superiors, most notably Generals George McClellan, Alfred Pleasonton, and Philip Sheridan. These senior officers possessed the insight to understand how to use Custer's talents,

how much initiative to let him have, and what risks he could reasonably take. The Custer they knew was a gifted tactician who had the ability quickly to sum up the shifting situation he faced and use the forces at his disposal swiftly and effectively. They set the stage for him, and he did his part to win their battles. And when necessary, they helped keep their adventurous protégé out of trouble.

Custer had a talent for getting into scrapes. As a cadet at West Point, he believed that rules were made to be broken. He was the merry prankster of the Corps of Cadets, the lovable rogue who did things his way, witty, charismatic, and popular. And while there were others like him who courted the retribution of the authorities, Custer had an uncanny ability to get himself out of trouble as artfully as he got into it. He racked up demerits but stayed just below the line that brought expulsion. He submitted to periodic punishments as the price of playing the game. Whether it was due to his charm, good fortune, or intuition, he managed to live the life of the cadet *bon vivant* and still graduate, albeit at the bottom of his class, and facing a court-martial the day before graduation.

Custer's West Point exploits give insights into his combat leadership. He was a creative thinker and dynamic problem-solver. The sense of adventure that led him to blow post in the middle of the night for the forbidden pleasures of Benny Havens's saloon was the same spirit that led him to volunteer for dangerous wartime scouting missions or lead dramatic charges against difficult odds. He could have done much better at the Academy if he had followed more rules, studied more lessons, avoided demerits, and played fewer pranks; but then he would not have been Custer.

Custer made things happen. He came from a humble background and got ahead on ability and pluck. He was a risk taker who traded on his accomplishments, not his background or birth. He would rather shape events than be shaped by them. He was at his best in situations where dash and quick decisions were needed. He was comfortable on the knife-edge of reality, where will, idea, and circumstance merge in an onrushing wave. He arrived on the national scene at the right time, a natural warfighter thrust into the greatest conflict of the nineteenth century. He wound up in situations where he could give full expression to his instinctive genius for war and was rewarded with rank, fame, and influence. But when the Civil War ended, Custer had trouble adapting. There were fewer battles to be fought, less opportunity to give expression to his spirit. He had to reinvent himself while staying true to his character. It was a challenge he faced for the rest of his life.

John M. Bulkley recalled Custer as the "genial, warm-hearted friend" from his childhood, and wrote that "under the garb of the soldier, and the sometimes austere exterior, there beat the warmest of hearts, and existed the most affectionate of natures." Bulkley believed that the Custer he knew would long be remembered. "The gallant bravery, the spirit, and the patriotism of Custer commended him to public favor," he wrote, "and it is not in the heart of the American people soon to forget those whose blood has been shed in their name."[5] Custer has not been forgotten, but he is commonly misremembered. This book explores the real Custer.

PART ONE

BEGINNINGS

The Innate Idea, in D. H. Strother, "Personal Recollections of the War, by a Virginian," *Harper's New Monthly Magazine* (1868).

CHAPTER ONE

"MY VOICE IS FOR WAR!"

George Armstrong Custer was born December 5, 1839, in the east Ohio town of New Rumley in Harrison County, which his great-uncle Jacob helped found in 1812. A period guide said New Rumley was "situated on a high, healthy site" and had a population of about 150 people in thirty houses, with a meetinghouse, a school, two physicians, three stores, and three taverns.[1] It was typical of the small towns found in that part of the country, where most people worked the land and community life was strong.

George—who was called Autie, for how he pronounced his middle name when learning to talk—was a charismatic child with bright blue eyes and curly red-gold hair. He was born into a growing, close-knit family. His father, Emmanuel Henry Custer, was a thirty-three-year-old blacksmith from Cresaptown in western Maryland, descended from Arnold Küster, from the northwest German town of Kaldenkirchen, who migrated to America sometime around the turn of the eighteenth century. Custer and his second wife, Maria Ward Kirkpatrick, would eventually have seven sons and one daughter, in addition to four children from his previous marriage.[2]

"Father was pretty strict," George's younger brother Nevin Custer recalled, "stricter than most fathers nowadays are, I guess. He made us ride to church a-horseback every Sunday morning, and mother and Margaret came in the cart, and we had to sit there and never so much as smile."[3] Nevin said his father "worked the farm just the same way. Everybody had his work cut out an' he had to do it without whimpering and do it promptly; sort of religious duty, yuh know." When the kids worked the family farm, Emmanuel would put them fifty yards apart in the corn field "so we couldn't loaf and talk." They worked hard, but young George hated to get his clothes smelly, so he split and carried wood while his brothers worked in the barns.

The Custer kids attended the local public school—Ohio had established a public education system under the 1787 Northwest Ordinance—and they received a decent education for those times. George was a studious child who loved to read, and he would occasionally get a talking-to if he took a book into the fields. George was "bright as a dollar and never missed a recitation," Nevin recalled. While the other kids were "swimmmin' and boatin' and all that," Autie "always wanted to stay home and read." But George had a fun-loving side. He was friendly, outgoing, and mischievous, the latter a quality he got from his father, who, for all his seriousness at church or in the field, said he was "always a boy with my boys."[4] George's cousin Mary said George was "full of life and always ready to do anything which had a semblance of daring in it."[5]

The children of New Rumley were taught by Mr. Foster, a strict disciplinarian who did not take misbehavior lightly. "Lawsey, how that man could whip!" Nevin recalled, decades later. He was punished for whispering in class, while Tom Custer was in frequent trouble for chewing tobacco at school. Tom "bored a hole in the school room floor with an auger to give him a place to spit," Nevin said. "He tried to keep it covered with his foot, but of course after [a] while Foster found it and Tom got licked." Foster would make children stand with their toes on one crack of the wooden floor and their hands on another while he lashed them with a birch rod. "No teachers like them nowadays," Nevin mused.

But George was one of Foster's favorites and somehow avoided punishment. "George kept his geography on top of his paper backed novels," Nevin recalled. "He used to read 'em all the time in school, but Foster never caught him. ... Foster'd come along and pat George on the head, and then yank up the rest of us." The kids got Foster back once by locking him out of the schoolhouse for not giving them the customary treats at holiday time. When Foster tried to come in a window, they kept him at bay with a coal shovel they heated in the stove. "I guess we all got licked for that," Nevin said, "except George. George wasn't in it. He was home studying. Always studying."

George was exposed to martial matters from a young age. His father, like most able-bodied men in the community, was a member of the local "cornstalk militia" unit, the confidently named New Rumley Invincibles. When he was four years old, Autie began to follow the men in their drills, running through the manual of arms with a small, wooden musket. Emmanuel had a little uniform made for George, and he became something of a mascot for the unit. The militiamen called Autie "a born soldier." After George mimicked some classic oratory his brother was learning at school, father Custer took George to the drill, and "the child, in uniform, was lifted to the counter of the village store among the militiamen and, waving his sword, announced what proved to be the watchword of his future. ... My voice is for war!"[6]

At age thirteen George moved to Monroe, Michigan, to live with the family of his older half-sister, Lydia Reed. Monroe was founded as Frenchtown and was the site of an 1812 battle in which the British and their Indian allies, led by the Shawnee chief Tecumseh, defeated the Americans.[7] Custer entered the recently founded Boys and Young Men's Academy, presided over by principal Alfred Stebbins, "an accomplished instructor from the eastern states," according to John McClelland Bulkley, who as a boy shared a desk with Custer at the academy.[8] Stebbins' Academy was advertised as a "school for boys, exclusively, where they could enjoy all the comforts and privileges of home, and at the same time be fitted for any of the colleges and universities of the United States."[9] Students came to the academy from as far away as Chicago, Cleveland, and Buffalo.

"In the school were some of the brightest young men of the day," Bulkley recalled, "and their names were found among the makers of history in the nation and honored in all the walks of civil life and military renown."[10] He believed that the "superior facilities of this school and the greatly improved social environments produced a most favorable effect upon the formation of [George's] character."[11] When the school closed, Bulkley purchased the old desk he had shared with Custer that bore the initials they had carved into it.

George was still studious, but even more mischievous. One of his boyhood teachers confronted the young man after being caught misbehaving:

> "I know it was wrong, but I could not help it."
> "Could not help it?"
> "No, Sir. I wanted to do it."
> "But could you not restrain your impulses?"
> "Don't know, Sir—never tried."

"But don't you think you ought to try?"

"What if I could; but I don't feel like trying."[12]

Monroe would have an enduring hold on young George because there he met the love of his life. Custer did odd jobs for Judge Daniel S. Bacon, a local civic leader and one of the organizers of Stebbins's school. One day, as he passed by the Bacon home, the judge's thirteen-year-old daughter, Libbie, called out to him from the gate, "Hello, you Custer boy!" and then ran into the house. It was their first meeting, and though they would not speak again for years, that brief encounter was memorable for both of them.

"I can remember about the days on the farm and how 'fraid George was of the girls and bashful," his brother Nevin recalled. "Why he'd blush as red as a tablecloth whenever a girl came his way." But when it came to Libbie, his bashfulness vanished. Her spontaneous greeting to him "just won George right over."

Several things conspired to keep the youngsters apart. One was their relative social standing: Elizabeth Bacon was from a leading family in the town, and George Custer, bluntly, was not. There was also a difference in ages. And there was timing; George was soon to graduate from Stebbins' Academy and return to Ohio. However, "it was love at first sight for Custer," one of his former officers later wrote, "and although they did not meet again for several years, he was determined to win the owner of those brown eyes."[13]

Back in Ohio, George used his Stebbins diploma to secure work as a teacher in the one-room Beech Point schoolhouse in the town of Hopedale, ten miles southeast of New Rumley. "Us younger boys always expected to grow up on the farm," Nevin said, "but George didn't. He wanted to teach school right off." In addition, George was apprenticing as a cabinetmaker. He would return home every other week, using part of his dollar-a-day teaching salary to help with the family finances. "He was handsome, tall, straight, well built, quick and agile," a local recalled, "with a clear and sparkling eye, well chiseled features, and a compact head, which made him a youth of mark even in that little town, among his play fellows."[14]

George was popular with the children, was very animated in the classroom, and as he was only a teenager himself, was known to roughhouse with the older boys. But his youth made it difficult for him to command respect. When he was teaching at a district school near Cadiz at age seventeen, he lost control of the situation and the boys took over the schoolhouse. "They tossed him about like a baby, and the girls themselves even joined in the melee to laugh at and abuse him."[15] George was so humiliated that he went home and cried. In those days he did not show qualities of daring or heroism, according to a contemporary: "Quite the reverse. He was more distinguished for good looks, quick movements and gentlemanly demeanor than for courageous boyish exploits."[16]

But after the humiliating incident at the school, George summoned the courage he previously lacked. One night at Hopedale, he was sitting near a window and "some big fellow on the outside was standing at the window making faces at him and calling him 'Baby!' 'Baby Custer!' 'Oh dear, little darling!'" Custer jumped up and "quick as lightning said, 'Damn you!' and ran his fist through the glass, striking the fellow full in the face." His tormenter was more surprised than injured, and George cut his hand badly. But as one observer noted, the incident "gave him a standing for courage that he had never maintained before."[17]

A local resident recalled that around this time, George was "remarkable only for brightness and aptness, and even in that not to an extraordinary degree. He was generally popular on account of his urbanity, and was sort of a favorite among the girls because he was rather good looking." He eschewed manual labor and "was more fond of roaming over the country and loafing at the corners than attending to the trade to which he was apprenticed." Custer did not seem to be destined for greatness. "I presume if Custer had not made such a famous career in his after life that his boyhood would have been passed over as one of perfect mediocrity," the townsman said. "At least then his future was not marked very high."[18]

But George harbored greater ambitions than being a rural schoolteacher or Ohio cabinetmaker. He wanted to be a famous soldier or, failing that, a great educator at an eastern college. Given his circumstances, the most direct route to achieve this was through the United States Military Academy. "I think [West Point] is the best place that I could go," he wrote his sister in 1856.[19] "Mother is much opposed to me going there, but Father and David are in favor of it very much." His mother had always envisioned George taking the cloth like the Methodist preacher he was named after. But Emmanuel approved of the idea in principle. The trick then was getting an appointment.

Custer's family lived in Ohio's competitive Twenty-First District, which had shifted over the years between Democratic, Whig, and other parties.[20] Emmanuel was a Jacksonian Democrat and a man of strong convictions. "He was an ardent, impulsive Methodist, and a staunch, uncompromising Democrat," one profile noted. "People who did not believe as he did in either way he would not even argue with, unless the argument was all on his side."[21]

"Father Custer was a man of fire and intense feeling," Elizabeth Custer recalled, "and though he exhorted in the prayer meetings Sunday, politics and patriotism were equally as much a religion to him weekdays."[22]

George followed in his father's outspoken partisan footsteps. Unfortunately, their member of Congress was John A. Bingham, elected in 1854 on the post-Whig Opposition party ticket and reelected in 1856 as a Republican.[23] Under most circumstances the congressman would not be expected to grant his allotted seat at West Point to a vocal member of the opposing party.

"Bingham was a Republican and Pap was a Democrat," Nevin said, "and we didn't think George would ever get anything." Father Custer recalled that George "asked me once to see Congressman Bingham about getting him an appointment to West Point. Bingham and I were opposed politically, and I didn't want to ask him to do anything for me or mine." But George went ahead anyway, "stole a march on his father and asked Bingham himself."[24]

"I received a letter, a real boy's letter, that captivated me," Bingham recalled. "Written in a boyish hand, but firmly, legibly, it told me that the writer ... wanted to be a soldier, wanted to go to West Point, and asked what steps he should take regarding it." The letter read,

> Dear Mr. Bingham: I am told you can send a boy to West Point. I am also told that you don't care whether he is a Democrat boy or a Republican boy. I am a Democrat boy and I want to go to West Point and learn to be a soldier so I can fight for my country.
>
> Sincerely yours,
> GEORGE A. CUSTER.

"Struck by its originality, its honesty," Bingham said, "I replied at once."[25]

Bingham "took a fancy to him," a local politician recalled. "He saw that there was something in the young man and so pushed him along. Bingham was a good judge of boys, as well as of men, and he could see that Custer's bright eyes, quick perception and fluent manners marked for him a successful career, if he ever had a chance to show himself. Bingham determined to give him a chance."[26]

Bingham's nomination letter for George describes him as "17, 5'9 3/4", good health, no deformity, reads well, spells correctly, writes a fair and legible hand, able to perform with facility and accuracy the ground rules of arithmetic, fully possesses all the qualifications physical, mental, and moral required." It was an accurate, if not dazzling description. But the hopeful applicant was also aided from an unexpected quarter.

While teaching, George roomed at the home of a local farmer named Alexander Holland, who was influential in Republican circles. Holland made an appeal to Bingham on Custer's behalf and helped secure the appointment. He might have fallen under the Custer charm and wanted to help the earnest young man realize his ambitions. Or he might have had another motive—namely, breaking up a budding romance. While staying at the Holland house, George formed a close relationship with the farmer's daughter Mary. In one letter to her, he wrote, "You occupy the first place in my affections, and the only place as far as love is concerned." After alluding to the possibility of marriage, he concludes, "I will talk with you about it when I see you next at the trundle-bed. Farewell, my only Love, until we meet again—From your true and faithful Lover, Bachelor Boy."

"Bingham appointed him in spite of politics," Nevin said. "Men was honester then than they are now—and if you ever saw a crazy youngster it was George." The congressman's recommendation was approved, and George's appointment letter for the Academy arrived in early 1857, signed by Secretary of War Jefferson Davis.

CHAPTER TWO

CUSTER THE GOAT

"I never heard anything of his successes at West Point," Libbie recalled. "It was a tale of demerits, of lessons unlearned, of narrow escapes from dismissal, of severe punishments, but all told in so merry a way and the very caressing tone of his voice proving that nothing was dearer to him than the four years of his life as a cadet."[1] George cautioned that his "career as a cadet had but little to commend it to the study of those who came after me, unless as an example to be carefully avoided."

Like most "animals" or "beasts," as the new arrivals were (and still are) called, George Custer's introduction to West Point life was three months of drill, servitude, and sleeping in tents. When he arrived at the Academy in the summer of 1857, the cadets were in their summer encampment on the Plain. One new arrival described encampment as "a time of joy and merriment to the old cadets, but a time of trouble and fatigue to the new ones. The new cadets are compelled to clean the parade ground, before the tents, in the tent, make the beds, clean the ditches, bring water, while the old cadets fiddle, dance, sing, get drunk and be merry."[2] But the indignities of the encampment did not seem to make an impression on young George, and a few months into his stay, he wrote his sister, "I like West Point as well if not better than I did at first."[3]

George easily made friends in the Corps. His natural charisma and easygoing, fun-loving personality resonated among his peers. Morris Schaff observed his inborn qualities: "His nature, so full of those streams that rise, so to speak, among the high hills of our being. I have in mind his joyousness, his attachment to the friends of his youth, and his never-ending delight in talking about his old home."[4] George quickly established himself as one of the Academy's lovable rogues. Then-plebe John Montgomery Wright recalled the scene in August 1859 when the cadets who had been on furlough were returning through the gate, and the cry went up "from a hundred throats … 'Here comes Custer!'" Wright saw "an undeveloped looking youth, with a poor figure, slightly rounded shoulders, and an ungainly walk…. an indifferent soldier, a poor student and a perfect incorrigible … a roystering, reckless cadet, always in trouble, always playing some mischievous pranks, and liked by everyone." A few nights later, in one of the traditional West Point initiations of the day, a laughing Custer "yanked" Wright from his tent, dragged him in his blanket across the Plain, and sent him flying down the slope.[5]

Like most cadets, Autie picked up nicknames, such as "Fanny," for his long hair and peaches-and-cream complexion. It was an unbecoming moniker for a warrior, but cadets could be harsh with those who too obviously paid attention to their grooming. He was called "Curly" for his curly locks, which coincidentally was Crazy Horse's boyhood name. He tried to keep his curls under control using cinnamon-scented hair oils, which were the style of the time, but this made matters worse, and he became known as "Cinnamon." He then sought to dispense with all hair-related names and shaved his head. However, now Custer faced reports for having his hair too short, so he wore a wig to stay within regulations until his hair grew out.[6]

The cycle of life at West Point was well established by the time Cadet Custer arrived. The structure, traditions, and importance of the Academy were firmly rooted. The academic system devised by Superintendent Sylvanus Thayer forty years earlier had remained largely unchanged. Cadets experienced a mix of academic and tactical instruction geared toward producing what the institution believed was the ideal officer. The academic curriculum was focused on mathematics, drawing, language, and some history and liberal arts. Military lessons included infantry, artillery, cavalry tactics, and practical leadership lessons. Discipline was strict, and daily life was highly regimented. The most notable difference between the Thayer system and the West Point of Custer's day was the addition of a fifth year, which was instituted a few years earlier by Secretary of War Davis, who was an 1828 grad. When Davis fought to preserve the extra year as a senator, a Georgia cadet wished he would go to hell, but then quickly said, "No, I take that all back; for I believe the day is coming when the South will have need of Mr. Davis' abilities."[7]

The first big hurdle in a cadet's academic career was the series of first-year midterm exams. This was the largest winnowing of any incoming class. "Our January examination is over now and I am glad of it," George wrote after the 1858 exam. "I passed my examination very creditably but there were a great many found deficient and sent off…. My class which numbered over 100 when we entered in June is now reduced to 69. This shows that if a person wants to get along here he has to study hard."[8]

The end-of-year exam was another milestone that could potentially be disastrous for an unprepared cadet. The trial lasted over two weeks and covered all aspects of the cadet curriculum. The 1858 exam claimed more plebes from Custer's class, but he was not among them. "I am glad that I can say that I went through my examination in a manner that did honor not only to myself but to my instructors also," George wrote from his second encampment.[9] He had come in fifty-eighth of the sixty-two who passed. "I am now one class higher than I was before," he continued. "I am well and have been well all the time. I would not leave this place for any amount of money because I would rather have a good education and no money than to have a fortune and be ignorant."

If Autie got a good education at the Academy, it was despite himself. Custer's poor academic performance at West Point is part of Academy lore. George was consistently in the last academic section, known as "The Immortals," and also performed poorly in tactical instruction. But not everyone who wound up at the bottom was there because they could not cope with the curriculum. Cadet Custer had a sound educational background and clearly could have done better if he had chosen to. But George was part of a long line of West Point cadets who did not care about class rank and were content to use the time they might have been studying (or "boning," as cadets said) to socialize, play pranks, or engage in other forbidden pursuits. The least able cadets and those with severe disciplinary problems would wash out early. Those left at the bottom were either working diligently to hang on or, like Cadet Custer, taking it all in a carefree spirit, knowing they could pull out a minimal passing grade at the last minute.

Custer might also have been gaming his likely branch assignment. In those days there was a fairly rigid system of branching, with top cadets being assigned to engineers, artillery, and ordinance, and those with lower grades sent to the infantry, dragoons, mounted rifles, or cavalry. George noted that "the cavalry offered the most promising field for early promotion,"[10] and he enjoyed his daily riding lesson. Custer was "the beau ideal of a perfect horseman," by one account. "He sat in the saddle as if born in it, for his seat was so very easy and graceful that he and his steed seemed one. At West Point he was at the head of all the classes in horsemanship and delighted in being on the tanbark. It is related of him that he could cut down more wooden heads on the gallop than any other one of the cadets."[11] But while Custer developed a reputation as an expert rider, this did not translate into military proficiency, and his worst grades in his final year were in cavalry tactics.

Anecdotes of Custer in the classroom relate his happy-go-lucky attitude toward his studies. He once asked his Spanish instructor how to say "class dismissed" in Spanish, and when the instructor answered, Custer led the class out of the room. In French class he was bidden to translate *Léopold, duc d'Autriche, se mettit sur les plaines de Silesie*, and began, "Leopard, duck and ostrich met upon the plains of Silesia."[12] John Montgomery Wright said that Custer's bravery in battle did not surprise anyone who had seen him "walking up with calm deliberation to the head of the section-room to face the instructors with the confession that he knew nothing of his lesson."[13]

Custer was not a great reader at West Point. While he read much in the years before he reached the Academy, he did not check out a library book once after his plebe year. Studying was something to be done only when absolutely necessary, usually before an exam. In the winter of his third, or "cow," year, while prepping for the January exam, he complained that the lessons were "twice as long in reviewing as when they first were given out" and that he was studying "almost night and day to make up for lost time."[14]

Tully McCrea of the Class of 1862, a fellow Ohioan who roomed with Custer his first year at West Point, observed that "the great difficulty is that he is too clever for his own good. He is always connected with all the mischief that is going on and never studies any more than he can possibly help." Yet, Tully "admired and partly envied Custer's free and careless way, and the perfect indifference he had for everything. It was all right with him whether he knew his lesson or not; he did not allow it to trouble him."[15]

In his first summer at the Academy, Custer noted that he was "becoming accustomed to the strict discipline and [had] escaped with but few demerit marks." In fact, he had earned twelve demerits in his first month, a reasonable total for a beast. "Though some find it difficult to avoid," he continued, "getting this number at one hundred and fifty marks [in a single semester] would dismiss a person and as some offenses give one a five demerit a person has to be very careful in his conduct."[16] Custer did not take his own advice to heart. Peter Michie, second in the Class of 1863 and for thirty years a leading professor at West Point, recalled that "Custer was constantly in trouble with the school authorities…. He had more fun, gave his friends more anxiety, walked more tours of extra guard, and came nearer being dismissed more often than any other cadet I have ever known."[17] Morris Schaff, of the Class of 1862, wrote that the Academy "has had many a character to deal with; but it may be a question whether it ever had a cadet so exuberant, one who cared so little for its serious attempts to elevate and burnish, or one on whom its tactical officers kept their eyes so constantly and unsympathetically searching as upon Custer."[18]

Custer's mischief was frowned on by the authorities but was part of cadet life and tradition. Cadets found a variety of prohibited ways to amuse themselves in their off-hours, such as smoking, drinking, playing cards, having "hash parties" of contraband food, and other amusements. They played cat and mouse with the tactical officers who tried to catch them in the act. The cadets used a variety of subterfuges to trick the Tacs, such as tapping codes on the barracks' heating pipes to alert others to surprise inspections. Cadets like Custer who lived on upper floors could quickly put their rooms in order before the officers arrived.[19] But institutional memory worked against them; some of the Tacs had been in their position years earlier when they were cadets and knew all the tricks. So for example Custer thought he had secured his cooking utensils by hiding them in the chimney, until an officer "hived" his hidden hash kitchen during an inspection. George A. Woodruff of Custer's class, fated to die at Gettysburg, tells the story of a cadet, probably Autie, "hanging outside a fourth-story windowsill by his fingertips to escape the inspecting officer who was hunting up students out of their rooms after 'taps,' engaged, in this instance, in making molasses candy."[20]

Many cadets smoked, but not Custer. "Nothing could induce me to use tobacco either by smoking or chewing as I consider it a filthy, if not unhealthy, practice," he wrote his father. "I can say what very few of my age can, and that is I never 'chewed' of tobacco in my life and what is more I do not think I ever will."[21] However, he sought a letter of permission to smoke from his father, explaining that he wanted to be able to barter with his roommate. Smoking in the barracks was forbidden, and George was skinned more than once for having tobacco smoke in his room, since the cadet in charge of the room the day of the infraction got the demerits.

Custer also engaged in the tradition of hazing plebes and other unsuspecting cadets, whether "deviling" cadets on guard duty or "yanking" them from their tents in the middle of the night. Custer once stole a rooster belonging to Lieutenant Henry Douglass because the incessant crowing bothered him. He got rid of the evidence by eating the bird. Another cadet volunteered to throw away the feathers but carelessly left a trail of evidence leading back to him, and took the punishment.

Custer's record of delinquencies contains self-explanatory entries such as the night of July 9, 1860, when during encampment he was cited for "being out of his tent without hat, coat, or pants after 10:00 p.m." (one demerit) and for "interfering with a new cadet on guard" (five demerits). But some pranks were much more elaborate. Cadet Thomas Rowland, who was first in the Class of 1863 before he resigned to join the Confederacy, recalled the night in 1860 when some older cadets snuck into the rooms of sleeping plebes and stole all their clothes. The consequence, he wrote, was "the Plebes were half of them absent from reveille; the rest presented a most ridiculous appearance. All of them without hats, some in their stocking feet, no man with his own coat on, while from the windows above the others looked down with long faces and wrapped about with blankets, terrified to death at being reported absent from reveille, but 'not even an umbrella in case of a fire.'"[22]

Of course, with pranks came consequences. With characteristic self-mockery, George sketched a picture of the cadet guardhouse, a face peering through the barred windows, with the caption, "G. A. Custer's Summer Home on the Hudson."[23] Custer said his "offenses against law and order were not great in enormity, but what they lacked in magnitude they made up in number."[24] The record bears this out. Of his five and three-quarters folio pages of demerits, most were one- to two-point violations, some three to four, and a few fives. He was marked down for being late, talking, napping, being absent, skipping class, neglect of studies, collar turned up on coat, long hair, room in disorder, idling, visiting, laughing, throwing bread at dinner, trifling, loitering, being unshaven at inspection, having his hair brush out of place in his room, throwing snow balls, throwing stones, having a rusty musket, playing cards, riding despite being on sick report, and being absent from hospital when sick. In his first year, he racked up 151 demerits, the fifth highest in his class, other than those who were expelled.

The Custer legend contends that he holds the all-time record for demerits, and his total of 726 in four years is an impressive—or notorious—achievement. But the absolute demerit record was set decades earlier. Charles H. Larnard of Rhode Island, Class of 1831, had a career total of 1,658 demerits, and even racked up 729 in a single year, three more than Custer's four-year total. But partly because of Larnard, the Academy imposed a two-hundred-point annual demerit limit his final year. Anyone straying over that line, or receiving one hundred "skins" in a semester, risked expulsion. So neither Custer nor anyone else could get near the Larnard record. Also in earlier years, firsties (seniors) had 50 percent added to their demerit totals because they were expected to know better. This was done away with by Custer's day; by then, plebes were forgiven a third of their demerits in recognition of being "less experienced, and more likely to err."[25] So for example Custer's 151 total at the end of his plebe year reflected an earned 226 demerits minus one-third.[26] Given the changing rules and the two-hundred-point limit, the matter of the demerit record becomes somewhat subjective.

However, for his era Custer set a strong demerit pace that continued with few breaks right up to the end of his West Point career. He had ninety-seven demerits in the six months up to June 6, 1861, when the term ended. In the next three weeks, suspecting his class would graduate early, he racked up fifty-two more.

Cadets had a safety valve to clean up their demerit records. They could voluntarily "walk an extra," which, in Custer's words, "consisted in performing the tiresome duties of a sentinel during the unemployed hours of Saturday; hours usually given to recreation."[27] A tour lasted four hours, walking back and forth on a thirty-yard interval in full uniform with musket. Each tour would eliminate one demerit. Custer estimated he walked sixty-six Saturdays total, to stay within the one hundred-point semester limits. This might be a low estimate; from January through March 1860, he accumulated 129 demerits (fifty-three in February alone) and over the full semester walked off thirty of them.

Tully McCrae said that "extra guard duty is severe punishment, as I know from experience." He preferred confinement to quarters.[28] But in a letter home, Custer noted that "everything is fine" after describing punishment tours. They were a way of cleaning up his record and showing the authorities that he was committed to the institution and its ultimate authority. Punishment was the price he paid for living the life he had chosen. "Military law is very severe," Custer once wrote, "and those who overstep its boundaries must abide the consequences."

Custer played by his own rules at West Point, but he also knew how far he could push the system. He had ways of getting into trouble, but he also had a talent for getting out of it, which was the greater skill. His repeated brushes with the authorities and near escapes from harsher punishment gave rise to an expression that would come to be known throughout the Army, "Custer's luck."

When required, George could toe the line. His cadet lifestyle was a matter of choice, not a compulsion. Custer demonstrated that he could be a model cadet in the three months of April through June 1860, when he received no demerits. As a reward he was given a day of extended limits. But after July 4, Custer reverted to his more familiar ways. He began accumulating skins again, and by December 1860 he was five demerits below the one-hundred-point limit for the semester. And the following month, it looked like Custer's luck had run out.

George was worried that he might not pass the January 1861 midterm exams. He was suffering from too much revelry, not enough study, or a combination of both. So Custer decided to collect some tactical intelligence. Professors prepared lists of questions for each cadet to be asked by the examining board. The exam questions were a closely guarded secret, and cadets tried a variety of means to get copies. In one case a cadet snuck into the professor of rhetoric's room and was copying the exam, when the professor returned. He dove into a trunk and hid until a sympathetic female servant distracted the professor, and he slipped out.

Custer infiltrated the room of one of his professors and found the notebook in which the questions were recorded. He was busily copying his page when he heard someone approaching. He tore out the page with his name on it, replaced the notebook, and fled the scene. Of course, when the professor later consulted the notebook and noted the missing page, he had a very good idea who had taken it.[29] Custer was arrested, along with some others who had been up to the same thing, and all the exam questions for everyone were changed. The result was one of the most difficult exams in West Point history, and thirty-three cadets washed out.

Proceedings were brought against the cadets who tried to cheat, and it did not look good for George. Tully McCrae wrote home that expulsion was unavoidable and that he was sorry to see Custer go. Three weeks later the verdicts came down, and most of the cheating cadets were dismissed. But not George. "Custer with his usual good luck was also reinstated, and he was the only one in his class, while the rest were sent off," McCrea wrote. "He does not know why it is he was more fortunate than the rest, but I am quite sure that he will be more careful in the future and study his lessons more."[30] That, of course, was wishful thinking.

Cadet life was strict, but it had its diversions. West Point of the 1850s was not as isolated as it had been in the past, and in fact it had become a tourist destination. Hudson River school artists, such as faculty member Robert Walter Weir, popularized the natural beauty of the area. The Hudson Valley was lined with hilltop homes—called "castles"—of the wealthy and influential. "A 'brownstone front' in New York and a home on the Hudson meant social distinction and great wealth," Libbie wrote.[31] Roe's Hotel, at the bend in the river that had made West Point a strategic asset during the Revolution, where chains were laid to prevent passage by British ships, was renowned to have one of the best views in the country. When George arrived in 1857, he called West Point "the most romantic spot I ever saw."[32] Visitors flocked to the Academy in the summertime to enjoy the setting and the social life. Glee clubs, excursionists, day-trippers, and dignitaries all arrived on a daily basis. And, fortunately for the cadets, they brought their daughters.

Young ladies would gather on the shady, tree-lined edge of the Plain and watch the cadets in their drills. During their off-hours, the cadets, freshly scrubbed and docked out in their crisp uniforms, would escort the young women around the post, telling tales of life at the Academy.

The cadets held "hops" three times a week during the summer encampment to make more opportunities to meet and mingle. "The large room
in the Academic Hall is filled with a crowd of gaily dressed ladies and
their attendant Cadets," one account noted. "Indeed during the summer
months West Point presents the appearance of a fashionable watering
place."[33] Another report from the fall of 1860 noted that "the cadets
have rather a glorious time than otherwise" with the many visitors, and
"as a crowning enjoyment, the young gentlemen have the satisfaction
of knowing that they are prime favorites with the ladies." The buttons
on the cadets' dress uniforms became special objects of attention and
conquest by the female visitors. The "spoony buttons" were given over
as tokens of favor, or marks of affection, or in return for some fleeting,
usually harmless, physical contact. Some of the ladies were quite brazen
in their pursuits. One reporter, sitting on the piazza of Roe's Hotel,
heard a "maiden coaxing her father to remain over Sunday. 'Just one
day longer, dear papa,' said she, exhibiting a jingling handful of bullet-
buttons, 'Here are five, and Sunday evening will surely make out the
half dozen.'"[34]

The more adventurous couples would take a stroll on "Flirtation
Walk," originally the access path to the Revolutionary War–era cross-
river defensive chains. The walk extended along the riverbank from the
wharf below the hotel, south to a spot known as Kosciuszko's Garden,
after Thaddeus Kosciuszko, the Polish engineer who had designed West
Point's fortifications for George Washington. It was wooded and rocky,
had many twists and turns, and was well hidden from view from the
Academy above. Here, especially on moonlit nights, nature frequently
took its course, and as one observer put it, "if trees had lips as well as
lungs, they could probably reveal some very tender secrets."[35] R. W.
Johnson of the Class of 1849 recalled that "many youthful maidens, with
their breasts heaving with emotions they could not suppress, and with

their voices tremulous with excitement, have said 'yes' when 'no' would have been far better for their future comfort and happiness."[36]

But there was fun to be had beyond formal dances and informal romances. When George first arrived at the Academy, he noted that some of the cadets donned civilian dress and "have the boldness to cross the sentinels posts at night and go to a small village two or three miles down the river for the purpose of getting things which are not allowed, such as ice cream, candies, fruit and (I am sorry to say) some even go for wines and other liquors."[37] Custer soon became an expert at these daring exploits, stealing out after the 10:00 p.m. bed check. As he noted, "Because we are in bed at ten o'clock is no reason why we should remain there until reveille [5 o'clock]." He and his cohorts would arrange things in their beds to make them look occupied in case there was an informal inspection in the middle of the night, some cadets even fashioning dummy heads for added realism. Then, donning civilian clothes, they would slip off post and make their way to the nearby town of Buttermilk Falls to while away the time until early morning when they had to return. On Thanksgiving 1859 George and his friends blew post to attend a ball where they "passed a very pleasant night, reached home a few minutes before reveille, changed our citizens' dress for our uniforms and were then safe. But I was in poor humor for hard study during the next day." He was "almost (*but not quite*) sorry" he had gone to the ball.[38]

One of the main centers of cadet off-post antics was a riverside saloon known as Benny Havens. "The forbidden locality of Benny Havens' possessed stronger attractions than the study and demonstration of a problem in Euclid," George wrote, "or the prosy discussion of some abstract proposition of moral science."[39] Benjamin Havens had been a vexing presence to the authorities since he had first been run off post for dispensing spirits to cadets forty years earlier. He had served libations to generations of future officers from his two-story tavern, and cadet Edgar Allan Poe said Old Ben was "the sole congenial soul in this God-forsaken place."[40]

William Woods Averell described Benny as "of uncertain age, over fifty and under eighty, with a ruddy clean-shaven face which displayed soft little wrinkles about his eyes and mouth." Old Ben was "full of wise saws and quaint stories" about former cadets who had gone on to fame as Army officers, "which he would relate with a merry twinkle of his eyes and a genial quaver of voice that made them fascinating to youngsters." He was assisted by his three grown daughters, and being recognized or asked for by name by Benny or his daughters "was an honor to which no cadet was indifferent."[41] During the Civil War, the West Point drinking song "Benny Havens, Oh!" sung to the tune of the Irish ballad "The Wearing o' the Green" became an Army standard, sung by soldiers who had never been to the tavern, and perhaps never knew it really existed.

Adventurous cadets who "ran it" to Benny's could find good meals, companionship, and a break from the Academy grind. And there was of course an opportunity to drink. Benny Havens was famous for his "hot flip," a hot rum drink he concocted by sticking a red-hot poker into a metal pitcher filled with his mix of secret ingredients. A few flips usually did the trick. Once George had to carry a fellow cadet who was too drunk to walk back from Benny's, drag him upstairs, and get him undressed and into bed just minutes before reveille. Bearing back the "well-developed young sinner deadened with liquor" was "the hardest and most perilous feat of his varied adventures," Libbie recalled.[42]

Benny Havens was the scene of many special events, such as a going-away party Custer organized in April 1860 for members of the class soon to graduate. The "firsties" being honored were Stephen Dodson Ramseur of North Carolina and Wesley Merritt of Illinois. Also present were Henry DuPont of Delaware, John Pelham of Alabama, Thomas Lafayette "Tex" Rosser of Texas, and of course Custer himself. It was a night of merriment and comradeship among young men who looked forward to bright futures as officers in their country's service. What they did not know was that they would soon face each other across bloody battlefields in a country torn apart by war. In a few short years, three of the six around the table would have left the U.S. Army for the Confederate cause, four would become general officers, and two would be dead.

John Wolcott Adams, *Benny Havens*, from "Old College Songs," *Century* 78, no. 181 (June 1909).

THE BROTHERHOOD BROKEN

In Raoul Walsh's 1941 biopic, *They Died with Their Boots On*, Custer and other West Point cadets gather on the Plain in the spring of 1861 to hear an announcement from visiting "Senator Smith." He asks them to sign an oath foreswearing all loyalties except to the national government. Those officers and cadets who felt they could not meet the requirements of the oath were allowed to depart. At the command, "Gentlemen of the South, fall out!" Custer—played by Errol Flynn, who personified the general for a generation—watches with concern as Southern cadets walk resolutely from the ranks.

Senator Smith grouses to the superintendent, Major Alexander H. Bowman, that he had "not been misinformed as to the preponderance of traitors at West Point" and that it was "high time that Congress acted to clean out this nest of secessionists." But Major Bowman corrects the senator. "We don't concern ourselves with the making of wars here," he says, "only the fighting of them." To the cadets, the Supe says, "We have lived as soldiers, and politics have had no place among us. Let us part then as we have lived, with the determination to do our duty, wherever it may lie." The Southerners form a column and march off the field led by mounted Captain Fitzhugh Lee, nephew of Robert E. Lee. The post band plays "Dixie," and the loyalist cadets present arms as their former classmates pass.

The Hollywood version of the Academy's sundering is moving, but manufactured. The severing of the West Point fraternity came about gradually; when the Southern cadets left, they did so by ones and twos. They were enthusiastic, but most had not rushed headlong into the split. American military officers were supposed to be above politics. Judson Kilpatrick of the Class of May 1861, later Custer's commander and rival, said there was a custom established among the cadets at West Point "which forbade the discussion of politics. The violation of this regulation was met with that severest of punishments, social ostracism."[1] The apolitical professionalism of the American soldier was based on long-standing concerns about the role of standing armies in the life of the Republic. West Point's critics had long raised this issue, and it was only partially quelled by the heroism of Academy grads in the Mexican War. For most serving officers, and especially for West Point cadets, politics was off-limits.

However, sectional feelings went beyond politics. They were expressions of the cadets' local and state pride, tradition, heritage, and community spirit. West Point was one of the few national institutions outside of the U.S. Congress where people gathered from every state, and naturally this generated friendly competition and a degree of culture clash. "Among the noticeable features of cadet life as then impressed upon me, and still present in my memory," Custer wrote years later, "were the sectional lines voluntarily established by the cadets themselves; at first barely distinguishable, but in the later years immediately preceding the war as clearly defined and strongly drawn as were the lines separating the extremes of the various sections in the national Congress."[2]

Over the decades, the Southern cadets had developed a reputation as forming a relaxed aristocracy. A British observer who stopped at West Point during the Thayer era commented, "There is a remarkable difference between the cadets of the Northern and Southern States: the former are generally studious and industrious; the latter, brought up among slaves, are idle and inattentive, so that they are almost all dismissed; consequently, the Academy is not 'in good odor' with the planters; for they imagine that favoritism prevails, and that the dismissals are not impartial."[3] In general, Southern cadets were regarded as less prepared and seen as underachievers.[4] Because of stereotypes like this, there was a widespread view among Northerners that most officers who hailed from the South were incompetent. This idea persisted until the dramatic Confederate victories in the early years of the Civil War, when suddenly the Southerners were considered martial geniuses, and the Northern officers were dismissed as bungling and ineffectual.

Sectional rivalries among cadets were initially relatively harmless, but in the late 1850s they began to reflect the intensity of the growing national division, particularly over the issue of slavery. The Southerners were especially motivated. "While the advocates for and against slavery were equally earnest and determined," Custer wrote, "those from the South were always the most talkative if not argumentative."[5] Francis Henry Parker of Custer's class noted during his first months at West Point that "a man's politics have a great deal to do with the opinion formed of a person by the cadets. There are very few Republicans here but they are all cut by the rest of the cadets…. Particularly are the Mass. men abused…. they have to fight continually, and in every way. But they are superior both mentally and physically and most always come off victorious."[6]

The Republican party was young at that point, having been organized three years earlier in response to the Kansas-Nebraska Act by a
coalition of abolitionists, former Whigs, and merchants. Other events
followed that heightened sectional tensions: the terror of Bleeding Kansas, South Carolina representative Preston Brooks's beating Massachusetts senator Charles Sumner with a cane on the Senate floor in May
1856, and the March 1857 Supreme Court decision in *Dred Scott v.
Sanford* that legalized the unhindered expansion of slavery into the territories.

The watershed event for sectionalism at West Point, and the country
generally, was John Brown's attempted slave insurrection at Harpers
Ferry and subsequent trial, which took place between October and
December 1859. "The John Brown raid into Virginia stirred the wrath-
ful indignation of the embryonic warriors who looked upon slavery as
an institution beyond human interference," Custer wrote, "while those
of the opposite extreme contented themselves by quietly chuckling over
the alarm into which the executive and military forces of an entire State
were thrown by the invasion led by Brown, backed by a score or two of
adherents."[7]

The Harpers Ferry raid affected the Corps personally; one of Brown's
hostages was Colonel Lewis Washington, great-grandnephew and closest living relation of George Washington and father of plebe James B.
Washington of Virginia. The troops that ended the siege and captured
Brown were commanded by the former superintendent Colonel Robert
E. Lee and his aide-de-camp, Lieutenant James E. B. Stuart of the Class
of 1854. Lieutenant Israel Greene, USMC, who commanded the Marine
platoon that stormed the firehouse where Brown was holed up, had
recently received artillery training at West Point. The cadets followed
reports of the raid, trial, and execution closely. On December 2, 1859,
the day John Brown was hanged in Charles Town, Virginia, he was also

hanged in effigy from a tree in front of the barracks. Afterward sectional feelings at the Academy became more acute and more overtly political, and they sometimes led to violence.[8]

"It required more than ordinary moral and physical courage to boldly avow oneself an abolitionist," Custer recalled of those days. "The name was considered one of opprobrium, and the cadet who had the courage to avow himself an abolitionist must be prepared to face the social frowns of the great majority of his comrades and at times to defend his opinions by his physical strength and metal."[9] One such cadet was Emory Upton of the Class of May 1861. Upton was appointed to the Academy from New York but for the previous two years had been a student at Oberlin College in Ohio. Oberlin was a noted center of progressive education, the first college to admit African American students (in 1835) and the first coeducational college (in 1837). "Upton was a bold fellow and thoroughly radical in his views," his classmate Jacob B. Rawles recalled.[10] Upton was the first cadet to openly declare himself an abolitionist, and as Morris Schaff stated, "this made him a marked man."[11]

Wade Hampton Gibbes, Class of 1860, was the son of a slave owner and had grown up on a South Carolina plantation. He was a vocal firebrand, and he disliked Upton intensely. He started a rumor that the young abolitionist had been involved with a black woman at Oberlin, and after it got back to Upton, he called out Gibbes.

"One noon we were drawn up preparatory to marching to the mess-room," Judson Kilpatrick recalled. "Upton stepped out from his position on the right of the battalion, walked deliberately down the line to the extreme left, where Gibbes was standing, and asked him if he had used the language attributed to him." Gibbes said he did, and Upton "brought his hand down on the face of the vilifier with a ringing slap." Upton was jumped by "a score of high-toned Southerners," and he was rescued by "those who were willing to see fair play." It was "a pretty plucky thing for one to do with all the odds against him, and only three friends in the Academy."[12]

They agreed to meet in the barracks and settle the matter as gentlemen. The two came to blows and cadets crowded around, cheering them on. Gibbes got the better of Upton, who eventually emerged, his face bloody, heading for the stairs up to his room. The Southern cadets were shouting threats and insults, when Upton's roommate, a big Pennsylvanian named John I. Rodgers, appeared at the top of the steps, his eyes "glaring like a panther's," according to Schaff, and said to the jeering Southerners, "If there are any more of you down there who want anything, come right up!"[13]

The Upton-Gibbes fight "was the most thrilling event in my life as a cadet," Schaff wrote, "and, in my judgment, it was the most significant in that of West Point itself." In it Schaff saw a prophecy of the war to come, reflecting both "the courage and the bitterness with which it was fought out to the bitter end."[14]

The fight stood out in memory because it was the exception. Northern and Southern cadets did not generally engage in brawls over politics. When fights did happen, they were usually over other matters. But sectional tensions continued to percolate at the Academy, and they came into sharp focus during the 1860 election campaign.

In October 1860, Southern cadets arranged an electoral straw poll. Senator Joseph Lane of Oregon, the father of John Lane, Custer's friend, classmate, and sometime-roommate, was the vice presidential nominee of the Southern Democrat faction headed by Breckenridge.[15] Custer, being a Northern Democrat, could be expected to support Stephen Douglas, the establishment Democratic nominee. But the real purpose of the straw poll was to root out the Republicans in the Corps' midst.

"A better scheme than this straw ballot to embroil the Corps, and to precipitate the hostilities between individuals which soon involved the

States, could not have been devised," Morris Schaff wrote. The ballot was secret, with a voting box inside a long shed near the barracks. "The balloting was generally secret, for several reasons," recalled Jacob B. Rawles of the Class of May 1861. The Northern and Southern cadets, especially roommates, held their friendships "in high regard, and as the feeling was very intense through out the country, before the impending crisis of that four years of fratricidal warfare, our personal opinions were more or less guarded."[16]

This was not the case with Emory Upton, who took the opportunity to provoke the Southerners. He walked to the shed waving his ballot over his head shouting, "I'm going to vote for Abraham Lincoln, and I don't give a rap who knows it!" Several Southern cadets rose to the provocation, and another brawl seemed imminent, but Charles C. Campbell of Missouri, later a Confederate major, intervened and insisted on a fair fight. Cooler heads prevailed and stopped a repeat of the previous bloodletting.[17]

Breckenridge won a plurality of ninety-nine votes out of 278, and Lincoln was second with sixty-four. The incensed Southerners then began to hunt out the "Black Republican Abolitionists in the Corps."[18] Only thirty cadets admitted they backed Lincoln, and all of them from west of the Hudson. Ohioan Schaff, a Lincoln backer, called the unwillingness of the New England Republicans to stand by their votes "the most equivocal if not pusillanimous conduct I ever saw at West Point."[19] Lincoln was soon hanged in effigy, like Brown, in front of the barracks.

As the election neared, Custer wrote, "the Breckenridge army of Southern Democrats did not hesitate to announce, as their seniors in and out of Congress had done, that in the event of Lincoln's election secession would be the only resource left to the South."[20] Lincoln's victory on November 6, 1860, demonstrated the breakdown of the national political system. Lincoln swept the free states and carried none of the slave states, the first and only such outcome in presidential electoral history. McCrea, another of the Lincoln supporters from Ohio, celebrated the Republican victory. "As we rejoiced the other parties mourned," he wrote, "the southerners [fumed] and (as is customary with a great many of them), they threatened to do all kinds of terrible things, and blustered around at a great rate." He thought that it "would be a blessed good thing" if the Southerners resigned, because "it would clear the institution of some of the worst characters."[21]

Not everyone was certain the coming division was a "blessed good thing." William A. Elderkin from New York, of the Class of May 1861, expressed the ambivalence some cadets felt in the days after Lincoln's election: "Election is at last over ... ominous signs of dis-union are plainly visible, and probably before we see each other again 'something will turn up'—I do not blame the 'south' for feeling as they do—nor would I wonder to see them take the sword, if necessary, to defend their just rights—still, I was born under a northern sun and have sworn to serve under the federal constitution, and so I must do—yet. God forbid that I should ever be called into a hostile field against my own countrymen."[22]

But among the Southern cadets, particularly those from the Deep South, it was clear that a long-expected revolution was imminent. "It seemed to have been a part of the early teaching of the Southern youth," Custer wrote, "that the disruption of the Union was an event surely to be brought about."[23] Thomas Rowland of Virginia, head of the Class of 1863, observed in a letter home that "a great many cadets have assumed the blue cockade, tying a small blue ribbon upon the cap button" in solidarity with the South.[24] Three days after the election, the Columbia, South Carolina, *Guardian* published an open letter from the West Point cadets of the Palmetto State pledging to stand by their homeland if it left the Union. "All we desire is a field for making ourselves useful," they said.[25] Ten days later South Carolinian Henry S. Farley resigned, followed four days later by James "Little Jim" Hamilton. The Janesville, Wisconsin, *Gazette* mocked these and other departing cadets, editorializing that "after their *chivalry* gets chilled, and their vacancies have been filled, these boys will be forced to the conclusion that they have made asses of themselves."[26]

Eighty-six of the 278 cadets at the Academy at that time were from states that eventually joined the Confederacy. Sixty-five of them left or were discharged for reasons connected to the war. Six left for other reasons, and fifteen sided with the Union.[27] The Southern cadets did not leave en masse, as portrayed cinematically, but departed in small numbers as the Union slowly disintegrated through the winter and spring of 1860–61. Custer observed that one important reason the Southern cadets were in a hurry to leave was because the Confederate government was organizing its armed forces, and "it was important that applicants for positions of this kind should be on the ground to properly present their claims."[28] Custer noted with some amazement that the Academy raised no barriers to the cadets' resignations and departures, even though their intentions to join the nascent Confederate forces were clear. Indeed, throughout the whole of the Army, officers and troops changed the blue for the gray with little difficulty.

"What is to become of our glorious Union?" Cadet Rowland fretted. "Disunion gains ground only because the conservatives remain inactive, and the violent meet with no opposition sufficient to check their impetuous course." He said he would remain loyal as long as he could, then "we must all cast in our lot with Virginia and hope for the best. I do not fear civil war," he continued, "for I do not think it is the spirit of the nineteenth century to fight over an abstract principle."[29]

Custer remembered things differently. "War was anticipated by [the Southerners] at that time and discussed and looked forward to ... with as much certainty as if speaking of an approaching season," he wrote. "The cadets from the South were in constant receipt of letters from their friends at home, keeping them fully advised of the real situation and promising them suitable positions in the military force yet to be organized to defend the ordinance of secession. All this was a topic of daily if not hourly conversation."[30] Rowland noted that discussion about "the prospect of dissolution interferes somewhat with the studying throughout the corps, among the excitable or the lazy."[31] But despite the prospect of cadets facing each other in deadly contest on future battlefields, there was no noticeable animus between them. "The approaching war was as usual the subject of conversation in which all participated, and in the freest and most friendly manner," Custer wrote. "The lads from the North discoursing earnestly upon the power and rectitude of the National Government, the impulsive Southron holding up pictures of invaded rights and future independence."[32]

George had always gotten along with the Southern cadets, in part because he was a strong Democrat and an anti-abolitionist who openly denounced the "Black Republicans." Also Custer knew the Southerners better; he was a member of D Company, most of whom were from the South or West. One of Custer's roommates and a close friend was Pierce Manning Butler Young from Cartersville, Georgia.[33] Schaff called him "a very good fighter, and a very good hearted fellow."[34] Young was also a strong Southern partisan. During the John Brown trial in 1859, he said he wished he had a sword as long as from West Point to Newburgh so he could cut off every Yankee head in a row. "I am devoted to my whole country," Young wrote to his father, "but to that portion of my country who array themselves under a black republican banner, I am a sectional enemy."[35] One day in the winter of 1860–61, while the cadets discussed current events, Young made a prediction:

> Custer, my boy, we're going to have a war. It's no use talking;
> I see it coming.… Now let me prophesy what will happen to
> you and me. You will go home, and your abolition governor

will probably make you colonel of a cavalry regiment. I will go down to Georgia and ask Governor Brown to give me a cavalry regiment. And who knows but we may move against each other during the war. You will probably get the advantage of us in the first few engagements as your side will be rich and powerful, while we will be poor and weak. Your regiment will be armed with the best of weapons, the sharpest of sabres; mine will have only shotguns and scythe blades; but for all that we'll get the best of the fight in the end, because we will fight for a principle, a cause, while you will fight only to perpetuate the abuse of power.[36]

Young resigned in March 1861, eventually becoming an officer in the Cobb Legion Cavalry in J. E. B. Stuart's Corps.[37]

"One by one the places occupied by the cadets from the seceding States became vacant," Custer wrote. "It cost many a bitter pang to disrupt the intimate relations existing between the hot-blooded Southron and his more phlegmatic schoolmate from the North. No schoolgirls could have been more demonstrative in their affectionate regard for each other than were some of the cadets about to separate for the last time, and under circumstances which made it painful to contemplate a future coming together."[38]

One Saturday in late December, Custer was, as usual, walking an extra, when he saw a group of cadets carrying two others toward the wharf on their shoulders. One was his classmate Cadet First Sergeant Charles P. Ball of Alabama, the other John Herbert Kelly of California, of Custer's company. As the men were borne away, they raised their hats to Custer across the plain in farewell. After looking to see if he was being watched, George saluted them by bringing his musket to "present."

"Those leaving for the South were impatient, enthusiastic, and hopeful," Custer wrote. "Their comrades from the North, whom they were leaving behind, were reserved almost to sullenness; were grave almost to stoicism."[39] Francis H. Parker wrote to his father that if war comes, "this government is going to have a pretty hard time to sustain it and *entres-nous* I think that the South stands as good a chance of coming out victorious as the North, if not a better.... I've heard many a northern cadet and soldiers say they never would go south and fight the battles of the Black Republicans."[40]

By February 1861 seven states had left the Union. On February 8, the Convention of Seceded States declared the formation of the Confederate States of America, and ten days later Jefferson Davis was sworn in as its president. Abraham Lincoln was on his way to Washington, still weeks away from his inauguration, and lame-duck president James Buchanan was doing little to prevent the continued dissolution of the country.

On the morning of February 22, 1861, the Corps of Cadets marched to the chapel to the tunes of the West Point band. An order had come down that in honor of Washington's birthday, they were to "listen to the friendly counsels, and almost prophetic warnings," in his Farewell Address.[41] Commandant John F. Reynolds led the group into the chapel. The cadets took their seats and listened as Washington's words were read, entreating them to "properly estimate the immense value of your national union" and to frown on "every attempt to alienate any portion of our country from the rest, or to enfeeble the sacred ties which now link together the various parts."[42] The cadets were then released for the customary holiday.

It was a cloudy day, and most spent it indoors, discussing the political crisis or studying. The cadet barracks, a stylized castle, had two major wings, east and west, with a sally port between the wings on the ground floor. Over the years, the cadets had—perhaps unconsciously, certainly without plan—segregated themselves: Northerners on the east side of the port, Southerners on the west.

At 9:30 p.m., the hour of evening tattoo, the post band formed near the gun on the north side of the plain and marched toward the barracks playing "Washington's March." Cadets gathered at the windows to watch and listen. As the band marched through the sally port, it struck up "The Star-Spangled Banner." When it emerged on the south side of the barracks, Custer, whose window faced that side, began a cheer that was soon taken up by the rest of the Northern cadets. The cheering was against regulations, but it persisted. The Southern cadets, led by Tom Rosser, responded with massed cheers for "Dixie." The Northerners "flung back a ringing cheer for the Stars and Stripes; and so cheer followed cheer," Schaff wrote. "Ah, it was a great night! Rosser at one window, Custer at another."[43]

Six weeks later the mirthful mood at West Point had changed. The idea that conflict could be avoided had given way to certainty that it would soon arrive. "The excitement is so great concerning the probability of war that I have scarcely thought of anything else," Custer wrote in a letter to his sister. "No one speaks of anything but war and everyone on this part of the country firmly believes that we will hear in a few days that hostilities have commenced."[44] Francis H. Parker echoed these sentiments. "It is the general opinion among cadets and officers on the Point," he wrote on April 7, "that President Lincoln intends to fight, or at least to adopt such measures and take such steps as will bring on the war."[45] Custer predicted, "I feel confident that we will have war in less than a week."[46] Two days later Confederate forces attacked Fort Sumter in Charleston harbor.

Events at Sumter electrified the North. "Opponents in politics became friends in patriotism," Custer wrote, "all difference of opinion vanished or were laid aside."[47] But the attack also unified the South, and George blamed the Republicans for tearing the country apart. President Lincoln's call for troops to occupy the seceded states after the Fort Sumter attack tipped the balance for the middle states that had yet to leave the Union. "Everything here is full of excitement and suspense," Virginian Thomas Rowland wrote two days after the attack. "There will be several resignations today, and the whole of the North Carolina delegation will resign this week. As soon as I hear that Virginia is going to secede I should like to resign immediately."[48] Virginia adopted a secession ordinance April 17, and Rowland left soon after. On April 18 the cadets were required to take an oath of allegiance, and ten Southern cadets refused and were dismissed. Thirty-three cadets resigned on April 22, 1861, the largest single-day group. Among them was Custer's friend Thomas Rosser, who headed to the then-Confederate capital, Montgomery, Alabama, to seek a commission.

With hostilities underway, the Class of 1861 petitioned to graduate early and were given their wish on May 6. They were sent to Washington immediately, being delayed briefly in Philadelphia by the chief of police, who suspected them of being a band of secessionists.[49] Custer's class also petitioned to leave early, which would mean missing their fifth and final year. Rather than being commissioned right away, the cadets were rushed through a compressed version of the fifth-year curriculum, a "course of sprouts" one said.[50] The cadets rose at 5:00 a.m. for two hours' study, then had breakfast. They continued in classes until 4:00 p.m., then had an hour's drill, parade, supper, and a half-hour break before studying again until lights out at 10:00 p.m. Many cadets put blankets over their windows and continued to study. "This method of cramming a year's course into two months time is rather hard on us," Francis Parker wrote, nine days into the course. "I never studied so hard and did so poorly as I am now."[51] One cadet estimated that they were reading about 125 pages of lessons a day.[52] Custer said the pace was so physically punishing that they were all becoming thin and pale, and he had lost five pounds in two weeks. "There was never an instance of so severe studying being done as is now done by my class," he wrote.[53] He stayed up studying until one in the morning, catching a few hours' sleep before rising again at five.

Despite his studiousness, Custer tested poorly in the 1861 exams, coming in at the foot of the class. George C. Strong, who graduated fifth in the Class of 1857, noted that "it is a favorite idea among many here that it requires an abler man to stand at the foot of his class throughout the course than at the head of it." The academic style of the goat—to study only when absolutely necessary and then to cram in just enough to pass—were "symptoms of that epidemic which is called Genius."[54] But even as the last man of his class, Custer was a survivor. In the ten years before the Civil War, the graduation rate was only 52 percent.[55] One hundred twenty-five cadets entered with Custer in 1857; of those, most washed out, twenty-two resigned to join the Confederacy, and thirty-four graduated. And as Custer liked to add, "Of these, thirty-three graduated above me."[56]

Custer later claimed that some of the Southern cadets, had they remained, "would probably have contested with me the debatable honor of bringing up the rear of the class."[57] Custer was last in his class in his third year, and the five cadets above him all fought for the Confederacy and could have dropped below him the final year.[58] The sixth was Charles Nelson Warner from Pennsylvania, who was found deficient in January 1861 and sent home, but recalled to finish his studies and graduated as the goat of 1862.

Custer had predicted that his class would be gone by June 25, "if not sooner," and he was close to the mark. On June 30, 1861, they were relieved of duty at West Point and ordered to "report to Washington City without delay." However, when his classmates departed, Custer was not among them. He had a final trick to play on himself.

On the evening before his class was set to graduate, Custer was serving as officer of the guard at the encampment. "I began my tour at the usual hour in the morning," he recalled, "and everything passed off satisfactorily in connection with the discharge of my new responsibilities, until just at dusk I heard a commotion near the guard tents."[59] He rushed over to find a crowd of cadets ringed around two of their fellows, yearling William Ludlow and an upperclassman, swearing oaths at each other. "Ludlow was a greeny," Custer later explained, "but he had pluck."[60] Just as Custer arrived, the two came to blows, "a good square out-and-outer."[61]

"I had hardly time to take in the situation when the two principals of the group engaged in a regular set-to," Custer wrote, "and began belaboring each other vigorously with their fists."[62] Custer should have arrested them, but as he later wrote, "the instincts of the boy prevailed over the obligation of the officer of the guard."[63] Some friends of the older cadet were trying to trip up Ludlow, so Custer waded into the mob of cadets and said, "Stand back, boys, let's have a fair fight!"[64] The contest resumed and "Ludlow was getting the best of it," when the crowd evaporated. Custer noticed too late the cause: Lieutenants William B. Hazen and William E. Merrill were approaching, the former the officer in charge.

"Why did you not suppress the riot which occurred here a few minutes ago?" Hazen demanded. Custer gave his opinion that a fight between two boys could not properly be described as a "riot," which was the wrong answer. The next morning Commandant Reynolds placed him under arrest. "I was in the guard house when my class graduated," he said. Custer's classmates bade him farewell as they departed for Washington, and he replied, merrily, "I'm the nest egg!"[65]

Custer remained at West Point for two long weeks before a general court-martial convened, presided over by Lieutenant Stephen Vincent Benét.[66] "I was arraigned with all the solemnity and gravity which might be looked for in a trial for high treason," Custer recalled.[67] Cadet "George

W. [*sic*] Custer" was charged with "neglect of duty" (for not breaking up the brawl) and "conduct to the prejudice of good order and military discipline" (for calling for a fair fight). He pled guilty on both counts. "The trial was brief," he recalled, "scarcely occupying more time than did the primary difficulty."[68]

Meanwhile, Custer's classmates were doing what they could in Washington to secure the release of their class goat. "Fortunately some of them had influential friends there," Custer observed.[69] He was also aided by the fact that trained officers were needed to assign to the units that were being hurriedly put together in anticipation of open warfare with the Confederacy. On July 17, Custer was ordered to report to the adjutant general in Washington. He left West Point the day after the telegram arrived, rushing off to war without waiting for a verdict from the court. "What the proceeding of the court or their decision was, I have never learned," he wrote.[70] In absentia, he was sentenced only to be reprimanded in orders. The court noted that it was being lenient "owing to the peculiar situation of Cadet Custer represented in his own defense, and in consideration of his general good conduct, as testified to by Lieutenant Hazen, his immediate commander."[71]

Shortly before his class graduated, Custer had written his sister that he was not certain when they would next meet. "I would not be surprised if I never visited home again," he wrote, "everything is uncertain, life is always so and at no time was it ever more so than at the present." Many people were expecting the war to be brief and bloodless. Woodruff, in the excitement after the attack on Fort Sumter, wrote he hoped soon to see "an army in the field which shall be sufficiently large to be absolutely irresistible by any force the south can bring against us."[72] But George was not convinced. "It is useless to hope or to suppose that the coming struggle will be a bloodless one or one of short duration," he wrote. "It is certain that much blood will be spilled and that thousands of lives lost, perhaps I might say hundreds of thousands. In entering the contest everyone must take his chance and no one can say that he will live through it, but this is a necessary consequence and cannot be avoided. If it is to be my lot to fall in the service of my country and in defense of my country's rights I have or will have no regrets."[73]

PART TWO

CUSTER GOES TO WAR

Custer's Charge at Aldie, from M. Quad and Henry Whittemore, *Field, Fort and Fleet: Being a Series of Brilliant and Authentic Sketches of the Most Notable Battles of the Late Civil War* (Detroit: Detroit Free Press, 1885).

CHAPTER FOUR

"A SLIM, LONG-HAIRED BOY, CARELESSLY DRESSED"

George Custer rushed from West Point to warfare faster than any graduate before him and probably since. In only days he went from the guardhouse at the Academy to the battlefield in Virginia. As he said, he got there in time to "run with the rest at Bull Run."[1]

George left West Point on July 18, stopping briefly in New York City to buy his lieutenant's kit, then took an evening train to Washington that was "crowded with troops, officers and men, hastening to the capital."[2] Crowds at the stations cheered the soldiers on their journey south, since it was believed that open warfare was imminent. George arrived the morning of July 19 and went to Ebbit House in search of some of his classmates. He found one of his former Academy roommates, James P. Parker of Missouri. Parker and Custer were, according to Morris Schaff, a "well-matched pair." They had "fooled away many an hour that should have been devoted to study." After George excitedly discussed the loom-ing confrontation in northern Virginia, Parker sheepishly showed Custer the letter from the War Department accepting his resignation for the Confederacy.

Custer camped out at the adjutant general's office seeking orders, though the fate of a freshly minted second lieutenant was a low priority with war imminent. Finally, at two in the morning of the twentieth, the officer on duty beckoned to George and said casually, "Perhaps you would like to be presented to General Scott, Mr. Custer?" to which George "joyfully assented." Winfield Scott was a figurative and, at six feet five, literal giant of American military history, with a career stretching back to 1808. "I had often beheld the towering form of the venerable chieftain during his summer visits to West Point," Custer wrote, "but that was the extent of my personal acquaintance with him."[3]

General Scott was very cordial to young Custer and asked him if he would like to join some of the Academy graduates who were busy train-ing new volunteers, or perhaps he had a "desire for something more active?" George said he wanted to join his unit, Company G of the 2nd Cavalry, at the front as soon as he could. Scott commended Custer for his enthusiasm and told him to find a horse to ride to Commanding General Irvin McDowell's headquarters. He could deliver some dis-patches before joining his unit.

Horses were in short supply, but Custer's luck held. He found a horse left behind by a West Point detachment. The horse turned out to be one he knew—Wellington, "a favorite one ridden by me often when learning the cavalry exercises at West Point," George recalled. That evening he rode his familiar friend to McDowell's headquarters at Centreville, arriv-ing after midnight on July 21. Battle was imminent.

The Union had pushed into Virginia "in deference to the incessant demands of a large portion of the press, calling for an attack upon Con-federate forces," Custer said.[4] Politics played an important role; it had been three months since the attack on Fort Sumter, and few overt moves had been made to assert federal power, other than the occupation of Alexandria, Virginia, on May 24. Politicians and newspaper editors pressed Lincoln to act. Furthermore, the ninety-day enlistments the president had called for shortly after Fort Sumter were expiring, for some units that very day. The Union had to use the troops or lose them. But there was still a general view in the North that the war would be brief, exciting, and victorious. "War was not regarded by the masses as a dreadful alternative, to be avoided to the last," Custer wrote of those early, heady days, "but rather as an enterprise offering some pleasure and some excitement, with perhaps a little danger and suffering."[5]

The Battle of Bull Run at first seemed to live up to the expectation of war as something brief and glorious, at least from the Union side. McDowell opened with a broad flanking maneuver west of the Confederate Army of the Potomac under General P. G. T. Beauregard, which was encamped near Manassas Junction across Bull Run. Union forces drove rebel units back onto Henry House Hill by afternoon. Custer was assigned to a cavalry squadron protecting an artillery battery and did not see heavy fighting, though his unit did come under counter-battery fire. He noted of his first moments under enemy fire that while he had heard the sounds of cannon shot at West Point, "a man listens with changed interest when the direction of the balls is toward instead of away from him."[6]

Late that afternoon Custer stood on a ridge with one of his classmates, watching the Union line advance. The two were congratulating each other on "the glorious victory which already seemed to have been won," when Confederate reinforcements, principally under Colonel Thomas J. Jackson, who would earn his nickname "Stonewall" that day, began a fierce assault that broke the Union line.

"No pen or description can give anything like a correct idea of the rout and demoralization that followed," Custer wrote. The confident

Union troops had become "one immense mass of fleeing, frightened creatures."[7] Custer's unit kept good order and was one of the last organized troops to cross back over Bull Run, keeping the advancing rebels at bay as best they could. That night, Custer's unit continued "hastening with the fleeing, frightened soldiery" back to Arlington, on muddy roads through driving rain. "I little imagined when making my night ride from Washington to Centreville the night of the 20th," Custer wrote, "that the following night should find me returning with a defeated and demoralized army." Reaching Arlington Heights the morning of the twenty-second, Custer lay down under a tree "where, from fatigue, hunger and exhaustion, I soon fell asleep, despite the rain and mud, and slept for hours without wakening."[8] It had been four days since he departed West Point.

"No battle of the war startled and convulsed the entire country, North and South, as did the first battle of Bull Run," Custer later wrote.[9] It exploded the myth of the short war and gave notice to the North that not only were the rebels serious about defending the Confederacy but they were more than able to fight. Custer took time in the gloomy days afterward to find his benefactor, Congressman Bingham. "I had never seen him," Bingham recalled. "I heard of him after the First Battle of Bull Run." Word had spread in the capital that Custer's delaying actions had helped prevent the disaster from being worse than it was. "I heard of his exploit with pride, and hunted several times for my boy, but unsuccessfully. Then one day a young soldier came to my room without the formality of sending a card.... He was out of breath, or had lost it from embarrassment. And he spoke with hesitation: 'Mr. Bingham, I've been in my first battle. I tried hard to do my best. I felt I ought to report to you, for it's through you I got to West Point. I'm ...' I took his hand. 'I know. You're my boy Custer!'"[10]

After the disaster at Bull Run, Custer's company was temporarily attached to the Jersey Brigade, commanded by the mercurial one-armed

Brigadier General Philip Kearny. Kearny, who had just organized the brigade, had no staff officers, and requested the junior officer in the company to be detailed to his staff. For Custer it was another stroke of luck.

"I found the change from subaltern in a company to a responsible position on the staff of a most active and enterprising officer both agreeable and beneficial," George wrote.[11] This began a series of assignments in which Custer served as a staff officer or aide to senior officers, positions that were critical to advancing his career. George learned how war was waged at the operational level, moving large units over great distances, not just the tactical level of the close-in battle. But more important, staff work gave him the opportunity to get into fights he would have missed had he been tied to the fortunes of his unit.

As a staff officer, Custer was called on to serve as a commander's eyes and ears. He carried urgent battlefield messages, did critical reconnaissance, and engaged in a variety of special missions. When battles were looming, he knew when and where to get into the thick of them. It was work that suited Custer's personality and skills and increased his freedom of action. It fed Custer's appetite for adventure and placed him in situations where he could not only demonstrate his courage but make sure it was noticed.

In the fall of 1861, Custer was ordered back to his company. General Kearny thought highly of Custer and predicted great things for his future. Unfortunately, Kearny did not live to see it. He was killed the following September at the Battle of Chantilly.

After a furlough for sickness in the winter of 1861–62, Custer saw his first serious action. In March 1862, General George McClellan, chafing under criticism from President Lincoln and others for not having taken concerted action against the rebellion, ordered a general movement toward Manassas, which had recently been evacuated by rebel forces. After reaching Manassas, General George Stoneman, McClellan's cavalry commander, ordered a movement south along the Orange and Alexandria Railroad to hit the rebel rear and, if possible, according to Custer, "drive him across the Rappahannock." On March 14, the Union cavalry column found Confederate pickets in force on a hill near Catlett's Station, twelve miles southwest of town. Orders came down to push them off the hill, and Custer, whose unit was conveniently at the front of the column, volunteered to lead the attack.[12]

"I marched the company to the front," Custer wrote, "formed line and advanced toward the pickets, then plainly in view, and interested observers of our movements." After leading the advance to a "convenient distance," he wrote, "I gave the command 'Charge' for the first time. My company responded gallantly, and away we went." The rebel skirmishers broke before the charging horsemen and ran across the bridge at Cedar Run, setting it on fire behind them. Custer's force pursued to the river-bank and opened fire. "The bullets rattled like hail," he wrote to his parents, and for a few minutes there was a spirited exchange. But with the bridge ablaze, no easy way to cross the river, and his men coming under increasing fire from the rallying Confederates, Custer pulled back. It was George's first action in command, and he could take credit for "the shedding of the first blood by the Army of the Potomac,"[13] which had been formed in the summer of 1861.

In late March 1862, at the onset of the Peninsula Campaign, Custer sailed from Alexandria to Fortress Monroe, where he was assigned to be assistant to Lieutenant Nicholas Bowen, Class of 1860, chief engineer for Brigadier General William F. "Baldy" Smith's division. During this period Custer achieved the distinction of becoming one of the first Army aviators. The Union Army Balloon Corps, under the leadership of Thaddeus S. C. Lowe, gave Federal commanders unprecedented intelligence on enemy positions and troop movements. Some, however, questioned the value of the expensive balloons and their highly paid civilian technicians. Since Lowe owned and operated the balloons, his men could "report whatever their imagination prompted them to," Custer wrote, "with no fear of contradiction," thus ensuring their "profitable employment."[14]

To check this potential conflict of interest, the Army decided to send officers aloft, and General Smith chose Custer to make the ascents. It was "an order which was received with no little trepidation," he wrote, "for although I had chosen the mounted service from preference alone, yet I had a choice as to the character of the mount, and the proposed ride was far more elevated than I had ever desired or contemplated."[15] He noted an event a few weeks earlier, when General Fitz John Porter ascended in a balloon and the tether rope broke, sending him on a three-mile drift over enemy lines and back until he leaked enough hydrogen from the balloon to make a rough landing in a tree. At Bull Run, a Confederate battery from the New Orleans Lafayette Artillery, commanded by his old friend Thomas Rosser, put a ball through some of the ropes holding the gondola of a Union balloon, forcing the craft down.[16]

Custer's first trip—which he made sitting nervously in the small basket—went without incident, and in time he was making almost daily ascents.[17] On the night of May 3–4, 1862, Custer observed heavy fires in the vicinity of Yorktown. Going up again on the morning of May 4, 1862, he noted that there were no expected campfires behind the Confederate lines. Custer informed General Smith the rebels had abandoned their positions, confirming intelligence Smith had just received from two "contrabands" who had wandered into the Union camp.

Union forces, led by Stoneman's cavalry, surged ahead, until being stopped by a dug-in rebel rear-guard at Fort Magruder under the command of James Longstreet, two miles from Williamsburg. During this movement Custer rode out ahead of the column and ran into a rebel cavalry rear-guard at Skiff's Creek. He exchanged fire with the horsemen, who retreated, leaving the bridge over the creek burning. Custer rushed ahead to put out the fire, blistering his hands in the process.

The Union right was held by one of Smith's brigades, commanded by Brigadier General Winfield Scott Hancock. Custer volunteered to join Hancock's force for the expected advance. The next morning, May 5, it appeared that rebel forces had abandoned a position across a dam to their front. Hancock assembled a volunteer force to take the rebel works, covered by artillery and infantry in case the position was still defended. But as the troops arrived for the assault, they saw that Custer and a captain had already ridden across and occupied the enemy trenches.

General Joe Hooker, on the Union left before Fort Magruder, kept the enemy busy while Hancock advanced. After a sharp action, Hancock's men occupied two enemy redoubts, seriously compromising the rebel defensive line. He sensed an opportunity to close the trap on Longstreet; instead, he was told to withdraw.

Hancock delayed his withdrawal several hours, hoping Sumner would change his mind. Late in the afternoon, when he was reluctantly preparing to pull back, rebel forces mounted a sudden, concerted assault. After a series of opening skirmishes, four heavy lines of Confederate troops emerged across level ground in front of Hancock's ridge crest position, "giving the Federal troops an opportunity, for the first time, of hearing the Southern yell," Custer recalled.[18] He watched the rebels "advancing rapidly and confidently" as Hancock, on horseback, rode the line encouraging his troops.

The enemy crossed over half a mile uncontested to within three hundred yards, then opened up. Hancock's men returned fire, and Custer said the "exultant yell of the Southron met an equally defiant response from his countrymen of the North."[19] Charging against lines of Union infantry, "the Confederates were losing ten to one of the Federals," Custer recalled, but they kept coming.[20]

The rebels closed to within twenty paces when they finally began to falter under the ceaseless fire from Hancock's line. Sensing the enemy was vulnerable, Hancock, "as if conducting guests to a banquet rather than fellow beings to a life-and-death struggle," Custer recalled, issued the order, "*Gentlemen*, charge with the bayonet." The Union line surged ahead, with Custer joining in. The rebels broke before the onrushing Union force, and Custer took six prisoners and "the first battle flag captured from the enemy by the Army of the Potomac."[21] The banner, from the 5th North Carolina Infantry, was given to French observer François d'Orléans, prince of Joinville, son of the French king Louis Philippe, to return to McClellan's headquarters. Joinville, a combat veteran in his own right who would come to know Custer well, said he "entertained so high an opinion, from the first day I met him, that I am proud of his achievements. I mean Custer. He is a noble fellow."[22] Both Hancock and Baldy Smith praised Custer for his initiative and daring over those several days that began up in a balloon.

With the Confederate forces retreating toward Richmond, the Union troops advanced to the Chickahominy River. McClellan's chief engineer, Brigadier General John G. Barnard, called the river "one of the most formidable obstacles that could be opposed to the advance of the army."[23] But Custer noted that while the river was "chargeable with some of the misfortunes of the Army of the Potomac, [it] was almost literally a stepping-stone for my personal advancement."[24]

The Chickahominy was not broad or swift, but it flowed through belts of forested swamp three to four hundred yards wide, and in the spring flood the river would spread across the entire area. The land was soft and spongy, unsuited for major military movements. There were a few widely separated and well-defended bridges. General Barnard was told that otherwise the river was not fordable.

The idea that the Chickahominy could not be crossed did not impress Custer. Given a scouting detail three-quarters of a mile below New Bridge, he found a good approach to the bank and waded right into the river. The water was four feet deep, but the bottom was firm, and Custer was able to cross without difficulty. A few days later, he made a more dangerous scout, wading from near the bridge downstream for half a mile, risking fire from enemy pickets who apparently did not see him.

Having determined that the river was crossable, McClellan ordered a reconnaissance in force to prove that operations could be conducted there. On the rainy morning of May 24, Custer and Lieutenant Nicholas Bowen led a picked force of seventy-five men from Companies A and B of the 4th Michigan Infantry to the ford site. The men of A Company were from George's adopted hometown of Monroe. They crossed the river, then moved in a skirmish line toward the bridge, with the rest of the 4th following on the other bank.

The area was defended by the Fifth Louisiana and Tenth Georgia regiments, and Manley's battery of artillery. The rebels in the vicinity outnumbered the attacking force four to one. But Custer's raiders had the element of surprise, and they rushed the rebel outposts near the bridge, overwhelming the defenders, capturing many, and chasing those who broke back toward their camps. Custer grabbed a large bowie knife from one of the prisoners and brandished it to the regiment across the river.

"The Rebels say we can't stand cold steel," he shouted. "I captured this from one of them. Forward and show them that the Michigan boys will give them all the cold steel they want!"[25]

The 4th fired a volley at the rallying rebels and pushed across the river. The bridge had been fired so the men waded through the armpit-deep water holding their bayoneted muskets and cartridges above their heads. The Union troops began firing from a bridgehead in a ditch behind a fence, knee-deep in water, but as ammunition ran low and rebel artillery appeared, the Union force withdrew, taking thirty-five prisoners with them. The attacking Federals lost only one killed and seven wounded, against twenty-seven killed, twenty-six wounded, and forty-three missing on the Confederate side.

In his report of the action, Lieutenant Bowen praised Custer, saying he was "the first to cross the stream, the first to open fire upon the enemy, and one of the last to leave the field."[26] General Barnard said that the "attack and capture of the enemy's pickets by [Second Lieutenant Custer] and Lieutenant Bowen was founded upon these reconnaissances, to which the successful results are due."[27] In a note to Secretary of War Stanton, General McClellan noted that Custer and Bowen made "a very gallant reconnaissance" and that the recon force "handled [the rebels] terribly."[28]

After the action, McClellan sent for Custer to thank him for his efforts, and recalled him as "a slim, long-haired boy, carelessly dressed." He was fresh from the engagement and covered in Chickahominy mud. The general thanked Custer and asked what he could do for him. Custer "replied very modestly that he had nothing to ask, and evidently did not suppose that he had done anything to deserve extraordinary reward." McClellan then offered Custer a position as his aide-de-camp at the rank of Captain of Volunteers, and George "brightened up and assured me that he would regard such service as the most gratifying he could perform."

"McClellan had, by a rare power peculiar to him, in that short interview, won Custer's unfailing loyalty and affection," recalled Lieutenant Willard Glazier, of the 2nd New York Cavalry, "and when Custer was asked afterwards how he felt at the time, his eyes filled with tears, and he said: '*I felt I could have died for him.*'"[29]

CHAPTER FIVE

"I PROMISE THAT YOU SHALL HEAR OF ME"

McClellan liked Custer as "a reckless, gallant boy, undeterred by fatigue, unconscious of fear" whose "head was always clear in danger," and who "always brought me clear and intelligible reports of what he saw when under the heaviest fire. I became much attached to him."[1] Custer, likewise, admired McClellan. But they were in many ways opposites. Where Custer was the goat of his West Point class, McClellan graduated second in the Class of 1846. Where Custer was bold and spontaneous, McClellan was cautious and methodical. Both, however, were men of strong will and independent spirit, which could also be taken as arrogance and feed the resentment of rivals. Custer believed that McClellan's wartime failures were not the fault of the general, whom he considered a master strategist. Rather, he thought they were imposed by Washington politicians who conspired against him. "Few persons can realize or believe at this late day the extent of the opposition which McClellan encountered from those from whom his strongest support and encouragement should have come," Custer wrote long after the war. "This opposition was well known at the time; in fact there was little if any effort to conceal it."[2]

Custer was with "Little Mac" as the general's ambitious plan to take Richmond and defeat the rebellion was itself defeated. The Federal advance was blunted five miles from Richmond on May 31, 1862, at the Battle of Seven Pines. The Confederate commander, General Joseph E. Johnston, was wounded and eventually replaced by Robert E. Lee, who, though outnumbered, went on the offensive during the Seven Days' Battles, taking place from June 25 to July 1. The Confederates suffered almost twice the number of Union killed and wounded, but Lee's string of victories demoralized McClellan's army, ended his Peninsula Campaign, and undermined his already soft political support in Washington. The Federals still had considerable forces in the field, backed onto Malvern Hill on the James River, but McClellan was effectively paralyzed as a commander, and the threat to Richmond was over.

On August 5, McClellan sent a three-hundred-man reconnaissance in force toward the White Oak Swamp Bridge, about four miles from Malvern Hill. Custer was part of a twenty-five-man advance force with orders to "dash at once upon the enemy as soon as he should be discovered" and to "engage to the best advantage while the main body was being brought up." Near the bridge, the shock troops encountered thirty to forty men of the 10th Virginia Cavalry and fell on them with a fury. They killed three and captured twenty-two, and the rest dispersed. While part of the Federal detachment rushed ahead to capture the bridge, Custer and Lieutenant Byrnes "took the road to the left toward Malvern Hill, chasing, shooting, or capturing all the pickets that came from that direction." When the Confederates formed for a counterattack, the Federals withdrew. Colonel William W. Averell, commander of the 3rd

Pennsylvania Cavalry, later commended "the gallant and spirited conduct of Captain Custer and Lieutenant Byrnes."[3]

During the Peninsula Campaign, Custer encountered several West Point friends who were now Confederates. George found that their friendship remained "most loyal and unchanged." When they had parted as cadets, "it never entered our minds that war could destroy a friendship cemented by our four years of intimate association."[4]

On May 31, just before the Battle of Seven Pines, Custer's former roommate Lieutenant James B. Washington was captured while taking a message from Joseph E. Johnston to James Longstreet.[5] He was taken to McClellan's headquarters, where he met Custer and a few other officers he had known at West Point and was greeted with "much cordiality and glee." McClellan ordered that "the prisoner should not be treated very severely, but allowed a cigar and other refreshments occasionally." That night the group of former cadets had "rather a jollification" in a command tent, "rehearing scenes at West Point in which they had mingled, 'skylarking' at Benny Havens, and other haphazard frolics, stories of study and drill, and mutual inquiries for friends scattered south and north amid the ranks of the confederate armies."[6]

Later, as George related, "a strolling artist came through camp taking photographs" and rendered a striking set of pictures of Custer and Washington sitting together.[7] Washington called over a small black boy who was watching the photographer and had him sit at his feet. The photo wound up in the *London Illustrated News*, captioned "Both sides of the war and the cause of the war." The image of the reunited West Point chums was republished throughout the United States. It was an early moment of national fame for Custer, and "James B. Washington" dog tags were minted and distributed as collectables in the North.

When Washington was departing for his detainment at Fort Delaware, Custer tried to hand him some Federal bills, saying, "You must have some money Jim, those pictures in your pockets [Confederate currency] don't pass up there." When Washington refused, Custer stuffed the money in his vest pocket.[8] Later in the war, Washington's stepmother hosted Custer at her war-wearied Virginia home. In gratitude for his kind treatment of her stepson, she gave Custer a button from one of George Washington's coats. Custer eventually had the button mounted on gold and gave it to Libbie as a brooch. Mrs. Washington later said, "I would not at one time have believed it possible for me to like, or even acknowledge myself pleased with anyone from the North."[9]

Confederate Captain John W. "Gimlet" Lea, I company, Fifth North Carolina regiment, and formerly of Custer's class, was wounded and taken prisoner on May 5, 1862, at the Battle of Williamsburg. Lieutenant Alexander C. M. Pennington, Class of 1860, found Lea lying in a barn stall, his wounds untended, and brought him to Custer. "When we first saw each other he shed tears and threw his arms about my neck," Custer wrote,

> and we talked of old times and asked each other hundreds of questions about classmates on opposing sides. I carried his meals to him, gave him stockings of which he stood in need, and some money. This he did not want to take, but I forced it on him. He burst into tears and said it was more than he could stand. He insisted on writing in my notebook that if ever I should be taken prisoner he wanted me treated as he had been. His last words to me were, "God bless you, old boy!" The bystanders looked with surprise when we were talking, and afterwards asked if the prisoner were my brother.[10]

Williamsburg resident Margaret Durfey, wife of Confederate Colonel Goodrich Durfey, agreed to take Lea in while he recovered from his wounds. During his convalescence, Lea and their daughter, also named Margaret, fell in love and were engaged. Lea wanted Custer to serve as his best man for the wedding, but the Union Army was preparing to withdraw, so Gimlet and Margaret moved the nuptials up to the next evening, August 19. The ceremony was held at the Durfey house, called Bassett Hall, the groom in Confederate gray, the best man in Federal blue, and the bride, Margaret, and her bridesmaid, cousin Maggie, in maidenly white. "I never saw two prettier girls," Custer later wrote.

Custer stayed a few days at Bassett Hall, entertained by Maggie at the piano—she played Southern patriotic tunes in a vain attempt to get Custer's goat; but he simply laughed—and playing cards with Gimlet. "He won, every time," Custer wrote.[11] George left when the last of the Union forces pulled back. By September, Lea had been exchanged and was again with the Confederates, "fighting," Custer said, "for what he *supposes* to be right!"[12]

Meanwhile, the war had shifted north. Lee, believing rightly that McClellan would mount no further attacks near the Confederate capital, decisively defeated Union General John Pope's Army of Virginia at the Second Battle of Bull Run, August 28–30, 1862, opening the way for Lee to advance into Maryland.

McClellan moved to block him, their armies meeting at Antietam on September 17, 1862, and fighting to a stalemate in the bloodiest day of the war. McClellan's caution during and after the battle worked to Confederate benefit, and while the Union Army paused, Lee escaped back to Virginia. Custer saw some action during this period, though he was not in the thick of the fight. He was on hand for President Lincoln's visit to McClellan's headquarters in early October, in which the president urged the general to drive south and harry Lee's army. But McClellan wanted more time, men, and supplies, and consequently did little. This was the last straw for Lincoln, who was convinced that McClellan had an incurable case of "the slows." He relieved "Little Mac" of command on November 5 and replaced him with the reluctant Ambrose Burnside.

Custer believed the entire matter was political. "No officer of either side ever developed or gave evidence of the possession of that high order of military ability which at that peculiar and particular time was so greatly demanded in the Federal commander," he wrote. "The defeat of McClellan was not the result of combinations made either in the Confederate capital or in the camp of the Confederate army, but in Washington."[13] However, D. H. Strother, an artist, writer, and staff officer who was sympathetic to McClellan, succinctly summed up the reasons for his dismissal: "he created an army which he failed to handle, and conceived plans which he failed to carry out."[14]

Strother knew Custer around this time and called him "one of the most agreeable acquaintances I have made among the juniors of the Staff." He described him as "rather a handsome youth, with light, curling hair and lithe figure," whose "friends, it seems are pushing him for a Brigadier's commission to serve in the cavalry, and his comrades frequently joke him on the subject." He said that Custer "takes their chaffing pleasantly, and replies, with a shake of his curly head, 'Gentlemen, I don't know whether or not I am worthy of such promotion; but if they give it to me, I promise that you shall hear of me.'"[15]

CHAPTER SIX

"CONSPICUOUS GALLANTRY"

Custer remained on McClellan's staff, but with no battles to fight and winter setting in, he was authorized a furlough and returned to Monroe, Michigan.

In Custer's adopted hometown, as in most places removed from conflict, the day-to-day hardships of war were somewhat abstract. Monroe and the surrounding area sent more than three thousand young men to the war. Scores of them died in combat, or of disease.[1] "In my joyous life it was only when sorrow came to the town that I realized something of what war really was," Libbie recalled.[2] Judge Bacon made a daily trek to the railway station to get the Detroit newspapers, and when the news was bad and the casualty lists were long, the entire community saw his sadness as he trudged back up the street. "The war aged him greatly," Libbie said, "and he never recovered from his grief."[3]

Libbie, like many young women of the era, entertained the young men back on leave at social events. At a Thanksgiving party in 1862, Captain George Custer showed up. They were introduced by mutual friend Conway Noble—"I assented merely to be rid of him," Libbie said—and passed only a few words. But after the party, George "went home to dream," and Libbie said, "How little did I think my fate would be sealed."[4]

The dashing captain and the young society girl may have made a pretty couple, but for Libbie it was not love at first sight. "With the critical and exacting eye of a girl," she remembered, "I decided I would never like him no matter how attentive he was because his hair was light, and because I despised his military overcoat as it was lined with yellow."[5] Libbie was unaware that, far from being a matter of bad personal taste, yellow was the regulation color for the cavalry. But when Custer promised to "tone down his hair, and his overcoat lining," Libbie said, "finally I consented to know him."[6]

George had been smitten with Libbie since she had hailed him from the garden gate, eight years before, so the story went . But there were still obstacles to overcome before he could pursue a serious relationship with her. One was Libbie's view of matrimony. "If I thought of marriage at all it was with a shudder over what it involved in practical details," she said. "I had seriously contemplated the then-despised life of an old maid." She also said she had "never known, nor particularly cared for officers or army life."[7]

An even more serious obstruction was Judge Bacon. To him George Custer was still the kid who did chores to help pay his way through Stebbins' Academy. Going to West Point and earning a commission helped matters somewhat, but Bacon did not envision his daughter as an Army bride, and certainly not wed to a mere brevet captain.

The judge had also witnessed an incident a year earlier when George was back on leave and had gotten publicly drunk and staggered past the

Bacon house. But that drunken spell had actually been George's last. His sister Lydia had sternly rebuked him and likely warned him about what Judge Bacon would think of a public drunk. George took the pledge because he realized "there was no future for him if he continued to drink, as like everything else he did at that time there was no likelihood of its being done with moderation."[8] He later wrote that abstinence is something "which, if more generally followed, not only in the army, but in all professions, would save to the public service and to private occupations some of the bright intellects which otherwise are soon squandered and destroyed."[9]

In the end, George returned to war without any formal arrangement with Libbie. "Father's opposition had compelled me to consider his wishes," she wrote, "and refuse clandestine intercourse."[10] But she told the judge she would not promise never to see him again.

In April, Custer reported to General McClellan's private residence in New York City to help write final reports of his campaigns. It was "the most magnificently furnished house I was ever in," George wrote his sister, and Mrs. McClellan was "one of the most amiable and agreeable ladies" he had ever met.[11] But life in the city was expensive ($2.75 a day for board, he noted), and he longed to have more active service than sitting from 10:00 a.m. until 3:00 p.m. writing reports.

Custer's career was at a crossroads. Being tied to someone powerful is a double-edged sword, because when the mighty fall, those around them share a measure of their fate. His close association with McClellan would thereafter raise questions among Little Mac's numerous political opponents in Washington whether Custer was truly loyal. And as McClellan began to move from being a stubborn general to Lincoln's open political opponent, it only made matters worse.

Custer wanted to be appointed colonel of a state volunteer regiment. These posts were plum positions that often went to those with political pull. Custer was hampered by his Democratic background, his close association with the politically unpopular McClellan, and his lack of ties to Republicans beyond Congressman Bingham. Custer sent letters of recommendation from Generals Ambrose Burnside, George Stoneman, and Joseph Hooker to the Republican governor of Michigan, Austin Blair, but to no avail. Custer noted, "If the Governor refuses to appoint me it will be for some other reason than a lack of recommendations."[12]

George even made an appeal to the troops of the 5th Michigan Cavalry regiment, then in need of a new commander. "About the 1st of June," recalled Captain Samuel Harris, "a slim young man with almost flaxen hair, looking more like a big boy, came to us and, as the line officers expressed it, with the cheek of a government mule, actually asked us to sign a petition to Gov. Austin Blair to appoint him as Colonel of the 5th. He said his name was George A. Custer, and that he was a West Pointer." Harris said, "We all declined to sign such a petition as we considered him too young."[13]

Custer's luck returned in the person of Brigadier General Alfred Pleasonton, one of Stoneman's cavalry division commanders, who picked Custer as an aide-de-camp in May 1863. Pleasonton was a District of Columbia native and graduate of the Class of 1844, a career horse soldier who fought with the famed 2nd Dragoons in Mexico and on the frontier. He was in a number of important engagements in the Civil War and was brevetted for bravery at Antietam. Pleasonton had seen Custer in action days before that battle when George rode with him and the 8th Illinois Cavalry pursuing the Confederates after the Battle of South Mountain. They caught the Confederate rear guard cavalry near Boonsborough, Maryland, on September 15 and "charged them repeatedly, and drove them some two miles beyond the town."[14] Pleasonton noted in particular Custer's gallantry in the charges, as well as that of his aide, Captain Elon Farnsworth, whose uncle commanded the regiment.

Pleasonton had seen young Custer at his best. War and battle very much agreed with him. He took to it naturally, and the danger and thrill of it spoke to something deep in his character. Custer wrote to his cousin Augusta that he would be glad when the war was over, and when he thought of the "pain and misery produced to individuals as well as the miserable sorrow caused throughout the land," he could not but "earnestly hope for peace, and at an early date." However, he wrote, "If I answer for myself *alone*, I must say that I shall regret to see the war end. I would be willing, yes glad, to see a battle every day during my life."[15]

Though a staff officer now, Custer still sought action. At the Battle of Chancellorsville (May 1–4, 1863), he took part in Stoneman's raid behind Confederate lines. General "Fighting Joe" Hooker, the Union commander defeated at Chancellorsville, asked for Stoneman to be relieved, saying that "one more raid like it would leave us no cavalry." But Custer thought Hooker was making Stoneman a scapegoat for his own failings. "Stoneman stands very high in the estimation of the entire army," Custer wrote, "but it has become a rule in this army, from custom, that when any failure occurs, someone must be found to bear the responsibility, and in selecting such a person it is not proposed to find that one who really is responsible but to discover the most *available* man."[16] In June, Stoneman was relegated to a desk job at the Cavalry Bureau in Washington, but his rough treatment was another lucky break for Custer, since General Pleasonton was tapped to take over command of the Cavalry Corps.

On June 8, the day after receiving his new assignment, Pleasonton was poised on the banks of the Rappahannock with a strike force of eleven thousand cavalry, three thousand infantry, and six batteries of horse artillery. Custer was up late as duty officer in Pleasonton's headquarters at the James Knox house near Beverly's Ford, with orders to awaken the general at 2:00 a.m. He wrote to his sister that he was about to embark on a major raid. "We could see the rebels in their rifle pits on the opposite bank before dark," he said. The Union cavalry had quietly moved into attack positions, and at four in the morning they would "ford the river and charge" the enemy emplacements. "It will be a daring undertaking," he wrote, and the raiders expected to make it as far as Culpeper, fifteen miles west, and thence beyond. "We can ride over anything that opposes us," he predicted.[17]

When the hour came for the attack, Custer and Colonel Benjamin Franklin "Grimes" Davis, Class of 1855 and a pro-Union Alabamian, rode down to the riverbank and quietly crossed the fog-enshrouded ford, pistols drawn. As they rode up the opposite bank, they were challenged and opened fire, which signaled the 8th New York Cavalry regiment to charge across the ford after them. The Union horsemen rode furiously through the Southern positions, slashing and firing as the surprised rebels attempted to mount a defense.[18]

Hooker devised the raid to beat Stuart's cavalry to the punch. The plan was to cross the river in two columns, one under John Buford at Beverly's Ford and another under David McMurtrie Gregg six miles south at Kelly's Ford; converge near Brandy Station; and drive on to Culpeper. Pleasonton expected to face some, though light, resistance. But the Union commanders were unaware that they faced not a small raiding force but 9,500 rebel cavalrymen. And Culpeper, rather than being lightly defended, was surrounded by Ewell's and Longstreet's corps and was serving as Lee's headquarters for his planned move north into Pennsylvania. So what both sides believed would be the start of a few days of raiding became the Battle of Brandy Station, the largest cavalry battle in the war.

Custer was mounted on a horse called Roanoke, an iron-gray stallion he had captured during a raid into Virginia's Northern Neck three weeks earlier. The horse was allegedly worth nine hundred dollars, and Custer wrote his sister, "I never intend to ride him into battle, he is too valuable." His preference was to send Roanoke home and "leave him there until the war is over." But his other horse, Harry, was "getting very fat and pretty," and the need for a strong mount in the planned-for raid changed his mind.[19]

Roanoke, however, was untested in war, and his first engagement showed him lacking in martial ardor. Custer and "Grimes" Davis, leading the 8th New York, slammed into the 6th Virginia Cavalry on the Beverly Ford road. A chaotic fracas ensued in which Davis was mortally wounded and Roanoke dashed into a roadside fence, where the horse "huddled in fright, neighing madly but budging not an inch"[20] until the Federals retreated. On the retreat, Roanoke cleared a stone wall clumsily and sent Custer flying. He remounted and hurried to join the main body of Union cavalry.

The Battle of Brandy Station raged for hours but was inconclusive: on the one hand, Lee's movement north was shielded by the costly engagement; on the other, the Union Cavalry Corps proved it could match Stuart's famed horsemen. Custer was singled out by Pleasonton as being "conspicuous for gallantry throughout the fight."[21]

About a week later, Custer was given another opportunity for battle. General Hooker ordered Pleasonton to break through the rebel cavalry screen, penetrate the Blue Ridge Mountains, and determine if Lee's forces were moving down the Shenandoah Valley. Pleasonton ordered Brigadier General Gregg's division west down the Little River Turnpike to the town of Aldie, a key crossroads in the Bull Run Mountains, eighteen miles east of both Ashby's and Snickers Gaps.

Custer rode along with Gregg and his staff. David McMurtrie Gregg was a scruffy, bearded cavalryman who had served on America's northwest frontier after graduating with honors in the West Point Class of 1855. He had a solid combat record in the Civil War, and his sturdy demeanor had earned him the nickname "Old Steady." Gregg was not known for dressing the part of a commanding general, and that day Custer blended in with his informal style.

"When Custer appeared he at once attracted the attention of the entire command," recalled Captain Henry C. Meyer of the 24th New York Cavalry. He was "dressed like an ordinary enlisted man, his trousers tucked in a pair of short-legged government boots, his horse equipments being those of an ordinary wagonmaster. He rode with a little rawhide riding whip stuck in his bootleg, and had long yellow curls down to his shoulders, his face ruddy and good-natured."[22] He also sported a broad-brimmed straw hat. After watering on the banks of Little River, Custer's horse Harry (he had returned to his trusty mount following Roanoke's less than ideal performance at Brandy Station) slipped coming up the bank, dumping George in the river. He emerged unharmed but soaking wet. "The dust at this time was so thick that one could not see more than a set of fours ahead," Meyer wrote, "and in a few minutes, when it settled on his wet clothes and long wet hair, Custer was an object that one can better imagine than I can describe."[23]

Kilpatrick's brigade led the advance and made contact with rebel pickets outside Aldie on June 17, sweeping them briskly through the town. They encountered firmer resistance from the 5th Virginia Cavalry under the command of Thomas Rosser, who were firing from behind a stone wall with artillery support. The rebels "received Kilpatrick's men with a murderous fire," wrote First Lieutenant Henry Hall, "which literally covered the field in front with dead and dying, and sent the others flying in disorder to the rear."[24] With Kilpatrick's offensive power spent, Confederate Colonel Thomas T. Munford sent the 3rd Virginia forward to counterattack. He hoped to seize Union guns and push the Federal cavalry back through Aldie. At that critical moment, the 1st Maine Cavalry arrived.

Kilpatrick, retreating with the remnants of his brigade and looking "a ruined man," saw Custer hastening the Maine cavalry to the field. "Forward First Maine!" Kilpatrick shouted. "You saved the field at Brandy Station, you can do it here!" Custer, who was with the cavalry's commander, Colonel Calvin Douty, waved his saber and charged ahead. The regiment followed.

"In an instant we were among them," Hall wrote, "and soon all who were on the road were on the run." They "charged up the road close at the heels of the enemy and midst such a storm of dust that it was impossible to tell the dividing point between friends and foes," wrote private William O. Howe.[25] Kilpatrick was stopped when his horse was shot through the throat. Douty rushed out far in advance of his men and was cut down. Custer, with Harry galloping uncontrollably, powered through the chaos reaching the enemy rear, fighting all the way, then circled the field and returned to the Union lines.[26] George might have been run down by the rebels, but with his dust-caked clothing and unorthodox hat, it was not clear which side he was on.

Colonel Munford reported of Aldie, "I have never seen as many Yankees killed in the same space of ground in any fight I have ever seen, or any battle-field in Virginia that I have ever been over."[27] But the Virginians withdrew and the Federals held the field. Captain Henry Meyer said at Aldie that Custer attracted "the attention of every one present by his conspicuous gallantry."[28]

By June 25, Lee had crossed the Potomac into Maryland with most of his army.[29] President Lincoln and Union General in Chief Henry Halleck lacked confidence in Hooker's ability to thwart Lee and relieved him of command on June 28, replacing him with General George Meade.

That day, Meade sent for Pleasonton—who had recently been promoted to major general—to discuss the growing crisis of Lee's invasion and how they could handle it. "I told him that Lee would make for Gettysburg," Pleasonton recalled, "and that if he seized that position before we could reach it we should have hard work to get him out, and that to prevent his doing so would depend more on the cavalry than anything else." He asked permission to reorganize the Cavalry Corps, and especially "to have officers I would name specially assigned to it, as I expected to have some desperate work to do." Meade agreed, and in his first dispatch to Washington three young captains were elevated to the rank of brigadier general: Wesley Merritt, Elon Farnsworth, and George Custer.[30] They were assigned to the 3rd Cavalry Division under Judson Kilpatrick.

Custer at twenty-three became the then-youngest general officer. In that respect he reflected a trend. The cavalry was an arm of experimentation and innovation on both sides of the war, and each had their twenty-something horse generals. All the members of the 3rd Division's command group were in their twenties: in addition to Custer, Kilpatrick and Merritt were twenty-seven, and Farnswoth was just shy of twenty-six. Custer's friend Pierce M. B. Young of Georgia became a Confederate general at twenty-six, and so did Thomas Rosser. Confederate General Stephen Dodson Ramseur had gained his promotion at age twenty-five. Former West Point Cadet John Herbert Kelly, whom Custer had saluted as he was being borne off on the shoulders of his friends to join the Confederacy, became a cavalry brigadier in November 1863, also at age twenty-three. He was killed near Franklin, Tennessee, in August 1864.

Custer received notice of his promotion June 29, and at first he thought it was a joke. When it became clear he really was being made a brigadier, he quickly penned a note to someone he felt needed to know immediately, Elizabeth Bacon. "I owe it all to Gen'l Pleasonton," he wrote. "He has been more like a father to me than a Gen'l."[31]

PART THREE

THE BOY
GENERAL

Custer at "Woodstock Races," from Frederick Whittaker, *A Complete Life of Gen. George A. Custer* (New York: Sheldon, 1876).

CHAPTER SEVEN

GETTYSBURG

Custer took command of the 2nd Cavalry Brigade, made up of four Michigan regiments.[1] Captain James H. Kidd of the 6th Michigan Cavalry first saw George on June 30, 1863, and the general made quite an impression. "An officer superbly mounted who sat his charger as if to the manor born," Kidd wrote. "Tall, lithe, active, muscular, straight as an Indian and as quick in his movements, he had the fair complexion of a school girl." Custer wore a black velvet jacket, trimmed in gold lace and fronted by a double row of brass buttons over a blue navy shirt, and "a necktie of brilliant crimson was tied in a graceful knot at the throat, the lower ends falling carelessly in front." His wide-brimmed black hat with a gold cord "was worn turned down on one side, giving him a rakish air. His golden hair fell in graceful luxuriance nearly or quite to his shoulders, and his upper lip was garnished with a blonde moustache. A sword and belt, gilt spurs and top boots completed his unique outfit."[2] Lieutenant Colonel Theodore Lyman, one of Meade's aides, said, "This officer is one of the funniest-looking beings you ever saw, and looks like a circus rider gone mad! … His aspect, though highly amusing, is also pleasing, as he has a very merry blue eye, and a devil-may-care style."[3] Custer explained, "I want my men to recognize me on any part of the field."[4] If any of Custer's men had doubts about the bravery of their brigade's eccentric-looking leader, they were dispelled later that day when Custer led a charge through the streets of Hanover, Pennsylvania, against rebel cavalry under the command of Jeb Stuart.

After several pitched cavalry battles in Virginia weeks earlier, among them Brandy Station and Aldie, Stuart moved the Confederate cavalry south, appearing to retreat back toward rebel lines on the Rappahannock. But this was a feint; Stuart swung around Manassas Junction and moved back north, crossing the Potomac at Rowser's Ford between Leesburg and Washington, D.C., on June 28.

First creating panic by moving toward the Federal capital, Stuart drove north into Maryland, raiding Union supply trains and skirmishing with Pleasonton's cavalry. His advance was slowed, however, by the 125 captured wagonloads of supplies he had in tow, and his route made it impossible to maintain contact with the right edge of the main body of the Army of Northern Virginia. Stuart was unable to provide General Lee with the necessary screening troops and intelligence regarding Union movements. Bereft of his "eyes and ears," Lee moved north, seeking to avoid a decisive engagement but uncertain where his enemy was maneuvering, and in what numbers. As Confederate General Henry Heth later said, "The failure to crush the Federal army in Pennsylvania in 1863, in the opinion of almost all the officers of the Army of Northern Virginia, can be expressed in five words—*the absence of our cavalry.*"[5]

On July 1, Heth stumbled into combat against Union General John Buford's 1st Cavalry Division at Gettysburg, and Lee consolidated his scattered forces. The next day, Kilpatrick's division was ordered to probe the Confederate flank on the eastern reaches of Gettysburg and perhaps find a way to disrupt Lee's lines of communication through the Cashtown Gap. Stuart had reached Gettysburg earlier that same day, having ridden as far north as Carlisle looking for the Army of Northern Virginia. Having word of the Union movement, Stuart ordered Wade Hampton's brigade to intercept and block the Federals along the Hunterstown road.

Union cavalry reached Hunterstown that afternoon. A brisk charge through the town by the 18th Pennsylvania Cavalry put to flight a small rebel holding force. Outside Hunterstown, Farnsworth's brigade deployed to the right on the road to Cashtown. Custer took the left, which led toward Gettysburg and Hampton's main body.

Spotting the enemy cavalry, Custer briefly surveyed their defenses and planned his attack. The 6th Michigan regiment was in the lead. Captain Henry E. Thompson of Company A prepared to charge up the road, with two companies dismounted in an adjacent wheat field to provide support should the assault force fail. Battery M, commanded by Custer's friend and now brevet Captain Alexander Pennington, was deployed to the rear.

When the attack force had readied, Custer rode to the front and took his place beside Captain Thompson. He was conspicuous in his black velvet jacket and gold-trimmed trousers, "the gilt stripes of a brigadier-general on his arm," Henry C. Meyer recalled. "He wore a man-o-war's man's shirt with the wide collar out on his shoulders, on each point of which was worked a silver star indicating his rank of brigadier-general. The neck was open, just as a man-o'-war's man has his, and he wore a sailor's tie."[6] Company A faced superior forces in a good defensive posture, but this did not deter Custer. He sounded the charge and led the men thundering down the road toward the Confederates.

"The charge was most gallantly made," Hampton later wrote. But the attack was doomed. The Rebels opened up as the Union cavalry closed. The Federals pressed on, passing the first line of dismounted Confederates and taking heavy fire in the flanks. Captain Thompson was felled, severely wounded.[7] His aide Lieutenant Stephen H. Ballard had his horse shot from beneath him and was taken prisoner. Custer's horse took a bullet in the head and fell, throwing him. Rebel troops rushed to capture or kill the general as he regained his footing. Private Norval Churchill rode to the rescue, shooting a Confederate who was closing on Custer before hoisting the general onto his horse and dashing back up the road.[8] Company A pulled back, with twenty-five wounded, leaving two dead.

Hampton's men counterattacked as the Michiganders withdrew, but they met heavy fire from Union skirmishers and artillery and were repulsed. An artillery duel then commenced that lasted a few hours. The fight died down, and the contending forces held their positions as night fell. Around midnight, Kilpatrick's division was ordered to retire south to the area around Two Taverns on the Baltimore Pike.

Custer's brigade arrived four hours later. They had been on the move and fighting continuously since June 29 and needed some rest. The men bedded down to the sound of cannon fire coming from the direction of Culp's Hill, about five miles northwest. It was "rather serious music to be lulled to sleep by," Major Luther S. Trowbridge remarked to his friend Major Noah Ferry, both of the 5th Michigan.[9] But after only three hours' rest, Custer and his men were readying again for action. Kilpatrick's division had been ordered to the southern end of the battlefield to strike at the Confederate right flank. Merritt's and Farnsworth's brigades moved out, and Custer was preparing to as well, when fate intervened.

That morning, General Gregg was in a position about five miles east of Gettysburg. General Pleasonton ordered Gregg to pull in closer to the right flank of the army dug in at Culp's Hill, which was then under attack and had seen bitter fighting. But Gregg hesitated, sensing that it was more important he hold the area to his front. He also knew that the part of his command on hand, a single brigade under the command of Colonel John B. McIntosh, would be insufficient to take on the full force of Stuart's cavalry should they attempt an end-run around the Union position.[10] Gregg's other brigade, commanded by his cousin Colonel J. Irvin Gregg, was further back on the Baltimore Pike. Gregg needed support, and Custer was available. On Gregg's order, Custer turned the Michigan Brigade north.

Gregg's instincts were good; Stuart was plotting another of his daring flanking maneuvers. He planned to sweep into the Union rear between the Hanover Road and the Baltimore Pike, creating confusion, raiding supply trains and encampments, disrupting Meade's stream of reinforcements, and supporting the massive infantry assault on the Union center that was about to be launched by General George Pickett. At mid-day, Stuart began moving south to the attack, and Gregg, more by design than chance, stood directly in his path.

Stuart paused on Cress Ridge, overlooking the Union lines. The ground between them, near the Rummel and Trostle farms, was not ideal for a cavalry engagement. There were trees to either side of the fields, which were crossed by stone and wood fences. Stuart's mobility would be limited, but he had the advantage of numbers. He ordered the Louisiana Guard Artillery battery to fire a round in each of the four directions of the compass, perhaps to flush out any other Union troops in the area, or to signal the Confederate main body that he was commencing the critical phase of his movement.

Pennington's battery answered Stuart's artillery, and the battle commenced. Dismounted rebel skirmishers from Ferguson's and Chambliss's brigades advanced across the fields against a similar line of men from the 5th and 6th Michigan regiments. The firepower edge of the Spencer rifles carried by the Michiganders stalled the initial Confederate movement. "Our boys held their fire until the rebs got within less than twenty rods, then they opened on them," Captain Harris recalled. "After the first volley the rebel officers called out, 'Now for them before they can reload.' But our boys did not have to stop to reload their Spencers, but gave them a second, third, and a fourth volley. Many a reb fell, either dead or wounded; the rest were unable to stand the rain of lead and the most of them got back faster than they came. … One tall, lean, lank Johnny, after he came in, asked to see our guns, saying: 'You'ns load in the morning and fire all day.'"[11]

"A stubborn and spirited contest ensued," Kidd recalled. "The opposing batteries filled the air with shot and shrieking shell. Amazing marksmanship was shown by Pennington's battery, and such accurate artillery firing was never seen on any other field. Alger's men, with their eight-shotted carbines, forced their adversaries slowly but surely back, the gray line fighting well, and superior in numbers, but unable to withstand the storm of bullets."[12]

As the scene developed on Rummel Farm, word came from General Pleasonton affirming Gregg's decision not to withdraw, and saying he should meet the enemy where he stood. But Pleasonton also ordered Gregg to release Custer to join Kilpatrick's planned attack on the Confederate right. Again Gregg stalled. He knew a major engagement was developing, and he had a report from General Oliver O. Howard of XI Corps that "heavy clouds of dust were seen rising above the trees on his right," indicating Gregg was facing the bulk of Stuart's cavalry. He sent word back that he required written orders to release Custer, and until he received them, the Michigan Brigade would stay where it was. Gregg noted that Custer, "fully satisfied of the intended attack, was well pleased to remain with his brigade."

Meanwhile, Union Colonel John B. McIntosh moved forward with dismounted troops of the 1st New Jersey and 3rd Pennsylvania, intending to relieve Custer's 5th and 6th Michigan. As they were exchanging positions they heard the opening of the great barrage in support of Pickett's Charge. James H. Kidd wrote, "The tremendous volume of sound volleyed and rolled across the intervening hills like reverberating thunder in a storm."[13]

At about the same time, Stuart began his attack in earnest, pushing up skirmishers as artillery rained on Custer's men. Pennington's battery gave covering fire, "the most accurate that I have ever seen," Gregg said.

Custer ordered a battalion in under Major Noah Ferry of the 5th Michigan to support McIntosh, but they rushed into an ambush laid by the 34th Virginia Battalion. "Rally boys!" cried Major Ferry as his men began to break. "Rally for the fence!" An instant later he was felled with a bullet to the head.

The battle around the Rummel Farm grew more intense. McIntosh committed the rest of his brigade, and Stuart more than matched him. Gregg directed an artillery barrage that blunted the rebel assault, and they fell back. But before the Union defenders could reform, Stuart's famed 1st Virginia Cavalry regiment, of Fitz Lee's brigade, charged without warning toward the Union right-center. "The impetuosity of those gallant fellows, after two weeks of hard marching and hard fighting on short rations, was not only extraordinary, but irresistible," Stuart wrote. "The enemy's masses vanished before them like grain before the scythe, and that regiment elicited the admiration of every beholder, and eclipsed the many laurels already won by its gallant veterans." McIntosh's men scattered to the protection of nearby woods.

Had Stuart moved immediately to support the 1st Virginia, the contest might have been decided. But before he could bring more force to bear, Custer's 7th Michigan Cavalry moved forward. The 7th was a small, inexperienced but eager regiment. Gregg ordered them to counterattack. This was Custer's moment. He rode to the front of the 7th, tucked his small hat into his pocket, drew his saber, and gave the order to charge.

"Come on you Wolverines!" he shouted and spurred his horse ahead. Custer rode bareheaded into battle, his golden locks streaming in the wind as the Michiganders raced after him across the field. The dismounted 9th and 13th Virginia regiments opened up on the Michiganders, half of whom veered into a fence. Major Luther S. Trowbridge of the 5th Michigan saw squadron piled upon squadron, "breaking upon the struggling mass in front, like the waves of the sea upon a rocky shore, until all were mixed in one confused and tangled mess."[14] Troops from the 1st Virginia jumped from their horses and attacked from the other side of the fence. Lieutenant George R. Briggs of the 7th Michigan recalled that "bullets were flying mighty thick at this time, and the air was filled with the shouts of men—the bursting of shells—the cries of the wounded—and the commands of the officers on both sides."[15]

"Custer's men had now warmed up to the work," observed Colonel William A. Morgan of the 1st Virginia Cavalry. "The fighting here was fierce, and terrible, they demanded our surrender, we telling them to go to that speculative country, generally supposed to be even hotter than the plains of Gettysburg were at that time."[16] Some officers of the 7th pulled down the fence, and the Virginians broke with the Federals in pursuit. "My men did not have time to reload their carbines," Colonel Morgan recalled, "but were clubbing them to ward off and return the sabre cuts, and thrusts of the maddened enemy."[17]

Custer had continued across the field with the rest of the regiment but lost contact with the enemy and was turning to pull back. As he did so, Colonel Laurence Baker of the 1st North Carolina Cavalry saw an opportunity and attacked. The startled men of the 7th Michigan stampeded back toward their lines, and another frenzied fight ensued as remnants of the 5th Michigan and McIntosh's men pitched in. "For God's sake men," McIntosh implored, "if you are ever going to stand, stand now, for you are on your free soil!"[18]

With the battlefield in chaos, Confederate Generals Wade Hampton and Fitzhugh Lee appeared from behind Cress Ridge leading their two battle-hardened brigades. "In superb form, with sabers glistening, they advanced," James Kidd wrote, "It was an inspiring and imposing spectacle that brought a thrill to the hearts of the spectators on the opposite slope."[19] Captain Miller said, "A grander spectacle than their advance has rarely been beheld! They marched with well-aligned fronts and steady reigns; Their polished saber-blades dazzling in the piercing rays of a bright summer's sun.... All eyes turned upon them and it seemed like folly to resist them."[20]

Gregg watched with growing concern as the rebel horsemen began thundering across the field. The only fresh unit he had left was the 1st Michigan regiment, which was heavily outnumbered. Nevertheless, he ordered them in. Custer, who had returned from the field, rode to Colonel Charles Town, commander of the 1st, to relay the order. "Colonel Town, I shall have to ask you to charge," he said, "and I want to go on in with you."[21] Custer repeated his rallying cry, "Come on, you Wolverines!" and they rushed forward, Custer four lengths ahead.[22]

"In addition to this numerical superiority," Custer wrote, "the enemy had the advantage of position and were exultant over the repulse of the 7th Michigan Cavalry. All these facts considered, would seem to render success on the part of the 1st impossible. Not so, however."

Custer's horse, Roanoke, fell, but George leapt onto another mount and rode into the clash. "Then it was steel to steel," Kidd wrote. "The fighting became hand to hand, blow for blow, cut for cut and oath for oath," recalled Colonel Morgan of the 1st Virginia Cavalry. With the sounds of cannonade and musket fire in the background from Pickett's assault, "it seemed as if the very furies from the infernal regions were turned loose on each other."[23]

"The First Michigan boys striking the rebs in the left flank, crowded them up in a heap," Captain Harris recalled, "so much so that the rebs could hardly do anything but try to defend themselves."[24] Captain William E. Miller of Company H, 3rd Pennsylvania Cavalry, said the sound of the collision of the two forces was "a crash like the falling of timber."

There followed "the clashing of sabers, the firing of pistols, the demands for surrender and cries of the combatants now filled the air."[25] Horses fell and crushed their riders; other unhorsed cavalrymen fought on foot. Miller, who had direct orders to hold his ground, disregarded them and struck the Confederate left. Miller was wounded, but his disobedience helped repulse the Confederates, and in 1897 he was awarded a Medal of Honor for his action.

"For minutes," Kidd recalled, "and for minutes that seemed like years—the gray column stood and staggered before the blow; then yielded, and fled."[26]

"For a moment," Custer wrote, "but only a moment, that long, heavy column stood its ground; then, unable to withstand the impetuosity of our attack, it gave way into a disorderly rout, leaving vast numbers of their dead and wounded in our possession, while the 1st, being masters of the field, had the proud satisfaction of seeing the much-vaunted 'chivalry,' led by their favorite commander, seek safety in headlong flight." Major Luther S. Trowbridge of the 5th Michigan thought the retreating rebels looked like "a flock of frightened sheep," and remarked that "the picture of that stubble field, with a thousand men scampering over it for dear life, our men in hot pursuit, while Pennington's battery sent its shrieking shells over our heads will ever remain most vividly photographed in my memory."[27]

Stuart's attack was broken. The outnumbered and disorganized Union troops had mounted a fierce enough resistance to frustrate the Confederate plan and bar the way to the Union rear. The Confederate cavalry withdrew, and Custer returned to Gregg, his face spattered with blood.

Things had not gone as well on the southern end of the field. Kilpatrick was ordered to harry the Confederate right flank, but rather than swing wide and deep, as Stuart was trying to do, he struck directly into the rebel flank, anchored in the rough ground near Round Top and Devil's Den. He first sent in Merritt's brigade, attacking dismounted on relatively open ground against Brigadier General George "Tige" Anderson's brigade of Georgia infantry, who handily checked the assault. Kilpatrick then ordered Elon Farnsworth and his brigade to attack on horseback to Merritt's right, across much rougher terrain and against Confederate infantry emplaced behind trees, fences, and walls.

After futile efforts by the 1st West Virginia and 5th New York regiments, Kilpatrick ordered in the 1st Vermont. Farnsworth protested, as Henry C. Parsons recalled, saying the members of his command were "'too good men to kill.' Kilpatrick turned, greatly excited and said: 'Do you refuse to obey my orders? If you are afraid to lead the charge, I will lead it.' Farnsworth rose in his stirrups and leaned forward, with his sabre half-drawn; he looked magnificent in his passion and cried: 'Take that back!' Kilpatrick rose defiantly, but repentingly said: 'I did not mean it; forget it.' For a moment, nothing was said. [Then] Farnsworth spoke: 'General, if you order the charge I will lead it, but you must take the awful responsibility.'"[28]

The result was a slaughter, a "mad charge by a mad leader," one rebel defender said. Farnsworth's brigade suffered a total of 183 casualties, and Farnsworth himself was struck down by five bullets. It was one of the episodes in his career that earned General Kilpatrick the nickname "Kil-cavalry."

Custer's brigade suffered even greater losses. Of the 254 Union casualties in the fight near Rummel Farm, 219 had been in Custer's command.[29] However, these men were not wasted, as Farnsworth and his command had been. Kilpatrick's assault was ill planned and poorly executed, and had Custer been on hand for the attack, it would have made no difference. But had Custer not been on the field with Gregg, Stuart would have had the edge, and rebel cavalry would have rampaged in the Union rear during the critical moments of Pickett's Charge. Whether it would have been enough to change the outcome of that assault is debatable, but Custer's critical role in the victory on east cavalry field is not.

General Meade, in his official report of the Battle of Gettysburg, summed up the cavalry fight against Stuart in one sentence: "General Gregg was engaged with the enemy on our extreme right, having passed across the Baltimore pike and Bonaughtown road and boldly attacked the enemy's left and rear." Stuart claimed victory, saying, "The enemy were driven from the field," and that "had the enemy's main body been dislodged, as was confidently hoped and expected, I was in precisely the right position to discover it and improve the opportunity."[30] Wade Hampton praised his men for keeping the Union cavalry in check. Edward Porter Alexander, Longstreet's artillery commander, gave his opinion that "the result [of the cavalry engagement] was a draw, each side claiming what it held at the close as a victory."[31]

Whatever the Confederates might believe, the Union cavalrymen knew they had achieved something significant. They had kept the Baltimore Pike open, held the Union right, and prevented Stuart from savaging the rear of Meade's army. John D. Follmer of the 16th Pennsylvania Cavalry said that "Custer was in his glory that day, if ever, and the Michigan Brigade proved itself to be the equal of any brigade in the service."[32] Custer later rather immodestly wrote in his report, "I challenge the annals of warfare to produce a more brilliant or successful charge of cavalry."[33]

CHAPTER EIGHT

THE "DARING, TERRIBLE DEMON" OF BATTLE

uster's star rose considerably after Gettysburg. General Pleasonton noted that the performance of young Generals Custer and Merritt "increased the confidence entertained in their ability and gallantry to lead troops on the field of battle." Custer was given a brevet promotion to major in the Regular Army for "gallant and meritorious services," and word began to spread about his achievements. A few weeks after the battle, James Kidd was riding a train to Washington and observed that "the name of Custer, the 'boy General,' was seemingly on every tongue and there was no disposition on our part to conceal the fact that we had been with him."[1]

Custer's natural flamboyance and charisma helped. Joseph Fought, a boy bugler who met Custer in the opening days of the Civil War, said he was "a conspicuous figure from the first, attracting attention wherever he went."[2] That included the attention of reporters, at a time when stories in East Coast papers were reprinted in smaller newspapers nationwide.[3] *New York Times* correspondent Edward A. Paul, who wrote extensively on the operations of the Army of the Potomac, often spent time with Custer's command and wrote comprehensive accounts of the operations of the Michigan Brigade.

Custer welcomed the attention. He allowed more access to reporters than most commanders did in those days. Many generals saw journalists as more trouble than they were worth, either passing along critical intelligence to the enemy through their stories or stirring up trouble with Washington by reporting incidents and shortcomings that did not make it into official dispatches. General Sherman famously court-martialed *New York Herald* reporter Thomas W. Knox after he violated an order not to accompany troops on what turned out to be a failed attack on Vicksburg. But Custer's press was generally good; a month after Gettysburg, the *Herald* published a glowing front-page profile:

> General Custer is not sufficiently known.... With a manly and weather-beaten face of severe expression, he wears the long flaxen curls of a girl of fifteen, and in lieu of the usual uniform dons a black velvet jacket, embroidered profusely on the back and arms with gold lace. He is proud of his Michigan men, and they fully return the sentiment. Whenever a charge is made, be it of brigade, regiment or company, he trots coolly at the head, spurs into a gallop, and the curls, gaily dancing time to each movement as a beacon followed with enthusiasm. Custer, added to unflinching bravery, has excellent judgment, and is universally esteemed by his brother officers. He is a man of mark, and would shine in any military sphere.[4]

The Custer who said he would be glad to see a battle every day of his life almost got his wish in the weeks and months after Gettysburg. The

Michigan Brigade was in constant action, first pursuing Lee's army as it withdrew to the Potomac, then continuing the fight into central Virginia. By August 1863, the Michigan Brigade was on the Rappahannock, opposite Fredericksburg. When Custer got word that his friend Thomas Rosser was across the river, he decided to pay him a visit. He asked Captain Samuel Harris to go to the river under a flag of truce (actually Custer's handkerchief) and negotiate a meeting of the two West Pointers. "I walked up the river road holding the handkerchief over my head," he recalled. "A large crowd very soon collected to see what the Yankee wanted." Harris told his rebel counterpart that "Gen. Custer was close by and would like to come over" to meet with Rosser. A half hour later, Rosser appeared and said, "Send him over." Harris escorted Custer to the river where Rosser sent a boat to fetch him. "At least 1000 cavalry and infantry from the rebel army thronged about the wharf as spectators when Gen. Custer landed," according to one report. "His reception by the officers was exceedingly cordial."[5]

"Custer staid over until about four o'clock," Harris recalled. "I was becoming anxious about him when he returned, saying that he 'had a fine time over there.'"[6]

On another occasion Thomas B. Beal of Company I, 14th North Carolina Infantry, was commanding the picket line in the morning when a Union officer "rode from the woods in our front and dashed straight for my picket post." The officer was accompanied by unarmed soldiers carrying newspapers and coffee for exchange. "The horseman rode up in a few paces of my post and came to a halt," Beal recalled, "at the same time crying out, 'Here is your papers, and I have a canteen of whisky for Col. [Gimlet] Lea, of North Carolina, who was in West Point with me. I am Gen. Custer.'"

Beal noted that Custer and his men were completely at his mercy, and orders had come down the previous evening to fire on any Union troops who showed themselves. But Beal had already decided during the night that his "sense of justice and honor" prevented him from killing men in cold blood who would not have known the risk. "I did not give the command to fire and close from right and left upon them," he said, "but I ordered one of my soldiers to tell him our orders changed in the night, and I would give him one chance for his life, and that was retreat in haste, or I would be compelled to fire, though they were unarmed and defenseless." Custer and his men quickly rode away. A year later Beal, wounded at Cedar Creek and left for dead by the retreating rebel troops, fell into Union hands. He wrote a letter to Custer relating the earlier episode and asking for parole, especially given his condition. He later received word that by Custer's order he was to be left at the residence in Strasburg where he was convalescing, and they bid him to "go home to my young wife I had married a short time before, who was thinking of me as dead."[7]

In September 1863, Confederate forces in the west faced serious reverses, and General James Longstreet's corps was detached from Lee's army to reinforce Braxton Bragg's Army of Tennessee. This gave General George Meade an opportunity. On the morning of September 13, Union forces pushed over the Rappahannock upstream from Fredericksburg and drove the rebels from Brandy Station to Culpeper, where at midday three cavalry divisions under Buford, Gregg, and Kilpatrick were set to converge.

Confederate guns were emplaced on a ridge outside of town. The 2nd New York Cavalry took "very severe artillery fire," said one report, "as great trees broken off and shattered clearly proved." Colonel H. E. Davies, commanding Farnsworth's old brigade, ordered a battalion of the 2nd New York under Lieutenant Colonel Harhaus and Major McIr-win to take the guns. The troopers galloped down a hill facing the battery, "a perfect avalanche of shot and shell crashing above them, and ploughing the ground around them," dressed the line at the base, then "charged up with such impetuosity that every thing gave way before them."[8]

Kilpatrick then tried to move left around Culpeper to capture a train that was departing in haste before the enemy onslaught. Custer's brigade scattered rebel skirmishers posted on the edge of the town, but the advance was frustrated by a stream swollen from recent rains. One hundred men from the 7th Michigan waded and swam the stream and charged up a hill on the other side, running off a rebel gun and some sharpshooters, securing that flank.

Meanwhile, Confederate cavalry had established a new defensive position in the woods just on the other side of the town, and rebel guns placed on a high hill began to punish the Union forces. Kilpatrick ordered a battalion of the 1st Vermont Cavalry, commanded by Major William Wells, to neutralize the threat. Custer dashed up to accompany the assault.

The charge was "of unequalled gallantry," one report read. The Vermonters were "obliged to dash through the town, and down a steep hill, through a ravine, and then up a steep and very high hill to the battery, which, meanwhile, was belching forth its shell and canister upon their ranks. But it could not retard the speed nor daunt the spirit of the 'Boy General of the Golden Locks' and his brave troops." The cavalrymen swarmed the rebel guns, and Custer, "armed only with his riding whip, compell[ed] many a man to surrender at discretion." Cavalryman Willard Glazier said that "no soldier who saw [Custer] on that day ... ever questioned his right to a star, or all the gold lace he felt inclined to wear."[9]

The battle continued for hours after, with a series of charges and countercharges. Shot and shell rained into Culpeper, and a Confederate account noted that "women were shrieking, soldiers were groaning with their wounds, and children were crying from fright, and the death-shots hissing from afar were howling and screeching over the town." At four in the afternoon, the rebels finally quit their defense and withdrew eleven miles to the Rapidan River. The assault netted numerous guns and over one hundred prisoners, but Custer was wounded by a Confederate shot, "which killed his horse and came near killing the general." A shell had taken off part of his boot and wounded Custer in the leg. He went up to General Pleasonton and said, "How are you, fifteen-days'-leave-of-absence?" referring to the leave granted a wounded man. "They have spoiled my boots but they didn't gain much there, for I stole 'em from a Reb." Colonel Theodore Lyman noted that "the warlike ringlets got not only fifteen, but twelve [additional] days' leave of absence and have retreated to their native Michigan!"[10]

The furlough was well timed. George had important business to attend to in Monroe. He had not been there since the previous spring, and this would be his first visit as a general. He had important matters to discuss with Libbie and was also determined to have a talk with her father, at the very least to make sure the judge was aware of his achievements. George and Libbie had honored her father's admonition against the two having any direct contact and had carried on correspondence through Libbie's friend Annette Humphrey. "Friend Nettie" and "Friend Armstrong" exchanged many letters, and in this way the indirect courtship continued. Libbie's friend Marguerite Merington said that George was "never allowed too abundantly to hope nor too utterly to despair," though at times he veered between the two.[11]

Libbie and her family had been away at Traverse City but by chance returned to Monroe the day after George arrived. Libbie wrote her cousin Rebecca Richmond that since George and Nettie were such good friends, "of course I saw him at once, because I could not avoid him. I tried to but I did not succeed." She confided that George "proposed to me last winter, but I refused him more than once, on account of Father's apparently unconquerable prejudice. I never *even thought of marrying him*. Indeed I did not know I loved him so until he left Monroe in the spring."[12] George wasted no time and renewed his intention to marry

Libbie. "The General's proposal was as much a cavalry charge as any he ever took in the field," she recalled. "Proposing the second time I saw him as a violent contrast to the ambling ponies of my tranquil girl-hood."[13] During this visit they made a pledge to each other, short of a formal engagement.

But nothing would happen without the judge's approval, and he was not yet ready to give his daughter over to George. Father Bacon sensed something was up during the furlough and artfully dodged the topic. He saw George off at the train station, where the young suitor said he had wanted to talk to the judge but would write instead. Mr. Bacon replied, "Very well." In Baltimore en route back to his command, George wrote Nettie that Libbie would have to intercede if there was any hope of getting her father's permission. "I feel her father, valuing her happiness, would not refuse were he to learn from her own lips our real relation to one another," he said.[14]

Back at the front, George was plunged almost immediately into battle. After the victory at Culpeper, the Union line moved up to the Rapidan. General Lee had no intention of letting it stay there. On October 9, he launched a massive flanking maneuver around Meade's right aiming for Centreville, an offensive that became known as the Bristoe Campaign. The next day, as Lee's forces pressed north, Custer was ordered to pull back from his forward position to Kilpatrick's headquarters at James City, west of Culpeper. He arrived that afternoon to find the town already occupied by rebel cavalry under the command of his West Point friend P. M. B. Young. There was a brief battle in which the 5th Michigan charged the rebel positions. The cavalrymen were turned back by sharpshooters from the 1st South Carolina firing from behind a stone wall. Custer noted that "most of my command rested on their arms during the night."

The next day Custer disengaged and headed east for Culpeper. On reaching the outskirts of the town, he learned that rebel cavalry were moving up behind him in force. The pursuers were Wade Hampton's division, under direct command of Jeb Stuart. Custer paused, expecting an attack that did not come. He then received urgent orders to make for the Rappahannock. The brigade moved through Culpeper with the band playing the "saucy air of Yankee Doodle," according to Colonel Edward B. Sawyer of the 1st Vermont Cavalry, and in the faces of the inhabitants they could "plainly read the expression 'good riddance.'"

The cavalry moved up the railroad line toward the river. Rebels again pressed from the rear, and more enemy troops emerged on Custer's left, "evidently attempting to intercept our line of march to the river," he wrote. By the time Custer's men reached the familiar field of Brandy Station, skirmishing in his rear forced him to move his guns to the head of the column to keep them from falling into enemy hands. Fire also erupted from the south; a reinforced cavalry division under Fitzhugh Lee was moving toward them but had mistakenly brought their artillery to bear on Hampton's men, an error they soon corrected. Then a courier arrived with more bad news: enemy horsemen under General James B. Gordon had rushed ahead of the column and cut the route to the river crossing. "The heavy masses of the rebel cavalry could be seen covering the heights in front of my advance," Custer wrote. "A heavy column was enveloping each flank, and my advance confronted by more than double my own number. The perils of my situation can be estimated." As Colonel Sawyer put it, "The scene began to grow interesting."

An artillery duel commenced while Custer weighed his options. Just then General Pleasonton rode up, having also been caught in the envelopment. Custer proposed a direct route out of the quandary: "cut through the force in my front, and thus open a way for the entire command to the river." Pleasonton approved, and the push was on. Custer formed the 6th and 7th Michigan as a holding force, with the 5th and

1st facing the front on the right and left. "I informed them that we were surrounded," Custer wrote. "We had either to cut our way out or surrender—which we had no intention of doing."[15]

Custer struck up the band before the attack, "which excited the enthusiasm of the entire command to the highest pitch," he said, "and made each individual member feel as if he was a host in himself." Willard Glazier recalled that Custer, "the daring, terrible demon that he is in battle, pulled off his cap and handed it to his orderly, then dashed madly forward in the charge, while his yellow locks floated like pennants on the breeze."[16] Custer's men made "a magnificent charge," Colonel Sawyer recalled, "but finding the rebel line formed beyond a ditch too wide for his horses to leap, had, after the exchange of a few rounds, been obliged to retire in considerable disorder."

By this time Buford's cavalry had joined the fight, along with the rest of Kilpatrick's division. They formed on the high ground of Fleetwood Heights with Buford on the left and Kilpatrick on the right. Buford's men faced more level ground and made a massed charge against the encroaching rebels. Custer's men regrouped and attacked the force to the right, along with the First Brigade commanded by Brigadier General Henry E. Davies. The Federals "fought desperately for self-preservation," Jeb Stuart recounted. "The woods near Brandy Station were speedily occupied by the sharpshooters of Lomax and Chambliss to resist the [Union] force moving from Fleetwood to the relief of the other column, and an engagement ensued of the most obstinate and determined character."[17]

"The scene had become wild and exciting," Colonel Sawyer wrote. "The batteries of the two divisions, and more than an equal number of guns on the rebel side (in all, probably forty), were vigorously playing. Charges and countercharges were frequent in every direction, and as far as the eye could see over the vast rolling field were encounters by regiments, by battalions, by squads, and by individuals, in hand-to-hand conflict." Glazier said that "no one who looked upon that wonderful panorama can ever forget it. On the great field were riderless horses and dying men; clouds of dust from solid shot and bursting shell occasionally obscured the sky; broken caissons and upturned ambulances obstructed the way, while long lines of cavalry were pressing forward in the charge, with their drawn sabres, glistening in the bright sunlight."[18]

Chaos grew on the field. Lines were indistinct, charges and countercharges were uncoordinated, and the two forces became mixed. "It was among the heaviest [fighting] of the war," recalled rebel John E. Cooke, "and for a time nothing was seen but dust, smoke, and confused masses reeling to and fro; nothing was heard but shouts, cheers, yells, and orders, mixed with the quick bang of carbines and the clash of sabres—above all, and the continuous thunder of the artillery. It was as 'mixed up' as any fight of the war."[19]

After two hours of fighting and maneuvering, the beleaguered Federal cavalry forced their way across the river, crossing in good order according to Custer. He had led his brigade on charge after charge during the battle, having two horses shot from under him but emerging unwounded.[20] The last Union horsemen were on the north bank of the Rappahannock after nightfall, having narrowly escaped a major calamity. Shortly after the two divisions reached safety and the men were preparing to make camp, General Pleasonton received an urgent order from Meade's headquarters—do not cross the river.[21]

CHAPTER NINE

THE BUCKLAND RACES

After escaping from the envelopment in the retreat from Culpeper, Custer sent for Major James Kidd of the 6th Michigan Cavalry to mount a reconnaissance mission on enemy forces near Gainesville. "It was my first personal interview with the great cavalryman," Kidd wrote. "He was at his headquarters, in the woods, taking life in as light-hearted a way as though he had not just come out of a fight, and did not expect others to come right along. He acted like a man who made a business of his profession; who went about the work of fighting battles and winning victories, as a railroad superintendent goes about the business of running trains. When in action, his whole mind was concentrated on the duty and responsibility of the moment; in camp, he was genial and companionable, blithe as a boy."[1]

Lee's unexpected drive north had forced Meade back forty-five miles to Centreville, and the campaign seemed to be a significant Confederate victory. But three days after the brutal Brandy Station fight, Lee's Third Corps, under the command of Lieutenant General A. P. Hill, was badly mauled by outnumbered yet well-positioned Union defenders at the Battle of Bristoe Station, southwest of Manassas. This blunted Lee's momentum and effectively ended the Confederate advance.

Lee began to pull back on October 18, and as the rebels moved south, Kilpatrick pursued Stuart closely, with Custer's brigade in the advance. Kilpatrick was "furious as a wild boar" by one report, looking for payback for the battle at Brandy Station the week before.[2] On the nineteenth Stuart's men made a stand on the south bank of Broad Run, at the village of Buckland Mills. Custer attacked the rebels head-on, but Stuart's artillery thwarted the assault. After a few more probes, Custer turned the rebel left flank and forced Stuart from his position, driving him a mile down the road. Custer's men paused in Buckland to rest while Davies's 1st Brigade continued the chase. Stuart's cavalry withdrew into the hilly country heading toward Warrenton, ten miles away.

Custer and his staff retired to a manor house called Cerro Gordo, located on a prominence on the north bank of Broad Run, overlooking Buckland Mills. The house belonged to Charles Hunton, a leading Virginia politician, and earlier that day had served as Jeb Stuart's headquarters. "At the time of our arrival at that point," Custer wrote, Stuart "was seated at the dinner-table, eating; but, owing to my successful advance, he was compelled to leave his dinner untouched—a circumstance not regretted by that portion of my command into whose hands it fell." The last of Stuart's commanders to leave was George's West Point friend P. M. B. Young. Stuart had advised Young not to tarry, and after a shell exploded nearby and an aide had called out, "They are coming, sir, we must hurry or be cut off from the bridge," Young and his men evacuated. Shortly after, Custer rode up. He politely asked Hunton's two daughters, who were minding the house, if he could have his dinner there. They said that it was already on the table, that General Young had just left it.

"Very well, ladies," Custer said, "Young and I are friends." Custer and his men sat down to eat and he regaled the sisters with tales of his and Young's exploits at West Point. Kilpatrick soon joined the group, visibly pleased with the turn of events. He announced that since Stuart had boasted of driving him from Culpeper, he was going to drive Stuart right back to Warrenton.

The congratulatory repast was interrupted by the sound of artillery fire. It came from a column of approaching cavalry that Kilpatrick assumed was Merritt's brigade. However, a short time later, a mile-long line of Confederate infantry emerged from the distant woods to the south across Broad Run, heading in their direction.

In his enthusiasm, Kilpatrick had ridden hard into a trap. As the Federal cavalry pursued Jeb Stuart and Hampton's division, Fitzhugh Lee, commanding a cavalry division reinforced with infantry, retired toward Auburn on a parallel track, the movement concealed by the rolling, wooded terrain. After the tail end of Davies's brigade disappeared down the Warrenton road chasing Stuart, Fitz Lee fired his artillery as a prearranged signal to commence the attack. Stuart turned his men and charged back on the pursuing Union cavalry, while Fitz Lee moved on the Federal rear to close the trap. The plan worked perfectly, Lee observed, because Kilpatrick "was easily misled."[3]

"I pressed upon them suddenly and vigorously in front," Stuart said, "with Gordon in the center and Young and Rosser on his flanks." Union troops strung out on the road at first resisted, but "the charge was made with such impetuosity … that the enemy broke and the rout was soon complete."[4] The confident Federal troops had been caught off guard by the unexpected reversal in fortune. Unable to rally and mount a coherent defense, they scattered north up the road toward Broad Run.

The situation was also heating up back near Buckland Mills. Custer had rushed the dismounted 6th Michigan under Major Kidd across the bridge toward the advancing rebels, along with Pennington's battery of artillery. Custer first thought the rebels were fielding a similar force of dismounted cavalry, but soon learned he was facing a determined infantry assault. "Pennington's battery, aided by the Sixth Michigan cavalry, poured a destructive fire upon the enemy as he advanced," Custer wrote, "but failed to force him back." The rebel infantry advanced to within twenty yards of his guns before Pennington limbered up and retreated back across Broad Run, followed by the 6th Michigan in good order.

The bridge soon became too hotly contested for the rest of the retreating Federals to cross. However, Custer's quick action had delayed Lee's advance just enough to prevent the trap from fully closing. Davies's retreating troopers, covered by Custer's well-placed artillery, were able to cross upstream from Buckland, and rallied miles away at Haymarket. Custer withdrew five miles east to Gainesville. As he evacuated his headquarters at Cerro Gordo, he paused at the gate and said to the Hunton sisters, "Ladies, give Young my compliments." Since he had taken Young's dinner, he said Young could have his breakfast.[5]

The Federal cavalry rout was soon dubbed the "Buckland Races." Total Union casualties in the engagement were 150 killed, wounded, and missing. It was a particularly stinging defeat for Kilpatrick, who saw his expected victory over Stuart melt away. The *Richmond Sentinel* crowed that the Union commander was "completely ruined. His command was killed, captured, or dispersed. When last heard from, he was at Alexandria, where he is supposed to have opened a recruiting-office for the enlistment of his command."[6] A Northern writer disparaged the "deplorable spectacle of the cavalry dashing hatless and panic-stricken through the ranks of the infantry."[7] Kilpatrick's favorite race horse, a thoroughbred mare named Lively, ran off and was captured by some of Mosby's raiders, who also took the Union soldiers sent to retrieve the horse. The *Sentinel* opined, "[D]riven out of Culpeper, ruined at Buckland's, the loss of his favorite mare must appear to him the 'unkindest cut of all.'"[8]

Fitzhugh Lee's turnabout ploy had worked perfectly. "I am justified in declaring the rout of the enemy at Buckland the most single and complete that any cavalry has suffered during the war," Jeb Stuart wrote. A rebel ditty, attributed to Stuart, mocked the Federal cavalry:

It was "the Buckland races," far-famed through old Faquier,
With Stuart before their faces, Fitz Lee came in their rear,
And such another stampede has never yet been seen.
Poor Kil led off at top of speed, and many a wolverine.[9]

Custer lost his headquarters baggage train, including his personal papers and uniforms, which had been sent ahead by Kilpatrick's order. However, his spirited defense at the Broad Run crossing was a bright spot in an otherwise embarrassing engagement, and the humiliation landed with Kilpatrick, which fanned the smoldering enmity between the two men. Whether by luck, ability, or a combination of both, it seemed Custer could do no wrong, and Kilpatrick increasingly resented it. There was no love lost on Custer's part either. He summed up the engagement in a letter to Nettie: "All wd have been well if Genl. K. had been content to let well enough alone."[10]

Custer's relations with General Pleasonton were much better. "I do not believe a father could love his son more than Genl. Pleasonton loves me," he wrote Nettie. "You should see how gladly he welcomes me on my return from each battle. His usual greeting is, 'Well, boy, I am glad to see you back. I was *anxious about you.*'"[11] In November Pleasonton gave Custer temporary command of the 3rd Division while Kilpatrick was in Washington on court-martial duty. Custer took the opportunity to mount a probing attack along the rebel front on the Rapidan. After his cavalry fell back, an artillery duel commenced along the river, and Confederate infantry advanced. Edward A. Paul of the *New York Times* captured a scene where Custer made an unorthodox contribution to the battle: "Gen. CUSTER, at Morton's Ford, fired two guns with his own hands at some men who occupied a rifle-pit in a position so as to annoy our advanced pickets. There were ten rebels in the rifle-pits. CUSTER's first shot struck the centre of the pit, killing or wounding all but four of the men, who ran back to another pit. His next shot fell directly among them, and persuaded them into a second flight out of sight."[12]

In Paul's telling, Custer comes across as a battlefield savior, an acting division commander single-handedly firing a cannon with pinpoint accuracy and taking out a threatening enemy position. Perhaps the shots were lucky—George was thirty-first in his West Point class in artillery tactics (better than his forty-fourth place showing in cavalry tactics, which placed him below nine cadets who resigned). But this incident along the Rapidan captured the Custer spirit, his willingness, even eagerness, to do whatever needed to be done to prevail in battle, even when it often meant doing it himself. Major Kidd, who had many opportunities to see Custer in action, said he was "brave, but not reckless; self-confident, yet modest; ambitious, but regulating his conduct at all times by a high sense of honor and duty; eager for laurels, but scorning to wear them unworthily; ready and willing to act, but regardful of human life; quick in emergencies, cool and self-possessed, his courage was of the highest moral type: his perceptions were intuitions."[13]

"Often I think of the vast responsibility resting on me," George wrote Nettie around this time, "of the many lives entrusted to my keeping, of the happiness of too many households depending on my discretion and judgment." When making a decision, he would say to himself: "'First be sure you're right, then go ahead!' I ask myself, 'Is it right?' Satisfied that it is so, I let nothing swerve me from my purpose."[14]

The same was true when it came to matters of the heart. George was unswerving in his pursuit of Libbie's hand, and amid the strife of battle in the fall of 1863, Custer faced one of his bravest moments—writing to Judge Bacon. After being nearly annihilated at Culpeper, the matter had become imperative. George wrote to the judge that he regretted that they had not been able to meet when he was in Monroe to address his intentions directly. He stressed that despite the previous impressions Mr. Bacon may have formed of him, he had grown as a man and officer. "It is true I have often committed errors of judgment," he confessed, "but as I grew older I learned the necessity of propriety." He said he had not broken his vow of temperance "with God to witness." George tried to make the case that he was responsible, mature, and "always had a purpose in life."[15]

Naturally, Custer fretted about how Judge Bacon would respond. He was also vexed by a young woman in Monroe named Fanny who had taken a shine to him and used her wiles to make Libbie jealous. "I am not surprised at Fanny's telling that my likeness is in her locket," he wrote to Nettie, on one of many exchanges regarding the prospective usurper. "I would be surprised at nothing she chooses to do." He worried too about Libbie's cousin Albert Bacon weighing in against him "because of his strong attachment for Libbie." But he stayed positive. "I am happy, happy in her love. Nothing can deprive me of that happiness, and I shall adhere to my long-established custom of looking on the bright side of things."[16]

After a few nervous weeks, Judge Bacon sent what Custer called a "straightforward and manly letter." It was lengthy, admiring, but nevertheless vague and noncommittal. "What does he mean?" George wrote Nettie in frustration.[17] He sent a reply to the judge asking flat out if he and Libbie could begin corresponding directly. His answer came in a letter from Libbie opening, "My more than friend—at last."[18]

Once Judge Bacon consented to the relationship between Custer and his daughter, he thought they should be wed soon. "You must not keep Armstrong waiting," he counseled Libbie, and of course George agreed. But Libbie intended to take things slowly. "Neither you nor he can know what preparations are needed for such an Event," she wrote her fiancé, "an Event it takes at least a year to prepare for."[19] Libbie was concerned that her mother had not fully signed off on the idea. "She is becoming reconciled," she wrote Custer, "but it is not resignation I want, but whole-hearted consent."[20] By Christmas, however, both parents were clearly happy with the romance. George sent a large photograph of himself to them to give to Libbie as a gift, and they secretly put it in her room and waited for her to discover it. "Father and mother were so excited, they thought I would never go upstairs to my room," Libbie wrote.[21]

Libbie also began to give ground on her yearlong timeline, because she was growing more certain of their future happiness. "I have often said because I love so many I could never greatly love one," she wrote George in December. "Foolish girl I was."[22] But she also fretted that the "worst about loveing [sic] a soldier is that he is as likely to die as to live," and they might not have a year to wait. [23] She eventually consented to a wedding in late winter.

"I am coming home in February for the purpose of getting married," Custer wrote to Isaac P. Christiancy, then an associate justice on the Michigan Supreme Court. "Libbie Bacon is the fortunate or unfortunate person, whichever it will be, who will unite her destinies with mine."[24] Isaac's son Jim was a lieutenant serving as an aide in the 9th Michigan Cavalry and planned to accompany George back for the wedding. But the wedding plans were still a family secret, and he asked Christiancy to keep it to himself.

In the rush of events, George forgot to ask his own father's consent to wed. Father Custer, of course, was in favor, even with Judge Bacon's first-rate Republican credentials. The Custers had moved to Monroe, and over the winter the two families got to know each other well.

Libbie had consented to marry quickly, but it would still be a major social event. She sent to New York for silks and trimmings for her dress and arranged an elaborate bridal tour. She wanted George to appear in full dress uniform, and to cut his hair. Her mother counseled there were some advantages to giving up on the dream wedding; with her first husband she agreed to hasten the ceremony, and she said she "always had my own way afterwards, in Everything!"[25]

When George left for the wedding, his officers gathered to wish him well. "Thank you, gentlemen," he said. "I'm going out to the Department of the West to get a command, or a new commander, and I don't know which."[26] Friend Nettie wrote in one of her final missives before the wedding, "You are worthy of her, the highest compliment I could pay you."[27]

The February 9 wedding date finally arrived. "There came to us such marveling," Libbie recalled, "that anyone ever dared to marry when perhaps a few months, as with us, of only occasional, hurried, and tremulous meetings on my part constituted our knowledge of each other."[28] George and Libbie were joined in the Presbyterian Church by Dr. Boydon at 8:00 p.m. Hundreds turned out for the wedding, the crowd overflowing outside the church. Libbie wore a rich white silk dress with an extensive train and a veil decorated with orange blossoms. George was in the dress uniform of a brigadier general. With Libbie were Nettie and her friends Anna Darrah and Marie Miller. Standing with George were Captain Jacob Greene of his staff, who was engaged to Nettie; Conway Noble, who had introduced Libbie and George on Thanksgiving in 1862; and John Bulkley, George's deskmate from Stebbins' Academy. "All went off remarkably well, and no mistake made," Judge Bacon wrote to his sister Charity. "It was said to be the most splendid wedding ever seen in the State."[29] The families and three hundred guests then retired to the Bacon home for the reception, which went long into the night. "The occasion was delightful, hilarious and social," Libbie's cousin Rebecca Richmond wrote.

For many it was the first time they were able to meet or spend any time with George, whom they had known only by reputation. Those who came expecting a vainglorious, pompous young general were pleasantly surprised. "Not one of us was prepossessed in [Custer's] favor," Rebecca said, "but in no time everyone pronounced him a 'trump'.... He isn't one bit foppish or conceited. He does not put on airs. He is a simple, frank, manly fellow."[30]

The bridal party left at midnight for Cleveland, where a reception was held by family friend Charles Noble, a trustee of the Young Ladies Seminary who had handed Libbie her diploma a few years earlier. They then went to Buffalo, stopped in Onandaga to visit Libbie's Aunt Charity and her husband, and continued east to New York City.

Once in the city, Custer received telegrams urging him to return early. But because the messages were not direct orders, and he wanted to continue the honeymoon Libbie had planned, he took his new bride to West Point. The Hudson was frozen, so they went first by train, then by sled, which George helped push over the icy, rough roads. The Military Academy, Custer's former "rock-bound highland home," charmed Libbie. "I never dreamed there was so lovely a place in the United States," Libbie wrote her father.[31] George was the returned prodigal son, and Libbie noted that "everyone was delighted to see Autie. Even the dogs welcomed him."[32] The superintendent was still Alexander H. Bowman, who had signed George's diploma. Some cadets knew him—as plebes they had suffered Custer's pranks. William Ludlow was in that class, for whom Custer had interceded the day before graduation to ensure a fair fight, and been court-martialed. George showed Libbie the grounds and buildings, the guardhouse and yard where he spent many hours suffering various punishments, and introduced her to some of the cadets from his day who were yet to graduate and to professors who had followed his rise with some pride and not a little amazement. "Custer! A General!" exclaimed one professor's wife. "Not that Cadet who used to tie tin pans to my dog's tail?" George was a bit miffed with Libbie for allowing some cadets to show her flirtation walk, but overall the visit was a success, and Libbie said that after visiting West Point she realized she had "married a man of distinction."[33]

The couple returned to New York City to take in some shows before beginning their leisurely journey south to Washington, when they were "brought to earth by orders to give up our brief play spell and go to the front."[34]

CHAPTER TEN

THE DAHLGREN AFFAIR

While George and Libbie were celebrating their nuptials, moves were afoot to sideline the newlywed general from one of the most dramatic actions of the war. Kilpatrick was planning a daring raid on Richmond, in which Custer would be given only a supporting role. Libbie later recalled that her "military life began and ended with the actual knowledge of perfidy in officers."[1]

Not everyone had been pleased with Custer's rapid rise in rank and national fame. Bugler Joe Fought noted that "all the other officers were exceedingly jealous of [Custer]."[2] Libbie wrote that the "usual swarm of enemies presented him with maligning and falsehoods, and there were deprecations of his ability." Such jealousies and rivalries were common during the war, and the young, dashing Custer was a special target for envy.

Kilpatrick was particularly displeased with the notoriety and success of his young brigade commander. In battle after battle, Custer was heralded as a hero while Kilpatrick bore the criticism, justly or not. An August 1863 newspaper profile of Custer gave a slap to Kilpatrick, saying, "a Cavalry Division General rarely charges. It would interfere with his duty. He sits either on his horse or a fence, smokes and claps his hands when a thing is handsomely done." The paper noted that elevating Kilpatrick to division command "has taken an electric leader of a charge from the service. It cannot also afford to lose Custer."[3] From Gettysburg through the Buckland Races, it seemed that Custer could do no wrong, and Kilpatrick was tinged with failure.

Kilpatrick was brave, and he behaved daringly in cavalry raids during the early years of the war, though usually at high cost to his commands. While bold, he had not shone as a division commander. He achieved high rank less through battlefield achievements than through ruthless self-promotion driven by his boundless ambition. Kilpatrick planned to make a career in politics after the war, and he thought that fame derived from battle might take him all the way to the White House.

Unlike Custer, however, who had ample natural charisma, Kilpatrick was not a charmer. He had an intense, angular face framed by scraggly facial hair, which grew oddly from his jawline. A fellow officer described him as a "wiry, restless, undersized man with black eyes [and] a lantern jaw."[4] Theodore Lyman said he was a "frothy braggart without brains" and that "it is hard to look at [Kilpatrick] without laughing."[5]

Kilpatrick also got into more trouble than Custer. He was a hard drinker and was detained for slandering government officials while on a bender in Washington. He was also suspected (though not convicted) of taking kickbacks from horse brokers providing mounts for his command.

Kilpatrick had married his West Point sweetheart, Alice Nailer, the day he graduated, and they had a son together. But he kept company with loose women during the war, which did not help his reputation.

Kilpatrick and Custer may have competed for the affections of an attractive young nurse from Cambridge named Anna Elinor "Emma" Jones, who was, in her own words, "a companion to the various commanding officers … a private friend or companion." She had appeared one day in the spring of 1863 at the headquarters of cavalry division commander Major General Julius Stahel, "ingratiated herself into the favor of the General," by one report, "and received an honorary appointment as a member of his staff. Anna rejoiced in the soubriquet of 'Major,' and as 'Major Jones' became an institution in the army." She became Stahel's constant companion and "thus lived and flourished. Every one knew Major Jones; officers would doff their hats, and privates would stand at full 'present,' as she rode by in military feminine dignity." When Stahel was relieved in June 1863, "Annie joined her fortunes with the young and gallant Custer, with whom she remained, retaining her rank and title." But Kilpatrick became jealous of her attentions to George and accused her of being a rebel spy. "Her whole object and purpose of being with the army seemed to be to distinguish herself by some deed of daring," Custer wrote. "In this respect alone she seemed to be insane."

Major Jones was removed from the command under an order banning all women from such unofficial positions, and she went off to adventures elsewhere. She boasted of her relationships with many general officers, but Custer said Anna's "claim of intimacy with me and General Kilpatrick is simply untrue."[6] Kilpatrick's wife, Alice, meanwhile, died of influenza in November 1863, and two months later their infant son perished.

Kilpatrick's Richmond raid originated with President Lincoln's desire to mount a cavalry operation to distribute copies of his December 8, 1863, amnesty and reconstruction proclamation. The president felt the document had received insufficient attention in the South and, for some reason, believed Yankee raiders might be able to get the word out. On February 12, Kilpatrick briefed the president and Secretary of War Stanton on a more ambitious plan. He suggested bypassing Lee's army encamped around Fredericksburg and mounting a swift surprise attack on Richmond. One column would attack the city from the north, and a second, smaller strike force would cross the James River and enter it from the south. Along the way the Union troops would destroy rail lines and other infrastructure, disrupt communication with Lee's forces, free Union prisoners at Belle Isle and Libby Prison, and sow confusion and chaos inside the lightly defended Confederate capital.[7]

Lincoln and Stanton signed off on the plan, though it met resistance from General Pleasonton, who told Stanton it was not feasible. But the White House favored the raid, and Kilpatrick bet Pleasonton $5,000 that he would pull it off.

Pleasonton's concerns were well founded. Even with most of the Army of Northern Virginia in the vicinity of Fredericksburg, Richmond's defenses were not as sparse as Kilpatrick seemed to believe. Three weeks earlier, Major General Benjamin F. Butler, in command of the Army of the James near Williamsburg, launched an expedition against Richmond with a similar aim. A brigade of cavalry moved northwest up the peninsula on February 6, intending to charge across the Chickahominy River at Bottom Bridge, then dash into Richmond to free prisoners and "tear up things generally." But the next day, to their surprise, the cavalrymen found the bridge planks taken up and the crossing stoutly defended by Confederate artillery, with nearby fords manned by rebel troops. Their mission thwarted, the raiders turned back to Williamsburg.[8]

Custer might have expected to lead the strike force hitting Richmond from the south. Instead, Kilpatrick gave that honor to twenty-one-year-old Colonel Ulric Dahlgren. Dahlgren was the son of Union Rear Admiral John A. Dahlgren, the head of Navy ordnance and developer of the

"Dahlgren gun." Ulric was a handsome, dashing, socially and politically connected young man who was charting a future in law when the war broke out. He joined the Army in the spring of 1861 and was commissioned a captain at age nineteen. Like Custer he served as a staff officer to several generals and engaged in the same types of high-risk adventures that made Custer famous. Notably, in November 1862, Dahlgren led sixty cavalrymen on a raid into Fredericksburg prior to General Ambrose Burnside's disastrous assault. He spent three days riding in and out of the town, gathering intelligence and prisoners, and dodging rebel fire in the city streets. Later, after the May 1863 Battle of Chancellorsville, he proposed a similar raid into Richmond, which Hooker, still smarting from the failure of Stoneman's Raid that April, rejected.

Dahlgren was a standout at the Battle of Brandy Station, where he attached himself to the 6th Pennsylvania Cavalry. General Pleasonton wrote that his "dashing bravery and cool intelligence are only equaled by his varied accomplishments," and the *New York Times* wrote that he was "a model of cool and dauntless bravery." As the Battle of Gettysburg commenced, Dahlgren scouted behind enemy lines and captured communiqués from Jefferson Davis intended for Robert E. Lee. This intelligence, which revealed there were no further rebel reinforcements headed north, was credited with influencing Meade's decision to fight it out on Cemetery Ridge. During the rebel retreat, Dahlgren spontaneously joined the 18th Pennsylvania, part of Kilpatrick's division, in an attack on Confederate cavalry in the streets of Hagerstown. Dahlgren was wounded in the leg during the wild urban fight, and he calmly reported to Kilpatrick afterward with blood leaking from his boot, before passing out. He lost his right foot and part of his leg, but while convalescing in his family home in Washington, D.C., Secretary of War Stanton personally delivered his colonel's commission.

Kilpatrick encountered Dahlgren at a Washington social event as plans for the Richmond raid were taking shape and offered him the command of the second strike force. The column was slated to follow a route similar to the plan Dahlgren had proposed to Hooker a year earlier. "There is a grand raid to be made," Dahlgren wrote his father days before the mission began, "and I am to have a very important command. If successful, it will be the grandest thing on record; and if it fails, many of us will 'go up.' I may be captured, or I may be 'tumbled over'; but it is an undertaking that if I were not in, I should be ashamed to show my face again.... If we do not return, there is no better place to 'give up the ghost.'"[9]

But the "grandest thing on record" was not to include Custer. He was shunted off to a diversionary attack, leading a picked force deep into enemy territory in the direction of Charlottesville. Ostensibly his mission was to cut the Orange and Alexandria Railroad between Charlottesville and Gordonsville, which would sever rail communications between Richmond and Lynchburg to the south, and also between Lee's army and the capital. Custer was instructed to cut telegraph lines, capture rebel stores, take prisoners, and generally create chaos. But Custer's most critical objective was to fix rebel attention west, drawing forces away from Richmond to open the way for Kilpatrick's raiders. It was a dangerous mission, and one trooper noted to Kilpatrick, "It looks as if there is not much chance for Custer." Kilpatrick replied, "What of it?"[10]

On February 28, Custer set out toward Charlottesville on the James City road with 1,500 men and a section of artillery.[11] To add insult to injury, Kilpatrick had assigned the choice men of the Michigan Brigade to his own command, leaving Custer with a force he had not previously commanded. He drove south, crossing the Rapidan and Ravenna Rivers over several days, fighting a few skirmishes, and making "as much noise as several batteries of artillery could consistently make," in order to draw maximum rebel attention.[12] Resistance was slight until they encountered elements of Stuart's cavalry three miles outside Charlottesville. Custer's men charged and routed the rebels, driving them off and overrunning a camp of sixty men. According to one account, it was "one of the boldest fights our cavalry has made during the war."[13]

However, Stuart's cavalry soon rallied, and rebel infantry converged on the scene by rail. Custer withdrew across the Ravenna, destroying a bridge and three flour mills, and set off for the Rapidan as night approached. Cold rain mixed with sleet fell steadily. In the darkness, the Federal column took a wrong turn and blundered into a muddy ravine, which stopped them for the night. By morning, Custer discovered that large numbers of rebels were closing behind him, and another force was concentrated ahead near his intended crossing at Burton's Ford.

Custer had to move quickly before the jaws of the trap closed. He rushed his command toward Burton's Ford and fired on the rebels with his two Parrot guns before leading a spirited charge that pushed them back. As the rebels consolidated their line and hurried men to the scene for the expected fight, Custer suddenly broke contact and wheeled his horsemen down the Standardsville Road toward Banks Mill Ford on the Rappahannock. He outran the pursuing rebels and crossed the undefended ford without incident.[14]

"By a series of brilliant movements," the *Soldier's Journal* reported, "including some fine charges and sharp fighting, our men got safely off."[15] The *New York Herald* wrote that General Custer "met another force of the enemy, and, after several dashing charges, drove them off."[16] The *Richmond Whig* made light of accounts by "Yankee letter writers" of Custer's bravery in the operation, saying he only fought because he "got lost" and was forced to make a stand. The *Whig* said accounts of his victorious charges were "the stereotyped form of Yankee lying" and that Custer owed less to "cold steel" than to "his two pieces of cannon and the heels of his horses."[17] But Custer completed his mission in fine fashion, doing significant damage to the Confederate rear and capturing fifty prisoners and five hundred horses. He adapted to shifting circumstances and brought his command back safely, suffering only four troopers wounded and none killed.

For Kilpatrick's raiders, things were going less smoothly. The main body of about four thousand set off on the evening of the twenty-eighth, moving quietly to maintain the element of surprise. They reached Spotsylvania the next morning, and Dahlgren's force of 460 split off for the swing around Richmond. "The men are in good spirits," a reporter wrote, "the weather excellent for campaigning, and the rebels are doubtless taken by surprise, with the bulk of their army away on furlough or looking for something to eat."[18]

That evening Kilpatrick's column crossed the North Anna River and burned Beaver Dam Station, an important railhead. But they failed to halt a train departing for Richmond, which may have been the same train that Dahlgren's force missed upriver at Frederick Hall Station. By one account Robert E. Lee was aboard and "narrowly escaped capture."[19] The passengers reached Richmond that day and spread news of the approaching Yankee raiders.

Northern papers also starting running stories on the supposedly secret mission. Kilpatrick took reporters with him, and on March 1, as the raiders drove deep into enemy territory, the *New York World* reported Kilpatrick was moving on Richmond with a large force of cavalry "in the hope of capturing that city by a coup de main, or compel Lee to leave his entrenchments at Mine Run, and march to its defense."[20] The *New York Herald* said that Kilpatrick was "speeding towards Richmond" and mused that the city "has so many times seemed ready to fall a prey to whosoever would 'grasp it like a man of mettle,'" implying that Kilpatrick was the daring soul who would finally succeed.[21]

By the time that report appeared, Kilpatrick had sped to Richmond's defenses. He swept through the outer line of skirmishers then paused, listening for sounds of Dahlgren's fight inside the city. Kilpatrick fired artillery and waited for a response, which was to be the signal to burst through the inner rebel lines, link up with Dahlgren, and sow panic in Richmond before withdrawing down the peninsula to safety. But there were no sounds of battle or signs of buildings burning, and the only alarm appeared due to the presence of his forces on the city's outskirts.

"The goal was in sight," James Kidd recalled. "That a dash into the city, or at least an attempt would be made nobody doubted."[22] Kilpatrick's men skirmished with the rebel defenders, and it seemed the prize was ready to be taken. However, with no evidence Dahlgren was in the city, Kilpatrick seemed to fade. At that critical juncture, he was "overcome with a strange and fatal irresolution," Kidd wrote.[23] It was the first indication that the raid might end in failure. J. W. Landern, one of Kilpatrick's scouts, said that until then the commander had "resolutely and skillfully carried out the plan," but at that point "he was 'not in it.' He did not seem to be himself." Kilpatrick had been complaining of not feeling well, and Landern said he "always thought his illness the cause of the feeble effort made to enter Richmond."[24]

At 3:00 p.m., after several hours waiting, Kilpatrick ordered his men to withdraw and regroup further east to let the situation clarify. The men were "tired, hungry, and disappointed," Landern recalled, "having had no sleep and but little rest for more than 48 hours."[25] They were chilled by intermittent rain and sleet, and gratefully set up camp at nightfall, awaiting news of Dahlgren.

Around 10:00 p.m. Kilpatrick's men were readying to head back toward Richmond when gunfire erupted on the perimeter. Wade Hampton's Confederate cavalry boldly charged in among them, and soon the camp was in chaos. Unbeknownst to Kilpatrick, rebel horsemen had been on his trail since the day after he set out. "The surprise was admirably effected," the *Staunton Spectator* reported. "Gen. Hampton was in advance, and he was fired upon by one of the enemy's videttes, which was the signal of the alarm. A wild panic immediately took place in the Yankee camp; the horses stampeded, and a scene of indescribable confusion ensued."[26] Hampton "furiously attacked our camp," Landern said, "and we were obliged to get." After a brief, sharp fight, and still with no word from Dahlgren, Kilpatrick withdrew his force toward Williamsburg.[27]

A few days later, when Kilpatrick was safely down the peninsula, a small, bedraggled group from Dahlgren's force finally appeared, led by Captain Mitchell. They bore grim news of the fate of their column. Dahlgren's force had moved south as planned, taking prisoners and capturing rebel supply wagons. The roads were muddy from the driving rain, making passage difficult, and they were uncertain where to make the critical James River crossing. But their guide, a freed slave from the area named Martin Robinson, assured them they could ford the James near Dover Mills.

Dahlgren's force was delayed a few hours at the plantation of the Confederate secretary of war, James Seddon, freeing his slaves and assisting them in looting the property. But when the raiders arrived at the riverbank, it was clear they would not get across; the James at that point was so swollen by rain it had become easily navigable, demonstrated by a sloop they watched sail by. Dahlgren was furious. Lieutenant H. A. D. Merritt of the 5th New York Cavalry related that the young colonel accused the freedman Robinson of "betraying us, destroying the whole design of the expedition, and hazarding the lives of every one engaged in it." Dahlgren informed Robinson he was to be hanged. The freedman begged for his life, claiming it was all a misunderstanding, but to no avail. "A halter strap was used for the purpose," Lieutenant Merritt recorded, "and we left the miserable wretch dangling by the roadside."[28]

Unable to cross the James without going miles upstream and doubling back, Dahlgren proceeded down the river road toward Richmond. He halted seven miles from the city, within sight of the outer works. His men could hear Kilpatrick's guns, and Dahlgren sent scouts to try to communicate with the main force, but they did not return. Yet even with the raid plan in tatters, Dahlgren mounted an attack and managed to penetrate the Richmond city limits.

Opposition soon coalesced, and Dahlgren withdrew, heading north. His men fought a skirmish at the farm of Benjamin Greene in northwest Richmond, then headed east in search of Kilpatrick as the evening deepened. "No one engaged in that night's search will ever forget its difficulties," Lieutenant Merritt wrote. "The storm had set in with renewed fury. The fierce wind drove the rain, snow and sleet. The darkness was rendered intense by the thick pines which overgrew the road, and which dashed into our faces almost an avalanche of water at every step."[29]

Around the time Kilpatrick was locked in a fight with Wade Hampton's men, Dahlgren and his band had moved past them to the north and were thirty miles east of Richmond, across the Pamunkey and Mattaponi Rivers, south of the crossroads town of Stevensville. But a band from the 9th Virginia Cavalry under the command of Lieutenant James Pollard, augmented by civilian volunteers, had caught up to them and blocked their way. When the rebels challenged Dahlgren, he fired his pistol and was met by a volley in return.

"Every tree was occupied," Lieutenant Merritt wrote, "and the bushes poured forth a sheet of fire."[30] Dahlgren went down immediately. "The Yankees attempted to charge through our lines, the charge being headed by Dahlgren himself," the *Staunton Spectator* reported. "He was shot dead before his column came in contact with our lines."[31] The rest of the command scattered. Many were captured, but enough made it back to Federal lines to tell the tale.

The Richmond raid was a failure, but the controversy had only just begun. A thirteen-year-old member of the Richmond home guard found papers on Dahlgren written in his hand calling for unrestrained violence once inside the city. With "the [Union] prisoners loose and over the river, the bridges will be secured and the city destroyed," he wrote. "The men must keep together and well in hand, and once in the city, it must be destroyed, and Jeff. Davis and Cabinet killed."[32]

The Dahlgren papers were printed in newspapers throughout the South and created a firestorm of debate. This apparent appeal to unlimited warfare was unprecedented in the war. Fitzhugh Lee in his report on Dahlgren's death decried the "ridiculous and unsoldierly raid" and the "insane attempt to destroy Richmond and kill Jeff. Davis and cabinet."[33] Washington quickly denied that the purpose of the raid was to assassinate members of the Confederate government, and General Meade said that the papers, if genuine, were Dahlgren's idea, and not official orders. Kilpatrick said the papers were fabricated "and published only as an excuse for the barbarous treatment of the remains of a brave soldier."[34] Kilpatrick was referring to a story that Dahlgren's body had been mistreated by the rebels. This was not true, and the body was returned unmolested. But Ulric's prosthetic leg went missing; it wound up on display in a Richmond department store window.

Kilpatrick and his command were shipped to Alexandria to convalesce, and while there one of his troopers added to the general's woes by killing a black sentry who was trying to enforce an order against carrying weapons inside city limits. But the Dahlgren affair was the end for Kilpatrick in the East. He was relieved of command and sent west, and by May he was commanding Sherman's cavalry for the upcoming march through Georgia. "I know that Kilpatrick is a hell of a damned fool," Sherman said, "but I want just that sort of man to command my cavalry on this expedition."

Once again Custer glided over it all. He was supposed to have played only a supporting role in the operation, but wound up enjoying another round of national fame. Compared to the failure and scandal of the Kilpatrick-Dahlgren raid, Custer's diversionary maneuver, in which he evaded superior forces and completed his mission with his command intact, looked like a work of genius. Official Washington needed a hero to take the sting away from the high-profile disaster, and Custer was made to order. He was received by the president and members of Congress and praised in the press.

"It astonishes me to see the attention with which he is treated everywhere," Libbie wrote to her parents in March. "One day at the House he was invited to go on the floor, and the members came flocking round to be presented.... The President knew all about him when Autie was presented and talked to him about his graduation."[35] George and Libbie were a hit on the Washington social circuit—a young, attractive, and engaging couple. George's rugged soldierly authenticity and practiced humility were well balanced by Libbie's beauty and sharp wit. When Libbie met Congressman Bingham, she joked, "Mr. Bingham, I want to thank you for transforming my husband from a wood-chopper into a general of the United States Army."[36] Libbie was impressed with the way George was received around town and said she found it "very agreeable to be the wife of a man so generally known and respected."[37]

Kilpatrick never forgave Custer for outshining him during the war. He served out the rest of the conflict in the West and later had a controversial run as U.S. minister to Chile. Years after the war, George heard Kilpatrick lecturing on the Battle of Gettysburg, altering facts to minimize the role of the Michigan Brigade in stopping Stuart. After the lecture Custer approached Kilpatrick, laughed, and said, "All right Kil, so long as you don't leave me out of the battle entirely."[38]

CHAPTER ELEVEN

LITTLE PHIL

uster's luck held through the Dahlgren affair and was about to get better. General Ulysses S. Grant assumed overall command of the Army in the East, the latest attempt by Lincoln to find a fighting general who could bring the war to an end. The Custers traveled from the front in Virginia to Washington in March 1864 on the train bringing Grant from the West. George introduced Libbie to the new commanding general, and she wrote about her impressions to her parents: "Sandy hair and moustache; eyes greenish-blue. Short, and, Mother, not 'tasty' but very ordinary looking. No show-off but quite unassuming, talked all the time and was funny."[1] The Custers had a second honeymoon in the city for a few weeks while Grant settled into his new position and planned for the spring offensive.

Grant reorganized the Cavalry Corps, yielding three divisions, commanded by General Gregg; General Alfred Thomas Archimedes Torbert, who had commanded the 1st Cavalry Division in the Army of the Potomac after the death of General John Buford in December 1863; and General James H. Wilson, an engineer who had served as Grant's inspector general. Custer's brigade was put in the 1st Division under Torbert, "an old intimate friend of mine, and a very worthy gentleman," he wrote Libbie.[2] The Cavalry Corps commander, Alfred Pleasonton, an unlucky victim of the Richmond raid he had opposed, was sent to the Trans-Mississippi theater, and the Union horsemen were handed over to Philip Sheridan.

Sheridan bore little resemblance to Custer's ideal, McClellan. Though both stood about five and a half feet tall, "Little Mac," by his bearing, intellect, and sense of self, projected an air of significance that few could ignore. Not so "Little Phil." David S. Stanley, who rode in a coach with Sheridan while on their way east to enter West Point, called him "the most insignificant looking little fellow I ever saw."[3] Wharton J. Green, who was acquainted with Sheridan at the Academy, recalled, "If, at that time, I had been called upon to designate the man on that historic spot who would later on reach the high rank Sheridan attained, he would probably have been one of the very last to have come under consideration."[4] Sheridan had a rough time at the Academy, being suspended a year for fighting, and graduating in the lower third of the Class of 1853. He served on the frontier in Texas, and at the start of the war was a captain in the Army of Southwest Missouri. He was nearly court-martialed for allegedly appropriating horses from private citizens but was saved by Major General (later Chief of Staff) Henry W. "Old Brains" Halleck, who made Sheridan a member of his staff. Shortly thereafter he was given a volunteer colonelcy and command of the 2nd Michigan Cavalry. By 1862, Sheridan was a division commander, and in 1863 he became a major general, noted for heroism at the battles of Murfreesboro and Chattanooga.

"There is no soldier of the Civil War with whom [Sheridan] can be fairly compared with justice to either," James H. Kidd wrote. There was nothing that stood out about Sheridan, and "if he had not the spark of genius he came very near to having it." Sheridan was calm, unhurried, thoughtful, and confident. "In his bearing was the assurance that he was going to accomplish what he had pledged himself to do.... The outcome to him was a foregone conclusion."[5]

Grant brought Sheridan east as a trusted subordinate who would make the cavalry a unified combat arm instead of a scattered force used chiefly for flank security and raiding. One day after he arrived in Washington, Sheridan stood on the porch of Willard's Hotel with Major John H. Brinton, a surgeon on Grant's staff, discussing the new seriousness he was going to bring to the Corps. "Doctor, I'm going to take the cavalry away from the bob-tail brigadier generals," he said. "They must do without their escorts. I intend to make the cavalry an arm of the service."[6]

"The art of war is simple enough," Grant said in 1862, commenting on French military theorist Antoine-Henri Jomini. "Find out where your enemy is. Get at him as soon as you can. Strike him as hard as you can, and keep moving on."[7] This had been Grant's way of war in the West, and with the Overland Campaign he brought that logic to the eastern theater. Grant planned a push similar to what Hooker had attempted a year earlier at Chancellorsville, seeking to break the stalemate along the Rappahannock and push Lee back toward Richmond. But instead of relying on Jomini's steady logic to overcome Lee, as Hooker had tried to do, Grant would use brute force. As he wired to Washington from Spotsylvania six days into the Wilderness Battles, having already lost twenty thousand men and eleven general officers, "[I] propose to fight it out on this line if it takes all summer."[8]

Grant had opened his campaign on May 4 and immediately became engaged in a hard fight in the woodlands west of Fredericksburg. After several days of pitched battle, Grant sought to flank Lee's forces and cut him off from Richmond. Sheridan was ordered to take the key cross-roads of Todd's Tavern, a position he had previously occupied. But when the Federals returned on May 7, rebel cavalry was there to meet them. Todd's Tavern became a bloody but inconclusive contest in which Custer and Rosser squared off again. After repeated attacks the road was kept open long enough for Lee to pull back to more favorable ground at Spotsylvania. Some say this single failed Union action extended the war for another eleven months.

Passions were high afterward: General Meade, commanding the Army of the Potomac under Grant, had arrived late to the battle, and on May 8 he and Sheridan got into a shouting match over the perceived blunder. Sheridan argued that if Meade cut him loose, he could take on Jeb Stuart's entire corps and whip the rebel cavalry. Grant decided to let Sheridan make good his boast. The cavalry set off the next day intending to drive deep into Virginia. "Our move would be a challenge to Stuart for a cavalry duel," Sheridan wrote, "behind Lee's lines, in his own country."[9]

Custer led the way. The first day, his men pushed to Beaver Dam Station, capturing and burning two trains of supplies headed for Lee's army, tearing up eight miles of track and freeing hundreds of Union prisoners captured in the wilderness. That night the "sky lighted up for miles with the glare of burning property," by one report. The next morn-ing, the cavalrymen were "awakened by the howling of rebel shells," but their horse artillery "soon drove the enemy to a respectful distance." They pushed south along the Richmond, Fredericksburg, and Potomac Rail Line toward the Confederate capital, "constantly fighting the rebels from our rear and flanks" and "at night bivouacked within twelve miles of Richmond."[10]

The Kilpatrick raid was still a fresh memory, and the Confederates may have thought Sheridan was attempting a similar move on the city. Stuart pushed ahead on Sheridan's left and established a blocking position on high ground about nine miles from the city center, a few hundred yards east of Brook Road, the main route into Richmond. The rebels made their stand just north of a junction and an inn called Yellow Tavern.

On May 11, Sheridan got his cavalry duel. As his force moved on the Confederate position, the enemy "poured in a heavy fire from his line and from a battery which enfiladed the Brook road, and made Yellow Tavern an uncomfortably hot place."[11] Custer, on the right of the Federal line, was taking brisk fire from rebel guns and sharpshooters in nearby woods, and he rode about his command ordering, "Lie down, men—lie down. We'll fix them!" He told Wesley Merritt he was going to attack on Stuart's left flank while Gibbs and Devin held the rest of the line. Merritt said he would support the move in any way he could. Soon Sheridan rode up, and Merritt told him of Custer's plan.

"Bully for Custer!" Sheridan said. "I'll wait and see it." Custer and his men set off toward the rebel lines as the band played "Yankee Doodle." His men descended into a depression at the trot, crossed a ditch over three small bridges, and then broke into a charge up the rising ground to the cheers of the men in the line behind them. The rebel guns on the crest could not be depressed enough to come into effective play, and Custer's men routed the artillerymen and their support troops and captured three guns. A rebel prisoner later said he "never saw such a man as 'That Custer,'" adding that "when he goes for a thing he fetches it in."[12]

"It was, without exception, the most gallant charge of the raid," a reporter wrote, "and when it became known among the Corps cheer after cheer rent the air."[13] As Custer broke the rebel left, Gibbs and Devin attacked in the center and right, driving the Confederates from their positions and scattering them. Casualties were heavy on both sides, but the Confederates suffered a particularly acute loss. Jeb Stuart, trying to rally his men against Custer's assault and stem the tide, was grievously wounded and carried from the field.[14] The shot was credited to John A. Huff of the 5th Michigan, who would be mortally wounded at the Battle of Hawe's Shop seventeen days later. Stuart was taken to Richmond to be tended by his brother-in-law Dr. Charles Brewer, but succumbed to his wounds. Thus Sheridan in his first head-to-head battle with Stuart not only defeated his cavalry but deprived the Confederacy of its *beau ideal.*

"We have passed through days of carnage and have lost heavily," George wrote Libbie days later. "We have been successful.… The Michigan Brigade has covered itself with undying glory.… I also led a charge in which we mortally wounded Genl. Stuart." Merritt told him the Michigan Brigade was "at the top of the ladder."[15] George enclosed a sprig of honeysuckle he said he plucked from inside the fortifications of Richmond. The battle had opened the approaches to the city, but Sheridan wisely chose not to try to enter Richmond proper, since he might not emerge afterward. He stuck to his plan and moved toward Butler's men on the peninsula.

The Overland Campaign pushed Lee back on Richmond, at high cost to both sides. However, Grant failed to destroy the Army of Northern Virginia, and by June the rebels were digging in around Richmond and Petersburg while Grant prepared for a siege. Railroads were critical for the Confederates to maintain communications and supplies, and Grant approved a plan for a sweeping raid up the Virginia Central Railroad to cut the vital line at Trevilian Station, fifty-five miles northwest of Richmond. Sheridan was then to proceed to Charlottesville to join

Major General David Hunter's forces campaigning in the Shenandoah Valley.

The raid launched on June 7. Sheridan, with Torbert's and Gregg's divisions, crossed to the north side of the Pamunkey River and headed northwest, parallel to the North Anna River. The raiders faced no serious resistance, and four days later they were poised a few miles due north of Trevilian Station. However, the Confederates had detected Sheridan's movement and rushed forces up the Virginia Central line to meet him.[16]

Both sides took the initiative. Early on June 11, as Union troops began their move south, two brigades of Wade Hampton's division engaged Sheridan's force in the woodland just north of Trevilian. Sheridan did not know how many troops he was facing or if there were other Confederate units in the area, but he was too close to his objective not to make a fight for it.

He planned a two-pronged attack. Torbert ordered Custer to take the Michigan Brigade along a wood road a mile to the right of the rebel defensive line, which led to the railroad, seven hundred yards from the station. Custer's mission was to run around Hampton's flank, turn right up the railroad, and get into the enemy rear, seizing the objective if possible. The rest of the cavalry would press Hampton in the front, heading south on the road through the woods leading directly to Trevilian Station, where the two forces would rejoin.

Custer's men moved forward against some light resistance. He quickly discovered he was not seven hundred yards from the station, but close to two miles. Undeterred, Custer moved up the tracks, and as he closed on the station, scouts reported Confederate supply wagons ahead, from Hampton's baggage train. He ordered Colonel Alger and the 5th Michigan to take the wagons. He sent the 6th Michigan in support, when rebel troops suddenly appeared to their rear and charged. Custer counterattacked and drove the enemy troops off, pressing on toward the station. But there he found more rebel troops with a battery to the right of the road. He charged them with the 7th Michigan, sending word to the 1st Michigan, which was delayed at the end of the column, to come up rapidly. But "this regiment was found fully employed in holding the enemy," he wrote, "who were making a vigorous assault on our rear." The 5th Michigan, which had charged too far while pursuing Hampton's rear guard, was cut off by fresh rebel forces coming onto the field under Rosser from Hampton's division. The Confederates retook the station, and there was still no sign of Merritt's and Devin's brigades, which were fighting through the woods.

Custer had a serious problem. "I was compelled to take up a position near the station from which I could resist the attacks of the enemy," he wrote, "which were now being made on my front, right, left, and rear." He found himself sandwiched between two rebel divisions—Hampton's, which was also engaging the main column, and Fitz Lee's, which had come up the tracks behind Hampton, unbeknownst to Sheridan.

Custer quickly consolidated what forces he could and established a defensive ring. "The smallness of my force compelled me to adopt very contracted lines," he wrote. "From the nature of the ground and the character of the attacks that were made upon me our lines resembled very nearly a circle." His men were in open terrain and lacking cover, with his entire position in range of the enemy's guns. The position was so small and precarious that the rebels had to restrict fire for fear of overshooting into their own units on the other side.

Rebel units charged and were repulsed. Custer had to keep shifting his position to keep a cohesive defensive line. A Southern newspaper report captured the chaos of the scene: "A regiment of Yankees went tearing down the road, and into the dust which rose in clouds around them, darted Col. Waring with his 'Jeff Davis Legion' in hot pursuit. Close on *his* rear pressed another Yankee regiment, followed by one of Rosser's—all thundering along together!"[17] The Federal officer in charge of the captured rebel wagon train sought to move to a safer position and wound up delivering the haul back to the enemy. (He was later relieved.) Rebels took Custer's headquarters wagon, also capturing his cook, Eliza, a freed slave who had joined George's camp around the time he was made a brigadier. Custer's aide and best man, Jacob Greene, was captured, and when a Confederate took Greene's spurs at Hampton's headquarters, he announced proudly, "You have the spurs of General Custer's Adjutant-General."

George was in the thick of the fight. When a trooper from the 5th Michigan was shot down in an exposed position, he ran out and picked him up to take him to safety. A rebel sharpshooter fired at Custer during the rescue, and the spent ball glanced off his head, stunning him briefly but otherwise leaving him unharmed.[18] Custer's standard-bearer, Sergeant Mitchell Beloir, was wounded but did not leave the line until overcome with blood loss. "General they have killed me," he said. "Take the flag!" Beloir rode off to die, and George tore the flag from its staff and stuffed it into his shirt.[19]

The rebels were pressing on all sides. One group seized a cannon and began to roll it off the field. Pennington reached Custer and said, "General they have taken one of my guns."

"No! Damned if they have!" Custer replied, and with Pennington and a few other men in tow furiously charged the piece and took it back.[20]

The rest of the command under Torbert and Gregg was still slogging through the woods north of Custer's position. "The men fought desperately," Torbert wrote, "but it was hard to drive the enemy from his cover, as my men could not see their foe."[21] They had no word from the Michigan Brigade but had heard the sound of musketry and guns from the direction of the station all morning long. They eventually powered their way through the woods, and, reaching open ground overlooking Custer's fight, they saw the Wolverines surrounded and in dire straits. Torbert and Gregg's men redoubled their efforts and forced Hampton's men back onto Custer's line. The scene grew even more chaotic as rebel units began to break to escape being surrounded themselves. "The Yankees swarmed over the whole country," according to one Southern account. The rebels drew their guns up "into the form of a hollow square, and blazed away in all directions."[22]

"So panic-stricken was [Hampton's] division and so rapidly was it pushed that some of it was driven through Custer's lines, and many captured," Sheridan recalled.[23] Hampton's force retired up the tracks, and Gregg's division drove Lee's troops back down the rail line toward Louisa Courthouse. Custer's brigade was saved.

That night the Union forces camped on the battlefield in exhaustion. Eliza had escaped her rebel captors in the confusion of the fight and returned. The elements of the 5th Michigan who had been cut off early in the battle eventually turned up after fighting through the rebels and riding a wide circuit back to the main body.

The next day, Sheridan's men set about destroying Trevilian Station and what railroad tracks they could. Overnight, Lee's men had circled around the Union force to join Hampton's division, blocking the way west. Late in the day on the twelfth, Torbert mounted a reconnaissance in force against the rebels, who were emplaced behind breastworks two miles away. After a series of fruitless charges, the Union forces pulled back.

From prisoners Sheridan learned that General Hunter, commanding Union forces in the Shenandoah, was near Lexington, not Charlottesville as he had thought. So, facing a strong, roused enemy deep in their territory, short on ammunition, and with supplies uncertain, Sheridan withdrew to the east.[24] The trip back was arduous; Sheridan was hampered by his train, the wounded, and hundreds of former slaves who spontaneously joined the Federal column from surrounding farms and plantations. They reached their start line by June 20.

Sheridan declared Trevilian a victory, even though he had suffered over one thousand casualties, compared with over eight hundred by the Confederates. The damage to the rail line was repaired in two weeks, foiling that aspect of the plan. And he came nowhere near Hunter's force. It was only a win in that he avoided a major disaster and escaped with his command relatively intact.

Grant's report suggested that Custer intentionally got surrounded so "when the assault was made, the enemy found himself at the same time resisted in front and attacked in rear, and broke in some confusion."[25] George wrote, in words presaging a battle then twelve years distant, "My Brigade was completely surrounded, and attacked on all sides. Had the others been prompt we would have struck the greatest blow inflicted by our cavalry."[26] He had lost all of his personal belongings except what he carried in battle and his toothbrush. Libbie's love letters were gone, and she later learned from a former POW at Libby Prison that, to her mortification, the surgeon there had been reading them. In a later battle, when Custer's men captured rebel Brigadier General Thomas T. Munford's baggage, Custer had the personal letters tied up and put off-limits to save his enemy the same embarrassment.[27]

The first Libbie knew of the Trevilian raid was in the newspapers. "The *Herald* says you are gone on a dangerous expedition, again," she wrote to her husband on June 10.[28] Libbie followed the war closely while living in Washington and came to know the rhythms of the city that portended a fight. Before the Overland Campaign kicked off in May, she noted the large numbers of troops and supply trains moving through the city. She said the "silence in the papers shows that a great battle is expected."[29]

Libbie said that Army marriages were happy because "there were so often, in those days of oft-occurring separations, repeated honeymoons."[30]

George told her that when it came to reports from the front, "no news is good news."[31] Sometimes the bad news was unavoidable, even if it was wrong. After the Battle of Trevilian Station, Congressman Bingham heard that Custer was dead and went to Secretary of War Stanton to confirm it. Learning George was alive, he rushed to Libbie and "found her pale and trembling. She had heard the newsboys under her windows crying 'Custer killed. All about Custer being killed.'"[32] Three times that summer, she heard reports of George being dead.

Wives of soldiers living in the city kept a close watch on the War Department, where a special flag was flown announcing battlefield victories. This was not necessarily good news, since victories always came at a high cost. Many casualties of battles fought in Virginia were taken to hospitals and cemeteries in and around Washington. "This is the saddest city," Libbie wrote her parents, "with maimed and bandaged soldiers in the streets, and the slow-moving government hearses."[33] She took a dim view of Washington in general, with its loose morals and no-go areas where unescorted women might be mugged, or taken for the wrong kind of lady. "This city is a Sodom," she wrote, "crowded with sin which the daylight sees as well as the night."[34]

After seeing President Lincoln at the theater, Libbie described him as "the gloomiest, most painfully careworn looking man I ever saw," and Mrs. Lincoln was "short, squatty and plain." But at a crowded White House reception, the president recognized her. "So this is the young woman whose husband goes into a charge with a whoop and a shout," he said, as they shook hands in the receiving line. "I am quite a Lincoln girl now," she told her parents afterward.[35]

In July, Michigan senator Zachariah Chandler invited Libbie to accompany a party of dignitaries taking the president's boat to the Union supply depot at City Point, at the head of the James between Richmond and Petersburg. She eagerly consented, having been separated from George for two months. The craft "seemed to crawl" down the Potomac, and a sightseeing stop at Fortress Monroe only increased Libbie's impatience. She wondered how she would get in touch with George when she got to the port, since she had not been able to send word in advance. But soon after the ship arrived, George appeared, standing in a small boat headed toward them, shouting and waving his hat to the cheers of the people at the rails. He bounded on the ship, ignoring the high-ranking dignitaries, "perfectly fearless in rushing for me as soon as he leapt on deck," Libbie recalled, "lifting me in [the] air, and overwhelming me with demonstrations of affection."[36] Poet Caroline Dana Howe of Maine witnessed the scene and immortalized it in verse:

> Out from the shore, a boat! A boat!
> With glistening oars, see, see! Custer there!
> Erect and firm, with locks afloat,
> With folded arms, and martial air.
>
> Our very breaths we almost check,
> His coming had for her such charms:
> One leap, he stands upon the deck,
> And has her in his brave, young arms.[37]

Soon other officers joined the party, and they danced on the deck to the music of Sheridan's band, against the booming of the Union siege guns bombarding Petersburg.

CHAPTER TWELVE

INTO THE VALLEY

As Grant pushed Lee toward Richmond in the spring, Union forces pressed south in the western part of the state. In May 1864, Major General Franz Sigel moved into the Shenandoah Valley, intending to cut the supply and rail head at Lynchburg to strain communications between Lee's forces, Richmond, and the rest of the Confederacy. Sigel was defeated at the Battle of New Market on May 15, but the campaign continued under sixty-one-year-old Major General David "Black Dave" Hunter, who reached Lynchburg on June 17. On the same day, Confederate forces under the command of Lieutenant General Jubal Anderson Early arrived from Petersburg and dug in. After a series of probing attacks, Hunter concluded erroneously that he was outnumbered and withdrew through West Virginia.

Seizing the opportunity, Early swept north unopposed, crossed the Potomac near Harper's Ferry, and by July was fighting inside the District of Columbia, on the outskirts of the City of Washington. He failed to enter the capital, but the movement had the desired effect: Early bragged that his men "didn't take Washington but we scared Abe Lincoln like hell."

Early's campaign convinced Grant that he needed a permanent solution to the Shenandoah Valley problem. In August, he chose Phil Sheridan to command the newly organized Army of the Shenandoah. His objective was to end the threat posed by Early and destroy the valley as a base of Confederate operations and supply. Grant ordered Sheridan to "do all the damage you can to railroad and crops, carry off stock of all descriptions and negroes, so as to prevent further planting. If the war is to last another year let the Shenandoah valley remain a barren waste."[1] He wanted the valley so stripped of supplies that "the crows flying over it will have to carry their provender with them."[2]

Sheridan put Torbert in command of his Cavalry Corps, with the 1st and 3rd Cavalry Divisions, commanded by Merritt and Wilson, along with Duffie's and Averell's cavalry divisions of the Army of West Virginia. Custer's Michigan Brigade was part of Merritt's command.

The rebels lost no time in giving Sheridan's men a baptism by fire. Confederate infantry under Brigadier General William T. Wofford met the Yankees as Devin's Brigade moved into the valley, and a spirited fight ensued along the Front Royal Pike. Rebel infantry and artillery was pushing Devin back, and Custer's brigade rushed through Chester Gap toward Front Royal to help in the repulse.

The enemy retreated back over the Shenandoah and rushed downstream to re-cross, seeking to mount a flank attack from Guard Hill, a commanding promontory between the Shenandoah's north fork and a creek called Crooked Run. Custer intuited their move and sent the dismounted 5th Michigan under Colonel Alger up the hill first, concealed by the rolling terrain. As the Confederates launched their attack with a spirited yell, Alger's men dashed up to the crest of the hill and began "pouring down upon the enemy a storm of bullets from their seven-shooters," as one report described, "before which the enemy again broke and fled towards the ford."[3] Custer had anticipated the retreat as well, and he sent the 1st Michigan to capture the crossing. Seeing their way blocked, many rebels threw away their weapons and swam for it, some drowning in the attempt. Over 250 simply surrendered. Confederate cavalry charged the ford to try to open it and free the prisoners, but Custer countered this with the 7th Michigan, and by evening "the enemy, foiled and whipped at every point, made no further attempt to cross the river."[4]

"The cavalry made some handsome saber charges," Sheridan reported, "in which most of the prisoners were captured. Colonel Devin was slightly wounded, but continued in the saddle. General Custer made a very narrow escape."[5] Merritt praised Custer for the "masterly manner" in which he conducted the battle. The *New York Tribune* ran a glowing description of Custer:

> Future writers of fiction will find in Brig Gen Custer most of the qualities which go to make up a first-class hero and stories of his daring will be told around many a hearth stone long after the old flag again kisses the breeze from Maine to the Gulf. With a small little figure, blue eyes and golden hair which will persist in curling loosely around his head; dressed in a navy blue shirt and dark blue pants, and wearing a black slouched hat ventilated by holes cut in the side, Gen. Custer is as gallant a cavalier as one would wish to see. No officer in the ranks of the Union Army entertains for his rebel enemy a more sincere contempt than Gen. C. and probably no cavalry officer in our army is better known or more feared by the foe than he. Always circumspect, never rash, and viewing the circumstances under which he is placed as coolly as a

chess player observes his game, Gen. Custer always sees "the 'vantage of the ground" at a glance, and like the eagle watching his prey from some mountain crag, sweeps down upon his adversary and seldom fails in achieving a signal success. Frank and independent in his demeanor, Gen. C. unites the qualities of the true gentleman with that of the accomplished and fearless soldier.[6]

A trooper who fought in the Front Royal battle summed it up more succinctly: "By G—d Custer is a brick!"[7]

Sparring continued between Sheridan's and Early's forces in the weeks that followed, with skirmishes and other engagements almost daily until mid-September. Each side sought advantage. Early raided in Sheridan's rear and disrupted the B&O Railroad at Martinsburg, while Sheridan probed Early's defenses and looked for an opening for a thrust down the valley. With increasing pressure from Grant and Washington to move south, Sheridan planned a major attack on Early at Winchester.

On September 19, Sheridan launched an infantry assault on the town from the east, moving VI and XIX Corps up the Berryville Pike. Sheridan hoped to exploit the dispersion of Early's regiments in the surrounding area, but the Union column was slowed crossing Opequon Creek five miles from Winchester town center, then blocked passing through a narrow gorge fronting the rebel positions. The slow advance gave Early time to establish lines east and north of town. The rebels were heavily outnumbered but mounted a spirited defense. Early's troops slowly withdrew and consolidated their lines, fighting among earthworks leftover from the battle fought there in 1862. The grinding fight continued into the afternoon with heavy casualties on both sides.

"Just at this critical period," a reporter noted, "above the roar of artillery and musketry, and the cheers and fierce yells of the contending armies, could be distantly heard the shrill notes of cavalry bugles sounding a charge."[8] Torbert's cavalry had arrived from the north, six thousand troopers in two divisions under Merritt and Averell, with Custer's brigade in the center. They moved quickly through the open fields on both sides of Martinsburg Pike, heading straight to Winchester. Chaplain Charles A. Humphreys of the 2nd Massachusetts Cavalry recalled that a "continuous and heavy line of skirmishers covered the advance, using only the carbine, while the line of brigades as they advanced across the open country, the bands playing the national airs, presented in the sunlight one moving mass of glittering sabres intermingled here and there with bright-colored banners and battle-flags. It was one of the most inspiring and imposing scenes of martial grandeur ever witnessed."[9]

Ahead of them were three brigades of Fitzhugh Lee's cavalry, and an infantry brigade commanded by Colonel George S. Patton, grandfather of the famous general who later bore his name. A Confederate soldier seeing the advance said, "I never saw such a sight in my life as that of the tremendous force, the flying banners, sparkling bayonets and flashing sabers moving from the north and east upon the left flank and rear of our army."[10]

The rebel cavalry, which had been driven back, regrouped to attack the Union horsemen. "As this column approached we prepared to meet it," one report read. "Sabres were drawn and all was got ready. On came the rebels with their sabres flashing and their hideous yells, scattering themselves so as to make their line of attack fierce as possible. Just as they got within pistol range of Custer, his brigade went forward recklessly upon the foe." Averell's division also charged ahead, overlapping the rebel flank. The Confederates pulled back, and "on went our chargers cutting and slashing through their ranks."[11]

"Both divisions advanced rapidly," Torbert wrote, "driving the enemy's cavalry pell-mell before them, on and behind their infantry."[12] The Union cavalry drove the rebels back toward their main defensive line, with the infantry anchored at a redoubt called Fort Collier. "Boot to boot these brave horsemen rode in," Merritt recalled.[13] The Confederate troops formed a square and prepared to make a stand. Their momentum up the left side of the Federal cavalry was ordered to charge the emplacement, with Custer at the front.

"Officers and men seemed to vie with each other as to who should lead," Custer wrote. "The enemy upon our approach turned and delivered a well-directed volley of musketry, but before a second discharge could be given my command was in their midst, sabering right and left."

The rebel left flank broke under the shock of Custer's attack. "Many of them threw down their arms and cried for mercy," Merritt wrote, "others hung tenaciously to their muskets, using them with their muzzles against our soldiers' breasts; a number took refuge in a house and fought through the doors and windows." But as the cavalry broke up the Confederate defenses on the left flank north of Winchester, a successful infantry attack by Crook's VIII Corps turned the left end of the line east of the town. Then, as Merritt put it, "the miserable remnant of Early's army fled madly through the streets of Winchester."

"The broken and demoralized divisions comprising Early's command now fled in confusion," a reporter wrote, "throwing away everything which could in any way impede their flight, and strewing the ground with their arms."[14] Early's controlled withdrawal had turned into a rout. Confederate Generals Robert E. Rodes and Archibald C. Goodwin were killed in the retreat, and Colonel Patton was mortally wounded trying to rally his broken brigade as his men dashed through the town. Other senior officers, including Fitzhugh Lee, were wounded. Sheridan took over 5,000 casualties killed, wounded, and missing, compared with Early's approximately 3,600. But Union losses were an eighth of their total force, compared with a quarter of Early's. "We have just sent the enemy whirling through Winchester," Sheridan reported to headquarters, "and shall be after them to-morrow."

Early pulled back twenty miles to Fisher's Hill, where he was routed again three days later, opening the valley to Sheridan. Custer played no direct role in the battle, but it would have an important impact on his career. Fisher's Hill was mainly an infantry fight, but Averell's 2nd Cavalry Division was on the Union right to shield against possible rebel cavalry movements and exploit the expected Confederate retreat. Averell failed to pursue the retreating rebels with vigor, however, causing Sheridan to relieve him of command on September 26. Custer was given command of his division. Sheridan explained in his memoir that Custer had been made a general officer in 1863 "with the object of giving life to the Cavalry Corps," and "though as yet commanding a brigade under Merritt, his gallant fight at Trevillian Station, as well as a dozen others during the summer, indicated that he would be equal to the work" of division command.

Four days later, Custer was shifted to command the 3rd Division. James H. Wilson—described by Custer as a "court favorite," who was promoted from the engineers solely because of his personal relationship with Grant and not because of any particular aptitude for cavalry operations—was promoted to brevet major general of volunteers and transferred West.[15] Custer had a dim view of Wilson, an "imbecile" who "nearly ruined the corps by his blunders," he wrote after a botched raid in May 1864. At the time, the 1st Vermont, then under Wilson's command, "asked if they could not obtain 'a pair of Custer's old boots' to command them."[16] With Wilson gone and Custer back with his old brigade as part of his command, he looked forward to having "the best Division in the Army."[17]

Custer took over his division in the midst of the scouring of the valley. The victories at Winchester and Fisher's Hill had opened the way to the upper Shenandoah and Luray Valleys, and Sheridan pushed his troops eighty-five miles to Staunton to commence the scorched-earth campaign. Union forces burned barns and foodstuffs, destroyed infrastructure, razed fields, and reduced one of the breadbaskets of the South to a charred, smoking ruin. The London *Guardian* reported on Grant's "characteristically cruel and ruthless" order to "do all possible damage to the railroads and the crops, to carry off the farming stock and the negroes, to take all available measures for preventing the cultivation of the soil, and, in view of the probability that the war would last for another year, to convert it into a 'barren waste,' where not even a blade of grass should be permitted to grow."[18]

On September 30, Custer reported that his command "destroyed 9 large mills and about 100 barns yesterday—the mills were filled with flour and wheat; the barns were filled with threshed wheat and hay. I also destroyed a large number of stacks of hay and grain found standing in the fields." His men also captured over 150 head of beef and 500 sheep. "No dwelling houses were destroyed or interfered with," he noted, though this policy was sometimes violated.[19] The effect was devastating; by one estimate Custer's and Merritt's divisions eliminated enough wheat in a single day to feed the entire Confederate Army for a year.[20]

Sheridan reported to Grant, "The whole country from the Blue Ridge to the North Mountain has been rendered untenable for a rebel army.... The people here are getting sick of the war. Heretofore they have had no reason to complain, because they have been living in great abundance."[21]

"Waving fields of yellow grain have been made a perfect waste, and overburdened barns burned to the ground," the *Philadelphia Evening Telegraph* reported. "The smiling valley of Virginia is now a desert for ninety miles."[22] Assistant Secretary of War Charles Henry Dana visited the valley and wrote approvingly, "[I]t is all a desert there; nothing is left except what corn was standing in the fields. All barns and their contents have been destroyed, and all stacks of hay and grain. All the cattle have been driven out, big and little, horned, hairy, and woolly.... Sheridan and Sherman are generals after the style I have always looked for in one respect at least—they devastate indeed."[23]

For Southerners the trauma of the burning mirrored Sherman's destructive march through Georgia. Captain Robert E. Park of the 12th Alabama regiment witnessed the devastation and bemoaned the "barbarous style of the barn-burner Sheridan and his robber followers. Sheridan laid the lovely Valley of Virginia to waste.... Such is Yankee civilization, humanity and Christianity!" Park wrote that it is a "matter of sincere congratulation that our chivalrous Southern leaders ... are made of far different material from that which makes up the bloody butcher Grant, the bummer Sherman, the barn-burner Sheridan, the mulatto-women-lover Custer, and the degraded Beast Butler."[24] Samuel Newton Berryhill, a Mississippian known as "The Backwoods Poet," encapsulated Southern attitudes in a poem entitled "Sheridan," which read,

> From Shenandoah's valley fair,
> Borne on the chilly midnight air,
> There comes a wail of wild despair—
> Sheridan.
> Women and babes—the old, the lame,
> Are shivering round the smouldering flame,
> And quivering lips pronounce thy name,
> Sheridan....
> Destruction o'er that land has past,
> And left the fields a blackened waste;
> No food is there for man nor beast—
> Sheridan....

The "crow" that flies on pinions fleet,
Need take no "rations" there to eat;
For Yankee flesh shall be his meat,
Sheridan.

Confederate cavalry, particularly troops commanded by Thomas Rosser, dogged Sheridan as he commenced his withdrawal from the ruined valley. Rosser joined Early on October 5, fresh from the successful "Beefsteak Raid" outside Richmond, in which rebel cavalrymen rustled 2,500 head of Union cattle from Grant's rear and herded them back to Confederate lines. Rosser was optimistically dubbed the "Savior of the Valley," and his self-named "Laurel Brigade" was expected to punish the Yankee invaders.[25] Rosser was given two more brigades to fill out a division and began pursuing Sheridan north.

The rebels were outraged at the scouring of the valley and eager for revenge. They harassed Union columns with hit-and-run attacks, picking off stragglers, turning back patrols, and generally keeping up the pressure. At first Rosser tracked the Federals at what Sheridan called "a respectful distance," but by the third day of the withdrawal he "had the temerity to annoy [the Union] rear guard considerably." Rosser dealt the Federal cavalry some smart blows on October 7 and 8, and "tired of these annoyances," Sheridan wrote, "I concluded to open the enemy's eyes in earnest." He sought to finish the "Savior of the Valley" and instructed Torbert that he "expected him either to give Rosser a drubbing next morning or get whipped himself."[26]

Custer had ridden six miles ahead of the army but was called back late on October 8, taking up a position west of the town of Tom's Brook Crossing with orders to "attack and whip the enemy" in concert with Merritt's division. Custer moved toward Rosser on Back Road, with Merritt's division to his left along the Valley Pike facing Major General

Lunsford Lomax's rebel cavalry. Sheridan watched the action unfold from a perch atop Round Hill north of town, expecting his men to "inflict on the enemy the sharp and summary punishment his rashness had invited."[27]

The Confederates were outnumbered, but Rosser was confident. "I'll drive [the Federals] into Strasburg [eight miles down the valley] by 10 o'clock," he vowed. Rosser had taken a strong position along Spiker's Hill, a steep ridge on the south bank of Tom's Run. "Near the base of this ridge the enemy had posted a strong force of dismounted cavalry behind stone fences and barricades of rails, logs, &c.," Custer wrote, "while running along near the summit was a second and stronger line of barricades, also defended by dismounted cavalry. On the crest of the ridge the enemy had six guns in position, strongly supported by columns of cavalry."[28]

The battle began early the morning of the ninth when a brigade under Pennington, then a volunteer colonel commanding the 3rd New Jersey Cavalry, pushed Rosser's pickets near the town of Mt. Olive back onto the main body. An artillery duel commenced, with neither side gaining significant advantage. Custer's guns were plagued by faulty ammunition but held their own. On the eastern side of the field, Merritt's division moved to battle, with Devin's brigade exploiting a gap between the two rebel formations along a creek called Jordan Run and flanking Lomax.

Custer sent Pennington forward with a strong line of mounted skirmishers to feel the enemy. From the stubborn resistance, it was clear that Rosser was in a strong position. Under close observation by the foe, Custer prepared two brigades under Pierce and Kidd for a frontal assault. When his line was ready, Custer rode out in front of his command, stopped his horse ahead of the line, doffed his wide-brimmed hat, and saluted Rosser with a flourish. Kidd wrote, "Custer and Rosser, in war and peace, were animated by the same knightly spirit."[29]

"You see that officer down there," Rosser said to his staff, watching the salute. "That's General Custer, the Yanks are so proud of, and I intend to give him the best whipping to-day that he ever got. See if I don't."[30]

"The entire line was ordered forward," Custer wrote, "and when sufficiently near the enemy the charge was sounded." It was a difficult assault, with Tom's Brook running across the field in front of them and the strong emplacements along Spiker's Hill. But Custer wasn't simply dashing in recklessly with drawn sabers. While Rosser's attention was fixed on his old West Point chum, Custer had already dispatched the 18th Pennsylvania, supported by the 8th and 22nd New York, to swing far to the right to mount a separate attack. They crossed Tom's Brook upstream and thundered in on Rosser's left flank and rear as Custer led the other two brigades forward on the front and right. "The enemy seeing his flank turned and his retreat cut off broke in the utmost confusion," Custer wrote, "and sought safety in headlong flight."[31]

Custer's men rushed after the retreating rebels for two miles where they formed a brigade to check the Union onslaught. The Federal cavalry were pushed back at first, but Pennington and Wells reformed their brigades for a massed charge. "Gen. Custer, attended by his staff and escort, dashed forward with his flag in the most heroic manner," a battlefield reporter noted, "and joined with his command in a grand charge and chase for the enemy's artillery. It was an extremely interesting and exciting scene."[32]

"Before this irresistible advance the enemy found it impossible to stand," Custer wrote. "Once more he was compelled to trust his safety to the fleetness of his steed rather than the metal of his saber."

Sheridan, who watched the battle from Round Hill, said, "The result was a general smash-up of the entire Confederate line, the retreat quickly degenerating into a rout the like of which was never before seen." The Federals captured eleven pieces of artillery, a few of which were brand new and seeing their first action. They also bagged over three hundred prisoners, a herd of cattle, and numerous wagons and supply trains. Among them were General Rosser's headquarters' wagons and papers and some of the items that Custer had lost at Trevilian Station.

The Confederates fled over twenty miles to Woodstock, and the battle soon became known as "The Woodstock Races." Thomas Munford called it "the greatest disaster that ever befell our cavalry during the whole war," based on the loss of so many guns and wagons.[33] Custer summed up the rebel loss, saying they were "deficient in confidence, courage, and a just cause."[34] Jubal Early notified Robert E. Lee that "the enemy's cavalry is so much superior to ours, both in numbers and equipment.... and it is impossible for ours to compete with his."[35] Commenting on the performance of Rosser's "Laurel Brigade," Early said tartly, "The laurel is a running vine."

That night Custer donned Rosser's captured uniform and paid a visit to the sleeping Brigadier General William Henry Seward Jr., son of the secretary of state. He woke the startled brigadier to announce that he was Rosser and Seward was his prisoner.[36] The next day, Rosser sent Custer a note:

Dear Fanny,

You may have made me take a few steps back today, but I will be even with you tomorrow. Please accept my good wishes and this little gift—a pair of your draws captured at Trevilian Station.

Tex

Custer sent Rosser's dress uniform coat to Libbie and replied to Tex:

> Dear friend,
>   Thanks for setting me up in so many new things, but would you please direct your tailor to make the coat tails of your next uniform a trifle shorter.
>
>   Best regards G.A.C.

CHAPTER THIRTEEN

"LET THE SWORD DECIDE THE CONTEST"

A fter Tom's Brook, the War Department sent Sheridan a note of thanks for his "brilliant victories" over the rebel cavalry, and the *New York Herald* reported that "it is believed that no organized Rebel forces will have the temerity to show themselves while General Sheridan is in the Valley."[1]

Ten days after Tom's Brook, Sheridan's men were encamped a mile and a half southwest of Middletown, in a defensive position along Cedar Creek. Custer's division was spread out over five or six miles, securing the right flank. On the night of October 17, Rosser had led a five-hundred-man raiding force to infiltrate Union lines and kidnap Custer, but they hit the wrong camp.[2] Private George Perkins of the Sixth New York Independent Battery saw the general the next day: "October 18, 1864: Met Gen. Custer and staff, who were going out doubtless to visit the pickets. I had a better view of him than ever before, and was struck by the extreme brightness of his yellow hair which he wears long in ringlets. He looks quite old in face in comparison with the remainder of his appearance."[3]

Sheridan had been called back to Washington days earlier and was spending the night in Winchester prior to his return. He had planned to launch a major cavalry action back into the valley after Tom's Brook, but he abandoned the idea after a dispatch was captured from Longstreet to Early saying that reinforcements were arriving and to "be ready to advance on Sheridan as soon as my forces get up, and we can crush him." To Early this sounded like a fine idea.

During the night of October 18–19, Early quietly moved three columns of over twenty thousand men toward the Union position on Cedar Creek. The night was foggy and still, so peaceful that one reporter said, "Even the mules seemed to be dozing." The first sign of trouble came at four in the morning when rebel forces attacked Union pickets on the extreme right of the army. Custer sounded "to horse" and readied his command for battle, but after the Confederates seized the ford at Cupp's Mill, they stopped their attack. Custer reported the incident and stayed at the ready, but for the next hour nothing else happened.

The attack on the right was a ruse to divert attention from the Union left. There, troops from Major General John B. Gordon's corps, spearheaded by a division led by Custer's West Point friend Stephen Dodson Ramseur, surprised and drove back Union pickets into the camps of Crook's VIII Corps. The rush of the enemy through the darkness and fog was so sudden and disorienting that Confederates were inside the Union perimeter before alarms could be raised. Hundreds of men were taken prisoner without firing a shot, many in their bedclothes. VIII Corps fell back in disorder, and the rebels pushed on to hit Emory's XIX Corps just over the Valley Pike. "The rebels hesitated not," a reporter wrote, "but pressed on, as a dashing cataract, over all barriers, completely surprising, and in a measure stampeding, the left of General Sheridan's line."[4]

The men of XIX Corps were also surprised, and their defense was hampered by rebel gunfire and the retreat of VIII Corps through their ranks. By then the sun was coming up. As the mist dispersed, Union troops saw the rebels under Ramseur had already flanked them and were in their rear. XIX Corps stood longer than VIII Corps had, but gradually began to break under the pressure on their left and from Kershaw's division on their front. General Emory had his horse shot from under him as he tried to form his troops against the determined assault. Unformed Union troops retreated, and supply trains were taken quickly north along the road to Winchester to keep them out of enemy hands.

General Horatio G. Wright, commanding the army in Sheridan's absence, ordered XIX and VI Corps under Major General James B. Ricketts to form on high ground on the west side of Meadow Brook, a tributary to Cedar Creek running west of Middletown. VI Corps set up a defense and fought stubbornly, but could not hold and soon retreated in good order.

Custer learned of the rolling disaster on the left shortly after daybreak from Torbert's aide Captain Coppinger. He brought in his scattered command and helped firm up the defense on the right and manage the retreat, rallying men who were "falling back in disorder and without any sufficient or apparent cause."[5] General Wright, bleeding from a musket ball wound to his chin, ordered Custer to the extreme left of the army to help Merritt's 1st Division stem the enemy advance. Custer left behind three regiments under Colonel Wells to manage the right, which thus far had not seen hard fighting.

The cavalry, particularly Merritt's men, helped secure the left flank while the infantry retreated and reformed a mile north of Middletown. Torbert praised the 1st Division for its determination, saying that while "many a horse and rider was made to bite the dust, they held their ground like men of steel." Custer's men engaged the enemy with sharp-shooting and artillery. Around 10:30 the fighting began to wind down, and was carried on mainly as an exchange of artillery fire. Rebel troops were resting from their long night's march and morning's fight, looting supplies from the Federal stores they captured. Had the battle ended then, it would have been a resounding Confederate victory. Union forces had been pushed back two miles; given up hundreds of prisoners, two dozen guns, and numerous wagons and supply trains; and suffered heavy casualties.

But around the time the fighting paused, cheers could be heard behind the Union lines, faintly at first, then growing stronger. Sheridan had appeared, riding a black pacer named Rienzi, waving his hat as he sped down the line, greeted with wild enthusiasm. Early that morning in Winchester, Sheridan had heard reports of artillery fire in the distance, but he assumed they were from a planned reconnaissance. But at 9:00 a.m. while he was riding through the town, he heard unmistakable sounds of battle. As he hurried south, "the head of the fugitives appeared in sight," he wrote, "trains and men coming to the rear with appalling rapidity." As the *New York Herald* put it, he "found a scene of skedaddles." Sheridan halted the retreat and, "taking twenty men from my escort, I pushed on to the front."[6]

Sheridan's dash to Cedar Creek became part of American military legend. American poet and portraitist Thomas Buchanan Read wrote a poem about the twenty-mile ride (actually closer to twelve miles), which was as much about the horse as the man, and rendered a painting to go along with it. "He seemed to the whole great army to say, / 'I have brought you Sheridan all the way / From Winchester, down to save the day!'" wrote Read. Rienzi, named for a raid Sheridan led on Rienzi, Mississippi, was renamed Winchester after this ride.

Sheridan restored order to the scene and began to reform his army. The right flank was coming under pressure as rebel infantry and Rosser's cavalry pressed Wells's brigade. Sheridan immediately shifted the 3rd Division to meet the threat, saying, "Go in, Custer!"

A gap had opened between the enemy cavalry and infantry. Custer, exploiting the rolling ground, pushed Pierce's battery to a position close to where the enemy had massed. "Being undiscovered," he wrote, "I caused my battery to open suddenly at short range; at the same time charged with about three regiments. The effect was surprising and to none more so than to our enemies, who, being entirely off their guard, were thrown into the utmost confusion by this sudden and unexpected attack." The cavalry charge by Pennington's brigade threw back Rosser's men for a mile and ended the threat to the right.

For the next few hours, Sheridan readied his men for an attack. Early did little to impede this work, though around 1:00 p.m. he made a half-hearted and short-lived move north. But he was outnumbered and no longer enjoyed the element of surprise. His three-mile line was thin and poorly defended on its flanks. The more numerous Union forces, on the other hand, were reinvigorated and had something to prove after their ignominious flight that morning.

Sheridan ordered a general advance late in the afternoon. The movement started well, but as the lines converged, Early's left overlapped the Union right and could have begun to roll it up. But Sheridan ordered a brigade under General McMillan to charge the angle of the flanking force, which cut them off from the main body. That charge was "the death-knell of the Confederacy," according to one observer.[7] Meanwhile, Custer's cavalry were forming for their own charge. Overcome with emotion, George rode up to Sheridan and threw his arms around him before returning to lead his cavalrymen against the disrupted rebel flank. "Custer's troopers sweeping across the Middletown meadows and down toward Cedar Creek, took many of them prisoners before they could reach the stream," Sheridan wrote, "so I forgave his delay."

"It was apparent that the wavering in the ranks of the enemy betokened a retreat," Custer recalled, "and that this retreat might be converted into a rout." Custer charged ahead, breaking the rebel left as the rest of the army made contact down the line. He fought across the same ground that had been contested earlier that day, pausing and reforming to press the increasingly disorganized foe. "Here mingled lay the dead and wounded of both armies," wrote Lieutenant Colonel John W. Bennett of the 1st Vermont Cavalry, "and as our men gazed upon the naked forms of their dead and wounded comrades—the former entirely and the latter partially stripped by our inhuman foe—the deep murmurs that ran along the ranks foreshadowed the impetuosity of the coming charge."[8]

Custer's men moved forward in plain view of the retreating enemy, who were being pressed back on Meadow Brook and Cedar Creek beyond. "Seeing so large a force of cavalry bearing rapidly down upon an unprotected flank and their line of retreat in danger of being intercepted," Custer wrote, "the lines of the enemy, already broken, now gave way in the utmost confusion." Rebels threw down their weapons and ran for it, and "in a headlong and disgraceful manner sought safety in ignominious flight." As one reporter put it, the charge "swept the enemy off the face of the earth before it every where."[9]

A small group of enemy troops rallied across Cedar Creek and delivered some hot fire to their pursuers at short range. Custer kept up the momentum and dashed forward with the 1st Vermont and 5th New York. "Hearing the charge sounded through our bugles," Custer wrote, "the enemy only stood long enough to deliver one volley; then, casting away his arms, attempted to escape under cover of the darkness."

"Confused and terrified the enemy threw down their arms and trampled upon each other in their frantic attempts to escape," Lieutenant Colonel Bennett recalled. "My men rushed upon them as though they were the appointed avengers of their comrades slain. Considering our numbers, the slaughter was fearful."[10] There developed what Custer called "an exciting chase after a panic-stricken, uncontrollable mob.... prisoners were taken by hundreds, entire companies threw down their arms, and appeared glad when summoned to surrender."

"The road was full of charging cavalry," Confederate Private George Q. Peyton recalled, "and I saw Custer with his long curls hanging down his back."[11] The pursuit continued into evening, through Strasburg and miles beyond. George said later, "The darkness of the night was intense, and was only relieved here and there by the light of a burning wagon or ambulance to which the affrighted enemy in his despair had applied the torch."[12] A bridge collapsed over a stream south of Strasburg, forcing many wagons to be abandoned. Others were ridden down and halted. James Sweeney and Frederick Lyons of the 1st Vermont Cavalry in Custer's division ordered one wagon to halt. The driver said, "The General ordered the ambulance to go on."

"What General?" Sweeney said.

"General Ramseur," the driver replied. Sweeney was wearing a light-colored jacket, and the driver had mistaken him for a rebel.

"That is the very man I am looking for," Sweeney said, and they captured the ambulance, the general, his surgeon, and his flag, which was emblazoned "On to Victory."[13]

Ramseur had been the hero of the morning's battle, rolling up the Union left flank and routing two Corps. He was a tested combat leader who had been in most of the major engagements in the east.[14] Morris Schaff described him as "dark eyed, stern [and] dignified."[15] In the course of that day's battle, he had two horses shot out from under him and was wounded in the arm but kept fighting until a musket ball pierced his lungs.

Custer learned of his friend's plight and had him taken to Sheridan's headquarters, at the Belle Grove mansion, to be tended to. There,

Ramseur saw his West Point friend Henry DuPont, first in the Class of May 1861, then a captain with the 5th U.S. Artillery. DuPont would be awarded a Medal of Honor for standing by his guns that day while the Union line collapsed in the face of Ramseur's assault. Henry had been present at the going-away party Custer hosted at Benny Havens for Ramseur and Wesley Merritt in April 1860. In fact, five of the six cadet revelers were on the field of Cedar Creek that day. They were missing John Pelham of Alabama, who had been killed at the Battle of Kelly's Ford, in March 1863. Ramseur asked for Merritt, but he was away with his troops and did not return in time.

Ramseur died the next day at Sheridan's headquarters. He asked Custer to cut a lock of his hair for his precious wife, Nellie. His last words were "I die a Christian and hope to meet her in heaven." The day before the battle he had received word Nellie had given birth to a baby girl.[16]

The victory at Cedar Creek had come at a high cost: over 5,700 Federals killed, wounded, or missing, compared with 2,900 of Early's men. But it ended up being a Union win, which is more than could have been said at midday. The Federals seized over fifty guns, numerous battle flags, countless wagons, and hundreds of prisoners. The mood at Belle Grove was exultant. When Custer saw Sheridan that night, he hugged him and whirled him about in the air, shouting, "By God, we've cleaned them out and got the guns!" He did the same to Torbert, who responded "There, there, old fellow; don't capture me!"[17]

There was gratitude all around for the near escape that changed a surprise defeat into an unexpected triumph. Grant ordered a salute fired and wired the secretary of war: "Turning what bid fair to be a disaster into a glorious victory, stamps Sheridan, what I have always thought him, one of the ablest of generals." Lincoln offered Sheridan "the thanks of the nation" and his "own personal admiration and gratitude" for the operations in the valley and "the splendid work of October 19."[18] Sheridan asked for "the brave boys, Merritt and Custer, [to be] promoted by brevet." And Custer praised his men that their "conduct throughout was sublimely heroic, and without a parallel in the annals of warfare."[19] Custer was chosen to escort a delegation of soldiers to Washington to present ten captured Confederate battle flags to the War Department.

Libbie had gone to Newark around this time to visit her cousins, saying as she left, "It would be my bad luck to have Autie come in my absence." A few days later, she read in the morning paper that George had arrived in Washington. She ran to her room and threw herself on her bed, crying, "I've missed him, I've missed him." But soon after, the front bell rang and George came bounding up the stairs, snatched Libbie from the bed, and carried her about the room.[20] They rushed back to Washington for the presentation on October 24.

Custer's men rode a bus up Pennsylvania Avenue to the War Department with a rebel flag flying out each window, to cheers from the passersby. "The soldiers in the city were jubilant," one report said, "and when they met Custer and his men in the street, would give the soldiers a hug, and some of the old soldiers would kiss Custer's hand."[21] Secretary Stanton met each of the men in turn and heard the stories of how they captured the flags.[22] Custer recounted tales of his men's heroism, saying their victory was "the most complete and decisive which has been achieved in the Shenandoah." The soldiers who had captured the flags were informed they would be awarded medals, and Custer was promoted to major general. Stanton shook Custer's hand, saying, "General Custer, a gallant officer always makes gallant soldiers."[23] "The third division wouldn't be worth a cent if it wasn't for him!" one of Custer's youthful lads interjected, to good-natured laughter.

Electoral politics hung heavily over the lighthearted scene. The 1864 presidential election was coming up on November 8, and Lincoln had needed victories in the field to boost his reelection chances. His challenger was George McClellan, who was still an officer on active duty, a War Democrat running on a peace platform as a means of unifying the fractured opposition party. Earlier in the year, Lincoln had doubted his chances for a second term; the war had dragged on longer than most anyone initially thought it would, and some Republican Radicals wanted to dump Lincoln because they thought he could not win. But ultimately the party rallied behind the president, who dumped Vice President Hannibal Hamlin and ran with War Democrat and former Tennessee senator Andrew Johnson under the National Union party banner. Their slogan was "Don't change horses in the middle of the stream."

McClellan was hampered by his running mate, Ohio congressman George H. Pendleton, a Peace Democrat whose desire to stop the war at any cost was viewed as too radical. McClellan's main selling point was that as a military leader he could bring peace with honor, something that had eluded Lincoln. But three days after McClellan was nominated, Sherman entered Atlanta, stealing much of his thunder. Sheridan's subsequent triumphs in the valley bolstered Lincoln's claims that he would soon bring the war to a close, achieving peace not only with honor but with victory.

Southern newspapers mocked the administration for exploiting military success for political gain. "The Sheridan Fight—Magnificent Election Bulletins" ran an October 31 headline in the *Richmond Daily Dispatch*. Anti-Lincoln Northern papers objected as well. But the facts on the ground were powerful arguments against McClellan's central campaign theme. If Lincoln could win the war, there was no need for Little Mac in the White House.

"My doctrine ever has been that a soldier should not meddle in politics," George wrote Libbie around this time.[24] But Custer was involved in the campaign whether he liked it or not. The same day Cedar Creek was fought, his name appeared, probably without his foreknowledge, in a newspaper article entitled "The Fighting Generals for Lincoln."[25] The presentation of the captured rebel battle flags at the War Department and Custer's promotion were a national news story. George had never supported Lincoln, but as a professional soldier he felt his political views did not matter. Lincoln was commander in chief, and Custer was subject to his orders. Furthermore he was well aware of the career risks he faced by being associated with McClellan.

Little Mac stirred passions among his supporters and detractors alike. There was always a lingering suspicion that George, having been on McClellan's staff, harbored a secret affinity for him, which of course he did. "Autie adored General McClellan," Libbie wrote. Even years after having served on his staff and while facing his own challenges as a general officer, "his worship of McClellan was still with him."[26]

Custer's reputation as a McClellan protégé had sometimes made things difficult for him in Washington. In the winter of 1863–64, he received a letter from a senator who was to vote on his much-delayed confirmation as a brigadier general. "Before I can vote for your confirmation," the senator wrote, "I desire to be informed whether you are what is termed, 'a McClellan man.'"[27] Libbie frequently faced the same question during her time in Washington in 1864, but she never rose to the bait, knowing that if she spoke the truth it would be all the worse for George. In January 1864, Custer wrote to his soon-to-be father-in-law, Judge Bacon, that he suffered "no little anxiety" over the confirmation vote. "You would be surprised at the pertinacity with which certain men labor to defame me," he said. "It was reported that I was a 'copperhead,' a charge completely refuted." He said he was "trusting to time to vindicate me."[28]

During his visit to Washington after Cedar Creek, George released a statement that was widely reprinted in the press, which was intended to remove all doubt about his views on the Democratic Peace Platform and proposals for an armistice: "I am a peace man, in favor of an 'armistice' and of sending 'Peace Commissioners,'" he wrote. "The

Peace Commissioners I am in favor of are those sent from the cannon's mouth. The only armistice I would yield to would be that forced by the points of our bayonets." He felt that proposing an armistice was "madness" given the successes of the armies in the field, and were a general to call for a halt to fighting when the enemy was crumbling on the battlefield, he would be "cashiered for cowardice and treachery." Rather than talking peace, he counseled that the armies at the front should be reinforced, and the matter pressed vigorously. Moreover, alluding to the election but not being able as a professional officer to make a political statement, he added, "Let the people, at the proper time, speak in such tones as will guarantee to the soldiers in the field a full and hearty support."[29] It was taken as an endorsement of Lincoln, but read literally it endorsed no one.

Emmanuel Custer disapproved of his son's public stance. George wrote a lengthy defense of his opinion, emphasizing the risks he had taken in battle and the need to press on to victory to justify the sacrifices that had been made. "Since the South has chosen to submit our troubles to the arbitrament of the sword," he stated flatly, "let the sword decide the contest."[30]

CHAPTER FOURTEEN

CUSTER'S COUNTER-INSURGENCY

W hile Union and Confederate main battle forces were contending in the valley, a parallel unconventional struggle was being waged that led to one of the most controversial events of Custer's Civil War career. "There are some things in the lives of all of us that we can't refer to with pleasure," Confederate cavalryman John W. Munson wrote, "and the hanging and shooting of some of our men, by order of General Custer, and in his presence, is one of those which Mosby's men rarely refer to. Neither it, nor what followed as a result of it, are happy memories to any of us."[1]

As Sheridan's army moved back and forth through the valley dueling with Early in the summer and fall of 1864, his rear areas were bedeviled by Confederate raiders under the leadership of John Singleton Mosby. Mosby commanded the 43rd Battalion, 1st Virginia Cavalry, raised under the Partisan Ranger Act of 1862, which authorized the formation of special units to conduct irregular warfare operations against Union forces. Mosby's Rangers operated principally in Union-occupied northern and northwest Virginia, an area that became known as Mosby's Confederacy.

Mosby's men were "a fit looking set of fellows," one reporter who spent time with the partisans wrote, "well dressed, and most of them commissioned officers of the rebel army, who prefer the romantic life of marauders to that of civilized warfare in the field. Some of them were well mounted, well dressed, and a majority of them were provided with Union overcoats. They were nearly all of them apparently highly intelligent and well-educated men, armed with sabres and revolvers, very few having carbines. They seemed well disciplined, and exhibited the utmost confidence in the Colonel."[2] Most of the Confederate ranger units had been disbanded by 1864 due to lax discipline and the sense in Richmond that their operations amounted to little more than state-sanctioned banditry. But Mosby maintained strict controls over his men and imposed the order of a regular military unit, which he consistently claimed they were.

Mosby's operations targeted Union supply trains, bridges, canals, and railroads. They raided lightly guarded encampments and Union depots, taking prisoners when possible, and generally made life difficult for the Northern occupiers. Federal forces hunted Mosby relentlessly, but they always came up short, and legends of his encounters and escapes grew over the years, earning him the nickname the "Gray Ghost." Libbie Custer related a story that Mosby was rumored to have given a lock of his hair to a girl near Washington to give to Lincoln with his compliments, "and he would take dinner with him within ten days."[3] Herman Melville's epic poem "The Scout toward Aldie" captures the air of uncertainty and dread in Union rear-areas in Virginia in those days:

> The cavalry-camp lies on the slope
> Of what was late a vernal hill,

But now like a pavement bare—
An outpost in the perilous wilds
Which ever are lone and still;
But Mosby's men are there—
Of Mosby best beware.

Custer's run-ins with Mosby began as soon as his command moved into Virginia after Gettysburg. In mid-July 1863 he reported "some little bushwhacking" going on, noting that "Mosby is reported at Aldie."[4] In August 1863, Custer formed "a party of 300 picked men, under an excellent officer, to hunt up Mosby." Pleasonton reported optimistically that Custer "has strong hopes they will either capture Mosby or drive him out of the country."[5] But Mosby eluded Custer's hunters as he had many in the past.

Mosby presented the same unconventional challenges that vexed regular force commanders before and since. Sheridan initially believed that it would not take much effort to secure northern Virginia. After the Battle of Cedar Creek, he claimed that "one good regiment could clear [Mosby] out any time, if the regimental commander had spunk enough to try."[6] It was the type of misconception that has plagued many American officers faced with insurgency: that a small amount of determined force would end the troubles.

Reporter E. A. Paul noted in 1863 that the "futile attempts to hold Mosby and his sixty men in check has probably cost the Government, during the last year, quite as much as any single army corps, and still Mosby's band was as active and destructive today as it was one year ago." The reasons why were common to any domestic insurgent force. Mosby drew support from the local population, who supplied him with manpower, horses, intelligence on the size and movement of Union troops, food, sanctuary, and medical assistance. "When any of these citizen soldiers are called to an account," Paul continued, "they are equally ready to make oath that they have done nothing to aid Mosby.... Remove these agents, and Mosby would soon be forced to seek another field to operate in."[7]

This was easier said than done. In August 1864, the 8th Illinois Cavalry regiment was ordered into the area near Upperville and Middleburg. Their orders were to "destroy, as far as practicable, the sources from which Mosby draws men, horses, and support"; to "arrest and bring in all males capable of bearing arms or conveying information, between the ages of eighteen and fifty"; and to "impress all wagons, and bring them in loaded with forage; destroy all crops of hay, oats, corn, and wheat which you cannot bring in, and seize all horses."[8] The regiment did its best to follow these expansive orders, but Mosby's network in the area remained intact, and actions taken against civilians only hardened the resolve of those secretly supporting the insurgents.

Custer employed rough tactics from the start. In August 1863 he sent a squadron to the home of one of Mosby's officers, a major named Williams, "with instructions to hang him to the nearest tree, if they caught him." Williams evaded capture, but Custer's men "removed his family from the house, and burned it down," freeing Williams's slaves and appropriating his horses and cattle.[9] Over time these punitive measures became more common and were used in an escalating war of tit for tat.

On the evening of October 3, 1864, Sheridan's chief engineer, Lieutenant John R. Meigs, and two other soldiers were waylaid by a like number of rebels along the road between the towns of Harrisonburg and Dayton, half a mile from Sheridan's headquarters. One soldier escaped, one was captured, and Meigs was killed. Meigs was a well-known and respected young officer, first in the West Point Class of 1863 and the son of Major General Montgomery C. Meigs, the quartermaster general of the Army. The surviving soldier reported that they had been attacked by surprise by men wearing Union uniforms, and Meigs "was killed without resistance of any kind whatever, and without even the chance to give himself up."[10]

The death shocked the Army and the Northern public. Young Meigs was held in high regard throughout Sheridan's command, and Sheridan also knew that Meigs's vindictive, rebel-hating father would expect some type of reprisal. "Determining to teach a lesson to these abettors of the foul deed—a lesson they would never forget," Sheridan later wrote, "I ordered all the houses within an area of five miles to be burned."[11]

Sheridan gave the job to Custer. It was not as extensive as the burning operations he had recently conducted further to the south, but its purpose was revenge, not military necessity. The area to be torched included the village of Dayton, Virginia, and Custer was prepared to wipe it out on Sheridan's order. However, shortly after he set about the burning, Custer received orders from Sheridan to "cease his desolating work." New facts had arisen in the investigation of Meigs's death that suggested that the ambush was fairer than originally reported, and Meigs had resisted capture and gone down fighting. Sheridan instructed Custer to spare the remaining buildings but nevertheless to "fetch away all the able-bodied males as prisoners."[12]

Union troops sometimes faced resistance on their reprisal missions. In August 1864, one of Custer's pickets was killed in a confrontation with Mosby's men, and some others were wounded and captured. In retaliation, he ordered Colonel Alger of the 5th Michigan to burn four homes of known rebel sympathizers near Berryville. A fifty-man detachment was dispatched under Captain Drake to go about the grim detail. They erected a barricade on the main road to prevent flight, then began the burning.[13]

When the first house was in flames, Captain Drake took a few men to another dwelling five hundred yards away. The residents, women and children, seeing what had happened to their neighbors, ran outside pleading with the soldiers not to torch their home. The soldiers, unmoved by the appeals, kept to their duty and lit the second house.

Nearby, concealed in a ravine, two hundred rebels had gathered and were observing the proceedings with growing outrage. An Irishman named Larry exclaimed to his fellows, "Jasus, if that wouldn't make a man fight, I don't know what would!" Larry leapt up and led a sudden, furious charge on the surprised Federals.[14] Williamson wrote,

> The man who could stand within the glare of burning dwellings, and witness unmoved the pitiful spectacle of pleading mothers with their frightened little ones clinging around them, and see the merciless savages who wrought this ruin gloating over the wreck they had made, and proceeding to a repetition of their cruel deeds of incendiarism, and not feel an impulse which would drive him to avenge such savagery, would not deserve the name of man. It seems hardly credible that men could be found in a civilized age, so lost to all sense of humanity as to thus rival the savage cruelties of Indian warfare.[15]

Mosby's men rushed Lieutenant Allen's group, which was near the first burning house. The overwhelmed Union soldiers broke and fled down the road but were blocked by their own barricade. They veered to the side but encountered a large stone wall running perpendicular to the road, and fleeing down it, they hit a corner and were trapped. The Federals attempted to surrender but were cut down to the last man. "Our men were demons that day," John Munson recalled. "Thirty of the burners were killed and wounded, mostly killed. We took no prisoners and gave no quarter."[16]

By this time Mosby's activities had become so troublesome that Grant ordered family members of his troops taken hostage and that Mosby's men be summarily executed if captured. "The families of most of Mosby's men are known, and can be collected," he advised Sheridan. "I think they should be taken and kept at Fort McHenry, or some secure place, as hostages for the good conduct of Mosby and his men. Where any of Mosby's men are caught hang them without trial."[17] Sheridan wasted no time implementing the order. "Mosby has annoyed me and captured a few wagons," he responded the next day. "We hung one and shot six of his men yesterday. I have burned all wheat and hay, and brought off all stock, sheep, cattle, horses, &c., south of Winchester."[18]

Subjecting Mosby's men to summary execution raised a critical legal question regarding their status as lawful combatants. Mosby's defenders argued that his men were part of an organized Confederate unit, and thus entitled to consideration under the laws and customs of war. But the Federals considered them brigands to be treated with summary justice. Mosby argued that his command "has done nothing contrary to the usages of war" and that "there was passed by the last U.S. Congress a bill of pains and penalties against guerrillas, and as they profess to consider my men within the definition of the term, I think it would be well to come to some understanding with the enemy in reference to them."[19]

Custer had already proved willing to mete out summary justice on partisans and soon had an opportunity to implement Grant's order. After the Third Battle of Winchester, when Custer was trying to break through Confederate defenses south of Front Royal, Captain Chapman of Mosby's command learned of a large Union supply train headed for the area. He arranged an attack, but Custer got wind of Chapman's designs. Rather than sending a small guard with the train, he personally led a much larger force not far behind it. When Chapman attacked the train, Custer quickly deployed forces to block his line of retreat. Realizing he had been trapped, Chapman turned his men and charged Custer's troopers, who had set up a line across a defile. Most of the Mosby men were able to cut their way out to freedom, but six were captured.[20]

Custer made a public example of the raiders. He paraded them through Front Royal, clearly intending to execute them. Custer led his troops through the town, "dressed in a splendid suit of silk velvet," a witness wrote, "his saddle bow bound in silver or gold. In his hand he had a large branch of damsons, which he picked and ate as he rode along. He was a distinguished looking man, with his yellow locks resting upon his shoulders."[21] The prisoners were "led through the streets of Front Royal with ropes around their necks—one poor fellow led before the very eyes of his mother pleading for mercy for her boy," one man recalled.[22] A rebel named Rhodes was "lashed with ropes between two horses," another eyewitness wrote, "and dragged in plain sight of his agonized relatives to the open field of our town."[23]

Trooper Rhodes was the first to die. A Union soldier volunteered to be the executioner and "ordered the helpless, dazed prisoner to stand up in front of him, while he emptied his pistol upon him." Two more were shot, while the rest were hanged from a large walnut tree.[24] A note attached to one of the hanged men read, "This would be the fate of Mosby and all his men."

The reaction among the partisans was electric. "There was at once a rumor set afloat that we were to fight thereafter under the black flag," Munson recalled, "and as a proof of it Custer's act was pointed to. Men examined their pistols more carefully."[25] Mosby wrote to Robert E. Lee to inform him of the "brutal conduct of the enemy" in his area of operations, against civilians and soldiers alike. He noted the Front Royal executions and proposed to "hang an equal number of Custer's men whenever I capture them."[26] Lee forwarded the proposal to Richmond, where it was "cordially approved."[27] *Lex talionis*, the law of retaliation, became the rule. From then on it would be an eye for an eye.

Mosby was already holding twenty-seven prisoners from Custer's command, and at a meeting of his officers at Rectortown on November 6, they decided to execute seven of them. The executions were in retaliation for the six killed at Front Royal and one other, A. C. Willis of Company C, who was hanged by Colonel William H. Powell in retaliation for Mosby's men executing a Federal spy.[28]

Mosby gathered the prisoners and informed them that he had "an account to adjust with Custer." They were ordered to draw lots from a hat, seven of which were marked for death. A witness wrote:

> It was a painful scene, and one never to be forgotten.... One of the captives laid his head on the shoulder of a comrade and wept like a child. Another prayed earnestly until it came his turn to draw, which he did with trembling hand. Holding up the paper and looking at it, his eyes brightened as he exclaimed: "Blank, by God! I knew it would be so." One said to a more fortunate companion: "Tell my mother I died like a man." Some could not overcome their feelings, and begged piteously for their lives.... It was not merely in a spirit of revenge that these men were condemned, but it was a measure to which Mosby was forced to resort, by the brutal acts of Custer and Powell.

"Our own men, too, were scarcely less affected," John H. Alexander recalled. "The prisoners had been in our company a day or two, and, as was always the case after the first embarrassment of capture had passed, quite pleasant relations had been established between them and us. We had ridden together, laughed and talked, and divided our rations and tobacco with them; and indeed between some of them and us quite a feeling of comradeship existed. The precipitation of the present state of affairs was a shock to all of us."[29]

A drummer boy who drew a death slip was spared on account of his youth, and the redraw condemned Lieutenant Disoway of the 5th New York Heavy Artillery. "And must I be hanged?" he said philosophically. The drawing done, the prisoners were marched off at nightfall toward Winchester by a guard led by Lieutenant Edward F. Thomson "with orders to execute them on the Valley turnpike as near General Sheridan's headquarters as possible." Along the way they encountered another party led by Captain Montjoy, who was bringing in some fresh Union prisoners. Lieutenant Disoway took a chance and made a Masonic distress signal. Montjoy, a Mason, convinced Lieutenant Thomson to hand over Disoway and another of the prisoners who was also a Masonic brother in exchange for two of the new prisoners. So Disoway survived, though Mosby later said critically to Montjoy that his command was "not a Masonic lodge."

On the way to the hanging, the Confederates realized they did not have enough rope, so they stopped at houses to collect bed cord from old-fashioned beds with which to bind and hang the men. It was a rainy night, and visibility was poor. Near Berryville, about ten miles east of Winchester, one of the prisoners escaped in the darkness, so the Mosby men decided to carry out the executions there rather than risk losing more of the condemned.

Three men were hanged by being hoisted by their necks and died cruelly of strangulation. This took a long time, so the captors decided to shoot the remaining three. The men were lined up and pistols aimed at them. At a command, two of the weapons discharged, but a third failed. "The revolver on my right went off, the revolver on my left went off, and the revolver that was in my face failed to explode," wrote Charles E. Marvin, acting quartermaster's sergeant in the 2nd New York Cavalry. "The click of the hammer on the tube went through me like an electric shock."[30] Marvin, who had meanwhile freed his hands, sprang on his intended executioner, knocked him down and fled into the trees. The other two prisoners fell, though one of them, named Bennett, was only wounded and was shot again. The Mosby men made a brief search for Marvin, who had hidden behind a tree, but they missed him in the darkness and gave up. Before leaving, the executioners pinned onto one of the hanged men a note written by Mosby reading, "These men have been hung in retaliation for an equal number of Colonel Mosby's men hung by order of General Custer at Front Royal. Measure for measure."[31]

Marvin later found refuge in the nearby house of an old woman, who said, "Have no fear; I had three of Custer's men in my house when Mosby's men were all over it, looking for them; and I had two of Mosby's men concealed in my house when Custer's men were here looking for them. Any one who comes to me for assistance gets it, if I can give it to them." Marvin was joined by one of the other men they tried to execute, who had been wounded and played dead. In time it turned out even twice-shot Bennett survived. So of the seven condemned Custer men, only the three who were hanged actually died.[32]

Mosby sent a note to Sheridan explaining that the intended executions were direct and proportional retaliation for the killings of his own men. "Since the murder of my men not less than 700 prisoners, including many officers of high rank, captured from your army by this command, have been forwarded to Richmond," Mosby wrote, "but the execution of my purpose of retaliation was deferred in order, as far as possible, to confine its operation to the men of Custer and Powell." He noted that future prisoners "will be treated with the kindness due to their condition, unless some new act of barbarity shall compel me reluctantly to adopt a course of policy repulsive to humanity."[33]

Mosby's letter had its intended effect. The tit-for-tat killings, at least the official ones, stopped. This was mostly in the Union's interest, since Mosby could take prisoner many more boys in blue than Sheridan could find Mosby men. A no-quarter policy was more deadly for Union troops than rebels.

Sheridan continued his operations in Mosby's Confederacy, though he refrained from revenge killings and to some degree paid more respect to the people in the area. In late November he sent three brigades on a scorched-earth mission, significantly more troops than the single regiment he earlier claimed could do the job. They "scoured the country completely between the Blue Ridge and Bull Run mountains."[34] Sheridan explained to Major General Halleck that he would have had to employ "ten men to his one" to "break [Mosby] up," and instead sought to make "a scape-goat of him for the destruction of private rights." Sheridan believed there would be "an intense hatred of him in that portion of this Valley which is nearly a desert" and that he would soon punish Loudoun County, "and let them know there is a God in Israel."[35] But he ordered Merritt, who commanded two of the brigades, that "no dwellings are to be burned, and that no personal violence be offered the citizens." He was to confine his activities to forage, barns, mills, and livestock. "This destruction may as well commence at once," he wrote, "and the responsibility of it must rest upon the authorities at Richmond, who have acknowledged the legitimacy of guerrilla bands."[36]

This campaign also failed. Some of Mosby's companies relocated for the winter, but they returned in the spring. Mosby was wounded in a fight but never captured, and Sheridan could only take solace in periodic and erroneous reports that he was dead. Later, in his official report on the Valley Campaign, Sheridan rationalized his failure, claiming incredibly that he had "constantly refused to operate against [Mosby's] bands," since they "prevented straggling and kept my trains well closed up, and discharged such other duties as would have required a provost guard of at least two regiments of cavalry."

The counterinsurgency in Virginia was one of the darker episodes of the war, noted on both sides for its brutality. Walt Whitman, who described the back-and-forth atrocities in his essay "A Glimpse of War's Hell Scenes," wrote,

> Multiply the above by scores, aye hundreds—verify it in all
> the forms that different circumstances, individuals, places,

could afford—light it with every lurid passion, the wolf's, the lion's lapping thirst for blood—the passionate, boiling volcanoes of human revenge for comrades, brothers slain—with the light of burning farms, and heaps of smutting, smouldering black embers—and in the human heart everywhere black, worse embers—and you have an inkling of this war.[37]

CHAPTER FIFTEEN

"CUSTER IS A TRUMP"

In the fall of 1864, George Custer was at the top of his game. In three and a half years of war, he had risen from being a second lieutenant to a brevet major general. He had fought in countless engagements large and small, some of which were among the great battles of the war, and in which he played a significant role. He had married the love of his life and was nationally known and acclaimed. In November, Private George Perkins of the 6th New York Independent Battery gave his assessment of Custer in part of a regular series of reports he wrote for the *Middlesex Journal*:

> In the whole of the campaign which commenced with the battle of Winchester, no general has won more praise than Custer, and in this last fight he has fairly doubled his laurels. He is a great favorite and everybody claims that he has nobly

earned the second star on his shoulder. He seems to possess
all the fire and courage of Kilpatrick, but infinitely more
judgment. In personal appearance he is the very model of a
dashing cavalry officer. His figure is slight and elegant and
he sits on his horse most gracefully. His costume is a dark
red velvet cavalry jacket, with pants of a light drab. His long
yellow hair flows out from beneath a broad brimmed hat,
and streams in ringlets far behind him as he rides along at a
swift canter. His features are strongly marked and pale. His
voice is heavy yet musical. The members of his old brigade
always cheer him when he passes, and he always returns the
compliment by waving his hat above his head. No wonder
he is admired when to graces of person he adds excellence
of mind. When he lifts his hat his fair complexion and hair,
and fine contour of head give him the look of a young
Apollo.[1]

The back-and-forth continued between the cavalry in the valley
through the fall. Custer and Rosser continued to spar, and at times the
contests seemed to take on a personal quality. During one fight, Custer
spied Rosser's battle flag among retreating enemy troops and led a
regimental charge to try to seize it. The charge lost momentum before
the riders could overtake the flag bearer, but Custer and three other men
kept riding hard for the banner and almost took it.[2]

As the year waned, the two armies settled into winter quarters. The
weather was severe, with frequent snow and bitter cold. "The rigor of
the season was very much against the success of any mounted operations," Sheridan recalled. But the winter was especially punishing for the
besieged Confederates in Richmond, and Grant wanted to increase their
misery by breaking up the railroads that fed the gloomy capital.

On December 19, two Union cavalry columns set off south. The larger, Merritt's and Powell's divisions led by Torbert, headed east through Chester Gap with orders to skirt the edge of the Blue Ridge Mountains south of Charlottesville, disrupting the Virginia Central Railway lines there, then moving on to Lynchburg and breaking that supply line as well. The second column, with Custer's division, would proceed straight down the valley as a diversionary force, engaging the Confederate units there and pushing on to link up with Torbert at Lynchburg 175 miles from Winchester. The columns were traveling light, with no artillery or wagons, carrying their supplies with them. "Nothing but extremely bad weather will prevent good results," Sheridan wrote optimistically to Grant.[3]

Early was holed up in Staunton, with a reduced force and uncertain will to fight. Custer was confident that he would be in Lynchburg for Christmas. But it was hard going for the men and their horses. Cold temperatures, ice, snow, and sleet slowed the column and did nothing for morale.

Two days later Custer's men were bivouacked at Lacey Springs, about sixty miles south of Winchester, outside of Harrisonburg. In the pre-dawn hours, word came from the picket line that rebels were advancing. Custer began to ready his men, and just as they were going to horse, "a yell and a simultaneous volley, and the flash of rebel carbines and rifles, gave warning that the enemy was already in their camp in large force." In the darkness Rosser's cavalrymen had infiltrated the Union perimeter wearing Federal wool overcoats. Troops fired almost randomly with pistols and carbines, while rebels engaged hand-to-hand with drawn sabers. Union troops fell back, re-formed, and charged the enemy. But between the darkness, the intermingled units, and the Confederates in blue, it was unclear how the contest was going. "The only way to distinguish friend from foe was by the sound of the voice," one report read.

"It finally came to a fight like that of the Irishman, every man 'on his own hook.'"[4] In the confusion, troops from both sides would make for camp with prisoners to find themselves among the enemy. At Custer's headquarters a rebel soldier came up and asked him which regiment it was. "Take off that blue overcoat," Custer ordered, and took the man prisoner.[5]

The weight of battle turned against them, and the Union troops withdrew, many men riding bareback because they had not had time to saddle their mounts. Custer captured two battle flags and took twenty-seven prisoners, but lost two killed, twenty-two wounded, and twenty prisoners to Rosser. Meanwhile, Torbert's column was checked by Lomax's cavalry and some infantry sent from Richmond near Gordonsville, and the two columns returned to Winchester, with hundreds of men frostbitten and with little to show for their efforts.[6]

As the winter of 1864–65 drew to a close, the war was looking bleak for the Confederacy. Around the same time Custer was being run out of Lacey's Springs, General Sherman arrived in Savannah, completing his march through Georgia. By mid-February he was in Columbia, South Carolina, and pressing north, sparring as he went with rebel General Joseph E. Johnston's weary troops. The siege of Richmond continued, and Jubal Early's command had been pared down to furnish defenders for the Confederate capital. At year's open he could only muster a few thousand troops to defend the Shenandoah Valley, and many of them were young boys and other replacements.

The valley was ripe for the taking. On February 20 Grant wired Sheridan, "As soon as it is possible to travel I think you will have no difficulty about reaching Lynchburg with a cavalry force alone." This movement, coupled with massed cavalry actions in Tennessee, Mississippi, and

Alabama, along with Sherman "eating out the vitals of South Carolina—is all that will be wanted to leave nothing for the rebellion to stand upon."[7]

Sheridan's force faced little opposition as they moved south. "Parties of the enemy made their appearance on our flanks," he wrote, "but no attention was paid to them."[8] Early's defensive force at Staunton consisted of "a local provost guard, and a company of reserves, composed of boys under 18 years of age."[9] Rosser attempted a delaying action but failed, and with the road to Staunton open, Early evacuated the city and fired the bridge over Christian's Creek.

Sheridan's force occupied the town on March 2, and he immediately ordered Custer to give chase to Early to prevent him from withdrawing to Richmond. Early had drawn up his forces, two brigades of infantry and Rosser's cavalry, in an entrenched defensive line outside the town of Waynesboro, ten miles east on the road to Charlottesville. The weather was inclement, cold and rainy. Early intended only to delay the Union forces while he withdrew his artillery, for which he had no horse teams.

The rebels had formed a line on the outskirts of the town, the left anchored near a bow in the South River. As Custer approached with his column, he noted that the flank was exposed in front of the river, inviting an attack. He hurriedly sent three regiments against Early's weak left while he assaulted the center with two brigades, swiftly breaking the line. "The rebels fired one volley," the *New York Herald* reported, "and then fled like sheep."[10] The 8th New York and the 1st Connecticut Cavalries charged through the town, "sabering a few men as they went along," and seized the river crossing at the opposite end, cutting off the main Confederate escape route. "The enemy threw down their arms and surrendered," Sheridan noted, "with cheers at the suddenness with which they were captured."[11] Early lost 9 pieces of light artillery, 13 battle flags, and over 1,200 of the 1,600 men he commanded.

Early and his general officers escaped the net, along with Rosser's cavalry. "It has always been a wonder to me how they escaped," Sheridan said, "unless they hid in obscure places in the houses of the town."[12] In fact, Early had been cut off from his command by Custer's sudden movement, and, climbing a hill outside of Waynesboro to view the battle, he said he "had the mortification of seeing the greater part of my command being carried off as prisoners."[13]

Custer pushed across the Blue Ridge through Rockfish Gap toward Charlottesville, fighting muddy roads and cold, driving rain. The city fathers met his mud-spattered troops outside of town and surrendered it without a fight. Custer paused there for a few days as the rest of Sheridan's force came up, and set about destroying the locks of the James River canal connector and tearing up the rail lines heading east, west, and south.

While in town Custer's men commandeered the presses of a local newspaper and published the *Third Cavalry Division Chronicle*, which contained the general's official reports of the recent days' actions. A notice called for people to furnish "donations" of provisions to Custer's division and was signed "Jubal Early, commissary for General Sheridan's army." An advertisement offered "Two Dollars Reward, Confederate Currency," for information concerning the whereabouts of a runaway slave, "Jube, answering to the name of Early," and a one-cent reward for Rosser.[14]

Rosser's house was nearby, and his wife, Betty, invited Custer in for a brief visit. She knew it would be her husband's wish to show some hospitality even though "she never supposed she could bring herself to speak to, much less invite a Yankee officer into her home."[15] As he was leaving, George held out a gold pen to her baby Sarah, whom she was holding, saying, "Give this to your Papa dear, and tell him it is from a friend who whipped him yesterday." Mrs. Rosser said no, but Sarah grasped the pen, and by the time Betty got it from her, "the Yankee was down the steps and in the saddle in a flash."[16]

With no strong force opposing him, Sheridan chose to move east rather than toward Danville and Sherman beyond, tearing up railroads and hunting the remains of Early's forces. Custer's division moved to Frederick Hall Station to break tracks, piling up railroad ties and heating rails on top, then wrapping the red-hot rails around telegraph poles. Custer inspected the telegraph office at the station and found a dispatch from Early to Lee indicating he was planning a surprise cavalry attack on Sheridan's forces near Goochland using 150 men of the 1st Virginia Cavalry under Colonel Morgan. Custer immediately set out to find and destroy them.

The chase was lively; when Early saw the Federal cavalry approaching in the distance, he knew he had been found out and scattered his force. Federal horsemen surged ahead with a whoop, and Custer shouted that the man who brought in Early would receive a thirty-day furlough. At one point Captain Burton of Custer's staff closed to within a few yards of Early and his orderly, but given the orderly's more pristine uniform, took him for the general and demanded he surrender. The orderly responded by shooting Burton's horse. Early finally escaped over the South Anna River, fleeing on foot; he was saved by the onset of night.[17] With a heavy heart, Robert E. Lee relieved "Old Jube" of command on March 30. With the destruction of Early's army complete and the valley secure, Sheridan remarked, "Custer is a trump."

CHAPTER SIXTEEN

"FIGHTING LIKE A VIKING"

Sheridan's cavalry rejoined the eastern army for the final push on Richmond. Torbert took command of the rump of the Army of the Shenandoah to maintain security in the valley, and Sheridan elevated Merritt to corps command over Devins's, Crook's, and Custer's divisions.

Richmond's last remaining supply lines were the Danville and Southside Railroads. Grant planned to swing forces four miles west of the rebel works around Petersburg, seize the ford over Hatcher's Run, then cut the Southside Railroad near Sutherland's Station. He could then move north and bottle up Lee's army and the Confederate government, ending the war. Grant's greatest fear in the weeks leading up to the campaign was that Lee would sense the growing danger, abandon Richmond, and move west to unite with Johnston's army in North Carolina. But the symbolic importance of Richmond kept Lee in place.

Sheridan began the movement on March 29 with the Cavalry Corps and infantry from II and V Corps. He was hampered by strong rains and muddy roads, and the going was slow. A key objective was the strategic crossroads of Five Forks, just south of the Hatcher's Run ford, which Merritt's scouts learned was lightly defended. He pushed two cavalry brigades forward against the mud and stubborn fire from rebel pickets, reaching the objective by mid-morning on the thirty-first.

But the Confederates had gotten wind of Sheridan's plan and were already on the move. A force of ten thousand men under Major General George Pickett crossed Hatcher's Run and swept down on Merritt's overmatched cavalry, pushing them south toward Dinwiddie Court-house.[1] Pickett had three brigades of cavalry under Rosser, Fitzhugh Lee, and W. H. F. "Rooney" Lee (second son of the Confederate commander); the three infantry brigades from his division; and two more from Bush-rod Johnson's. After a check administered by Gregg's and Gibbs's bri-gades, Pickett reformed and continued to push south.

Custer had been at the rear with the baggage train as the battle devel-oped. As Pickett's men drove the Union troops, Sheridan sent riders back to bring Custer forward on the double. "Custer never required more than simple orders on such an occasion," Sheridan's adjutant general, Colonel Frederick C. Newhall, recalled, "for he had in himself the vim which insured a prompt response to the wishes of the commanding general."[2] He rushed to the front with Capehart's and Pennington's brigades following, and when he arrived, "a scene of the wildest excite-ment prevailed," a reporter wrote.[3] Custer set the band to play "Gar-ryowen" to rally the retreating cavalry and ordered dismounted troopers of Capehart's brigade to tear down fences to assemble breastworks.[4]

Pickett's troops soon emerged from the woodline across a long field, in a "handsome and imposing line of battle" according to Major Henry E. Tremain of Crook's staff. Union guns brought them under long-range fire, but the "long, single, unsupported line of infantry [swept] over the undulating plain and scarcely deigning a reply to the warning compliments from our artillery."[5]

Custer set his available command to horse and assembled them for a charge. After conferring with Sheridan, he rode to his men, but Sheridan called him back.

"General! General!" Sheridan said firmly. "You understand? I want you to *give* it to them."

"Yes, yes, I'll give it to them," Custer replied hurriedly.[6] He readied his line for the saber charge and set out. But the ground was soft from the days of rain, and the horses became stuck, some falling, others throwing their riders. A charge was impossible, and Custer would have to find another way to "give it to them."

The rebels came on. "They were the flower of the Army of Northern Virginia," Chaplain Charles A. Humphreys of the 2nd Massachusetts Cavalry recalled, "and were led by one of its best fighting Generals—Pickett. They seemed to us utterly reckless of death. In the face of our severest fire they would swoop down upon us across an open field with such a careless swing, it seemed as if they enjoyed being on the skirmish line, and we suspected that they had such a miserable time of it in camp that they preferred standing up to be shot at."[7] The Union line firmed up with the arrival of Pennington's brigade, and the troopers prepared for contact behind their hastily erected defenses.

As Pickett's men came on, Sheridan, Merritt, Custer, and their staffs galloped down the Union line, hats aloft and colors flying, as the band played "Hail Columbia." The troops cheered wildly. Rebel sharpshooters took long-range shots at the party, scoring some hits among the junior staff and wounding *New York Herald* correspondent Theodore C. Wilson (who was "out of place," Sheridan observed gleefully).[8]

The rebels advanced in the teeth of fire from Union horse artillery, but the outnumbered cavalrymen lay low behind their breastworks until Pickett's men were within yards of their position. "Then they opened,"

Sheridan wrote, "Custer's repeating rifles pouring out such a shower of lead that nothing could stand up against it." The Confederates "recoiled in dismay" and pulled back quickly to the safety of the wood line. "For that night, at least," Chaplain Humphreys recalled, "Dinwiddie was safe."[9]

Sheridan was uncertain whether Pickett would continue the advance the next day, but he was ready for him if he did. Pickett's force was extended beyond the Confederate line, leaving his left flank vulnerable. Sheridan rushed word to Warren commanding V Corps, east of Dinwiddie, to "attack instantly and in full force" if the rebels advanced, and even if they didn't, to "attack anyway" at first light. Sheridan would hold the front with Custer while Warren swept in behind, and they would bag the lot of them.[10]

But Pickett understood the danger as well and pulled back to a position around Five Forks. An order came down from Robert E. Lee to "*hold Five Forks at all hazards. Protect road to Ford's Depot and prevent Union forces from striking the south-side railroad. Regret exceedingly your forced withdrawal, and your inability to hold the advantage you had gained.*" But even Five Forks was too far extended. Pickett was about four miles out from the end of the rebel works with no flank support. The Five Forks defense did not allow him to anchor on Hatcher's Run, which was two miles to his rear. Fitz Lee believed that "Pickett's isolated position was unfortunately selected" and thought it would have been better to establish a "line behind Hatcher's Run or at Sutherland Station [that] could not have been flanked."[11] But his uncle's order to Pickett was unambiguous, and the rebels dug in. "I immediately formed line of battle upon the White Oak Road and set my men to throwing up temporary breastworks," Pickett wrote. "Pine trees were felled, a ditch dug and the earth thrown up behind the logs."[12] As one report described it, "they fortified this empty solitude as if it had been their capital."[13]

The next morning a thick, cold fog lay on the Dinwiddie battlefield. When the mist had lifted enough to see to their front, Custer's men spotted some soldiers but could not tell who they were, friend or foe. Some thought they were Pickett's command, others believed they were troops from Warren's V Corps that had moved between them and the rebels in the early morning darkness. After some debate, one of Custer's staff said he saw "most unmistakably blue, and dashed boldly down toward a mounted officer" who was riding between the lines. There followed a challenge, some questions, then the report of a pistol. Custer's officer came galloping back to report that the opposing line was "positively gray—a very gray gentleman having shot at him and called him some highly improper names."[14]

Pickett's skirmishers were still to Custer's front, and hours into the morning there was no indication that Warren had launched his attack. Sheridan went off to investigate, but by midday there was still no sign of battle. On the Confederate side of the field, Pickett was also surprised, having expected Union forces to have moved against him sooner. His defenses prepared, he accepted an invitation from Rosser for a shad bake along Hatcher's Run, a tradition among the Tidewater Virginians.

Meanwhile, Sheridan angrily confronted Warren over the delay in launching the attack.[15] V Corps was disorganized; bad maps and poor communications had left Warren's divisions out of position and uncertain where to strike the rebel line. Sheridan righted matters and got the attack going by 4:00 p.m. But flawed intelligence on Pickett's location led Brigadier General Samuel W. Crawford's division to march past the point of contact, and Brigadier General Romeyn B. Ayres's division suffered flanking fire when he thought he was moving to hit the rebels head-on. The momentum of the assault slowed. Sheridan, dissatisfied with Warren's performance, took personal control of the battle, and later would relieve Warren of command. Sheridan rode to where the fight was most critical and, with his command standard in hand, jumped his horse into the rebel works, where surprised enemy troops immediately gave up. The Confederate left began to break. Pickett, who had learned too late that the battle was under way, rushed under fire to the front to try to rally his beleaguered troops.

Custer's division was moving on the opposite side of the rebel line, and Pennington's dismounted brigade engaged the enemy in the front while Wells's and Capehart's brigades swung wide to the left, seeking a gap. They were thwarted by Rooney Lee's outnumbered but dogged cavalry. "The fighting was fearful I never yet heard such a terrific fire of musketry," Federal trooper George E. Farmer wrote. "But every soldier said this is the ending of the war and we are bound to whip them."[16]

In the center a desperate struggle was under way. Union Private Theodore Gerrish from Maine wrote, "It was hot work, and in many places it was a hand to hand fight. Men deliberately pointed their rifles in each other's faces and fired. Clubbed muskets came crushing down in deadly force upon human skulls. Men were bayoneted in cold blood. Feats of individual bravery were performed on that afternoon which, if recorded, would fill a volume."[17] The rebels fell back from their original line to a new position to consolidate their defense, but it was of little use. "Our left was turned," Pickett wrote, "we were completely entrapped. Their cavalry, charging at a signal of musketry from the infantry, enveloped us front and right and, sweeping down upon our rear, held us as in a vise."[18]

As the rebels fought desperately, Custer made a final, determined charge on the faltering right. The Confederates were "strung out in a single line three feet, or more, apart," a rebel soldier recalled, "yet they repelled all the charges of Sheridan's picked horsemen, until Custer led. They all bear witness that his charge, which he led in person, was the most gallant and determined they ever saw, and that they were astonished to see Custer and his men ride on and over them, although the head of the charging column seemed to crumble and sink under their fire."[19] "Bodies of cavalry fairly mounted their intrenchments, and charged down the parapet, slashing and trampling them, and producing inextricable confusion," one report read. "Close by fell the long yellow locks of Custer, saber extended, fighting like a Viking, though he was worn and haggard with much work."[20]

The Confederates were "overpowered, defeated, cut to pieces, starving, [and] captured," in Pickett's words.[21] Rooney Lee's cavalry held back the Union pursuit long enough for some rebels to escape, but as evening drew on, Federal cavalrymen swept the surrounding countryside netting thousands of prisoners. In all, the Confederates lost nearly three thousand killed, wounded, and captured, against Union losses of just over eight hundred. But more important, the rebel right was broken, and the Richmond defenses compromised. Five Forks was later called the "Waterloo of the Confederacy." Custer was on the verge of one of his finest weeks, harrying Lee's forces, harassing his baggage trains, reeling in prisoners, destroying whole regiments. And in the chaos of the pursuit, Custer was again reported killed.

CHAPTER SEVENTEEN

"CUSTER AGAINST THE WORLD"

The Union victory at Five Forks spelled the end for Confederate Richmond. Rebel supply lines were cut, and Robert E. Lee informed Jefferson Davis that further defense of the city was untenable. The army and government fled west. Federal forces gave chase, trying to prevent the Army of Northern Virginia from linking up with Johnston's army, which was withdrawing before Sherman's forces in North Carolina. The Cavalry Corps rode hard, attempting to stay ahead of Lee's retreating troops, and Custer was in the van, skirting the Confederate left, anticipating the inevitable shift south toward Johnston. Colonel Newhall of Sheridan's staff penned a description of Custer in these final, frantic days:

> At the head of the horsemen rode Custer of the golden locks, his broad sombrero turned up from his hard, bronzed face,

the ends of his crimson cravat floating over his shoulder, gold galore, spangling his jacket sleeves, a pistol in his boots, jangling spurs on his heels, and a ponderous claymore swinging at his side—a wild, dare-devil of a General and a prince of advance guards, quick to see and act. Seeing him pass by, a stranger might smile and say, "Who's that?" as he noticed his motley wear, his curls, and his quick impetuous way, but would wonder to see him in the thick of a fight; for Custer loves fighting, and hated his enemies then.[1]

Newhall described the general's war fighting during the pursuit as "Custer against the world."

The men of Lee's once-lethal army were still ready to fight if they had to; but they were on their last legs, and the further they fled, the more hopeless their situation seemed. "No Confederate soldier who was on and of that fearful retreat can fail to recall it as one of the most trying experiences of his life," Robert Stiles recalled. "Trying enough, in the mere fact that the Army of Northern Virginia was flying before its foes, but further trying, incomparably trying, in lack of food and rest and sleep, and because of the audacious pressure of the enemy's cavalry."[2] The retreating units were crowded onto a few muddy roads, short of food and ammunition, cold and tired. General John B. Gordon, who commanded at the leading edge of the Confederate flight, wrote: "Fighting all day, marching all night, with exhaustion and hunger claiming their victims at every mile of the march, with charges of infantry in rear and of cavalry on the flanks, it seemed the war god had turned loose all his furies to revel in havoc."[3]

On April 5, Lee found his hoped-for route south along the Danville Railroad blocked by Crook's cavalry at Jetersville. His army continued west, in search of rations expected at Farmville, but the trains had been diverted to Appomattox Station by a Union ruse. En route to Farmville, two divisions under B. R. Johnson and George Pickett, and under overall command of Richard Anderson, ran headlong into Union cavalry near a stream called Sailor's Creek.[4]

Custer's division came on the field moving toward a road junction, Marshall's Crossing. They first encountered skirmishers guarding some Confederate supply wagons, which had been put in the front of the column to protect it from Union forces harassing the rear. Custer drove the train and its escorts back toward a stone wall across an open field near the road, behind which crouched waiting rebel infantry from Pickett's division. Pickett wrote that his men were "weary, starving, [and] despairing" when they reached Sailor's Creek from Five Forks, and that for "forty-eight hours the man or officer who had a handful of parched corn in his pocket was most fortunate."[5]

But Pickett's men still had some fight left in them. As the cavalry galloped near, the rebels opened fire in a fusillade that "made many a rider bite the dust, and sent the whole column staggering back," Chaplain Humphreys recalled. Custer, however, was "not the kind of leader to be balked by a single defeat," and "as soon as he could form his men again he made the assaulting column more solid by doubling it, and then sent it off up the slope on a gallop."

"Away we went," wrote E. G. Marsh of the 15th New York Cavalry, "with our sabres swinging at our wrists, ready to grasp at a moment's warning, and our carbines at an advance, ready for use. We had not gone more than forty rods, when the rebels opened fire upon us from three points, with grape and canister, solid shot, and shell, and musketry."[6] This charge, too, was futile; the assault withered as it reached the wall, the men "flung back in forceless fragments of defeated valor, and the earth … strewn with death." But the enemy was before Custer and he meant to break him. He again doubled his force, lined them up across the field, and rode the length of the line to show his men he was with them.

"Drawing his sword and putting spurs to his steed, he dashed along the front of the whole line of serried soldiery," Chaplain Humphreys wrote, "his brown sombrero turning up its broad brim from his bronzed forehead, his long yellow curls floating on the wind, the ends of his crimson cravat flying like tongues of fire over his shoulders, his face aflame with the eager joy of battle. He seemed utterly oblivious to danger and to bear a charmed life amid the shower of bullets, and gave us an inspiring example of death-defying valor."[7] He bade the band play "Yankee Doodle" and led the massed cavalry toward the rebel redoubt.

"There had been no cavalry charge during the war which has surpassed that of Custer's in this attack, in energy and power," one news report read. "It was terrible to the foe. With sabers drawn, with horses upon the run, goaded by spur and quickened by shouts til they caught the wild enthusiasm of their riders; til, horses and men became fiery centaurs, the line swept on." The rebels loosed more grapeshot and musket fire on the rushing line of cavalry, inflicting more damage, but the mass of the attack was too great. Custer's men reached the rebel line and "leapt the intrenchments, shooting and sabering all who resisted."[8]

George's brother Captain Tom Custer rode with him in the charge. Tom had enlisted as a private in the 21st Ohio regiment in September 1861, at age seventeen. Nevin Custer had also joined up but was discharged for rheumatism. Tom campaigned in the West in the first years of the war, participating in some of the major battles and serving briefly as an escort for General Grant. In October 1864, George petitioned to have Tom transferred to his command, and he was commissioned a second lieutenant in the 6th Michigan Cavalry, joining George in November. He had fought by his brother's side since, having a horse shot out from under him at Five Forks and capturing a rebel standard three days earlier at the Battle of Namozine Church. Now he thundered across the field, heading for the enemy works.

"Tom led the assault on the enemy's breastworks, mounted," George wrote to Libbie. He was "first to leap his horse over the works on top of the enemy while they were pouring a volley of musketry into our ranks."[9] Colonel Capehart, who was a few feet away, saw the rebel color-bearer of the 2nd Virginia Reserve Battalion raise a pistol and shoot Tom in the face at close range. The shot "knocked him back on his horse," Capehart recalled, "but in a moment he was upright in his saddle."[10] Tom grabbed the flag while drawing his revolver and shot the enemy infantryman in the chest, killing him. Tom rode back through continuing fire seeking his brother. The side of Tom's face was bloody and spotted with burned powder. An officer he had served with in the West saw Tom and exclaimed, "Why you're wounded, man!"

"Not much," Tom replied, spitting out blood. He found George, who had been unhorsed in the charge.

"Armstrong," Tom said as he came up, "the damned rebels have shot me, but I've got my flag."[11] George told Tom to go to the rear to have a surgeon attend to his wound. "Damn it, there isn't any rear!" Tom exclaimed, readying to charge back into the fight. George shouted at him to halt and gave him a direct order to seek assistance before he bled to death.[12]

For this fight and for his valor at Namozine Church, Tom Custer was awarded two Medals of Honor, the only soldier in the war to receive the medal twice for separate actions.[13] By that point in the conflict, it had become a convention that soldiers who captured enemy flags would be so recognized, though it was the type of thing that George had done as a junior officer—without receiving any medals. But George never begrudged his brother the honor. "Do you know what I think of him?" he wrote Libbie after the fight. "Tom should have been the General and I the Lieutenant."[14]

While Custer's cavalry was breaking the front of the Confederate column, Wright's VI Corps was battering the rebel rear, facing two divisions under Custis Lee and Joseph B. Kershaw, commanded by Richard Ewell. "The 6th Corps, changing direction, followed like hounds," a reporter wrote, "until the enemy, finding he could not get past Custer, turned on them again."[15] It was a brutal fight. "We were attacked simultaneously, front and rear, by overwhelming numbers," Stiles remembered, "and quicker than I can tell it the battle degenerated into a butchery and a confused mêlée of brutal personal conflicts. I saw numbers of men kill each other with bayonets and the butts of muskets, and even bite each others' throats and ears and noses, rolling the ground like wild beasts."[16] A quarter of Lee's remaining force was lost, along with most of their supplies, and those who escaped death or capture were "broken down, nearly famished, and mostly without arms."[17] Observing the rout of his troops from a high point to the west, Robert E. Lee said to Major General William "Little Billy" Mahone, "My God! Has the army dissolved?" On the side of one of the captured Confederate wagons a rebel had written, "We uns has found the last ditch."

Seven thousand Confederates were captured, including eight generals, among them Ewell, Custis Lee, and Kershaw. At the Federal field headquarters after the battle, Kershaw recorded that "a spare, lithe, sinewy figure, bright, dark, quick-moving blue eyes; florid complexion, light, wavy curls, high cheek bones, firm set teeth—a jaunty close-fitting cavalry jacket, large top-boots, Spanish spurs, golden aiguillettes, a serviceable saber … a quick nervous movement, an air telling of the habit of command—announced the redoubtable Custer whose name was as familiar to his foes as to his friends."[18]

Kershaw presented his sword to Custer, saying "I have met you on several occasions in battle, and I know of no officer to whom I would rather surrender my sword." But Custer refused the honor, asking instead that it be given to the corporal of the 2nd Ohio who had captured the general. Ewell also tendered his sword, as did others, but Custer took none of them. General Ewell said, "Further fighting is useless; it is a wanton waste of life." He told Custer that "if a white flag were to be sent out, the 30,000 men in our army would surrender." But Custer said he had no authority to seek a truce.[19]

The Spanish spurs Kershaw noted Custer wearing may have been the pair loaned that day by captured Confederate artilleryman Colonel Frank Huger, a friend from the Class of 1860. He was the son of Confederate General Benjamin Huger of the Class of 1825. The intricately carved spurs originally belonged to Mexican General Antonio Lopez de Santa Anna, and the elder Huger had received them from General Winfield Scott during the Mexican War. General Huger gave the spurs to his son Frank when he graduated from West Point. Young Huger was captured by his friend Custer at Sailor's Creek, and George kept Huger with him for the rest of the day, as he said, "to let you see how I am going to take you fellows in."[20]

Also among the prisoners was Brigadier General Eppa Hunton, a brigade commander in Pickett's division, of the Hunton family whose home, Cerro Gordo, had been Custer's headquarters during the October 1863 debacle at Buckland Mills. Hunton was very sick and doubted he would survive imprisonment. Hearing about Hunton's condition, Custer sent his physician "with a bottle of imported French brandy," Eppa recalled, "and furnished me with a hair mattress to sleep on. He was as kind as a man could be, and I shall never forget his generous treatment."[21] After the war Hunton served as a member of Congress from Virginia, and Eppa's son recalled that when some charges against Custer were referred to the House Military Affairs Committee, Hunton became his chief defender. "I never saw him more deeply and earnestly interested than in Custer's defense," he recalled. "I think nothing came of the investigation and that the charges were never pressed."[22] Also on the committee with Hunton in the Forty-Third Congress was former Confederate cavalryman Pierce M. B. Young, elected from Georgia, who had traded meals with his friend Custer at Cerro Gordo the day of the Buckland Races.

Sheridan openly praised Custer for his conduct in the battle. He sent word of the victory to Grant, adding his opinion that "if the thing is pressed I think Lee will surrender."[23] Word came back shortly from President Lincoln: "Let the thing be pressed."

Sheridan had already moved. Cavalry and infantry that had not been engaged in Sailor's Creek continued to harry Lee's men, and the day after the battle, Sheridan pressed on with the rest. Custer set off flying a red and blue silk banner with crossed sabers, a personal standard that Libbie had sewn for him weeks earlier and that already bore the scars of battle from its "glorious baptism" at Dinwiddie. George assembled a personal escort of men who had captured Confederate battle standards, bearing their trophies in ranks behind him. After Sailor's Creek the honor guard carried over thirty rebel flags, and in the next few days they would have forty. Seeing Custer ride past with his colorful escort, an old soldier of the VI Corps observed, "Oh, yes, my boy, you have picked up the apples, but the Sixth Corps shook the tree for you."[24]

As Custer set off in pursuit of the rebels, he passed General Kershaw and a group of Confederate prisoners and raised his hat to them. "There goes a chivalrous fellow," Kershaw said, "let's give him three cheers." Custer then had his band strike up the unofficial Confederate anthem, "The Bonnie Blue Flag," to the whoops and yells of the prisoners.[25]

After Sailor's Creek, Lee's army crossed to the north bank of the Appomattox River and pressed west toward Lynchburg, pursued by II and VI Corps. V Corps and Merritt's cavalry stayed on the opposite bank, moving along the Southside Railroad and seeking to cut off Lee's retreat at Appomattox. "Lee's army was rapidly crumbling," Grant wrote of these last days. "Many of his soldiers had enlisted from that part of the State where they now were, and were continually dropping out of the ranks and going to their homes."[26] But most of Lee's men were willing to fight as long as he led them.

Late in the afternoon of April 8, Custer came in sight of Appomattox Station, where he spied locomotive smoke. Four trains were at the station, their cars loaded with supplies for Lee's hungry army—the provisions the rebels had expected at Farmville. Custer quickly sent a regiment around the station to block the track toward Lynchburg, then galloped down the road and "enveloped the train as quick as winking."[27] They took the trains without losing a man, but the alert crew of one engine managed to fire it before it could be seized. Custer assembled engineers and brakemen from his ranks and ordered the trains east down the line toward the advancing Federal infantry.

The timing was critical. As Custer was arranging the trains' movement, artillery fire broke out. Confederate Brigadier General R. Lindsay Walker had been sent with twenty-five guns from the Third Corps Reserve Artillery to secure the trains for Lee's approaching troops, and was firing on Custer from a nearby hill. "Not expecting a fight at that place, the enemy was somewhat disturbed and demoralized by the appearance of our forces," Augustus Woodbury of the 2nd Rhode Island regiment wrote, "and especially indignant at the loss of his supplies, upon which he had almost laid his hand."[28]

Custer hastily organized an assault, which made little progress against the grapeshot and canister from the massed guns. After several attempts and with the hour growing late, Custer grew impatient. "Boys," he said, "the Third Division must have those guns. I'm going to charge if I go alone." Custer led a final charge on the rebel artillery, overwhelming the defenders, and, said Captain Luman H. Tenney of the 2nd Ohio Cavalry, "our boys did not stop until they had passed the Court House where the camp-fires marked the location of the rebel army along the hillsides."[29] In addition to the twenty-five guns he had faced, plus five others, Custer's men seized a hospital train, between 150 and 200 supply wagons, and 1,000 prisoners from the reserve artillery and the lead elements of Lee's army heading for the station.[30]

As the rest of the Cavalry Corps arrived, Sheridan pressed toward Appomattox Court House as far as he could without infantry support, bidding Generals Ord, Gibbon, and Griffin to move up quickly to close the trap.[31] "If General Gibbon and the Fifth Corps can get up to-night we will perhaps finish the job in the morning," Sheridan wrote Grant. "I do not think Lee means to surrender until compelled to do so."[32]

Sheridan was right. That night Lee held a war council with his Corps commanders, Longstreet, Gordon, and Fitz Lee. Earlier in the day, he had told a doubting General Pendleton that "we have yet too many bold men to think of laying down our arms." And even after the loss of their supplies to Custer, Lee wanted to make a final attempt to break out toward Lynchburg. Fitz Lee and Gordon would strike Sheridan with Longstreet guarding the rear, then the entire army would push through west. When Gordon asked where he should stop to make camp, Lee replied, "The Tennessee line."[33]

That night Custer worked himself to exhaustion preparing for the critical day to come. His men were "so near the enemy they could almost hear each other breathe in the midnight darkness."[34] The general sat by a campfire waiting for the dawn and fell asleep upright with a coffee cup in his hand.

"It was a beautiful Sunday morning, fair dawn of a fairer day," Chaplain Humphreys wrote of April 9, 1865. "The country was white and pink with the beautiful blossoms of the plum, the peach, and the pear."[35] But as Captain Tenney of the 2nd Ohio Cavalry penned in his diary, "9th. Sunday. Fighting commenced early."[36] Gordon's rebel infantry advanced strongly against the dismounted Federal cavalry, who pulled back slowly. Custer spied some men from the 10th Connecticut sheltering by a fence during the move and shouted to them, "Boys, this is your last fight. There is nothing but a battery over there. When you take that the war will be over."[37] The 14th Virginia Cavalry regiment claimed to have captured Custer around this time, "but in the confusion [he] made his escape."[38]

The Confederates pushed ahead and managed to clear one of the roads to Lynchburg, allowing Fitz Lee's cavalry to try to flank the Federals on the left. But Charles Griffin and the V Corps had moved up behind the withdrawing Federal cavalry and mounted a vigorous counterattack. The rebels were pushed back hard, and when Lee sent word to Gordon asking how the battle was proceeding, he replied to the courier, "Tell General Lee I have fought my corps to a frazzle, and I fear I can do nothing unless I am heavily supported by Longstreet's corps."

Lee knew the end had come. "There is nothing left me but to go and see General Grant," he said to Lieutenant Colonel Charles S. Venable, "and I had rather die a thousand deaths." Lee sent word to Grant, who was approaching from the east, asking for terms. But along the front, the battle continued. Longstreet, seeing Gordon's Corps weakening, set his final battle line. Men dutifully fell into their places in the ranks, but this was not the army it once was. "Their faces were haggard, their step slow and unsteady," a member of McGowan's South Carolina Brigade wrote. "Bare skeletons of the old organizations remained, and those tottered along at wide intervals."[39]

Custer's division had moved to the right of the Union line, opening the way for the attack by V Corps. But his men were not out of the fight. He called his troops to mount and assembled them for a charge into the weakening rebel left flank and to their camps beyond. As Custer was waiting for Devin's division to deploy to his right, a Confederate soldier appeared on the field on a running horse with a white towel on the end of his sword. Captain Robert Sims, of Longstreet's staff, had been sent by Lee to inform Gordon that talks were under way with Grant, and then to request a halt to the Federal attack.[40]

"The enemy perceiving that Custer was forming for attack," Sheridan wrote, "had sent the flag out to his front and stopped the charge just in time." E. G. Marsh was with the 15th New York Cavalry at the front of the line when Sims rode up. Custer "did not wish to halt," Marsh recalled. "He wished to whip them completely; but we had to stop and wait the arrival of the flag of truce, and listen to the message from Lee."[41] When Sims delivered his message asking for a cessation of hostilities, Custer replied, "We will do no such thing. We have your people now where we want you, and will listen to no terms but unconditional surrender."[42]

"Well sir," Sims replied, "we will never submit to that." But he agreed to take Custer's message to Gordon. Sims rode off with Custer's chief of staff, Lieutenant Colonel Edward Whitaker, and presently Custer followed with an orderly, holding a white handkerchief. They reached the Confederate line at a position held by the Rockbridge Artillery, and the rebels, "not exactly appreciating the situation and covetous of good boots," dismounted the orderly to acquire his footwear and were about to do the same to Custer. George looked about for the commander of the unit; by chance it was Major Wade Hampton Gibbes, Class of 1860, Emory Upton's tormentor at West Point. "Gibbes I appeal to you for protection," he said. Gibbes intervened and escorted Custer and his orderly to General Gordon's headquarters.

Custer repeated his demand for unconditional surrender to Gordon, who refused. "Sheridan directs me to say to you, General," Custer said, "if there is any hesitation about your surrender, that he has you surrounded and can annihilate your command in an hour." Gordon replied that since the senior commanders of both armies were engaged in surrender talks, if Sheridan "decides to continue the fighting in the face of the flag of truce, the responsibility for the bloodshed will be his and not mine."

Custer then asked to be taken to Longstreet and was escorted by Major R. W. Hunter of General Gordon's staff, and Gibbes. As he approached Lee's old warhorse, Custer said, "In the name of General Sheridan I demand the unconditional surrender of this army!"

Longstreet was unimpressed. "I am not the commander of the army," he replied, "and do not have the authority to give its surrender. Nor do you have the right to request it. And you are within the lines of the enemy without authority, addressing a superior officer, and in disrespect to General Grant as well as myself; and even if I was the commander of the army I would not receive the message of General Sheridan."

"If you do not surrender you will be responsible for the bloodshed to follow," Custer barked, using Gordon's line.

"Go ahead and have all the bloodshed you want!" Longstreet snapped back, and began to give orders to his staff to bring up divisions that he knew, but maybe Custer did not, existed on paper only.

Custer, surprised, said, "General, probably we had better wait until we hear from Grant and Lee. I will speak to General Sheridan about it. Don't move your troops yet." Custer, having failed in his attempt to bluff his way to bagging Lee's entire army, returned to Union lines escorted by Gibbes. When he was out of earshot Longstreet laughed. "Ha! ha! that young man has never learned to play the game of 'Brag!'"[43]

The fighting slowly ceased as word of the truce spread along the front. Gunfire was replaced with cheers on the Union side. "Lee has surrendered!" Captain Tenney wrote. "Oh the wild and mad huzzas which followed! Pen can not picture the scene. The four years of suffering, death and horrid war were over. Thank God! Thank God!! was upon every tongue. Peace, home and friends were ours. Yes, thank God! What wonder that we were crazy with joy?"[44]

"We all dismounted, and such a scene of handshaking and embracing I have never elsewhere witnessed," Chaplain Humphreys recalled. "Some tossed their hats and cheered; some rolled on the ground, yelling like Indians; some sobbed like children, only with exuberance of happiness. It was the very madness of joy."[45] Across the field the rebels were sobbing in grief at the idea they were to surrender, even half-starving and faced with a superior force.

Grant was awaiting Lee at the house of Wilmer McLean in Appomattox. Sheridan had ridden to town and met with Gordon, and other Union officers converged on the scene for what was to be one of the most important meetings in American history. In his memoirs General Horace Porter placed Custer in the room, and he appears there in a well-known painting of the surrender conference by Tom Lovell.[46] But while others were drawn to McLean's parlor to witness history, Custer, who was responsible for so much of it, was back near the truce line indulging his boyish instincts. After returning from Longstreet's headquarters, Custer sought out Alexander Pennington.

"Let's go and see if we can find Cowan," he said. Colonel Robert V. Cowan of North Carolina, formerly of the Class of 1863, was the tallest man in the Corps in Custer's day. He had been found deficient in English and mathematics in his plebe year of 1860 and sent home. Cowan commanded the 33rd North Carolina in Wilcox's division, was wounded at Chancellorsville, and participated in Pickett's Charge under Trimble. Custer and Pennington went to the picket line on a stream bank and asked for Colonel Cowan. A messenger went back, and presently Cowan rode up and jumped his mount across the ditch.

"Hello, you damned red-headed rebel!" Custer said, and the three laughed. They were soon joined by Lieutenant Colonel Orville E. Babcock, third in the Class of May 1861, and then on Grant's staff. But Babcock did not come to relive old times; he was a member of the party escorting Robert E. Lee to McLean House. Lee had spotted the small gathering as he crossed a bridge 150 yards away and sent Babcock to tell them he did not want fraternization. The West Pointers separated, and Babcock rode back to Lee, who was soon out of sight.[47] Then the group reconvened. They chatted for quite a while, no doubt remembering West Point days and refighting the battles of the previous four years. Meanwhile, the conference at McLean House assembled and concluded, after which Custer and the others heard cheers erupt from the Confederate lines. They watched as General Lee rode back down the road.

"As he proceeded into his lines there was a grand rush toward him of his men and officers," Pennington wrote, "cheering, I suppose, to give him heart, for he seemed very much depressed as he rode by us."[48] Custer and Pennington bade Cowan goodbye and headed toward the town. That was the last they saw of the "damned red-headed rebel." When the time came formally to surrender his regiment, Cowan refused; he handed over command to Major J. A. Weston, and rode off south.[49]

At McLean House the souvenir hunt had begun. McLean had moved to Appomattox from Manassas after the first engagement of the war, to get as far from the conflict as he could. But now the war had come to him, and Horace Porter saw him "charging about in a manner which indicated that the excitement was shaking his nervous system to its center."[50] Officers began bargaining with him for objects from his house. Every item in the parlor—tables, chairs, pens, papers, even young Lula McLean's doll called the "silent witness"—became targets for relic hunters. Reporter Edward A. Paul, present at the surrender, noted, "Before twenty-four hours I doubt if there is much of the [McLean] house left—such a penchant have Americans for trophies."[51]

General Ord paid forty dollars for the marble-topped table at which Lee sat. Custer's chief of staff, Lieutenant Colonel Edward Whitaker, bought the chair Lee sat in, and Colonel Henry Capehart bought the one used by Grant. McLean had refused to sell the chairs, throwing to the floor the money that was pressed into his hands. The colonels forced their way out with the chairs anyway, and later a cavalryman appeared, handed McLean a ten-dollar bill, and rode off.[52] Horace Porter had loaned his pencil to Lee and retrieved it afterward. Mrs. McLean "sold everything in the room that day except the … red and green carpet," Libbie Custer noted, adding that if she had had the foresight to cut the rug into small squares and sell them individually, she could have "bought the adjacent farm from the proceeds."[53]

When Custer arrived at McLean House, Sheridan presented him with a small, wooden, oval-topped table to give to Libbie. His note to her read,

> My Dear Madam: I respectfully present to you the small writing-table on which the conditions for the surrender of

the Confederate Army of Northern Virginia was written by Lt.-General Grant, and permit me to say, madam, that there is scarcely an individual who has contributed more to bring about this desirable result than your very gallant husband.

Sheridan also gave Custer the white linen dishtowel Sims had carried to the Union lines as a flag of truce.[54] George left McLean House in high spirits, holding the table slung over his back; Horace Porter said he looked like Atlas carrying the world.

CHAPTER EIGHTEEN

"LIKE THE CHARGE OF A SIOUX CHIEFTAIN"

The two armies awoke to a cold, drizzly morning on April 10. The sense of calm was disorienting; after the previous frenzied week, there was no urgency, no sense of expectation or danger. It was the first slow morning many of the men had experienced in some time. Porter Alexander said that the day after the surrender "seemed to usher in a new life in a new world. We had lived through the war. There was nobody trying to shoot us, and nobody for us to shoot at. Our guns were gone, our country was gone, our very entity seemed to be destroyed. We were no longer soldiers, and had no orders to obey, nothing to do, and nowhere to go."[1]

Custer issued a general order to the soldiers of the 3rd Cavalry Division. "With profound gratitude towards the God of Battles, by whose blessings our enemies have been humbled, and our arms rendered triumphant," he began, he wished to express his "admiration of the heroic manner in which you have passed through the series of battles which to-day resulted in the surrender of the enemy's entire army." Custer went on to praise their courage, noting they had "never lost a gun, never lost a color … never been defeated … [and] captured every piece of artillery which the enemy has dared open up on you." He hoped that these actions had finally brought the war to a close "and that, blessed with the comforts of peace, we may soon be permitted to enjoy the pleasures of home and friends.… Speaking for my self alone," he concluded, "when the war is ended and the task of the historian begins, when those deeds of daring which have rendered the name and fame of the Third Cavalry Division imperishable are inscribed upon the bright pages of our country's history, I only ask that my name be written as that of the Commander of the Third Cavalry Division."[2]

Along the lines, the troops from the opposing armies were visiting each other's camps; the rebels in particular were looking to barter for breakfast. "Our camp was full of callers before we were up," Joshua Chamberlain recalled. They came to "see what we were really made of, and what we had left for trade." The visiting and trading grew to the point "that it looked like a county fair, including the cattle show."[3] William Swinton of the *New York Times* wrote, "Hostile devisement gave place to mutual helpfulness, and the victors shared their rations with the famished vanquished. In that supreme moment these men knew and respected each other."[4] Grant soon had rations issued to Lee's men from their own captured stores.

After another meeting between the senior leaders, officers from both sides began congregating in the center of town. Grant recalled, "[They] came in great numbers, and seemed to enjoy the meeting as much as though they had been friends separated for a long time while fighting battles under the same flag. For the time being it looked very much as if all thought of the war had escaped their minds."

The gathering at Appomattox Court House on April 10 was a pantheon of American heroes unlike any in history. Grant chatted with longtime rebel friends Pete Longstreet, Harry Heth, and Cadmus Wilcox, who had been a groomsman at his wedding. Lee met with his old friend George Meade, and Colonel Theodore Lyman of Meade's staff was reunited with his Harvard classmate "Rooney" Lee. George Pickett was there, talking to his friend from their northwest frontier days Rufus Ingalls, Grant's quartermaster general and West Point roommate. Other friends and family members, rebel and Federal, high-ranking officers and orderlies, met and renewed the bonds forged in the Old Army, in civilian life before the war, or at West Point. "Great God!" Longstreet wrote. "How my heart swells out to such magnanimous touch of humanity. Why do men fight who were born to be brothers?"[5]

Custer was his usual ebullient self. The previous night he had two tents pitched on a hill near the McLean House, and seven of his West Point friends from Lee's army stole away to spend the night there. "I remember their embracings and the genuine hearty reception given them by the General," one of Custer's officers recalled.[6] When morning came he sought out other friends and acquaintances from both sides, sharing stories and reminiscences. Gimlet Lea was there, and Custer provided a hamper of food for him and his staff. Fitz Lee came riding into town, and Custer, who had known him as a tactical officer at West Point before facing him in many battles, grabbed him; the two wrestled on the ground laughing and rolling about like boys.

The ceremonial stacking of arms and final pass in review of the Army of Northern Virginia were yet to come, but Custer was not present for it. Later on the tenth, Sheridan assembled the cavalry and moved twenty miles east to Prospect Station, then continued toward Richmond.

Libbie Custer was also heading to the former Confederate capital. The morning of April 10, she was "awakened to more joy than I believed I would ever know by the clang of bells, whistles, calliopes, firings of cannons and the shouts of the newsboys." She jumped from bed and ran half-dressed to hear the news of Lee's surrender. "I wanted to scream and dance with joy," Libbie recalled.[7] She was invited to accompany a delegation of members of Congress from the Committee on the Conduct of the War and their wives on a visit to Richmond. They sailed in the president's dispatch boat *Baltimore* to City Point, then were guided by Admiral Porter through the Confederate mines up the river to the city.

"It was a great relief at last to see the spires and roofs of Richmond," Libbie wrote. The once-beautiful city was a wreck: buildings were gutted, and ruins still smoldered from the fires lit during the evacuation a week earlier. Masses of cheerful, hungry, and uncertain freed slaves roamed the streets. The delegation did some sightseeing before reboarding the *Baltimore* to continue their voyage south to Charleston. But Libbie, upset at the prospect of being "whisked off to a city she cared nothing about" when George was so near, was allowed to stay in Richmond. She spent the night in the Confederate White House, in Jefferson Davis's bed.

On her second morning in Richmond, Libbie was "awakened by the sound of a saber knocking against the stairs." She leapt from bed and saw through the cracked door George "leaping up the stairs two at a time." Sheridan had given George permission to travel to Richmond to meet Libbie and bring her back to the command.

"I cried, I laughed, and then I began to realize that war was over," she recalled, "and with the sanguine heart of youth I was sure that we would never be separated again."[8] After their reunion they went to catch a train at City Point, where some officers good-naturedly chided George that "it was a pretty how-do-you-do that after four years of fighting, his wife had beaten him" to Richmond.[9]

Meanwhile, George's former adjutant and best man, Jacob Greene, unexpectedly showed up, having spent six months in several Confederate prison camps after his capture at Trevilian Station. He was paroled and allowed to return north, and that January he had finally married "Friend Nettie" Humphrey.[10] When word came that he was officially exchanged and freed for combat duty, he rushed to the front, missing the surrender by one day. The mood was light as the division rode back north through the Virginia countryside. Even Southerners flocked to the road to see the famous Custer, waving handkerchiefs and clapping.[11]

Weeks later, Custer's men were encamped at Bladensburg, near Washington, D.C., preparing for the Grand Review, a two-day tribute to the victorious Union Army ordered by President Johnson. The first day, May 23, featured the troops of the Army of the Potomac, with Sherman's Army of the West the day after. The troops marched a mile and a quarter down Pennsylvania Avenue, from the Capitol to the reviewing stand outside the White House: 160,000 soldiers over two days, with six hours of parade each day. Women also marched, wives of officers and other "Daughters of the Regiment" who had helped care for the men in camps and hospitals. Horatio Nelson Taft described it as "the most magnificent spectacle of the kind ever witnessed on the continent."[12]

"It was a clear, bright morning," Joshua Chamberlain recalled, "such as had so often ushered in quite other scenes than this."[13] Several thousand school children gathered at the north end of the Capitol singing patriotic songs and giving flowers and garlands to the troops as they passed. "A mighty spectacle this," Chamberlain wrote, "the men from far and wide, who with heroic constancy, through toils and sufferings and sacrifices that never can be told, had broken down the Rebellion, gathered to give their arms and colors and their history to the keeping of a delivered, regenerated nation."[14]

President Johnson, Generals Grant and Sherman, and many other officers and cabinet members watched from the reviewing stand outside the north porch, which was wrapped in star-spangled bunting. Grant later sketched the scene:

> The National flag was flying from almost every house and store; the windows were filled with spectators; the door-steps and side-walks were crowded with colored people and poor whites who did not succeed in securing better quarters from which to get a view of the grand armies. The city was about as full of strangers who had come to see the sights as it usually is on inauguration day when a new President takes his seat.

Spectators were hanging from windows and sitting on rooftops along the parade route, everyone cheering and throwing flowers. Many carried umbrellas to escape the hot sun and the morning rain, which helped keep the dust down. Bands played martial tunes, horses clattered on cobblestones, officers barked commands. A sign on the Capitol proclaimed in large letters, "The only national debt we never can pay is the debt we owe to the victorious Union soldiers."[15]

Still, the joyous atmosphere was tempered by remnants of a recent tragedy. The Capitol was still hung with black crepe from President Lincoln's lying in state, and the flag flew at half-staff in his honor. The flag of the Treasury Guard regiment, which had hung below the presidential box at Ford's Theatre the night Lincoln was shot, draped the portico of the Treasury Department. A large tear at the bottom of the flag showed where John Wilkes Booth's spur had caught as he jumped from the balcony before falling onto the stage and breaking his leg.

The Cavalry Corps began moving at 4:00 a.m. for the review. They paraded down Maryland Avenue, passing the Capitol then turning up Pennsylvania. The cavalry led the parade, fronted by Wesley Merritt and his staff, General Sheridan having been called to New Orleans to organize occupation forces. Custer's 3rd Division followed in a column eight horsemen across, and behind them the rest of the Corps, eight thousand horses strong.[16] Custer rode at the head of his division, leading the first combat unit in the parade of what at the time was the most powerful land army in the history of the world.

The cavalry rode on "splendid horses," Taft wrote, "generally the officers and the Staffs rode horses which had been trained to the Service, but there was a great deal of prancing and dashing to and fro of officers on the Avenue."[17] General Sherman disagreed, grousing that Custer's cavalry "would not have passed muster on the Champ de Mars in Paris. The horses were good, the men were fine, but not good-looking for review."[18] Another observer said the cavalry review was "the shabbiest and least attractive of all. The horses of the generals and other mounted officers were fine brutes, and in excellent condition; but oh! ye unnamed rank and file, ye dragoons who charged with Sheridan and doubled up Lee's right wing at Five Forks, how did ye manage to do it with the sorry jades ye bestrode at Washington?... There were no curvetings, no high and boastful neigh; very tamely did they jog on, more like word-down dray-horses than the spirited chargers we had looked for."[19]

Others, however, saw in the war-worn horses and their weathered riders a reflection of the hard and noble service they had undergone. Walt Whitman, who marched with his brother George and the 51st New York Volunteers, having served as a nurse in Washington, described the cavalry as he had seen them two days earlier during a review for the departing Sheridan: "[A] strong, attractive sight; the men were mostly young, (a few middle-aged,) superb-looking fellows, brown, spare, keen, with well-worn clothing, many with pieces of water-proof cloth around their shoulders, hanging down. They dash'd along pretty fast, in wide close ranks, all spatter'd with mud; no holiday soldiers; brigade after brigade. I could have watch'd for a week."

"Custer's division, which had the advance, was the chief attraction," one report read, "and its appearance was the signal for vociferous cheers and continued applause. Throughout the army as well as among the people, the dashing and never-failing Custer is regarded as the Murat of the war."[20] Custer's men rode in platoon columns with drawn sabers, all wearing the crimson cravat. "His long golden locks floating in the wind," Horace Porter recalled, "his low-cut collar, his crimson necktie, and his buckskin breeches, presented a combination which made him look half general and half scout, and gave him a daredevil appearance which singled him out for general remark and applause."[21]

"General Custer, a dashing fellow with youthful look and long yellow hair, lead the cavalry," Reverend H. M. Gallaher recalled. "The ladies near by assured us he was a very handsome officer."[22] George was at the high point of his fame as he passed up Pennsylvania Avenue to the cheers of the crowd: "Custer! Custer! Hurrah for Custer!"

The column turned up 15th Street, went around the Treasury Building, and headed for the reviewing stand. Custer doffed his hat as he passed a chorus of three hundred young ladies in white, who threw flowers as they sang "a pleasanter shower than the leaden one through which Sheridan's squadrons had so often and so boldly rode."[23] One girl tossed up a wreath of roses and evergreens, but the thorns pricked Custer's spirited mount, Don Juan, and the former racehorse reared up and bolted down the road to the cries of spectators.

The viewers were "enchained breathlessly by the thrilling event," a reporter wrote, and the "perilous position of the brave officer."[24] Custer attempted to salute as he rocketed by the reviewing stand, dropping his hat and saber. But he stayed calm and steady in the saddle, and once he regained control of Don Juan, he turned his mount and trotted back to his men. "Round upon round of hearty applause greeted him," said a report, and the officers and officials in the reviewing stand joined in the clapping.[25] Custer's final Civil War charge had stolen the show.

Don Juan's bolting sparked a debate. One former staff officer alleged "it was merely a little theatrical display by the gallant trooper" who afterward "pranced back to his position at the head of his column."[26] Another witness argued "the true cause of the runaway was combined in the profuse display of bunting, the sudden shouts of ten thousand people and music from several bands (on the high stands) which greeted the head of the column of the Army of the Potomac."[27] Dr. Pulaski F. Hyatt wrote Libbie that the thorny wreath had caused the problem. George himself believed the thoroughbred thought the parade was the prelude to a race, and "the moment he saw the stand the old turf days came back to his memory and the judges giving the start ... and he was off."[28]

Theatrics or not, "It was a pretty picture," a reporter wrote.[29] Another noted, "In the sunshine his locks unskeined, stream a foot behind him.... It is like the charge of a Sioux chieftain."[30]

After passing the reviewing stand, the 3rd Division trotted back east on K Street, stopping at a field on the edge of the city. There the men lined up in their regiments "to take leave of the young and gallant General whom they had learned to follow with a perfect confidence of victory, and had learned to love as few commanders have been loved by cool-headed American soldiers."[31] George handed his hat to an aide and, along with Libbie, rode along the front of the division, followed by his colors and staff, to the cheers of each regiment as he passed.

In a voice choked with emotion and with tears in his eyes, Custer thanked his troops for their courage, loyalty, and kindness. "I shall now leave you for another field," he said, "but before doing so I take pleasure in transferring this standard, which you have so bravely followed, to the hands of General Capehart, than whom you cannot ask a more gallant and capable commander. Farewell! God bless you!"

The band struck up "Auld Lang Syne," and George, Libbie, and an escort rode off toward the Capitol.

FALL FROM GRACE

Albert Berghaus, *General Custer at His Desk in His Library*, from Elizabeth
B. Custer, *Tenting on the Plains* (New York: Charles L. Webster, 1893).

CHAPTER NINETEEN

THE "LONG-HAIRED HERO OF THE LASH"

In the summer of 1865, George, Libbie, and Eliza went south to join Sheridan's new command in the Military Division of the Southwest in Texas. The Custers traveled west by train then south by riverboat, meeting homeward-bound Confederate General John Bell Hood along the way. During a stop in New Orleans, they were warmly received by General Winfield Scott, then seventy-nine years old and nearing the end. He died the following May at West Point.

Sheridan met them in his mansion headquarters. He had left Washington before the Grand Review due to the perceived urgency of the situation in Texas, where the rebellion had lingered. Confederate units under General Edmund Kirby Smith had kept up the fight after Lee's surrender, and the last battle of the war, at Palmito Ranch, took place a month after Appomattox. Even when Kirby Smith fled to Mexico after negotiating his army's surrender on May 26, there were concerns that conditions in Texas would remain chaotic. Sheridan wrote that "there is not a very wholesome state of affairs in Texas. The Governor, all the soldiers, and the people generally are disposed to be ugly."[1] Grant believed that "the whole State should be scoured to pick up Kirby Smith's men and the arms carried home by them," but given the size of the state and the few Federal troops on hand, this was clearly impossible.[2]

Some also worried the French-backed government in Mexico might take advantage of the volatility in Texas to press claims to lands lost twenty years earlier in the Mexican War. Sheridan wrote Grant of the "rascality of the Rio Grande frontier," where there was "no government and a questionable protectorate." He believed that "this portion of the late rebellion should be crushed out in a manly way and with the power of a great nation, as a contrast to this French subterfuge to assist in the attempt to ruin our country."[3]

Sheridan planned a show of force to quell any military action by unruly Texans, the French, or the Mexicans. He planned to send two columns west: 5,000 men under Wesley Merritt, riding from the Shreveport to Austin, and 4,500 under Custer, heading from Alexandria, Louisiana, to Houston. If necessary, they were to unite with Merritt in San Antonio to form a division for movement south. The troops were to carry pontoon bridges "to cross streams on the line of march, and for the additional object of being able to cross the Rio Grande."[4]

When Custer arrived in Alexandria on June 23, 1865, he took command of five cavalry regiments: the 7th Indiana, 1st Iowa, 5th and 12th Illinois, and 2nd Wisconsin. He might have expected he could immediately take up with the style of command he used with his old division. But these troops had fought mostly in the West during the war, under their familiar officers. All they knew of Custer was what they read in the papers. Custer had not shared their hardships or bled with them.

There were no battles looming where Custer could prove his mettle. The war was over. President Johnson had declared an end to hostilities on May 10, 1865, when Jefferson Davis was captured, and again on June 13. But he excepted Texas, where the rebellion would continue into August 1866. This technicality, however, made no impression on the men serving in the volunteer regiments. With the rebel armies disbanded and the Confederate government dissolved, they expected to go home. "Now that the war was ended," Philip E. Francis of Company B, 1st Iowa Cavalry wrote, "and we were to separate in a few days, never again to meet as a military body, never again to live over those experiences which had made us a band of brothers, the future of each seemed the concern of all and plan-making was mutual. We were all heartily glad the end of the bloody contest had come, yet loth to separate."[5] Troops gathered at Memphis fully expecting to board ships headed north. But when the transports heaved downriver instead of up, "then the men *did* yell," one reporter wrote. "The men were mad—and pandemonium *was* let loose, but nevertheless down the broad bosom of the Mississippi we glided— destination unknown."[6]

"Tired out with the long service," an officer recalled, "weary with an uncomfortable journey by river from Memphis, sweltering under a Gulf-coast sun, under orders to go farther and farther from home when the war was over, the one desire was to be mustered out and released from a service that became irksome and baleful when a prospect of crushing the enemy no longer existed."[7]

Worse than not going home, the men learned that they might be sent into a war they had not volunteered to fight. Rumors that they might be part of an invasion of Mexico had a ruinous effect on troop morale. "A feeling amounting almost to mutiny existed throughout the command," Custer wrote, "occasioned by their determined opposition to remain longer in the service, and particularly was this opposition heightened by an impression that they were to be required to go to Mexico, a measure that they would not consent to under any circumstances. They claimed that they had enlisted for the present war, that the war was over, and that they were entitled to their discharge from service."[8] Many promptly deserted.

Custer's column remained in Alexandria until July, awaiting horses and equipment for the expedition. This delay created problems. The men had too much time on their hands, no pay, and meager supplies. There was none of the discipline imposed by facing an enemy army with prospects of battle. Returning Confederates, unhappy with the war's outcome and the impact of the struggle on their homes, came home to find Yankee troops roaming the streets. There was also the challenge of caring for freed slaves who had no guidance about what to do or where to go, seeking food and other forms of relief with no sympathy from the locals and no established Federal infrastructure to support them. "Between the troublesome negroes, the unsubdued Confederates, and the lawless among our own soldiers, life was by no means an easy problem to solve," Libbie wrote.[9] Custer had to deal with the types of complex problems that over a century later would be called the "Three Block War," requiring him to serve as soldier, diplomat, and humanitarian relief worker simultaneously.

Sheridan sent glowing reports back to Washington, claiming that "the columns of cavalry which start from Shreveport and Alexandria ... are perhaps the best equipped and handsomest of the war."[10] Custer's inspector general, James W. Forsyth, had a different view of the handsome troops: "Robbery, plundering and murdering was of daily occurrence," he wrote, "and nearly the entire division was in open mutiny."[11]

"The conduct of these troops while at Alexandria was infamous," Custer recalled,

> and rendered them a terror to the inhabitants of that locality, and a disgrace to this or any other service. Highway robbery was of frequent occurrence each day. Farmers bringing cotton

or other produce to town were permitted to sell it and then robbed in open daylight upon the streets of the town—this, too, in the presence or view of other soldiers than those perpetrating these acts. No citizen was safe in his own home, either during the day or night. Bands of soldiers were constantly prowling about the surrounding country for a distance of twenty or thirty miles, robbing the inhabitants indiscriminately of whatever they chose, and not unfrequently these squads of soldiers who were so absent from camp, not only in violation of orders but of articles of war, were accompanied by officers.[12]

The supply problem was critical. Clothes and uniforms were dilapidated, pants frayed from the knee down, shirts torn and tattered (if worn at all in the subtropical heat), boots worn out. "It was with the greatest difficulty that they could be made to wear any clothing," Forsyth wrote. "When I joined, large numbers of the men were riding horses about the country, and to water, with nothing on their persons but a pair of drawers and an undershirt, and a chip or straw hat. In this disgusting way they rode through the streets of Alexandria. A lady could not appear on the streets."[13] An officer explained to Custer that "the boys think they ought to be allowed to go home, and if not allowed to go home they ought to have a little liberty." Custer interpreted this "liberty" as "unrestrained permission to go where they pleased and rob whoever came in their way."[14]

Custer quickly and harshly sought to impose order on his raucous command. Three deserters who had been captured and one man who had engaged in mutiny were sentenced to death. The mutineer, Sergeant L. L. Lancaster of the 2nd Wisconsin, had a grudge against their commanding officer, Lieutenant Colonel Dale. He had ordered Dale to take a boat and leave the command, also intending to send Custer off, "and if he did not go quietly they would make him go or throw him in the river."[15] On the day of the execution, the command was assembled in a square, and the prisoners led in. "The wagon, drawn by four horses, bearing the criminals sitting on their coffins, followed at a slow pace, escorted by the guard and the firing-party, with reversed arms," Libbie wrote of the sanguinary scene. "The coffins were placed in the centre of the square, and the men seated upon them at the foot of their open graves. Eight men, with livid countenances and vehemently beating hearts, took their places in front of their comrades, and looked upon the blanched, despairing faces of those whom they were ordered to kill."[16]

Before the execution was carried out, Custer ordered the mutinous Lancaster taken out of the line.[17] Lieutenant Colonel Dale had interceded on his behalf for his "little drunken wordy mutiny." But another story had it that Custer was responding to threats from the 2nd Wisconsin that if the sentence was carried out, he and his staff "would be slaughtered."[18] Lancaster's death sentence was commuted to life imprisonment on the island of Dry Tortugas, west of the Florida Keys, and he was later pardoned by Andrew Johnson. The deserters were executed as planned.

The march into Texas in August hardly improved matters. The column left Alexandria on the morning of August 8, arriving on the twenty-sixth in Hempstead, Texas, 240 miles distant, "with rations exhausted, many of the soldiers barefooted, almost naked and without blankets, and with no supplies provided." One member of the division said that "the march from Alexandria to this place [Hempstead] was the most severe and uncomfortable, and attended with more suffering than any the regiment has experienced during its four years service in the field."[19] Philip E. Francis summed up the ordeal: "We had gone through the war; had camped in Missouri with a foot of snow on the ground; had lain down in the mud in Arkansas at night to find ourselves frozen to the earth in the morning; we had wrestled with vermin in Southern trenches, and doubled up on the discomforts of cold and the pangs of hunger—but, until after the war had closed and we entered Custer's division, the real hardships of camp life had never stared us in our faces."[20]

"We left the valley of the Red River, with its fertile plantations, and entered a pine forest on the table-land, through which our route lay for a hundred and fifty miles," Libbie wrote. "A great portion of the higher ground was sterile, and the forest much of the way was thinly inhabited."[21] This was not verdant Virginia, where Custer had spent most of the war campaigning. He was used to different climate, forage, and weather, and more reliable supplies. General Order 15, Custer's order for the movement through Texas, stressed keeping the command in tight order, to dissuade desertion and be prepared for action should the need arise. "Soldiers were ordered to report in ranks with coats buttoned, and to carry carbine, revolver, seventy rounds of cartridges, and saber," Philip E. Francis recalled. "The temperature was about 120 degrees, and there wasn't a rebel in the land."[22] The men were miserable, riding with full kit bunched together over dry, dusty trails. One angry trooper called Custer's order "another monument to the supreme ignorance and stupidity of the commanding General."[23]

Lieutenant Colonel McQueen of the 1st Iowa Cavalry said, "I never saw troops so badly managed and provided for, both in regard to outfit and rations, as this division of cavalry was while it remained under the command of General Custer, or such a lack of common sense in orders and in the exercise of discipline, as was displayed by its commander."[24]

Custer attempted to mitigate the heat of the march by setting out in the cool before dawn. "The General had reveillé sounded at 2 o'clock in the morning," Libbie wrote. "It was absolutely necessary to move before dawn, as the moment the sun came in sight the heat was suffocating. It was so dark when we set out that it was with difficulty we reached the main road, from our night's camp, in safety."[25] The horses sometimes wanted for forage and water, and their guide, a local named Stillman, would promise ahead a "bold flowin' stream," which inevitably would be "the bed of a dried creek, nothing but pools of muddy water, with a coating of green mold on the surface."[26] The command also had to deal with annoyances like mosquitoes, centipedes, pine ticks, and scorpions, one of which killed a teamster. Sheridan, who had served in the area before the war, said, "If I owned Texas and Hell, I would rent out Texas and live in Hell."[27]

Libbie bore the hardships with her usual pluck. She rode a horse named Custis Lee, which had been captured from one of Robert E. Lee's general staff officers, and other times she rode in a wagon. "My life in a wagon soon became such an old story that I could hardly believe I had ever had a room," she wrote. She recalled her father's early opposition to her becoming an army wife; he said that "after the charm and dazzle of the epaulet had passed, I might have to travel 'in a covered wagon like an emigrant.'" It became a matter of mirth for the young couple, and when Libbie was "lifted from my rather lofty apartment, and set down in the tent in the dark … the candle revealed a twinkle in the eye of a man who could joke before breakfast, 'I wonder what your father would say now.'"[28]

Some griped that Custer was playing favorites rather than seeing to the welfare of his men. "The best ambulance teams were taken to transport the General's camp equipage, staff and hunting dogs," M. P. Hanson recalled, "while sick men were transported on unloaded provision wagons without springs."[29] Custer's eccentric flair was also on full display, which did not go over as well with men who had not seen his fury in battle. "One afternoon while on the march we espied a man sitting on his horse," George W. Stover of the 7th Indiana said. "When we came up I saw it was Custer. He was dressed in cow-boy style, broad rimmed grey hat, linen duster, and a double-barreled shotgun across the pommel of his saddle, and the boys took him for a Texan."[30] George took offense when the men, not recognizing him, greeted him disrespectfully, but Libbie talked him out of punishing them.

Rations were the biggest problem on the march. "The full rations of fresh beef were generally issued at this time," Lieutenant Colonel McQueen recalled, "but not any more than the legal ration of beef, while all other rations were damaged and unfit for use, especially the hard bread, which was full of worms and bugs."[31] Soldiers boiled horse fodder to try to give substance to their dinners. A trooper from the 7th Indiana recalled, "There was a cynical child in our regiment, who declared that he had fresh meat every meal." Responding to the incredulous men, he got a piece of hard tack, "broke it, and counted us *eleven maggots* and fourteen *small* red bugs, very fresh and lively."[32]

Foraging was frowned on; the same general who helped lay waste to the Shenandoah and took delight in capturing enemy supply trains now had to enforce orders intended to conciliate the locals and reduce the footprint of the Federal occupation. Nevertheless, the men, driven by hunger and boredom, occasionally went out in parties to see what they could rustle up in the countryside. "Search of camp was made every morning," trooper Francis recalled, "and woe to the unlucky regiment which left evidences of foraging."[33]

In one case, a calf was stolen from a herd owned by Doctor R. R. Peebles, collector of the Port of Galveston. It was killed and made into soup for a sick soldier. This led to an incident that would haunt Custer for years afterward. Back in Alexandria, Custer had issued General Order 2, urging all officers and soldiers "to use every exertion to prevent the committal of acts of lawlessness, which, if permitted to pass unpunished, will bring discredit upon the command." Owing to the impracticability of formal courts-martial under the circumstances, he ordered that "any enlisted man violating the above order, or committing depredations upon the persons or property of citizens, will have his head shaved, and in addition will receive twenty-five lashes upon his back, well laid on."[34] This became known as "the whipping order."

Custer later explained that he "never found it necessary or desirable to issue such orders … simply because I have never been in command of troops whose conduct, both as regards officers and men, so nearly resembled that of a mob as was the conduct of these troops when I assumed command of them."[35] And orders of this type were not unprecedented. Ambrose Burnside, when he was commanding the Army of the Ohio, ordered that anyone caught looting be "stripped of his uniform, his head shaved, then branded on the left cheek with the letter T as a thief, and drummed out of the service."[36] Nevertheless, Custer's order transformed the "Boy General of the golden locks" into the "long-haired hero of the lash."

Private Horace C. Cure, Company M, 1st Iowa Cavalry, was arrested for having information about Dr. Peebles's stolen calf and not divulging it. In accordance with General Order 2, his head was shaved and he was given twenty-five lashes "by command of the author of the slave driver order," according to another member of the regiment. After Cure was whipped, "the men gathered in squads with carbines in hand, determined to avenge the ignominious insult thus offered to the old regiment." Lieutenant Colonel McQueen calmed them down but said that he would not tolerate any further violence against his men. "I will here say his hide will not hold corn, by God!"[37] Seven men of the 12th Illinois Cavalry and five of the 7th Indiana were given the same treatment. George Stover of the latter unit said that afterward, "It was a common occurrence to see soldiers at any time in the day draw up and shoot at Custer and staff" from a distance. "One time in particular they made him turn back. I was officer of the day at the time and saw the whole transaction. General Custer asked, 'Who in the h-ll was doing that shooting?'"[38]

A correspondent from the *New York Times* wrote that Custer had "tried every humane way to save his army from going to pieces, but failed" before resorting to flogging. "I leave it to everyone if Custer didn't do right." The flogging "had the desired effect, but brought down the friends of these soldiers upon him, who charge him with being disloyal, inhuman, and everything that is bad."[39] Inspector General Forsyth had a more jaundiced view of the events. "With reference to General Custer's order whilst I was with the command, I have simply to say that he made a great mistake," he wrote. "Instead of whipping he should have shot."[40]

Problems decreased when the cavalry encamped at Hempstead. The troops no longer had the rigors of the daily march, and supplies became more regular. Occupation duty was less taxing than expected; there were no major uprisings among the Texans, and the crisis on the Rio Grande never escalated to the point of war.

Sheridan came up by way of Galveston, bringing along George's father. But Father Custer soon came down with malarial fever, and George did too, though he was loath to show it. Libbie was amazed by his powers of endurance. George "seemed to have set his strong will against yielding to climatic influences," she wrote, "but after two days of this fighting he gave in and tossed himself on our borrowed lounge, a vanquished man. He was very sick. Break-bone fever had waited to do its worst with its last victim. Everything looked very gloomy to me." George eventually consented to taking doses of quinine and was "so racked and tormented by pain, and burnt up with fiery heat, that he hardly made the feeblest fight about the medicine." But he bid Libbie take a taste, "to be sure that I knew how bitter it was."[41]

Life for the Custers became more settled, and George got to know the local plantation owners. Even though he was a Yankee general, his charm won most of them over, and he and his officers were invited to society events and hunting excursions. Horse racing was a daily pastime in Custer's command, particularly among his father, his brother, and members of his staff. "General Custer himself always appeared on the race track as chief manager," Lieutenant Colonel McQueen recalled, "and generally dressed in the uniform of a private soldier or citizen acting (pardon the expression) the 'bohoy' among the boys."[42]

"We are running out to the stables half our time," Libbie wrote. "Armstrong has the horses exercised on a quarter-of-a-mile track, holds the watch and times them, as we sit round and enjoy their speed."[43] They became attached to a stable boy, "a tiny mulatto, a handsome little fellow, weighing about eighty pounds," whom George thought was "the finest rider he has ever seen." Libbie made him a "tight-fitting red jacket and a red-white-and-blue skull cap, to ride in at races."[44]

On October 21 there was a run between Custer's racehorse, Jack Rucker, and a steed belonging to the 1st Iowa. Large sums were bet on the contest, and when the Iowa horse lost, it was blamed on the Mexican rider, Private Nicholas LaCosta, who was openly alleged to have received "a liberal compensation from General Custer or his friends."[45] Custer and his staff were so elated at the outcome that they visited the regiment's camp that night to indulge in some celebratory poker, but in the process they lost most of the money they had won in the allegedly fixed race. Later, Custer had the Iowa horse transferred to the quartermaster general of his staff.

The Iowans sought revenge by bringing in a ringer. They got to know a sympathetic breeder in Austin who raised the finest horses in the state. He set up a race with General Custer at the city track, putting up a wager of $1,500, and quietly told the Iowans to place all the bets they could with Custer's staff. A few days before the race, a trooper went to the horse breeder, supposedly on behalf of General Custer, offering to pay the full $1,500 if he let Custer's horse win. "I was not brought up to run horses that way," the breeder responded. "If your horse is the fastest he takes the money; if my mare is the fastest she gets it."[46]

On the day of the race, Custer and his staff were certain of victory. The mood was light, the division band played tunes, and the officers and wives had gathered for the event. The race started and "off went the beautiful Texas horse, like an arrow from a bow," Libbie recalled. "But our Jack, in spite of the rider sticking the spur and cruelly cutting his silken neck with the whip, only lumbered around the first curve, and in this manner laboriously made his way the rest of the distance."[47] The track was six hundred yards long, and the little Texas mare beat Jack Rucker by sixty feet.

"Cheer upon cheer went up from the boys and citizens assembled there to witness the race," a soldier wrote, "intermingled with such expressions as, 'How are you, General Custer?' 'Couldn't steal the race this time!' 'Why don't you make your band blow?' and many other expressions."[48] The mood in the general's party turned less bright, and "the General and his staff, and the band and ambulances retreated in disorder and confusion."[49]

"Of course it was plain that we were frightfully beaten," Libbie wrote, "and with loud and triumphant huzzas, the Texans welcomed their winning horse long before poor Jack dragged himself up to the stand." She claimed that Jack Rucker had been drugged.[50]

In November the command moved from Hempstead to Austin, where they were generally welcomed.[51] The war had not touched Texas as it had other Confederate states, and many in the countryside refused to recognize Federal authority, or in some cases any authority. Custer's cavalry was a necessary stabilization force. "The citizens are constantly coming to pay their respects to Armstrong," Libbie wrote. "You see, we were welcomed instead of dreaded, as, Yankees or no Yankees, a man's life is just as good, preserved by a Federal soldier as by a Confederate, and everybody seems to be in a terrified state in this lawless land."[52] They passed several months in Austin without serious incident, and the Austin *Southern Intelligencer* said that Custer "won the admiration and esteem of all of our citizens who have been associated with him, either socially or on business." The paper said his conduct was marked by "uniform justice, kindness and courtesy."[53]

Elsewhere Custer was not regarded with such esteem. The Iowa state legislature, after investigating the whipping of Private Cure and the general treatment of the 1st Iowa Cavalry, passed a resolution denouncing "such ill-treatment as no other Iowa soldiers have ever been called upon to endure" and concluding that "such treatment or punishment was dishonorable to the General inflicting it, degrading to the name of American soldier, unworthy of the cause in which they were engaged, and in direct and flagrant violation of the laws of Congress and the rules and articles of war."[54]

A history of the 1st Iowa Volunteer Cavalry noted that "the hero of many a mad charge [sank] into the hero of the lash, [and] justly received the indignant condemnation of the people of Iowa." Iowa governor William M. Stone, who had risen from the rank of private to colonel in the war and had helped carry the wounded President Lincoln from Ford's Theatre to the house where he died, protested the "barbarous code adopted by the long-haired young general." He requested his unit be mustered out. Iowan Major General Fitz Henry Warren, the editor of the *New York Tribune* who had coined the expression "On to Richmond!" in 1861, took the matter to Secretary of War Stanton personally, and the unit was allowed to disband on February 15, 1866.[55]

But by then Custer had moved on. General Order 168 of December 28, 1865, mustered out 101 volunteer major generals, brevet major generals, and brigadiers, effective January 31, 1866. (In typical U.S. government fashion, the Senate finally confirmed George as a major general of volunteers three weeks later.)[56] The Custers left Texas by Galveston, in an old blockade runner.

"They hated us, I suppose," Libbie reflected on the morale problems in George's command. "That is the penalty the commanding officer generally pays for what still seems to me the questionable privilege of rank and power. Whatever they thought, it did not deter us from commending, among ourselves, the good material in those Western men, which so soon made them orderly and obedient soldiers."[57]

Charles Bertrand Lewis, who had served in the 6th Michigan Cavalry and accompanied the "expedish *a la Custer*" with the 7th Indiana, disagreed. He wrote that the men being good soldiers was never the issue and thought it appalling that they were "brought down here and drilled and worked nearly to death after they have done their duty and now they wish to go home to their families and friends." He said it was "a disgrace that the American Government will permit a lot of Regular Army Officers to domineer it with a high hand over American citizens who, according to their enlistment papers are free." As for his former commander, he concluded that Custer was "a Potomac officer trying to learn western men what duty is now the war is over. Potomac and Mississippi do not agree."[58]

CHAPTER TWENTY

THE "SWING AROUND THE CIRCLE"

Custer now faced a challenge he had not had to consider since he was commissioned: What does a natural-born warrior do in peacetime? For his entire professional career, George Custer had only known war. He had gone from the Military Academy to the battlefield. He had thrived in the wartime environment; it was the ideal setting to harness his abilities and proclivities in the interests of the Army and his country.

But with the conflict over, Custer had to adjust to life in a very different force. Libbie said that "the stagnation of peace was being felt by those who had lived a breathless four years at the front."[1] Volunteer units disbanded, and the professional officers who led them reverted to their Regular Army ranks. Wartime "brevet" ranks also disappeared. Custer was a major general of volunteers and brevet major general of the Regular Army when the war ended. But when he mustered out of the volunteer service, he was once again a Regular Army captain, and his salary dropped from $8,000 to $2,000. "Hurrah for Peace and my little Durl," George wrote Libbie after Lee surrendered. "Can you consent to come down and be a Captain's wife?"[2]

George Custer was at a critical decision point in his career. He could continue to serve in uniform, but as a noted war hero, he was offered many other opportunities. "The temptations to induce General Custer to leave the service and enter civil life began at once, and were many and varied," Libbie wrote. After they returned to Monroe from Texas, "all sorts of suggestions were made. Business propositions, with enticing pictures of great wealth, came to him. He never cared for money for money's sake. No one that does, ever lets it slip through his fingers as he did."[3]

"I think it probable that I shall leave the army," George wrote in March, "but will not decide till assured of success."[4] At the time, he was in Washington testifying before Congress, meeting important government officials, and pondering numerous offers from artists and photographers interested in recreating his likeness. He was in great demand and could have directed his interests profitably in a number of directions, whether civilian business opportunities or a government appointment. At one point he considered seriously a post as a foreign envoy. "I would like it for many reasons," he wrote Libbie, including the salary of $7,000 to $10,000 per year. He could have gone into politics but turned down a chance to run for Congress in Michigan in 1866—a race he certainly would have won.

"The old soldiers, and civilians also, talked openly of General Custer for Congressman or Governor," Libbie wrote. "It was a summer of excitement and uncertainty. How could it be otherwise to a boy who, five brief years before, was a beardless youth with no apparent future before him?"[5] He might have had a career like his former subordinate Russell

Alger of the 5th Michigan Cavalry, who served as governor of Michigan, secretary of war, and U.S. senator.

George also had an opportunity to keep fighting. Expatriate Mexican president Benito Juárez offered Custer a major general's commission in his rebel army, which would have put him in the field against the French-backed forces of self-styled Emperor Maximilian I. The U.S. Navy had established a blockade of Mexico, and Grant and Sherman liked the idea of Custer's having a hand in defeating Maximilian's army. The offer promised high pay and high adventure. But Libbie opposed the idea, as did Secretary of State William H. Seward. He thought the move would create further diplomatic complications with the French and prevailed upon President Johnson to block the appointment.

Libbie was tempted to urge George to resign. But her father, who had originally opposed her being an Army wife, talked her out of it. "Why, daughter," he said, "I would rather have the honor which grows out of the way in which the battle of Waynesboro was fought, than to have the wealth of the Indies.... My child, put no obstacles in the way to the fulfillment of his destiny. He chose his profession. He is a born soldier. There he must abide."[6] Judge Bacon had fully accepted George and Libbie's relationship, and lying ill in the spring of 1866 said that she had "married entirely to her own satisfaction and to mine. No man could wish for a son-in-law more highly thought of!"[7] Judge Bacon passed away on May 18, casting a pall of sadness over the two families, and George rushed back to Monroe from New York to support his grieving wife. "I should be far more miserable but for Armstrong's care," she wrote. "I do not wear deep mourning. He is opposed to it."[8]

Ultimately, Custer decided to continue his Army career. The postwar force was larger than the one Custer had expected to serve in while he was a cadet at West Point. In 1866, Congress tripled the size of the small prewar Army to undertake the military occupation of the former Confederate states, meet frontier security needs, man the coastal defense force, and deter the perceived threat from French-controlled Mexico.[9] But the larger force did not necessarily mean ample opportunities, as there were many senior officers, professionals, and volunteers with distinguished war records, all jockeying for assignments. Once the key billets were filled, promotions would not take place until a slot opened. "Death, dismissal, resignation, and retiring from illness or from age are the causes that make vacancies," Libbie wrote. Officers would look through the Army register to see who outranked them "and to estimate how many years it would take for those in the way to be removed, either by Divine Providence or by dismissal."[10]

Patronage had been important during the war and proved no less critical afterward. Connections—and skill in the slippery art of political infighting—could be more valuable for career advancement than a sterling war record. As Mrs. Custer noted, "though safe from the dangers of battle it did not mean peace, for that public life was usually a perpetual fight, and so often the foe in the dark."[11]

Custer was fortunate to have some powerful, high-level patrons. Secretary of War Edwin Stanton greeted him very cordially when he visited Washington in March 1866, gushing, "It does me good to look at you again!"[12] Stanton approved many suggestions from Custer for filling junior officer vacancies. Sheridan—who had been a first lieutenant at the time of Fort Sumter and emerged from the war a full major general—argued for a generalship for his young protégé, or at the very least command of a cavalry regiment. But Sheridan's entreaties and Custer's other connections were not enough. On July 28, 1866, Custer was commissioned lieutenant colonel of the 7th U.S. Cavalry, a new regiment based at Fort Riley. The coveted colonelcy was given to Brevet Major

General Andrew Jackson Smith, the son of a Revolutionary War veteran and member of the West Point Class of 1838. He fought in Mexico and on the frontier and served in the West under Grant during the Civil War. Grant had singled him out for heroism in the fighting during the approach to Vicksburg, and he ended the war a corps commander.

Custer was naturally disappointed. Being made a regimental deputy seemed like a rebuff. Smith arguably lacked Custer's exceptional record of achievement in the war, but he was typical of the generation receiving command billets in postwar regiments. The Army had a wealth of young, motivated officers like Custer, with impressive backgrounds, seeking to get ahead, but took a long-term view toward institution building. Seniority was still a guiding principle, and the Young Turks would have to wait their turn.

The new colonels were a mixed bag. Command of the 8th Cavalry went to John Irvin Gregg, cousin of General David M. Gregg; he had fought in Mexico, pursued a career in the iron industry between the wars, and rose to the rank of brevet major general as a cavalry commander in the Civil War. The 6th Cavalry colonelcy went to James Oakes of West Point's Class of 1846, brevetted for bravery in Mexico but with an undistinguished Civil War record. The 9th Cavalry went to Edward Hatch, a former brevet major general who had commanded a division in the West in the Civil War. And the 10th went to Benjamin Grierson, another brevet major general, division commander, and Westerner, whose raid before the siege of Vicksburg General Sherman called "the most brilliant expedition of the war."

Custer was not the only bright light of his generation whose career hit a slowdown. Wesley Merritt, who had been in higher command positions longer than Custer, was made lieutenant colonel of the 9th Cavalry under Hatch.[13] Like Custer, Merritt's highest Regular Army rank had been captain. But even if officers of Custer's and Merritt's caliber were not given regimental commands, neither were they being punished. Jumping two ranks to the regular rank of lieutenant colonel was the sort of career mobility that would have been nearly impossible in the Old Army.

Some were not so lucky. Custer's old corps commander General Pleasonton, who had graduated from West Point in 1844, was a Regular Army major before and during the war, and was offered the lieutenant colonelcy of the 20th Infantry, which he declined, before leaving the service in 1868. Alexander Pennington went from a volunteer cavalry brevet brigadiership to a Regular Army artillery captaincy, reaching the rank of major only in 1882; he made lieutenant colonel ten years later and returned to the rank of brigadier general in the Spanish American War, thirty-eight years after graduating from West Point.

Custer may have been given some hope by the treatment of 1855 West Point graduate William W. Averell, whose removal after the Battle of Fisher's Hill in August 1864 had opened the way for Custer's first division command. Averell resigned from the military in March 1865, but on July 17, 1866, President Johnson recommended Averell be promoted from the regular rank of captain all the way up to major general. The U.S. Senate confirmed the elevation on July 23. Averell did not return to the colors, accepting instead the post of consul general to the British North American Provinces, and afterward earning fame as the inventor of asphalt paving.[14] But he proved such promotions were possible.

Custer had supporters, but questions persisted. Rumors that he was politically unsound continued to dog him. He had achieved celebrity in part through the patronage of Radical Republicans, particularly Secretary of War Stanton, but was still of a Democratic bent. In March 1866 he was forced publicly to address a claim that while in Texas he had made pro-secession speeches. "I have made no speeches since coming to Texas," he wrote in an open letter, "and if I had, my voice would not have been

raised in support of and in sympathy with the statement and the doctrine of whose hostility to the Government is now as strong and openly
manifested as at any time during the rebellion. I hope my course during
the war will be accepted as bearing me out in this statement."[15] Custer
was called to testify before Congress on conditions in Texas, and he toed
the Radical Republican line, warning strongly against removing occupation troops, due to lingering hostility against the Union.[16] However, after
his Republican patrons failed to deliver the rank Custer wanted, he
decided to hitch his fortunes to Democrat Andrew Johnson.

In early August, Custer met with President Johnson to discuss getting
another assignment, perhaps command of one of the more numerous
new infantry regiments. "But in whatever branch of the service I may
be assigned," he wrote afterward to Johnson, "I most respectfully request
to be attached to an organization composed of *White* troops, as I have
served and wish to serve with no other class."[17] (Custer had earlier been
looked at for the lieutenant colonelcy of the 9th Cavalry, one of the new
black regiments, later famed as the Buffalo Soldiers, but Grant had
shifted him to the 7th Cavalry, and Merritt went to the 9th.) Johnson
was not immediately forthcoming, but he did ask Custer's assistance in
shoring up his shaky political fortunes going into the 1866 midterm
congressional elections.

Johnson was in a difficult position. The most destructive conflict in
the nation's history had fundamentally reshaped the political landscape.
"A new political era is being inaugurated," Custer wrote, "an era which
is destined to remodel and develop the character of our political structure."[18] But exactly what that era would look like was a matter of speculation. Some believed that *ante bellum* sectionalism was a thing of the
past and that with the end of slavery, both the Southern Democratic
faction and Republican party had lost their reasons for being. By this
calculation the future belonged to centrist Democrats like Johnson. He
had run with Lincoln in 1864 under the National Union banner, cutting

into McClellan's moderate-Democratic support. Johnson believed that he could keep the movement alive and build a new centrist party composed of disaffected Democrats, former Confederates, Northern Copperheads, and moderate Republicans alienated by the party's dominant Radical wing.

The plan seemed to make sense. The Republican party had made its name as an anti-slavery party. Lacking the cohesion and fervor supplied by abolitionism, it was feasible that the decade-old party would fracture, and Johnson's Union movement, championing moderate reconstruction policies, could pick up the pieces.

But the Republicans had several important factors working in their favor. They were the party of the martyred Lincoln, who was revered in death far more than he was while in the White House. Johnson by contrast struggled against the perception that he was never supposed to be president. Republicans also established networks of friendship and influence through war service that would prove to be long lasting and politically beneficial. Republican governors gave key volunteer regimental commands to trustworthy political allies, a factor that had worked against Custer earlier in the war, and these relationships remained solid for decades.

This was the dawn of an era of Republican preeminence at the national level. During the period in which the generations that fought the war dominated American national politics, from the 1860s to 1910, only one Democrat, Grover Cleveland, was elected president. There was also a sense among many Republicans, particularly among the Radicals, that the mission of the war was not yet complete. The South had to be punished, or at least the sacrifices made by the North had to be recognized. The 1866 election was the first peacetime opportunity to "wave the bloody shirt." It was not yet time to forgive and forget.

Reconstruction had replaced slavery as a dominant national political issue. The issue broke along institutional lines: Congress and the executive departments dominated by Radical Republicans appointed by Lincoln sought a punitive peace, while Johnson and the Democratic congressional minority favored a more moderate course of reconciliation.

The Radicals on Capitol Hill moved ahead with their program. On June 11, Congress passed the Fourteenth Amendment, authored by Republican Ohio congressman John A. Bingham, who had secured Custer's appointment to West Point. Supporters of the amendment said it was necessary to secure the rights of freed slaves and political minorities in the South, but opponents called it a Federal power grab. Johnson agreed to a plan to hold a National Union convention in Philadelphia from August 14 to 16 to defend "states' rights" against the "usurpation and centralization of power in Congress."

Custer attended the convention and became an open spokesman for reconciliation. He shook hands with a delegate from South Carolina, former Confederate Brigadier General Samuel McGowan, saying, "General, we have been looking at each other often during the war through field glasses and amid the smoke of battle. If we can now shake hands, these civilians who have stayed at their homes in safety surely should."[19]

Custer served as an honorary vice president of a Union conference in Michigan, which approved a resolution praising "the restoration policy of Andrew Johnson, and that the Southern States, which were not admitted to be out of the Union in time of war, are now that the rebellion is suppressed, as right-fully and should be as effectually in the Union as they were before the madness of their people attempted to carry them out."[20] In an open letter to a National Union party mass meeting in Washington, D.C., on August 23, Custer said he believed that the policies of the Radicals were so punitive they could start a second civil war. "I have had enough of civil war," he wrote, "and believing that the great National Union party is the only one whose efforts look to a permanent and honorable peace, and by whose aid only the Union can be restored under the Constitution, I have enlisted under its banner, beneath whose broad folds I propose to battle until the victory is won."[21]

Around the same time, Custer became involved with the Soldiers' and Sailors' Union (SSU), a veterans' organization formed in January 1866 by Northern and Southern troops seeking reconciliation. The organization was closely tied to the National Union movement. Custer, along with scores of other former general officers, signed an SSU statement that said he believed "the South is sincere in its declarations," and that he was "unwilling that the Southern people shall be held in vassalage, and that they cannot be denied representation in Congress without a plain violation of the Constitution."[22]

Custer's vigorous show of loyalty to Johnson was a far cry from his earlier political statements. In January 1864 he wrote to Republican Senator Jacob M. Howard of Michigan that he would "hang every human being who possesses a drop of rebel blood in their veins whether they be men, women, or children." And in May 1865 he had said that "extermination is the only true policy we can adopt toward the political leaders of the rebellion, and at the same time do justice to ourselves and to our posterity."[23] His abrupt change in tone, even if it reflected his true, private political views, was seen as hypocrisy and opportunism. "Gen. Custer, who flogged and shaved the heads of Iowa soldiers in Texas, is now the leader of the military wing of President Johnson's supporters," one newspaper observed. The *Detroit Free Press* charged that Custer had "deserted to the Southern ranks."[24] Custer denounced such articles as creating "false impressions regarding my past and present position," which he said were "being so assiduously disseminated throughout the country by a subsidized, unscrupulous, and fanatical press."[25] But the attacks intensified.

In late August, President Johnson embarked on a public relations tour of the North and Midwest that became known as the "Swing around the Circle." A pro-Johnson newspaper wrote that "the best answer to the unnumbered slanders which radical lips and radical sheets have hurled at The President will be his own presence among the American people."[26] Johnson took along a number of luminaries, including well-known cabinet officials, Admiral Farragut, and Generals Grant, Stedman, Stoneman, Crook, Rousseau, and Custer, who joined the party on its way through West Point.[27] Libbie accompanied her husband, and a press report described her as "among the most sprightly ladies of the presidential party. She is about 24, but looks not over 17, and is quite girlish and charming in her manners."[28]

Navy Secretary Gideon Welles, who accompanied Johnson on the tour, wrote that "the President made brief remarks at nearly every stopping-place to the crowds which assembled to meet and welcome him…. The authorities in some of the cities—Baltimore, Philadelphia, Cincinnati, Indianapolis, and Pittsburgh—declined to extend courtesies or participate in the reception, but the people in all these cases took the matter in hand and were almost unanimous in the expression of their favorable regard and respect for the Chief Magistrate."[29]

In reality, Johnson's public relations tour was more difficult than Welles would admit. In the East the president was well received, but the Republican governors of Ohio, Indiana, Illinois, Michigan, Missouri, and Pennsylvania all refused to appear or meet with him. Republican House members were also notably absent. And Johnson's public receptions were not always so positive or enthusiastic. Most people were more interested in seeing the heroic General Grant and others in the party than hearing from the accidental president.

In Indianapolis on September 10, the presidential party was given a welcome that "beggars all description," by one report. "A few faint hurrahs were given for Johnson, while continued yells were heard on every side for Grant and Farragut." Johnson tried to speak but the crowd would not let him. Custer, "who seemed to be running the show," came onto the balcony and admonished the crowd. "Hush, you damned set of ignorant Hoosiers!" he shouted, and the crowd answered with even louder calls for Grant. When Grant finally appeared, he was "received with a perfect storm." Afterward, the president tried to address the crowd again, but "the yells were terrible, and he was again forced back and the balcony closed for the night." Later a riot broke out, and one man was shot and three others wounded. Johnson delivered his speech the next day to a more temperate crowd, but Grant had to leave the presidential tour to prevent further distractions.[30]

This was fine by Grant, who was uncomfortable with the president using active military officers as political props. He might also have been wary of the political drift of the Johnson backers; a letter circulating at the Philadelphia National Union convention had called for arch-Radical Secretary of War Edwin Stanton to be removed from office. Grant was invited to speak at the Pittsburgh SSU meeting in September but declined, saying he saw "with regret the actions of any officer of the Army taking a conspicuous part in the political dissensions of the day."[31]

But Custer had no compunction about getting involved in politics. At the SSU convention in Cleveland on September 17, he boldly disagreed with Grant: "It has been said in certain quarters that a soldier who is in the army has no right to interfere in political questions. I think, however, that the real objection is that we do not coincide with the particular views of those people."[32]

However, the SSU was not generating the response its organizers had hoped. The Cleveland meeting was sparsely attended—Custer blamed the weather—and attacks from Republican papers were relentless. The *Toledo Blade* lampooned the proceedings, noting that "there wuz Custer uv

Michigan, with his hair freshly oiled and curled, and buzzin about ez though be hed cheated hisself into the beleef that he reely amounted to suthin."[33]

Republicans concluded that Custer was finally showing his true colors. They had always suspected he was a "McClellan Man," and they were right. Custer praised McClellan as the finest general he had ever known and had a picture of Little Mac on prominent display in his quarters (beside Libbie's portrait of him). The previously supportive *Detroit Tribune* denounced the "crack-brained folly of General Custer's recent performances" and referred to him sarcastically as "George Adonis Custer."[34] A cartoon by Thomas Nast entitled "Amphitheatrum Johnsonianum" portrayed Johnson as a Roman emperor at the arena surrounded by other notables in period garb, with Custer prominent in the foreground, dressed as a Roman warrior, watching the scene placidly while leaning on the fasces, the symbol of imperial power.[35]

Custer's "motives are easily understood," an Indiana paper editorialized, under the headline "The Soldier Whipper." He "desired promotion in the regular army" and found that "active support of Mr. Johnson's peculiar policy was a prerequisite to military as well as civilian appointments." Rumors spread that a grateful Johnson would give Custer general officer rank by brevet.

After the Cleveland convention, Custer was part of the delegation from the SSU that visited the White House to discuss the convention's outcome. Perhaps Custer hoped that the president would reward his good works with a higher rank or a better assignment. But Johnson was not in a mood to dole out favors. The "Swing around the Circle" had been a public relations failure, and the SSU was turning out to be something of a liability. The *Chicago Tribune* speculated that Johnson held Custer somehow responsible for the "ignominious failure of the Cleveland convention."[36] The day after the White House meeting, Custer received orders to report to Fort Riley.

Custer did not leave the stage without stirring some more controversy. He pulled back from his full-throated support of Johnson and
went on the record opposing the congressional candidacy of Democratic
state representative J. Logan Chipman "on account of his disloyal record
during the war." Chipman was the Democratic city attorney of Detroit
before the war and had written commentaries opposing the conflict.
Custer said he refused "to support Northern traitors and declares they
are unworthy of the confidence of the people."[37] The White House noted
Custer's change of tune and considered it a veiled attack. Detroit postmaster and newspaperman Henry Barns wrote to President Johnson
denouncing Custer's "Judaslike conduct."[38] The pro-Johnson *Dubuque
Herald* opined,

> Gen. Custer, whom the radicals were so fiercely denouncing
> a few weeks ago, it would seem has got sick of a little pure
> political atmosphere, and is already wallowing around in the
> congenial stenches of radicalism, where he feels at home.
> Gen. Custer, or Custard, or whatever it is, was one of those
> kind of men whose only achievement before he blundered
> into some kind of reputation before the war closed, was to
> wear his hair long. He shakes his gory locks magnificently,
> but the chief value of his head is on the outside. While pro-
> fessing to be a conservative man and par excellence a Johnson
> man, he is writing letters to defeat the conservative candidate
> for congress in his district in Michigan, and to aid one of the
> very men who propose to impeach the President. Custer
> evidently understands a good deal more about the hair busi-
> ness than he does about politics, and he had better confine
> himself to his brush and his pomatum.[39]

David Ross Locke, writing as the satirical character Petroleum V. Nasby, a lazy former Copperhead malcontent, noted that "them wich we bought up with appintments diskivered on a sudden that an Abolition Senit hed to confirm em, and to sekoor that they hev gone back onto us. Custer is a shinin example."[40] He mused that Custer was given a promotion to "keep him in posishen," but "now the Kernelcy wuz gone and Custer too, and wat wuz worse, there wuz no such thing to be thot uv ez dissmissin him."[41]

The November 6 election for the Fortieth Congress was a field day for the Radicals. Republicans gained thirty-seven seats in the House, and states sent eighteen more to the Senate. Democrats lost nine seats in the House, and dropped from eleven seats in the Senate to nine. The Republicans enjoyed veto-proof majorities in both chambers—in fact they had the largest percentage of House and Senate seats ever for a single party—and could push ahead with their radical program. President Johnson was left a helpless onlooker, soon to be impeached over trying to remove Stanton in violation of the Tenure of Office Act. The National Union party, and the possibility of a postwar centrist political alternative, was dead. Sectionalism emerged from the war stronger than ever, and the South remained solidly Democratic for the next century.

If nothing else, the election results showed the depths of Custer's political miscalculation. His foray into the world of high-level patronage had failed, and he was lucky to report to his new unit at Fort Riley with his lieutenant colonelcy intact.

CHAPTER TWENTY-ONE

COURT-MARTIAL

he Custers arrived at Fort Riley in late October 1866 to join the newly formed 7th Cavalry regiment. George was disappointed at not being named regimental commander; but his superior, Colonel Andrew Jackson Smith, also served as the chief of the District of the Upper Arkansas and was often on detached duty, leaving Custer in de facto command. And though he had lost his old rank, Custer and other wartime brevet officers were given the courtesy of their former titles, so Lieutenant Colonel Custer was still referred to informally as "General."

Fort Riley, established in the 1850s, was an important Plains post after the war, particularly after the Union Pacific Railroad reached nearby Junction City. Supplies and amenities were plentiful compared to conditions in Texas or at the front during the war. In a letter written that December, Libbie said they were "living almost in luxury" at the fort. She said that the well-organized, relatively new buildings, including barracks, stables, officers' and other houses, sutler's store, post office, mess hall, chapel, and billiard house, "give the post the appearance of a little city." They had "five dogs, cow & chickens—and such a nice new cow house & chicken coops. So, you see, we are comfortable. I have a carpet on my bedroom also and expect to have one on the dressing room. Eliza never did better than now.... I have scarcely a care."[1] There were also regular social events and periodic visits by friends and dignitaries seeking a taste of the "Wild West."

Still, the postwar Army faced considerable challenges. The glory and sense of mission of the Civil War days was gone. Frontier duty was very much what it had been for decades—long stretches of routine activity in an unchanging landscape, with periodic outings against the elusive natives, who usually gave battle on their own terms. "There were but two kinds of Indian battles," Major Martin Maginnis said, "one where the troops surprised and killed the Indians, and the other where the Indians surprised and killed the troops. If an Army officer failed in an expedition he was ridiculed and sneered at, and if he succeeded he was vilified as a barbarian and murderer."[2] There were few medals or incentives for the enlisted men, and no brevet promotions for the officers. John Gibbon noted dryly that glory was "a term which, upon the frontier, has long since been defined to signify being 'shot by an Indian from behind a rock, and having your name wrongly spelled in the newspapers.'"[3]

In the more remote areas, amenities were few and rations substandard. At one point on campaign in 1867, Custer's regiment was issued tack baked in 1861, "probably in honor of the year I graduated," he quipped.[4] The troops supplemented their provender by hunting, fishing, and gardening. Sickness was a constant problem, especially venereal disease, for which there was no convenient cure.[5]

The soldiers could not count on much sympathy from the American people. The postwar frontier force was not held in high regard. "The rank and file of the army is the most debased in the world," the *Burling-ton Hawkeye* opined. "The refuse and scum of our great cities is raked into it. No amount of information or competence—no length of ser-vice—no merit of the private, can avail him anything in any respect. There is no emulation or pride to appeal to. He is a dog of the basest kind."[6]

The enlisted force was a mixed group. Military service attracted immigrants (32 percent of the 7th Cavalry were Irish), criminals, and people who wanted free passage west. Low morale and rebelliousness were constant challenges, and the relative lack of major combat actions offered little inspiration or motivation. "Insubordination among the men was the certain consequence of the half-starved, discouraged state they were in," Libbie Custer observed. "One good fight would have put heart into them to some extent, for the hopelessness of following such a will-o'-the-wisp as the Indians were that year, made them think their scouting did no good and might as well be discontinued."[7]

There was up to 40 percent turnover every year due to death, deser-tion, and end of enlistment.[8] Desertion alone took around a third of the enlisted force annually, as men sought better opportunities in the mines, goldfields, or railroads. The 7th Cavalry lost nearly eight hundred men to desertion in under a year.[9] Secretary of War Stanton joked that "the best way to populate the west was to keep sending recruits out there."[10]

Of course, desertion was no joking matter. Besides the obvious dam-age to the force, deserters sometimes turned to banditry. In August 1865, John Pope, then commander of the Department of the Missouri, noted that "overland routes are new and will for some time be infested by wandering parties of lawless white men, lately bushwhackers and desert-ers from the army, and men from the disbanded rebel armies. These men prowl through that whole region of country and are more dangerous to travelers than the Indians themselves."[11] In 1866 the *New York Times* reported that deserters "turn murderers and robbers and horse thieves and are a terror to the travelling community. Scarcely a night passes but that some poor fellow is waylaid and killed."[12] And deserters did not always slip off quietly in the night. Albert Barnitz noted several cases where well-armed fugitives from the 7th Cavalry exchanged brisk fire with the sentries as they departed.[13] Custer's classmate Captain David H. Buel, commander of the arsenal at Fort Leavenworth, was murdered by a deserter named John M. Malone, whom Buel had reprimanded for drunkenness on duty.[14]

The frontier began to heat up shortly after the Custers arrived. On December 21, 1866, a column of eighty soldiers from the 18th Infantry under the command of Captain William Fetterman were ambushed and wiped out in the northern Wyoming Territory by Oglala Sioux, led by Chief Red Cloud.[15] The massacre inflamed a conflict that had been smoldering for years.

The northern Plains tribes had become incensed by the increasing number of whites traveling through Sioux, Cheyenne, and Arapaho lands on the Bozeman Trail, heading for the Montana goldfields. The Civil War was partly to blame; in 1864 General Pleasonton, then in Missouri, had begun paroling Confederate prisoners on the condition they went north to the Dakota and Montana Territories. John Pope, commanding the Military Division of the Missouri at the end of the war, noted in June 1865 that these men were as problematic as the Indians themselves. Pope believed that "the continued rush of emigration to the mines, making highways through the entire Indian country, and attended with outrages upon the Indians which are never heard of except in acts of retaliation, makes it pretty certain that Indian hostilities will continue."[16]

Meanwhile, the Indians had taken advantage of the power vacuum on the Plains during the Civil War. "Never before have the Indians been allowed for eighteen months to have their own way to murder, rob, and plunder indiscriminately and successfully, without check or hindrance," Major General G. M. Dodge wrote in the summer of 1865. "They seem confident of success, fight well, and believe to-day that one Indian is equal to five white soldiers. It takes almost man to man to whip them, and will until the conceit is taken out of them by severe chastisement."[17]

Captain Fetterman had assumed such "chastisement" would be easy: "Give me 80 men and I can ride through the whole Sioux nation." The Sioux quickly took that conceit out of him. But the Fetterman massacre became a rallying cry for those who wanted to settle the Plains issue once and for all. "Should this reported massacre prove to be a fact, it may wake the Government up to the necessity of remodeling the whole Indian Bureau," the *Philadelphia Evening Telegraph* editorialized. "It is certain that these roving savages cannot be allowed much longer to impede the development of this great branch of the nation's industry."[18]

General Sherman, now commander of the Military Division of the Missouri, ordered an expedition against the Indians in the spring of 1867, commanded by Winfield Scott Hancock. Hancock assembled a force of 1,400 men, including Custer and the 7th Cavalry, to take to the field with orders to find and punish any hostile Indian bands. Custer and his men moved 150 miles west to Fort Hays to make ready for the expedition. Libbie stayed behind at Fort Riley, though Custer was eager to have her join him. "Come as soon as you can," he wrote in May. "I did not marry you for you to live in one house, me in another. One bed shall accommodate us both."[19]

On April 12, Hancock met with Cheyenne chiefs at Fort Larned, fifty-five miles south of Fort Hays, near the junction of the Arkansas River and Pawnee Fork. With Hancock were 7th Cavalry commander Colonel Smith, Custer, Major Alfred Gibbs, and Lieutenant Colonel John W. Davidson of the 10th Cavalry. Tall Bear led a Cheyenne delegation of twelve chiefs. Colonel Ned Wynkoop, the Indian agent for the Cheyenne, was also present. Wynkoop was "an Indian agent *par excellence*," by one report. "The Indians have every confidence in his integrity, and respect him for the 'heap fight' that he is known to be capable of making."[20]

They gathered around a fire, the Indians passing a peace pipe, the whites smoking cigars. Hancock wanted to discuss the troubles on the Plains and warned the Indians that while he desired peace, he would fight any who went on the warpath. Tall Bear was focused on his people's suffering. It had been a hard winter with little food. Hancock told them that the bison were "going away very fast, and that they would all disappear eventually." Tall Bear, "wrapped gracefully in his buffalo robe, replied that they were becoming scarce, that they had never been so scarce as during the past winter, adding significantly, that the white men had made them scarce."[21] He blamed the railroads pushing through traditional Cheyenne lands and hunting grounds, and the white settlers who came in their wake.

The conference was inconclusive. Hancock requested to meet with more and higher ranking chiefs. Meanwhile, he wanted to move his force closer to the Indian village so they would understand the threat they faced. The next day he marched up the Pawnee Fork toward the village. Within six miles of the encampment, three hundred mounted Cheyenne warriors met him, drawn up in line of battle. Hancock halted, deployed some of his troops, then moved forward with Colonel Smith and Custer to parlay with the Dog Soldiers' domineering war chief, Roman Nose.

The six-foot-tall chief rode up dressed in a U.S. Army officer's uniform. "From his manner it was quite evident that he was indifferent whether he talked or fought," wrote reporter Theodore R. Davis, who was present at the scene. A Spencer carbine hung from Roman Nose's saddle, four revolvers were stuck in his belt, and he held a strung bow and a clutch of arrows in his left hand, "ready for instant use."[22] Hancock said he had come to talk and wanted to set up a camp where there was better wood and water. Roman Nose left some men with Hancock and rode off with the rest toward the village. After some delay Hancock resumed his march, over land that the Indians had burned, forcing him to make camp within a mile of the village. The Indian encampment was partially deserted; the chiefs explained that the women and children had grown frightened and left, and many of the young men were away on a hunting party.

Hancock grew suspicious; that night he ordered Custer and six hundred men to surround the village. They moved cautiously around the lodges in the darkness. "We all closed in on it, with carbines advanced," Albert Barnitz wrote. A reconnaissance party presently returned to report that the village was abandoned. "The Indians had left," Barnitz wrote, "just as noiselessly as wolves!"[23] The only remaining occupants were numerous dogs, a lame old man, and a little half-breed girl not more than nine years old. She was "almost insensible, covered with blood," Custer wrote. "When able to talk she said, 'Those Indian men did me bad!'"[24] Custer and his men went after the Cheyenne but only found the ashes of nearby Lookout Station and the half-consumed bodies of the station-men. Hancock ordered the Indian village burned in retaliation.

After this, the conflict was on. Custer took his command northeast to Fort Hays to ready for the coming campaign. An Iowa newspaper chided him for not being able to bring the fight to Roman Nose's band: "Gen. Custer, the celebrated soldier whipper, is after the Indians, but as usual the savages were too fast for him and succeeded in getting out of his way."[25] But Custer knew the challenges facing the cavalry in irregular warfare against the Indians. He opposed the impending conflict and advised his superiors against it. "I regard the recent outrages as the work of small groups of irresponsible young men eager for war," he wrote. He thought a general war on the Plains would further disrupt construction of the railroad and lead only to more innocent lives being lost. But "should a war be waged, none would be more determined than I to make it a war of extermination"—the same blunt language Custer used regarding the Confederates during the Civil War.[26]

However, chasing Indians across the Plains was nothing like engaging the Army of Northern Virginia. If anything, it was more akin to Custer's operations against Mosby's raiders. And the area he was patrolling was considerably vaster than Mosby's Confederacy—the state of Kansas alone is about fifty times the size of Mosby's area of operations. Custer had far fewer men, and the enemy moved with their whole communities, so the only scorched earth was when the Indians torched the plains to deny grass to Army horses.

The expected supplies for the regiment were slow in coming, and the wait at Fort Hays dragged on for weeks. Libbie, her friend Anna, and Eliza reached the fort in mid-May, which made the stay more tolerable for Custer, but the delay was hurting the unit. An outbreak of scurvy prompted Custer and his officers to buy anti-scorbutic foods for the men with their own funds, and they also mounted bison hunts and other measures "to secure for the men a beneficial change of rations."[27] But sometimes the hunting parties never came back. Albert Barnitz wrote his wife, Jennie, about a group that went out in search of buffalo and "forgot to return. Query, were they all gobbled by the Indians? We think not." He said that desertions were "a nightly occurrence."[28]

As in Texas, Custer had a difficult time coming to grips with the lack of discipline among the men. Barnitz wrote his wife that Custer "spares no effort to render himself generally obnoxious."[29] He called Custer "the most complete example of a petty tyrant that I have ever seen. You would be filled with utter amazement, if I were to give you a few instances of his cruelty to the men, and discourtesy to the officers."[30] In one case, six men went to the sutler's post a half mile from camp in search of canned fruit during the scurvy epidemic. But they did not have a pass, so Custer had their scalps half-shaved and paraded them through the fort in a wagon to "the exceeding mortification, disgrace and disgust of all right-minded officers and men in camp." Barnitz concluded that "no man but an incarnate fiend could take pleasure in such an abuse of authority."[31]

The 7th mounted periodic patrols but did not find any Indians. Once Custer had a report of a large war party at Lookout Station and led a nighttime patrol of three hundred troopers to engage them. But all he found were the men rebuilding the station passing the time playing poker, with no sign of alarm and unaware of any Indians. As Custer left, one of the poker players remarked, "Fellers, did yer ever see 'Wild Bill?' That was the chap; purty boy, wasn't he? Looked as ef he wanted a hand in, didn't he though?"[32] Custer did bear a superficial resemblance to James B. "Wild Bill" Hickok, who was scouting for Hancock at the time and won George's admiration.

Custer's expedition finally set off on June 1, heading for Fort McPherson, 250 miles north, with 350 men and 20 wagons. He was to scout the area between Fort Hays and the Platte River, then move west toward Fort Sedgwick, south to Fort Wallace, and east back to Fort Hays. It was believed that there were large numbers of Cheyenne and Sioux in the area, and Custer's orders were to "hunt out and chastise" them.

The first week of the scout, they saw few signs of Indians, but there was some drama. One night the troopers found they had camped amid a large colony of rattlesnakes, which they used to augment their rations after some quick work with their sabers. Days later Colonel Wickliffe Cooper, a well-regarded officer but an alcoholic, shot himself in the head in a drunken fit and died. And when they reached the Platte after six days in the field, thirty-five men deserted in twenty-four hours—10 percent of Custer's total force.

Late in the afternoon on June 7, thirteen more men "deliberately shouldered their arms and started off for the Platte," Custer wrote, "in the presence of the entire command, in open day."[33] This bold action threatened the cohesion of the entire unit, and Custer determined that "severe and summary measures must be taken." He ordered Major Joel

Elliot, Lieutenants Tom Custer, William W. Cooke, and Henry Jackson, and a few enlisted men to "pursue the deserters who were still visible … and then bring the dead bodies of as many as could be taken back to camp."

The pursuers set out. Seven of the thirteen deserters had opened up a two-mile lead and got away. Three of the remaining six were shot and wounded, and the other three surrendered. All six were placed under arrest and hauled back to camp in a wagon. Custer at first said the wounded would not be treated, but half an hour later quietly instructed the surgeon to tend to them. One of the men, Charles Johnson, who was shot in the head and abdomen, subsequently died of his wounds. "The effect was all that could be desired," Custer wrote. "There was not another desertion as long as I remained with the command."[34]

The column resupplied at Fort McPherson, then moved up the Platte valley, passing abandoned ranches and numerous rough graves, "all that told of the fate of the poor mortals who had ventured to make a home on the Plains," as Davis put it.[35] Twelve miles up the valley, they made camp near Jack Morrow's ranch. A Sioux war leader named Pawnee Killer arrived unexpectedly with a half dozen braves, saying they "loved their white brothers" and wanted food and protection from the Cheyenne. Pawnee Killer promised Custer he would encamp quietly near Fort McPherson if permitted, and when he left, Custer gave him a supply of coffee, sugar, and hard tack.

General Sherman, who arrived the next day, was skeptical that Pawnee Killer could be trusted. He ordered Custer south to the headwaters of the Republican River to search for Indian bands, then encamp and await further instructions. Sherman had a high opinion of George; earlier that year he wrote his brother that Custer was "young, *very* brave, even to rashness, a good trait for a cavalry officer. He came to duty immediately on being appointed, and is ready and willing now to fight the Indians." Sherman said he was "bound to befriend him."[36] Sherman encouraged Custer to be ruthless with the Indians, but as the column moved up the river there were none to be found—except when they wanted to be.

At dawn on June 24, the troopers were "busy grooming and feeding our stock, at peace with all the world," one of Custer's men recalled, when "suddenly came bang, bang, bang! and most unearthly yells." They saw "hundreds of Indians, all mounted on fleet ponies, and coming for us with a vengeance." The Indians wounded a sentry and attempted to drive off the cavalrymen's horses, "until the guard opened on them such a galling fire that they were obliged to retire." Custer was impressed with the skill the Indians displayed in mounting their attack. "We had often heard of the high perfection of some of the Indian tribes in military evolutions and discipline, but here we saw evidences which went far to convince us that the red man was not far behind his more civilized brother in the art of war."[37]

A truce was called, and Custer rode out with a half dozen men to talk to the leader of the war party. It was Pawnee Killer. He recognized Custer and asked him why he had left the Platte. Custer asked where Pawnee Killer's village was and why he was not near Fort McPherson as promised. Neither got a satisfactory answer. Pawnee Killer said his heart was good and asked for more sugar and coffee, and also some ammunition, none of which was forthcoming.

After the uncomfortable parlay, Custer rode back to his camp and ordered his men to make ready for a fight. They chased Pawnee Killer and his braves, but the Indians outran the cavalrymen, and Custer returned to camp. "This was the way they returned the favor" of the supplies, Custer's trooper wrote. "Pawnee-killer said it was a mistake, and Gen. Custer let him off scot free. The peace the old fellow wanted was a piece of our hair, I presume."[38]

Later that day a small group of Indians returned and watched the camp from a nearby bluff. Captain Louis McLane Hamilton, grandson of Alexander Hamilton, and, like his grandfather, handsome and ambitious, took a party of twenty men and rode after the Indians, chasing them eight miles from camp. But this was the same ruse that had fooled Fetterman; Hamilton rode into an ambush of three hundred Sioux. His group fought doggedly for an hour and somehow managed to get back to camp suffering no losses other than one horse.

Meanwhile, things were heating up elsewhere. One of Custer's supply trains, escorted by a detachment led by Lieutenants Samuel M. Robbins and William W. Cooke, fought a three-hour, fifteen-mile running battle with around eight hundred Sioux and Cheyenne warriors, suffering two wounded. And a detachment under Captain Barnitz got into a brutal, hand-to-hand scrape with a large group of Indians near Fort Wallace, losing some killed with many wounded.[39]

In the garbled way that news was sometimes passed along from the remote frontier, the *New York Tribune*, which was skeptical of the Plains campaign, reported that "there are no signs of a speedy end to the Indian war. Five thousand Sioux forbid white men to enter their country, the Utes threaten new disturbances, and it is reported that Gen. Custer has been overpowered and killed."[40] A British newspaper echoed this report, saying, "A large force of Indians had surrounded a small body of cavalry under General Custer, and killed the whole party."[41] The *St. Cloud Journal* responded to the false report: "If Gen. Custer had killed a pack of Indians the *Tribune* would have raised a fearful howl. This Indian worship is one of the most disgusting features of Eastern sentimentalism."[42] Sherman, long an enemy of the press, said that "journalists should endeavor to ascertain the truth before shocking the public with such terrible announcements."[43]

Awaiting further orders from Sherman, Custer moved his command along the Republican, then overland to the Platte, then to Riverside Station, forty miles west of Fort Sedgwick. There he learned by telegraph that orders had been sent out with Lieutenant Lyman Kidder and a party of ten, guided by a friendly Sioux named Red Beard. Custer was ordered to continue to Fort Wallace as originally planned; en route on July 12 near Beaver Creek, he found the mutilated remains of Kidder and his party. Red Beard had been scalped but the trophy left behind, a sign that it had been a Sioux ambush, probably Pawnee Killer's band.

The next day Custer arrived at Fort Wallace. He had expected to find Libbie there to greet him. But there was no word from her, and he learned that a flash flood on the Smoky Hill River at Fort Hays where she was last staying had taken nine lives. (In fact Libbie had a harrowing experience and narrowly escaped being swept away, not that he knew.) This was too much for him. After learning that the civilians from Fort Hays had been evacuated further downstream to Fort Harker, Custer assembled a group of seventy-five officers and men led by Captain Hamilton, and on July 15 they set out.

Custer drove his men mercilessly, 150 miles in fifty-five hours. The weather was hot and the way dangerous. "The Indians swarm along the route," one report noted, "and are bolder and more determined than ever before."[44] Near Downer's Station some of Custer's men who had lingered to the rear a few miles were attacked by a band of Cheyenne, and two were killed. Custer refused to take the time to send back a party to retrieve the bodies of the dead.

He arrived at Fort Harker early on the morning of July 19 and learned that Libbie had been sent safely to Fort Riley. He reported to Colonel Smith and asked permission to continue east. Smith, half-asleep and not knowing whether Custer was operating on orders from Sherman, allowed him to take the first morning train.

Several hours later George was reunited with Libbie. She closed her memoir, *Tenting on the Plains*, with a description of the scene, echoing the romance of her reunion with George in Richmond at the end of the Civil War:

> After days of such gloom, my leaden heart one morning
> quickened its beats at an unusual sound—the clank of a saber

on our gallery and with it the quick, springing steps of feet, unlike the quiet infantry around us. The door, behind which I paced uneasily, opened, and with a flood of sunshine that poured in, came a vision far brighter than even the brilliant Kansas sun. There, before me, blithe and buoyant, stood my husband! In an instant, every moment of the preceding months was obliterated. What had I to ask more?... There was in that summer of 1867 one long, perfect day.[45]

But at the end of the "long, perfect day," George Custer received some alarming news. Colonel Smith had made inquiries regarding Custer's journey and, finding he had no orders to leave his command at Fort Wallace, had Custer placed under arrest.

The Custer court-martial convened September 15 at Fort Leavenworth. The prosecutor was Captain Robert Chandler, judge advocate. Custer was defended by a West Point classmate, Captain Charles C. Parsons.[46] The presiding officer was Colonel William Hoffman, an 1829 Academy grad, and seven other officers served on the court, including another Custer classmate, Captain Stephen Lyford.

Custer faced three charges with eight specifications, most importantly conduct prejudicial to good order and military discipline, and absence without leave from his command. Conduct prejudicial included marching his men on "private business" (his search for Libbie). He was also taken to task for not returning for the bodies of the men killed near Downer's Station or pursuing the Indians who killed them.[47]

Captain Robert M. West raised the additional matter of shooting deserters without a trial, since Charles Johnson, the man who had died from the wounds he received while being apprehended, had served in his company. He also said the prisoners were treated cruelly, being denied water in the heat and forced to ride tied up in rough wagons.

Custer believed Hancock had prompted West to press this part of the case in order to shift attention from the fact that the Indian campaign had been a failure.

Hancock—known as "the Superb" for his Civil War exploits—was having trouble adapting to Plains warfare. The Indian Commission had held hearings at Fort Leavenworth shortly before Custer's court-martial, and most of the testimony was negative. "It would have been far better for the interests of all concerned had [Hancock] never entered the Indian country with his soldiers," Superintendent of Indian Affairs Thomas Murphy assessed. "Indians who at the time he got into the country were peaceable and well disposed towards the whites, are now fleeing with their women and children, no one knows whither, and what the final result will be is doubtful."[48] Given this backdrop, Custer and those sympathetic to his case thought he was being used as a scapegoat.

Custer pleaded not guilty to all charges and specifications, and the trial commenced. Many witnesses were called, including the officers involved in the events (including Tom Custer), some of the enlisted men, and the surgeon who treated the wounded men (who backed Custer's story). Captain West, a spree drinker, was considered too volatile to be an effective witness, and the prosecution kept him off the stand. Generally the case came down less to the facts, on which many agreed, and more to whether Custer's actions were justifiable.

Custer never took the stand but submitted a lengthy written statement, which sought to lend reasonable context to what happened. He argued he was out on the frontier commanding a relatively small force, unsupported by other units, with hostile Indians on the warpath. His command had already suffered many desertions, and a scheme was afoot for a mass break of perhaps a third of his force. Of the thirteen men who deserted on the day in question, over half got away. When the pursuers neared the remaining six, three of them dismounted and raised their carbines at them—actions not unusual in these cases, and meriting the use of deadly force in return. Three were wounded in the ensuing shootout, one seriously. The wounded were taken in wagons as opposed to ambulances because the ambulances were unserviceable. If faced with another such desertion, Custer said he would do the same thing. His determined action stopped desertions from the unit, at least for the time being.

From Custer's point of view, a "shoot to kill" order made sense under the circumstances. Peacetime executions for desertion were outlawed in 1830, but Custer's defense produced orders, including from General Hancock, saying if men were caught in the act of deserting to "shoot them down when taken."[49] As for the charge of cruelty, it had to be put in context. This was still the era where being "branded a deserter" was not just a figure of speech. Tattooing and branding were legal forms of punishment until 1872—including being branded with the entire word "deserter."[50] The men could get over a bumpy wagon ride.

Custer also maintained that he was never absent without leave from his unit; he acted on his own discretion when temporarily without orders. And his team raised technical objections to the composition of the court, noting that four of its members were inferior to him in rank and another was a commissary officer he had censured for corruption.[51] Equally problematic, Custer pointed out that Captain Lyford was one of his classmates and a close friend.

On September 26 Custer wrote with confidence, "The prosecution have examined about half their witnesses, including the most important. I would not hesitate to let my case go to the court on the evidence addressed by the prosecution.... Everything is working charmingly."[52] But Custer was in more trouble than he thought. The monthlong trial drew to a close on October 11, and after deliberating a few hours the court returned its verdict. Custer was found guilty on almost all the charges and specifications, except for those related to intentional cruelty. However, the court attached no criminality to his actions, and Custer was sentenced to be suspended from rank, command, and pay for one year.

Some, such as General Grant, thought Custer got off easy. Others, such as Sheridan, believed that he never should have been brought to trial. Libbie believed "the sentence is as unjust as possible. Autie merits acquittal."[53] For George himself, it was the low point in his career. With the 7th Cavalry drawn up in parade, Custer had to sit on horseback before the command as the orders of the court were read. He sat stiffly, showing no emotion, looking out at the horizon. He was a long way from the cheers of the Grand Review in Washington two and a half years earlier.

PART FIVE

REDEMPTION

THE SEVENTH U.S. CAVALRY CHARGING INTO BLACK KETTLE'S VILLAGE AT DAYLIGHT, November 27, 1868.—[See Page 811.]

The Seventh U.S. Cavalry Charging in Black Kettle's Village at Daylight (Battle of Washita), from *Harper's Weekly*, December 19, 1868.

CHAPTER TWENTY-TWO

WASHITA

Custer met the guilty verdicts with a brave face, but privately he was fuming. "All with whom I have conversed decree the sentence unjustly severe," he wrote. "It is not sustained by the evidence." But he asked Sheridan not to try to review the case or lessen the sentence, "as I will not accept it."[1] Libbie dismissed the affair as "nothing but a plan of persecution for Autie."[2]

The court-martial was another blow to Custer's reputation. One Michigan paper said that the trial "very materially changes our opinion of the man" and that it was "sufficient in itself to justify the dismissal of any officer."[3] Custer's affidavit in defense was summarized and reprinted in various papers, but he did not have a deep well of support. His excesses in Texas in 1865 and foray into politics in 1866 had alienated many editors and politicians on both sides of the political divide who otherwise might have spoken up in his defense.

Sheridan, who took over command of the Department of Missouri from Hancock just as Custer's trial began, remained an important and durable Custer ally. He graciously let George and Libbie use his quarters at Fort Leavenworth while he was on leave, and the couple settled in for the winter.

"I have nothing to do but to kill time," George wrote, "which I manage to do quite successfully."[4] It hardly seemed like punishment. Libbie's cousin Rebecca Richmond, who visited the couple during this period, wrote in her diary that their time was taken up with singing, games, hunting, theater, hops, and parties.[5] A typical entry, from January 3, 1868, read, "Armstrong and Libbie, Charles, Mary and I rode over to town this morning in the flanigan [carriage]. A bright, beautiful day but a trifle cooler than yesterday.... Sang as we rode, also ate an apple which was presented by an outrider, a cavalryman." But then Rebecca notes, "This evening just before retreat, Gen'l Custer was arrested by two officers from town on a charge of murder."[6]

Shooting the deserters still came back to haunt Custer. Captain West pressed the state of Kansas to charge Custer and William W. Cooke for the murder of Charles Johnson, the deserter who had been shot in the head and later died. Custer was implicated as an accomplice for giving the order to shoot and denying medical care afterward. Cooke was charged with pulling the trigger.

The case was initially dismissed for lack of jurisdiction, since the incident took place in Nebraska. But a second attempt led to a court hearing at Fort Leavenworth, including testimony from Clement Willis, one of the deserters. As in the court-martial, however, witnesses were vague or conflicting on key aspects of the events, and one newspaper concluded that "there appeared little doubt but the officers would be acquitted."[7] On January 18 the judge dismissed the charges for lack of sufficient evidence.[8] Custer retaliated by having West brought up on charges of drunkenness, garnering him a two-month suspension.

After the winter at Fort Leavenworth, the Custers went back to Monroe, where George spent time writing, fishing, tending to his horses, and on other pursuits. Meanwhile, after failing to bring about a military solution to the troubles on the Plains, the government sent a peace commission to try negotiating. Members of the commission included, among others, General Sherman, Brigadier General Alfred Terry, and old Indian fighter General William S. Harney, now retired, who had become an advocate for fair play with the tribes.[9]

In October 1867 at Medicine Lodge River, the commissioners met with the leaders of many of the southern Plains tribes, including Black Kettle of the Cheyenne, Satanta or White Bear of the Kiowa, and Ten Bears of the Comanche. The peace delegates opened with an apology for the burning of the village at Pawnee Fork that started Hancock's campaign, an implicit admission that the entire effort had been a mistake. The Indians were willing to deal, and tribal leaders agreed to move south of the Arkansas River and to end raids into Kansas and other settled areas. This would clear the main route west for railroads and settlements. They also agreed to move onto reservation lands in exchange for food, periodic payments, guns and ammunition for hunting, and other forms of support. The series of agreements was known collectively as the Medicine Lodge Treaty.

Peace was made with the northern Plains tribes under the Treaty of Fort Laramie in February 1868. Under this agreement the forts along the Bozeman Trail were abandoned, and whites were banned from the Power River country. The government established the Great Sioux Reservation, which comprised all the land west of the Missouri River in the southern part of the Dakota Territory, including the Black Hills. In addition, hunting lands were reserved for the Sioux, Cheyenne, and Arapaho in Wyoming, Montana, western Kansas, and eastern Colorado. It was a victory for Red Cloud, who achieved all his war objectives—but only if both sides honored the treaty.

Hopes for a peaceful year on the Plains began to wilt as the new grass grew. Headlines in the summer told of Indian raids, rapes, kidnappings, burnings, scalpings, mutilations, and attacks on wagon trains and settlers. A lieutenant and five men from Fort Larned were ambushed and killed. The government responded by holding back the arms and ammunition promised to the Indians for hunting; the Indians saw this as a betrayal. "The hope which was cherished," the *Philadelphia Evening Telegraph* opined, "that difficulties with the Indians on the Plains would be avoided during the present year, has proved delusive. The savage fondness for plunder and scalps has again been displayed.... It is as difficult for the bold spirits of the predatory tribes to restrain their murderous proclivities as it is for the hardened professional criminals of civilized life to become honest men."[10]

One attack that gained national attention took place in October. Seventy-five Indians waylaid a large wagon train along the Arkansas River, heading from Kansas to Colorado. Four wagons were captured, some of the others were lit with flaming arrows, and the ox teams were run off. The Indian band swelled to around two hundred warriors, and a weeklong siege commenced. Eventually soldiers arrived and the Indians withdrew, but they took with them twenty-year-old Clara, wife of settler Richard Blinn, and their two-year-old son, Willie. A note found four miles away read, "Dear Dick, Willie and I are prisoners. They are going to keep us. If you live, save us if you can."

Sheridan said that Clara was kept alive "to gratify the brutal lust of the chief, Satanta." Satanta, a signatory of the Medicine Lodge Treaty, was a noted Kiowa warrior with a dramatic flair. During the 1867 campaign, Hancock had been so impressed with the chief after meeting with him that he gave him a U.S. Army jacket with the rank of major general, a yellow sash, and plumed hat. A month later Satanta's men raided Fort Dodge and drove off the garrison's horses; the chief raised the plumed hat as he rode away.[11]

In another, longer letter in November, Clara wrote that the Indians told her, "When the white men make peace we can go home." She urged, "Do all you can for me. Write to the peace commissioners to make peace this fall. For our sakes do all you can and God will bless you.... I am as well as can be expected, but my baby is very weak."[12] The letter was sent to Colonel William B. Hazen of the 38th Infantry regiment, on special Indian duty at Fort Cobb. (This was the same Hazen who had arrested Cadet Custer in June 1861 for the fistfight incident the day before graduation.) He was involved in negotiations for Clara's release; the deal at that point stood at five ponies for the woman and her son. He forwarded the letter to Sherman, who sent it to the secretary of war, who used it to lobby Congress to keep up the fight against the Indians.

To many Americans the continued violence on the Plains seemed to violate the letter and spirit of the peace treaties. However, that was open to interpretation. Indians understood treaties differently than whites, and some bands could rightly claim not to be party to agreements they did not sign, even if others in their tribe did. And there were generational conflicts in the bands that agreed to the terms. The young men with something to prove were vexed by the old chiefs telling them to abandon the ways of the warrior. "The Indians feel that they are rich when at war and poor while at peace," noted Theodore R. Davis, who rode with Custer on the Hancock expedition. "There are many old chiefs who prefer peace, but the young men are invariably for war. The chiefs cannot control the 'bucks,' who take the war-path as naturally as the quail does the bushes or the young ducks to the sedge."[13]

Such nuances did not impress General Sherman, who wrote to Secretary of War John M. Schofield, "All the Cheyennes & Arapahoes are now at war. Admitting that some of them have not done acts of murder, rape, etc., still they have not restrained those who have; nor have they on demand given up the criminals as they agreed to do. The treaty made at Medicine Lodge is, therefore, already broken by them." Sherman said that "after a reasonable time given for the innocent to withdraw, I will solicit an order from the President declaring all Indians who remain outside of their lawful reservations to be outlaws, and commanding all people—soldiers & citizens—to proceed against them as such."[14]

After the failure of Hancock's wandering expedition the previous year, the Army experimented with other tactics. At the end of the summer of 1868, Sheridan organized a fifty-four-man mobile force of experienced frontiersmen commanded by brevet Colonel George A. Forsyth, his former chief of staff during the Shenandoah Valley campaign. The concept was to send out a light mobile force without baggage trains, carrying their supplies and ammunition with them, to match the Indians' mobility and fight them in their own manner.[15] But this increased mobility came at the expense of firepower; even if Forsyth found the Indians, his men could not bring on a decisive fight.

In any case, they did not have to track down the enemy—the Indians came looking for them. On September 17, after two weeks in the field, Forsyth's group was waylaid on an island in the Arikaree River in Colorado by Cheyenne Dog Soldiers under the command of Roman Nose. The Army troops were quickly pinned down and surrounded. They fought a three-day siege, eating meat from their fallen horses and drinking muddy river water. By the time a relief party arrived, they had suffered six men killed (one of them, Beecher, gave his name to the island) and fifteen wounded. Forsyth was severely wounded and reported dead, but he recovered. The Indians lost an estimated ten to thirty, including Roman Nose, who died charging the soldiers on horseback.[16] Custer later called it "the greatest battle on the plains."[17] But other than killing Roman Nose, the Battle of Beecher Island only showed the limits of trying to fight Indian style.

So Sheridan turned to a new strategy. The Indians lacked the capacity and inclination to campaign in the winter. The signing of the

Medicine Lodge Treaty in October underscored the traditional pattern of Indian warfare, with intervals of peace in the winter followed by renewed activity once the grass reappeared in the late spring. In the summer of 1865, Major General Grenville M. Dodge laid out the logic of striking the Indians off-season, observing that the Indians on the warpath were "not making any provisions for winter; are not hunting, planting, laying in meat, or in any way providing for the future as they usually do. The consequence will be that we will in the fall and winter have them at great disadvantage."[18]

Reporter Theodore Davis interviewed a messenger heading for Hancock's command in April 1867. The seasoned Plainsman thought talk of treaties was an attempt to buy time. "The soldiers will learn what nonsense it is to undertake to fight Indians during the summer season," he said, offering that winter was "the time to go for their villages. They know they can't escape, because their ponies are too poor to carry them; so they will stay by and fight." Defeating Indian mobility was the key to victory. "If the Indians are whipped at this time of year there will be some show for peace for the rest of the summer; otherwise they will fight all summer, and make peace in the fall."[19] Everything the anonymous messenger predicted came true.

As the fall of 1868 approached, Sheridan began planning for a winter campaign. Some thought the plan was too risky, but Sheridan reasoned that "as the soldier was much better fed and clothed than the Indian, I had one great advantage." He planned to "fall upon the savages relentlessly, for in [winter] their ponies would be thin, and weak from lack of food, and in the cold and snow, without strong ponies to transport their villages and plunder, their movements would be so much impeded that the troops could overtake them."[20]

Sherman approved the concept. He wrote to General Dodge, then a member of Congress from Iowa, "[W]e propose not to let up all winter

& before spring comes I hope not an Indian will be left in that belt of country through which the two railroads pass."[21] It was the same rapacity he had brought to his march through Georgia.

Sheridan wanted Custer to lead the winter campaign. He appealed to Sherman, who approved Custer's reinstatement in late September, cutting about eight weeks off his sentence. He was ordered "to report in person without delay to Maj. Gen. Sheridan for duty." George left Michigan immediately, eager to validate the trust that Sheridan and Sherman were placing in him. "I rely in every thing upon you," Sheridan wrote, "and shall send you on this expedition without giving you any orders leaving you to act entirely upon your judgment."[22]

"I can whip the Indians if I can find them," Custer wrote, "and I shall leave no effort untried to do this. I have a difficult task before me but I am confident that if the Indians can be found I can do it as well as most persons could."[23]

The impending winter campaign was by no means a secret. The Army would have preferred the Indians come onto the reservations, so they spread the word. In late September, Sherman instructed Colonel Hazen to "give out general notice that all Comanches, Kiowas, Cheyennes, and Arapahoes, that wish to escape the effects of the present Indian war, should now remove to the Reservation assigned them in their treaty at the Medicine Lodge." He went on to say, "General Sheridan shall prosecute the war with vindictive earnestness against all hostile Indians till they are obliterated or beg for mercy, and therefore all who want peace must get out of the theatre of war."[24] Indian agents Boone and Wynkoop would be on hand to distribute annuities to Indians who came in. They were supplied with $50,000 to make the arrangements for food, blankets, and other materials. Hazen was to establish himself at Fort Cobb after sending word out, and "if the Indians do not come, it is not his or our fault."[25]

Hazen got the word out as ordered, but it offended more Indians than it attracted. Part of the problem was that the Indians did not know the limits of the reservations, and some of the agents had established their headquarters far outside reservation lands, defeating the purpose of keeping the Indians stationary.

On November 20–21 Hazen met with a delegation of Arapahoe and Cheyenne chiefs headed by Little Big Mouth and Black Kettle. Both said they wanted peace, but they could not control every band in their tribes. "I do not represent all the Cheyennes," Black Kettle said. "I come from a point on the Washita River, about one day's ride from Antelope Hills. Near me there are over one hundred lodges of my tribe, only a part of them are my followers. I have always done my best to keep my young men quiet, but some of them will not listen." Black Kettle said he would "like to stop fighting, and come here soon with my people, and stay here with these Indian friends of mine, and be fed until the war is over."[26]

Hazen warned the chiefs he faced a similar situation. "North of the Arkansas is General Sheridan, the great war-chief," he told them. "I cannot control him, and he has all the soldiers, who are fighting the Cheyennes and Arapahoes. … You must go back to your country, and if the soldiers come to attack you, you must remember they are not from me, but from that great war-chief, and with him you must make Peace."

Hazen quickly sent word to Sherman that a deal with these two bands would bring in most of the Indians "on the war-path south of the Arkansas." But Hazen was unclear what he could promise them, or whether he had any authority to negotiate peace. "I should prefer that General Sheridan should make peace with these parties," he wrote, and feared that "as General Sheridan is to punish those at war … a second Chivington affair might occur which I could not prevent."[27]

Hazen was referring to the incident that took place November 29, 1864, near Sand Creek in southeastern Colorado, when the Colorado

Militia under Colonel John Chivington attacked Black Kettle's camp without provocation and killed over 150 men, women, and children. Black Kettle thought his people were safe and flew an American flag to show loyalty to the Union. Indian agent Ned Wynkoop, then a major in the 1st Colorado Volunteer regiment, had tried to broker a peace deal, but Chivington attacked anyway. The Sand Creek Massacre became a notorious incident in the history of relations with the Indians.

Despite Hazen's wish for peace, the next day Custer was on the march. On November 23, his regiment moved south from their base at Camp Supply on the North Canadian River in what today would be western Oklahoma. The weather was cold, and as the column began its march, a fresh snowstorm blew in, adding to the foot-deep snow blanket that covered the countryside. But Custer's force of around eight hundred was well trained and motivated, and the fresh snow would make tracking the Indian bands that much easier.

Custer's column was accompanied by *New York Herald* reporter DeBenneville Randolph Keim, a friend of president-elect Grant's who had accompanied Sherman on the march to the sea.[28] He wrote that Custer's operations order from Sheridan was straightforward: "To proceed south, in the direction of the Antelope hills, thence towards the Washita river, the supposed winter seat of the hostile tribes; to destroy their villages and ponies; to kill or hang all warriors, and bring back all women and children." Sheridan believed this no-quarter approach would level the playing field with the Indians and represented "two parties playing at the same game."[29] He declared he would march over the Indian villages "if he had to go all the way to Texas."[30]

Custer's column moved toward the Indian winter villages along the Washita River led by Osage scouts, the traditional enemies and frequent victims of the more numerous and warlike Cheyenne. Also along were experienced trackers "Old California Joe" Corbin, Raphael Romero, and Little Beaver. On November 26 the scouts "called our attention to a trail resembling a 'buffalo path' which was covered with snow," Albert Barnitz wrote. But "it should have been deeper, if the path had been made by buffaloes"—the track had actually been made by a band of Indians, but "whether a war party or a hunting party we could not tell." They followed this trail for some distance until they came to another, fresher trail, "which had obviously been made in the afternoon of the previous, by a war party of from one to two hundred Indians. It was known to be a war party from the fact that the Indians had no dogs with them, whereas hunting parties are always accompanied by dogs."[31] They sent word to Custer that they were going to follow the trail until they received further orders, and made sure their weapons were loaded and unfrozen in case of trouble.

That night the Osage scouts reported that they had tracked the war party back to a village on the Washita, where they had seen "heaps ponies." Custer went forward to scout the location himself. He crept through the snow along a ridgeline to look down on the valley by the light of the half moon. They were looking at the pony herd, but the figures were indistinct in the dim light; one officer said they were buffalo, until they heard the tinkle of a bell. The leader of the Osages repeated, "Heaps ponies."

"I am satisfied they are ponies, the herd of the village," Custer whispered back. "Buffaloes are not in the habit of wearing such ornaments as bells in this country."[32] Below them, across the Washita on a high bank in a strip of trees, stood the fifty-one lodges of Black Kettle's band.

Custer left eighty men back with the baggage train, and as quietly as possible brought up the rest. He divided them into four columns, which would attack the village from separate directions. They moved cautiously into position in the darkness, making as little noise as possible, to preserve the element of surprise. When they reached their attack positions, the men waited, standing in the deep snow, some of them sleeping leaning on their horses. As dawn approached, Captain Francis M. Gibson recalled listening intently for the attack signal, the regiment's trademark song, "Garryowen": "At last the inspiring strains of the rollicking tune broke forth, filling the early morning air with joyous music. The profound silence that had reigned through the night was suddenly changed to a pandemonium of tumult and excitement; the wild notes of 'Garryowen' which had resounded from hill to hill, were answered by wilder shouts of exultation from the charging columns."

"We had just reached the edge of a shallow ravine beyond which we could see the clustered tepees, situated among wide-branching cottonwood trees," Albert Barnitz wrote,

> when a shot was fired in the village, and instantly we heard the band on the ridge beyond it strike up the familiar air "Garry Owen" and the answering cheers of the men, as Custer, and his legion came thundering down the long divide, while nearer at hand on our right came Benteen's squadron, crashing through the frozen snow, as the troops deployed into line at a gallop, and the Indian village range with unearthly war-whoops, the quick discharge of fire-arms, the clamorous barking of dogs, the cries of infants and the wailing of women.

"We played one strain through," band member Henry Meder recalled, "then our instruments all froze up."[33]

"With cheers that strongly reminded me of scenes during the war," Custer wrote to Sheridan, "every trooper, led by his officer, rushed toward the village."[34] George led from the front as the four columns converged on the lodges. He was the first in the village, and fought through to the south side where he directed the battle from atop a low hill. Captain Hamilton, charging by his side, was shot from his mount and killed.

"The sleeping and unsuspecting savages were completely surprised by the onset," Sheridan wrote.[35] Some warriors were killed as they emerged from their teepees. Others managed to fight back, with rifles or hand-to-hand. Women and children ran about the village in fear, or hid in the lodges, and many fell victim to the hail of gunfire. "In the excitement of the fight, as well as in self defense," Custer noted, "it so happened that some of the squaws and a few children were killed and wounded." One count had around ninety-two women, children, and old men killed, along with ten warriors, but Cheyenne chiefs later told Custer thirteen men, sixteen women, and nine children were killed.[36]

Black Kettle rushed from his lodge and jumped on a horse, pulling up his wife Medicine Woman Later behind him. They tried to cross the river but were felled in a fusillade of bullets, killing them and the horse. Little Rock, the second senior chief after Black Kettle, tried to mount a defense until he was shot down by Major Elliott.[37] Seeing a small group of Indians fleeing downstream, Elliot rode off in pursuit with nineteen troopers shouting, "Here goes for a brevet or a coffin!"[38]

The battle subsided as the morning wore on. "Light skirmishing is going on all around," Frederick Benteen wrote. "Savages on flying steeds, with shields and feathers gay, are circling everywhere, riding like devils incarnate. The troops are on all sides of the village, looking on and seizing every opportunity of picking off some of those daring riders with their carbines."[39] A few charges scattered whatever organized resistance remained. The troopers took time to eat and rest as the Indian scouts collected scalps.

Custer took stock. He had successfully attacked what he believed to be a hostile band, and demonstrated that offensive operations in the winter were possible. His losses had been slight—only a few killed that he knew of, and some wounded, including his brother Tom and Captain Barnitz. Fifty-three women and children were taken captive. Custer's men sorted through the camp and discovered evidence suggesting that some in the group had been raiding. They saved various artifacts; Custer later sent the Detroit Audubon Club a buffalo hide shield, a bow and arrows, a beaded buckskin dress, and a ten-inch knotted scalp, said to be that of Little Rock.[40]

After picking over the camp, they prepared the rest for burning. "The plunder having been culled over, is hastily piled," Benteen wrote, "the wigwams are pulled down and thrown on it, and soon the whole is one blazing mass. Occasionally a startling report is heard and a steamlike volume of smoke ascends as the fire reaches a powder bag, and thus the glorious deeds of valor done in the morning are celebrated by the flaming bonfire of the afternoon."[41]

"All that was left of the village were a few heaps of blackened ashes," Custer wrote. The eight hundred ponies and mules in the herd were killed to deny them to other Indian bands, Custer himself picking off a few that were straggling through the village.

Sounds of the battle had echoed down the valley and alerted Indians in nearby camps. Presently warriors appeared along the ridgeline, watching the soldiers and taking some pot shots. "The firing was kept up by the Indians out, on the bluff, on our left front, all day," Henry Meder recalled.[42] Custer established a defensive ring around the village and distributed ammunition. He did not know how many Indians were in the vicinity, but he assumed they outnumbered his force. His supplies and ammunition were limited, and his pack train was miles away. He could not stay at the village; there was no relief column coming or even a prospect of other forces being sent to secure the position. The day was wearing, and Custer concluded he had to leave or be surrounded and put under siege.

Custer assembled his men and prisoners and began to march loudly downstream toward the next village, of Arapahos. This had the intended effect; the warriors who had been observing his force withdrew quickly and rushed ahead to spread the alarm. But after the Indians disappeared,

Custer abruptly turned his column back toward his pack train and made for Camp Supply, the band playing "Ain't I Glad to Get Out of the Wilderness." The Indians did not give chase, and Custer returned to the post on December 2.

"The head of Custer's column made its appearance on the distant hills," Sheridan recalled, "the friendly Osage scouts and the Indian prisoners in advance." Sheridan noted their "wild and picturesque performance in celebration of the victory, yelling, firing their guns, throwing themselves on the necks and sides of their horses to exhibit their skill in riding, and going through all sorts of barbaric evolutions and gyrations," and that night "the rejoicings were ended with the hideous scalp dance."

The rest of Custer's column arrived after the scouts, but Major Elliott was missing. He and his small band had vanished down the Washita. Days later, Custer, Sheridan, and one hundred soldiers returned to the site to learn their fate. The bodies were found in a small circle two miles from the village, "stripped as naked as when born, and frozen stiff," Frederick Benteen recalled. "Their heads had been battered in, and some of them had been entirely chopped off; some of them had had the Adam's apple cut out of their throats; some had their hands and feet cut off, and nearly all had been horribly mangled in a way delicacy forbids me to mention."[43]

"The little piles of empty cartridge shells near each body showed plainly that every man had made a brave fight," Sheridan wrote. "None were scalped, but most of them were otherwise horribly mutilated, which fiendish work is usually done by the squaws." The bodies were identified and buried.

Clara Blinn and her son turned up at an abandoned Kiowa village ten miles away. She had been shot twice in the forehead, and the back of her skull was smashed. "The body presented the appearance of a woman of more than ordinary beauty," one report noted, "small in figure, and not more than twenty-two years of age."[44] Sheridan, who was present at the discovery, noted that the powder from the weapon used to kill her had "horribly disfigured her face." One of her hands gripped a piece of corn cake, indicating she may have been eating or feeding her son when she was killed. Willie, who showed signs of starvation, had been grabbed by the feet and his head smashed against a tree. The bodies were wrapped in blankets and taken from the site, eventually being interred at Fort Arbuckle. A piece of Clara's calico dress and a lock of Willie's hair were sent to her husband.

"The Kiowas have been engaged in the war all the time, and have been playing fast and loose," Sheridan threatened after he returned. "I will take the starch out of them before I leave them."[45] Satanta, the Kiowa leader who had captured Clara, surrendered to Custer on December 17 along with Chief Lone Wolf, hoping to avoid the fate that befell Black Kettle. Instead, Custer had Satanta placed under arrest and sought permission to hang him for murder. Satanta was held until February when Chief Tene-angopte negotiated his release, promising that the Kiowa would return to the reservation.

Custer called Washita a "complete and gratifying success" and "a regular Indian 'Sailor's Creek.'" Once again he had redeemed himself through battle. The *New York Times* also praised the outcome of Washita. "Gen. Custer, in defeating and killing Black Kettle, has put an end to one of the most troublesome and dangerous characters on the plains," the paper said. "A permanent peace can now be obtained through energetic and successful war.... 'stout hearts' will do much; and one or two repetitions of Custer's victory will give us peace on the Plains."[46]

Sheridan said the battle sent a message to the Indians that there would be no traditional winter truce. He justified the attack on Black Kettle, saying his group was "one of the most villainous of the hostile bands," and if the sixty-eight-year-old chief did not personally participate in the depredations of the braves, he "freely encouraged them by 'making medicine,' and by other devilish incantations," and it was age alone that kept him back from joining them.[47]

Hazen said that Black Kettle had admitted to him less than a week before the battle that "many of his men were then on the war path, and that his people did not want peace with the people above the Arkansas."[48] But Hazen also criticized the campaign in a pamphlet entitled *Some Corrections of "My Life on the Plains,"* a direct response to Custer's published account.

Critics condemned the non-combatant casualties, the women, children, and elderly who were caught in the crossfire. In January 1869 the Cherokee, Creek, and Choctaw Indian delegates in Washington called for an investigation. Custer denied having specifically targeted women and children, but the bloody reputation he gained at Washita stuck in some quarters. Agent Ned Wynkoop maintained that Black Kettle thought he was on the reservation when his band was attacked and could have been reasoned with instead of attacked, with no loss of life. Wynkoop resigned his position two days after the battle—he had not yet heard what happened, but he anticipated the outcome. The Cheyenne had initially blamed him for the 1864 incident at Sand Creek, and he would not be left in that position again. He said he refused to be "the instrument of the murder of innocent women and children."[49]

Custer was also criticized for leaving the battlefield without determining what happened to Major Elliott or mounting a rescue operation. This built on the charges raised at his court-martial that during the forced march to Fort Harken he had in effect abandoned some of his straggling troops to the Indians. Frederick Benteen wrote a pathos-laden letter to his friend William J. De Gresse, imagining the death struggle of Elliott and his men and painting Custer as negligent. De Gresse gave the letter to the St. Louis Democrat, which published it anonymously, and it was later reprinted in the *New York Times*. Benteen's letter made this aspect of the battle very public, and Custer told his officers he would horsewhip the author if he found him. Benteen then admitted he had written it. Custer eyed him for a moment, then dismissed him saying, "Mr. Benteen, I will see you later."

Sheridan's campaign continued after Washita, with other officers gaining similar results. On Christmas Day 1868, six companies of the 3rd Cavalry and one of the 37th Infantry led by brevet Lieutenant Colonel A. W. Evans descended on a Comanche village south of the junction of Salt Fork and Elm Creek. They captured and burned sixty lodges as most of the Indians fled. "The Indians kept up fighting during the day and the next morning," one report read, "but there was not much fight in them."[50] On the last day of 1868, a delegation of twenty-one Arapahoe and Cheyenne chiefs arrived at Fort Cobb begging for peace. They asked for no terms, "but for a paper to protect them from the operations of our troops while *en route*. They report the tribes in mourning for their losses, their people starving, their dogs all eaten up, and no buffalo." Sheridan said his campaign was "the final blow to the backbone of the Indian rebellion."[51] An old chief complained that the winter campaign allowed the Indians no time "to get their seats warm."[52] In January 1869, when Comanche Chief Toch-a-way or Turtle Dove finally came to Fort Cobb, he struck himself on the chest and told Sheridan, "Me Toch-a-way, me good Indian." Sheridan replied, so the story goes, "The only good Indians I ever saw were dead."[53]

Custer had not lost his taste for taking risks. Over the next few months he would place himself in danger a number of times, meeting with Indians who might just as well have sought vengeance on him. "Yesterday a grand council was held near my tent," he wrote Libbie. "All the head chiefs of the Apaches, Kiowas, Arapahoes, Comaches, Cheyennes were present. I was alone with them except for an officer who took stenographic notes."[54] He campaigned into the spring, trying to bring in the last of the recalcitrant bands. He talked Sheridan into allowing him to take a small force into what had been Cheyenne country at the headwaters of the Red River, not to fight but to negotiate. "At first I was inclined to disapprove Custer's proposition," Sheridan recalled, "but he urged it so strongly that I finally consented, though with some misgivings." Sheridan was concerned that Custer's appearing with "so small a party might tempt the Cheyennes to forget their pacific professions and seek to avenge the destruction of Black Kettle's band."

Custer set out with a few officers, forty men, and intermediaries Yellow Bear and Little Robe. But after days of searching, Custer could not find the Indians he sought. He set out again with a much larger force, a column of 1,500 that the Cheyenne could not as easily ignore. Early reports from couriers promised success. Then the news turned grim. Major Ames at Fort Lyons was reported saying Custer was captured by Indians around March 10.[55] Two weeks later, the *New York Times* reported that Custer was "corralled" by the Indians. Custer's men were "nearly without horses, and the impression prevailed among those best informed, that the General and his command were in a tight place." He was supposedly waylaid by Kiowa under Lone Wolf and Satanta seeking payback for his imprisonment, Arapahos led by Little Raven, and Cheyenne out for vengeance after Washita. "One of the most terrible Indian wars that has yet been waged on the Plains will break out this spring," the paper speculated.[56]

But none of this was true. The same day the *New York Times* reported Custer basically done for, he sent word to Sheridan his expedition had been a success.[57] He had pressed his force swiftly across the Plains, outpacing the Indians, and eventually ran down a village of 260 lodges. Custer first thought to attack, but then learned that the Cheyenne held two white women, Mrs. Morgan and Miss White, and it would have been certain death for them if he just went in with guns blazing.

Custer rode up to the village with a small party, and Chief Stone Forehead, the Keeper of the Sacred Arrows, came out to meet him. After a brief parlay they repaired to his lodge. Along the way Custer saw that the village was in a great state of excitement, ready for a fight. Among them were the Dog Soldiers, which one paper called "the most mischievous, bloodthirsty and barbarous band of Indians that infest the Plains."[58] This was another reason for caution; Custer did not think his weary men would be up to the fight.

Custer sat with the tribal chiefs and smoked a long sacred pipe. He describes the solemn ceremony in detail in *My Life on the Plains* from the perspective of a "disinterested observer" even though he was a central part of the proceedings. "A desire to conform as far as practicable to the wishes of the Indians," he wrote, "and a curiosity to study a new and interesting phase of the Indian character, prompted me to obey the direction of the medicine man, and I accordingly began puffing away with as great a degree of nonchalance as a man unaccustomed to smoking could well assume."[59] Custer admits he almost got sick from having to smoke almost an entire bowl, but he persisted and the pipe made the rounds. Yet Custer failed to mention in his account that when the pipe returned to Stone Forehead, he tapped out the ashes from the bowl on Custer's boots, cautioning him that if he ever broke faith with the Cheyenne, he would become like those ashes.

Custer did not take long to wound Cheyenne pride. Later in the day, after returning to his camp, he took Chiefs Big Head and Dull Knife hostage and threatened to hang them unless the white hostages were released. "Only when the rope and tree were chosen did the Indians deliver up their captives," the *New York Herald* reported.

Sheridan was exultant with Custer's performance in the campaign. He promised to press for a promotion for his young protégé and told Custer to take a long leave, "as long as you please." Custer said that the campaign "taught the Indians that they are safe from us in no place, and at no season, and also what some of our people may doubt, that the white man can endure the inclemencies of winter better than Indians."[60] He reported back to headquarters that he held "captive Cheyenne chiefs as hostages for the good behavior of their tribe, and for the fulfillment of the promise of the latter to come in and conform to the demands of the government."

He concluded, "This I consider is the end of the Indian war."[61]

CUSTER ON THE PLAINS

"How many military men have reaped laurels from their Indian campaigns?" George Custer wrote, years after Washita. "Does he strive to win the approving smile of his countrymen? That is indeed, in this particular instance, a difficult task."[1] The press and politicians both exalted and condemned Custer for his role in the 1868–69 Indian campaign. But he may well have expected some official recognition for his achievements. He had succeeded where others had failed; he had validated the concept of winter war against the Indians; and he had forced many of the dissident bands onto the reservations. Moreover, he had, so he hoped, rescued his reputation from the missteps and mortification of the previous few years.

The timing seemed opportune. On March 4, 1869, Ulysses S. Grant was sworn in as eighteenth president of the United States, and William

T. Sherman assumed Grant's former position of commanding general of the Army. Sheridan, coming off the successful Plains campaign, was promoted to lieutenant general, and moved into Sherman's former command of the Division of the Missouri. Sheridan had promised Custer he would do what he could to get him promoted, and given his patron's influence, George had every reason to expect good things. The stars appeared to be aligning two months later, when Colonel Andrew J. Smith retired from command of the 7th Cavalry to become postmaster of St. Louis. It was the ideal opportunity to elevate Custer both to the open colonelcy and to command the regiment he had led successfully into battle.

Instead, both went to Samuel Sturgis. Sturgis was an 1846 Academy graduate and wartime volunteer brigadier general with a commendable though not stellar combat record. A complicating factor in the new arrangement was a misunderstanding between Custer and Sturgis in the summer of 1865, which they had papered over. Sturgis's receiving the command Custer wanted reawakened the resentment.

To escape the indignity, in June 1869 Custer requested appointment as commandant of cadets at West Point. It would be a dream assignment both for Custer and the cadets, and Libbie would enjoy life on the post, especially as wife of the second-ranking officer at the Academy. But that assignment went to Emory Upton, who as a cadet in Custer's day had been persecuted for his abolitionist beliefs and then gone on to serve bravely in the Civil War. Upton was a noted military intellectual who literally rewrote the book on infantry tactics based on his wartime experiences. In 1870 Custer, disappointed at losing out to Upton, reportedly threatened to resign.[2]

Custer's frustration at not attaining additional rank and responsibility is understandable given the commands he held during the war and what he achieved with them. On the other hand, he was still the highest-ranking member of his West Point cohort. Of the thirty-four graduates of the Class of June 1861, nineteen were still serving at the end of 1870, and of them, seventeen were captains. One of them, Joseph C. Audenreid, served as an acting colonel as an aide to General Sherman. Peter S. Hains was the only major, promoted in 1870. Of the rest of the class, three had left the service for civilian life, and three resigned after graduation to fight for the Confederacy. Nine were dead—four of wounds received in battle, two from other causes, and three, O'Rorke, Cushing, and Woodruff, killed in action at Gettysburg.

From that perspective, Custer was excelling in his Army career. Furthermore, he was the deputy commander of a cavalry regiment that frequently saw action, rather than a garrison commander in the East, a staff officer pushing papers in the War Department, or, like Major Hains, superintending engineer of the 5th Lighthouse District.

Despite his misgivings, Custer stayed in the West with the 7th Cavalry and made the best of it. Sturgis, like his predecessor, was often on detached duty, leaving George in command. He reinvented himself for the West, fully embracing his public identity as a frontier warrior. The Boy General in blue making mad charges against the rebels was replaced with the buckskin-clad frontiersman, vanquisher of the Indian and the buffalo. The new image was much like the old—dashing, warlike, romantic. And he kept the red cravat.

Custer's makeover was not superficial; he took well to the Plains, with its wide-open spaces, boundless opportunities for riding and hunting, and an appealing sense of adventure. He stalked the game the region provided, accompanied by his loyal hounds. "Although an ardent sportsman, I had never hunted the buffalo up to this time," Custer wrote of his first pursuit of the bison. He was eager to try it. During a lull in the Hancock expedition, he went off by himself on a hunt and found a lone buffalo, the first and largest he ever saw. Custer stalked the animal, and when he and his dogs emerged from concealment in a ravine, the beast "set off as fast as his legs could carry him." The chase continued for miles,

until the bison, with George's pistol pressed in its side, "suddenly determined to fight, and at once wheeled, as only a buffalo can," to gore
Custer's horse. His mount, Custis Lee, a favorite of Libbie's that he had
ridden in the war, veered wildly to avoid the attack. George grabbed the
reins with both hands, and "unfortunately as I did so," he wrote, "my
finger, in the excitement of the occasion, pressed the trigger, discharged
the pistol, and sent the fatal ball into the very brain of the noble animal
I rode." Custer was thrown to the ground. The bison broke off the attack
and departed. The dogs ran up and "with mute glances first at the dead
steed, then at me, seemed to inquire the cause of this strange condition
of affairs." Custer set off on foot, and fortunately a detachment of cavalrymen found him before the Sioux did. It was an inauspicious start to
a successful period as a buffalo hunter.[3]

Custer was the informal chief huntsman for his regiment, helping
keep the larders stocked with fresh meat. He was an amateur naturalist,
keeping live animal specimens on post and sending others to zoos in the
East. He also saved fossils from rich western beds that he forwarded to
scientists. And he took up taxidermy, a useful art to while away the winter months.

Libbie was with George whenever possible, in established posts or
tented encampments, at all times except during active operations. The
two enjoyed each other's company on long rides and quiet evenings, as
well as at the many social events they attended with the command or on
trips back "to the states." Libbie adapted well to life on post and in camp.
She was gracious in her important though informal role as the commander's spouse, and patient with their hardships. The couple faced
some financial difficulties; George dabbled unsuccessfully in land ven-
tures in Kansas, and the Bacon estate, which was supposed to support
Libbie's mother, turned out to have been mismanaged by its executor
and was in a shambles. Their cook and companion, Eliza, who had been
with the couple through many challenges during the Civil War and after,

departed late in 1869. The loneliness of the Plains had gotten to her, and as she explained to Libbie, "You's always got the ginnel, but I hain't got nobody."[4]

But Libbie kept a good attitude over the years, seeming to relish the challenges the couple faced. "How we have managed to preserve the romance … after nine years of married life and all our vicissitudes," she wrote in the summer of 1873. "Though we have had our trials, you have the blessed faculty of looking on the sunny side of things. Dear Autie, you are the richest of men."[5]

Yet, years after George was gone, a Navy officer opined to Brigadier General Edward S. Godfrey that "Custer was a brave man but a brute to his wife."

"That is a new one to me," Godfrey wrote. He had joined the 7th Cavalry in 1867 as a second lieutenant, fresh out of West Point. "Frequent visits and in camp gave me as fair opportunities to judge the home life and personal or family relations of his household as probably his critics had." He said Libbie's devotion to George's memory, and the continued loyalty of their close friends and associates, argued otherwise. "In the old days of garrison life of a regiment," Godfrey recalled, "there was an intimacy and inter-relation between families at different posts that was wonderful, and probably difficult for people outside to understand, and was often misrepresented." He said that "there was not much that could be hidden for any length of time" and he "never had any reason to believe that the family relations were other than happy contentment."

"On the march, in camp, in garrison, at great and small social functions of garrisons, in the home life, I've seen considerable of both Gen. and Mrs. Custer, and never discovered that their relations had cause for unhappiness," Godfrey wrote. "They were always chummy and seemed in perfect harmony."[6]

George, charismatic and naturally flirtatious, attracted the attentions of women wherever he went, particularly when Libbie was absent. He wrote to his wife about his various innocent encounters with a candor that would shock contemporary husbands for the inevitable sharp questioning they would face later in the same circumstances. ("There is a beautiful girl, eighteen or nineteen, blonde, who has walked past the hotel several times trying to attract my attention," George wrote Libbie during a trip alone to New York City. "Twice for sport I followed her.")[7] This frankness reflected George's ingenuousness and open nature but did nothing to quell stories of his wandering eye.

In September 1873, Custer attended a reunion of the Army of the Tennessee in Toledo, Ohio, to network with Grant, Sherman, and Sheridan. In the receiving line after the banquet, "a certain familiarity grew up between the visitors and ladies," and the girls started kissing the generals. This "opened an excellent opportunity for the fair belles of Toledo and the sunny daughters of the rural districts to kiss the president and some of the military heroes of the late war," the *Toledo Commercial* reported, "and they took advantage of the opportunity." Sheridan and Custer competed to see who could get the most kisses, and George, "whose position was on the left, made a brilliant charge, and for ten minutes kissed every lady that passed him." According to the reporter's informal, tongue-in-cheek count, Custer won the contest 417–410, with President Grant coming in at 393, and Sherman with 297.[8] *Frank Leslie's Illustrated Newspaper* ran a full-page engraving of the scene entitled "The Generals Kissing the Girls," with George accepting the attentions of a swooning maiden, a scandalized matron looking on.[9] This event no doubt helped solidify George's public reputation as a ladies' man.

There were less innocent accounts of Custer's waywardness. One concerned a Board of Inquiry allegedly held late in the Civil War regarding a dozen or more prostitutes Custer had put on the Federal payroll, listing them as "mule skinners." When it was uncovered, Custer was not punished but forced to repay the money. There was no finding that George personally availed himself of the women's services. The records of the proceeding were made secret, but according to Harry S. Truman's friend Keith Wilson Jr., the president enjoyed looking through old classified documents in his spare time and "got a big kick out of reading about Custer's womanizing."[10]

A better-known story of George's alleged waywardness concerned his relationship with a pregnant Indian woman captured at Washita named Meotzi, also known as Monahsetah or "Spring Grass," daughter of the slain chief Little Rock. George called her "an exceedingly comely squaw, possessing a bright, cheery face, a countenance beaming with intelligence, and a disposition more inclined to be merry than one usually finds among the Indians."[11] Frederick Benteen said that Custer "slept with her all the time" in the winter of 1868–69 in camp and when she accompanied the campaign as a translator, and she was also allegedly intimate with Tom Custer. According to scout Ben Clark, Raphael Romero was put in charge of the rest of the captive squaws and sent them around to officers' tents every night.[12]

However, Clark's and especially Benteen's motives in telling these stories have been questioned, and there are no other such accounts. Cheyenne gossip attributed Meotzi's eventual son to George, but since the timeline made no sense (the baby was born in January 1869), Custer was then called the father of a purported subsequent child, of which there is no record. But it is likely that George could not father children in any case, due to sterility caused by gonorrhea he had contracted during his 1859 West Point furlough.[13] And if he was up to something with Meotzi, he was not very circumspect; he mentioned her extensively in *My Life on the Plains* and even wrote Libbie about her at the time. And whatever the truth of George's relationships with other women, Libbie never sought greener pastures and never remarried after he was gone.

The Custers had no children, and George never showed any indication of wanting to be a father. At news of a mutual friend's new baby, he wrote Libbie that he "pitied him and congratulated myself that it was his wife and not mine who was the victim." He said he had "love enough for you but none to spare upon someone who I have never seen and don't want to see," and who would give him "much more anxiety & troubles than pleasure. You are all I desire, let those who must then have children. You are my wife and my baby I ask for no more."[14] Perhaps George's unsympathetic attitude was a rationalization of his disappointment in being unable to have children, since he probably would have been a loving and caring father.

Instead, the 7th Cavalry became part of Custer's extended family. Tom Custer was in the regiment, and George lobbied unsuccessfully for a commission for their young brother Boston. Bos later accompanied the unit on several expeditions as a civilian. Handsome Lieutenant James Calhoun—the shy "Adonis" of the regiment—met George's sister Margaret in 1870, and they were married two years later. Captain Myles Moylan married Calhoun's sister Charlotte. Fred Calhoun, James's brother, married George's niece Emma Reed, and Custer tried but failed to have him transferred to the unit. It was common for families to accumulate in regiments in those days, since under the old system an officer would sign on with a unit and stay with it for most if not all his career. Custer said service on the frontier amounted "almost to social exile," so it was natural for officers to take a romantic interest in their colleagues' eligible visiting sisters and cousins. Other friends and favorites of his included George W. Yates (who was from Monroe), Thomas B. Weir, and Algernon E. Smith.

George did not play favorites with regimental members of the "Custer Clan." He would even discipline brother Tom if it was warranted. But there was some resentment of what Lieutenant Charles W. Larned referred to as Custer's "royal family" and the perception of favoritism. Libbie called the officers of the 7th Cavalry "a medley of incongruous elements," among whom Custer had his critics and detractors.[15]

"Custer is not making himself at all agreeable to the officers of his command," Larned wrote at Camp Sturgis, Yankton, Dakota, in 1873. "He keeps himself aloof and spends his time in excogitating annoying, vexatious and useless orders which visit us like the swarm of evils from Pandora's box, small, numberless and disagreeable."[16] Custer "wears the men out by ceaseless and unnecessary labor.... We all fear that such ill advised and useless impositions will result in large desertions when the command is paid off, as it will be tomorrow morning." Larned said that "Custer is not belying his reputation—which is that of a man selfishly indifferent to others, and ruthlessly determined to make himself conspicuous at all hazards."[17]

Edward S. Godfrey recalled that "Gen. Custer in matters of discipline gave little or no attention to the enlisted men" but rather "held his officers responsible" for the infractions of the men and would punish whole units. Godfrey said that "those who sympathized with his principal aim, discipline, were at first dumbfounded and then outraged."[18] Colonel Sturgis's periodic returns to the 7th were met with joy, according to Larned, "for how long no-one knows ... perhaps only for a few days— any time would be a relief." Sturgis said, "Custer was not a popular man among his troops, by any means. He was tyrannical, and had no regard for the soldiers under him."[19]

One of Custer's most important critics was Captain Frederick William Benteen, a Virginian who had sided with the Union during the Civil War and fought bravely at Pea Ridge, Vicksburg, and other battles in the West.[20] He ended the war the commander of the 138th Colored U.S. Volunteers, and after was assigned to the 7th Cavalry as a captain. "I've been a loser in a way, all my life," Benteen wrote, "by rubbing a bit against the angles—or hair—of folks, instead of going with their whims; but I couldn't go otherwise—'twould be against the grain of myself."[21] His contrarian spirit was certain to clash with Custer's ego, and the two quickly developed an enduring enmity. Benteen took Custer to task for, as he saw it, abandoning Major Elliot at Washita. In 1873, during the Yellowstone expedition, Custer disallowed a request for emergency leave so Benteen could visit his desperately ill daughter, who later died. But Custer was not the only person with whom Benteen had bad blood; his private letters revealed him to be "a man of monumental vindictiveness and cancerous bitterness toward almost all his old comrades."[22]

Living in the West brought Custer in frequent close contact with Indians, especially the friendly tribes and bands that congregated near the forts, often for protection from the more warlike groups. "It is pleasant at all times, and always interesting, to have a village of peaceable Indians locate their lodges near our frontier posts or camps," he wrote. "The daily visits of the Indians, from the most venerable chief to the strapped pappoose, their rude interchange of civilities, their barterings, races, dances, legends, strange customs, and fantastic ceremonies, all combine to render them far more agreeable as friendly neighbors than as crafty, bloodthirsty enemies."[23]

Custer studied the people of the Plains and wrote accounts of their daily life and culture. He learned some of their sign language but mostly communicated through intermediaries, often mixed-race tribal members with a foot in both cultures. He forged good relationships with his scouts, often Osage, Delaware, Crow, and Arikara, frequent victims of larger and fiercer tribes, who worked with the Army against their traditional enemies. He respected the scouts and their innate knowledge of the Plains, and they generally liked and respected Custer. His Indian nicknames included Long Hair, Creeping Panther, and, after Washita, Son of Morning Star.

Custer's interest in Indian ways was partly intellectual but also practical. He needed to understand them to live among them, pacify them, and if necessary fight them. He was far from the stereotype later ascribed to him of a brutish Indian killer motivated by scorn and hatred. This is not to say he was without prejudice: Custer was a product of his times and had the predispositions of a white soldier, and he was also a believer in American civilization and progress, which in those days was synonymous with taming, settling, and harnessing the frontier.

Custer wrote that "in studying the Indian character," he was "shocked and disgusted by many of his traits and customs."[24] He critiqued the myth of the "noble savage," which had been a staple of Western literature since the seventeenth century, and described Indian life as he observed it. "Stripped of the beautiful romance with which we have been so long willing to envelop him," he wrote, "transferred from the inviting pages of the novelist to the localities where we are compelled to meet with him, in his native village, on the war path, and when raiding upon our frontier settlements and lines of travel, the Indian forfeits his claim to the appellation of the 'noble red man.'" Custer said that the white men on the Plains saw the Indian "as he is, and, so far as all knowledge goes, as he ever has been, a savage in every sense of the word." He added that the Indian was "not worse, perhaps, than his white brother would be similarly born and bred, but one whose cruel and ferocious nature far exceeds that of any wild beast of the desert."

Nevertheless, Custer said that among the Indians he found "much to be admired, and still more of deep and unvarying interest."[25] He said that Indian life, "with its attendant ceremonies, mysteries, and forms, is a book of unceasing interest. Grant that some of its pages are frightful, and, if possible, to be avoided, yet the attraction is none the weaker." He believed that the Indian was a unique type of person possessing an enduring attraction. "Study him, fight him, civilize him if you can," Custer wrote, "he remains still the object of your curiosity, a type of man peculiar and undefined, subjecting himself to no known law of civilization, contending determinedly against all efforts to win him from his chosen mode of life."[26]

Challenges arose from the Indians' sense of nationalism. "The Indians have a strong attachment for the land containing the bones of their ancestors," Custer wrote, "and dislike to leave it. Love of country is almost a religion with them.... there is a strong local attachment that the white man does not feel, and consequently does not respect."[27] This attachment to the land set up the fundamental conflict, since settlers, miners, and industrialists coveted the fields and the mineral wealth of the West. But Custer did not want perpetual war on the Plains. "I have yet to make the acquaintance of that officer of the army who, in time of undisturbed peace, desired a war with the Indians," he wrote. "On the contrary, the army is the Indian's best friend, so long as the latter desires to maintain friendship."[28]

Custer believed that the most enduring friendships with the Indians were based on interest. In dealing with any tribe, the whites had to first demonstrate that they could not be driven away, but then to act fairly and "observe strict justice in all dealings" with them. Indians "are naturally cruel to each other as well as to the whites," Custer said. "It is their nature." Achieving greatness through committing "acts of barbarity" was an idea "instilled into the Indian's mind from his birth to his death." Hence, force was needed to meet the Indians on their own terms and to make them "respect the whites and comprehend the power of the government." But Custer noted that even when an Indian submitted to government power, "he keenly feels the injustice that has been done him, and being of a proud, haughty nature, he resents it."[29]

Like many if not most Army officers, Custer believed many of the Indian problems on the Plains were caused by whites, particularly corrupt bureaucrats in the Indian Bureau. A vast and expensive Federal apparatus was erected to manage the reservation system, which became, as it was said, a means for whites to use Indians to rob both whites and Indians. Graft, influence peddling, and kickbacks were common. Federal payments to the tribes became targets for private traders and those in government-mandated monopolies who sold overpriced food, clothing, and tools, not to mention whiskey, rifles, and other things that made life difficult for the soldiers. Custer summed up his skeptical view of Indian agents with an anecdote from a tribal chief, who asked him to "see the Great Father and make a statement of their wrongs." Custer said he would do what he could, and maybe the government would send a new agent. "'No,' said the chief, 'we don't want a new agent. Agents come here poor and get rich in a few years. This one has everything he wants. If a new one comes we will have to make him rich also.'"[30]

Custer criticized the reservation system for its effect on Indian character. He contrasted the Indian "where Nature placed him … the fearless hunter, the matchless horseman and warrior of the Plains," with the denizen of the reservation, "grovelling in beggary, bereft of many of the qualities which in his wild state tended to render him noble, and heir to a combination of vices partly his own, partly bequeathed to him from the pale-face." Subjected to a life shaped by white civilization, the Indian loses that which defined him and made him who he was; as Custer said, "He fades away and dies."[31]

The Indians' natural identity was what Custer most admired about a people whom fate had made his enemies. "If I were an Indian," he wrote, "I often think that I would greatly prefer to cast my lot among those of my people who adhered to the free open plains, rather than submit to the confined limits of a reservation, there to be the recipient of the blessed benefits of civilization, with its vices thrown in without stint or measure."[32] To Custer, the renegades, the Indians who kept far from the reservations, the bands who would follow Sitting Bull into the wilderness to live the traditional way of life and await the white cavalrymen, represented freedom. They were motivated by the same spirit that animated him, the thirst for life, adventurous and unbounded. He saw them as he saw himself—fearless hunter, matchless horseman, and warrior of the Plains.

CHAPTER TWENTY-FOUR

THE GREAT BUFFALO HUNT

In the winter of 1871–72, Grand Duke Alexei Alexandrovich of Russia, the twenty-one-year-old fourth son of Tsar Alexander II, arrived for a grand tour of the United States. Diplomatic visits of this level were rare in the American interior, and at the time Russia was well regarded, if mysterious.[1] The duke was greeted with acclaim in every city he visited, across the Northeast, throughout the Great Lakes, and into the Midwest. Crowds turned out to see the handsome, young Russian royal, and local politicians rushed to be seen with him. "Alexis fever" broke out; during his visit to West Point, one newspaper reported, "by some happy combination of circumstances the company included an extraordinarily large proportion of very beautiful ladies."[2]

Alexis met with President Grant and other political leaders in Washington, and during a White House dinner Sheridan suggested the grand duke take a trip to the American West to participate in a buffalo hunt.

Alexis agreed, and Sheridan notified George Custer, then on temporary duty in Kentucky, that he would be master of the hunt.[3]

The Custers were the couple of choice to entertain visiting politicians and other dignitaries on the frontier. They gave their company a taste of the open Plains, seeing and meeting actual Indians and witnessing the pageantry of the cavalry drill. For the Custers it was an opportunity to maintain their links to the East and reinforce George's celebrity status. Custer's natural sense of showmanship, and personal charm, guaranteed a memorable time.

Alexis arrived in America just in time to see the vanishing West. The plains were changing, and the frontier of old was giving way to civilization and order. The expression "the Wild West," first popularized in the 1830s, paradoxically grew more common as the West became less wild. By the 1870s most of the country had been surveyed and mapped, and with maps came boundaries. The West was being tamed and contained. Railroads brought settlers and commerce. Barbed wire enclosed vast tracts of land. The remaining Plains Indian tribes were being herded onto reservations. Yellowstone National Park was founded in March 1872 in an effort to preserve some of the dwindling wilderness. The *Witchita Eagle* editorialized, "Here, where five years ago the buffalo had scarcely disappeared, and Texas herds roamed at will, great fields of wheat of brightest green now greet the eye, and young orchards and forest trees are growing finely. Thus is the wilderness tamed. Thus are new empires formed."[4] Poet John Greenleaft Whittier wrote of the march of progress,

> Behind the scared squaw's birch canoe,
> The steamer smokes and raves;
> And city lots are staked for sale
> Above old Indian graves.[5]

By the 1870s, whites who wanted to experience the romance of buffalo hunting had to hurry. An 1859 travel guide to the Plains noted that the "monarch of the prairies" was fast disappearing. "Not many years since they thronged in countless multitudes over all that vast area lying between Mexico and the British possessions," Captain Randolph B. Marcy noted, "but now their range is confined within very narrow limits, and a few more years will probably witness the extinction of the species."[6]

The bison herds had more than a few years left from when Marcy wrote, but in 1872, buffalo killings increased dramatically. A combination of factors were to blame. Railroads brought easier access to the hunting grounds as well as more reliable means of shipping bison products back east. Rifles, produced by Sharps, Remington, and the Springfield Armory, became more accurate and less expensive. Industrialization increased demand for bison hide to make tough leather transmission belts to run machines. There was a fad for Indian-made buffalo robes, and bison tongue and marrow were delicacies in high demand. Bison bones were used for fertilizer, and bison heads for decoration. Buffalo hunting seemed to be an easy way to make quick money, and hunters, sportsmen, and others descended on the Plains.

"The buffalo melted away like snow before a summer's sun," Lieutenant Colonel Richard Irving Dodge wrote of those days. "Congress talked of interfering, but only talked. Winter and summer, in season and out of season, the slaughter went on."[7] In May 1872 an estimated thirty thousand bison were killed, mostly for their hides, and sold for two dollars apiece. At the end of that summer, one newspaper noted that "as the bison are driven into narrow limits their destruction becomes greater, and it is highly probable that the animal within the next thirty years will become entirely extinct."[8] Two years later the killing dropped off because there were hardly any bison to be found. "Comparatively few buffalo are now killed, for there are comparatively few to kill," Dodge wrote. "In October 1874 I was on a short trip to the buffalo region south of Sidney Barracks. A few buffalo were encountered, but there seemed to be more hunters than buffalo."[9]

It was not just white hunters who were destroying the buffalo herds. Indians, particularly the Sioux, were lured by the demand for buffalo robes and began killing with abandon. Dodge noted that after the Pawnee retreated to a reservation and relinquished their previous hunting grounds, "the Sioux poured into this country" and "made such a furious onslaught on the poor beasts, that in a few years scarcely a buffalo could be found in all the wide area south of the Cheyenne and north and east of the North Platte."[10] Over the peak years of slaughter, 1872–74, an estimated 4.4 million bison were killed—3.2 million by whites and 1.2 million by Indians.[11]

European hunting parties were common on the Plains, since there was no sport like it to be had in their home countries. "Hundreds of the best shots from all over this country and Europe," an observer wrote, "were on hand to take a farewell hunt before the shaggy bison became extinct."[12] Not just bison but antelope, elk, wolves, bears, coyotes, and other game fell to the avid hunters.

Alexis was not the first European aristocrat the Custers had encountered on the hunt. In December 1866, the Russian prince Nicholas Ouroussoff, Count Montaigne of France, and some English nobles visited Fort Riley seeking buffalo. Libbie noted in a letter to Rebecca Richmond, "Prince Qusosoff nephew of the Saar of Russia (the small dictionary don't say Sar so I cant spell it) has been on a buffalo hunt. He visited us and so we found his highness the Prince quite like other dutchy boys. The English party of noblemen have not returned I think."[13] The *Junction City Union* reported that the Englishmen had enjoyed "fair luck in hunting the bison and extra good luck in not seeing 'ye savages.'"[14]

One report had it the prince killed thirty buffalo, and altogether his party accounted for 150 "of our noble American bison."[15] Later, in 1869, an Irish peer named Lord Waterpark visited Fort Riley. The hunts were not just for show; during one outing someone was gored, a few dogs were killed, and Libbie was almost taken out by charging a buffalo.[16]

Alexis and his party arrived at Omaha on January 12, 1872. There were a number of Russian notables along, including Vice Admiral Posslet, commander of the Russian fleet. They brought a vast number of servants—"almost as many servants and valets in the retinue of the Russians as there were troopers in the expedition" by one report. Among the Americans were General Sheridan; his brother Colonel Michael V. Sheridan; Sheridan's aide and Custer's former inspector general in Texas, Major James W. Forsyth; Colonel George A. Forsyth, hero of Beecher Island; General Ord commanding the Department of the Platte; Colonel Innis N. Palmer, commander of the 2nd Cavalry; and Dr. Asch of Sheridan's staff.

Custer met them dressed "in his well known frontier buckskin hunting costume, and if, instead of the comical seal-skin hat he wore, he had feathers fastened in his flowing hair, he would have passed at a distance for a great Indian chief."[17] The next day they took a train to the North Platte and then embarked on a fifty-mile ride over the snowy prairie to Red Willow Creek. Buffalo Bill Cody led, in fur-trimmed buckskin and black slouch hat, hair to his shoulders, and they were escorted by two companies of cavalry. The grand duke stayed long in the saddle, while others of his party did not. "There was so much real roughing it," one report noted, "that the frills, the band, and the champagne wagons could not take the edge off the adventure for the Grand Duke."

Near sunset they arrived at the well-provisioned, tented four-acre encampment dubbed Camp Alexis. Custer came loping in an hour late with his buffalo rifle over his shoulder, along with Ord, camp commander

General Palmer, and Lieutenant Starlagoff of the Russian Navy. Their wagon had broken down five miles out, and they had walked the rest of the way through the snow.

The main tents at Camp Alexis were "elegantly carpeted," and even the smaller tents were "furnished with a degree of comfort and elegance rarely found out here on the wild plains of Nebraska."[18] A banquet was held that evening, featuring game hunted on the prairie. Custer had shot a prairie chicken on the way there, taking its head off, and Alexis insisted it be cooked and eaten as well. Alexis asked George and Buffalo Bill many questions about how to hunt the bison, and Bill loaned him his reliable hunting horse, Buckskin Joe, so that "when we went into a buffalo herd all he would have to do was to sit on the horse's back and fire away."[19]

Custer's scouts located a herd about fifteen miles away, and the next day—Alexis's twenty-second birthday—they set out after it. Custer, the duke, and Buffalo Bill rode together, "all large and powerful, and all hardy hunters—they attracted the attention and admiration of everyone."[20] Custer and Cody were dressed in their frontier garb, and Alexis wore a grey outfit trimmed in green with brass buttons bearing the Russian imperial coat of arms and a dark pillbox hat. Alexis had a Russian hunting knife and a Smith & Wesson revolver with the coat of arms of the United States and Russia on the grip. They rode under a brilliant, sunny, cloudless sky, and it was warm enough that they did not have to wear overcoats.

They found the herd, which covered several square miles, and readied for the hunt. Russians were paired off with experienced American hunters. Alexis was given the opportunity to make first kill. Accompanied by Custer, Buffalo Bill, and two Brulé Indians, he approached downwind, concealed by a ravine that opened a quarter mile from the buffalo.

"Of course, the main thing was to give Alexis the first chance and the best shot at the buffaloes," Buffalo Bill recalled, "and when all was in readiness we dashed over a little knoll that had hidden us from view, and in a few minutes we were among them." Alexis emptied his pistol at some bison twenty feet away but did not score a significant hit. Bill handed him another pistol, but Alexis again failed to drop a buffalo. Fearing the buffalo would run off without Alexis getting a trophy, Bill handed him his rifle "Lucretia" and "gave old Buckskin Joe a blow with my whip" to urge him toward a large bull.

"Now is your time," Bill said. Alexis raised the rifle and felled the bull. Then he waved his hat, his party came riding up, and "very soon the corks began to fly from the champagne bottles, in honor of the Grand Duke Alexis, who had killed the first buffalo."[21] Then others were released to the hunt, "a wild rush of counts and cowboys, troopers and Indians." Some riders went down but none was seriously hurt. There was more excitement than hunting, and at the end of the day, only four buffalo were taken. Alexis cut the tail from his kill as a trophy, and the head was cut off to send to a taxidermist. The hunting party returned to camp, announcing their arrival back with Indian-style whoops. A courier was sent to the nearest telegraph station to send a message to Tsar Alexander II that Alexis had "killed the first wild horned monster that met his eye on the plains of North America."[22]

Not everyone was impressed with the royal hunt. The *Leavenworth Weekly Times* satirized the event, saying "the buffaloes, fully appreciating the distinguished honor done them by being the recipients of a visit from royalty, are turning out in great numbers, and in their best robes, to welcome his Highness with the right hoof of fellowship." An ancient cow who had "gamboled with Pocahontas when she was a heifer, that is, the cow, came to the imperial camp on Monday evening, and waited patiently about, like Mary's lamb, for his Highness to come out and shoot her." The paper noted that "instances of such great respect for royalty are very rare on the frontier. He shot her."[23]

That night there was a festive, champagne-fueled dinner in camp. They were joined by fifty Brulé warriors, along with numerous squaws and children, who had come at Sheridan's request to meet and entertain Alexis. Among the leaders were Spotted Tail, Red Leaf, Black Bear, Fast Bear, Conquering Bear, Little Wound, Brave Shield, and Custer's old adversary, Pawnee Killer. After the dinner, the young braves painted their faces and put on a war dance around a massive log fire. The chiefs held a powwow, and they, Alexis, Custer, Sheridan, and others smoked the peace pipe. Alexis generously gave the Indians silver coins, blankets, and hunting knives. Sheridan provided them with tobacco and other supplies and gave Spotted Tail an embroidered red cloth cap, a scarlet-trimmed brown robe, an ivory-handled hunting knife, and a gilt-inlaid general officer's belt of Russian leather. The mood was festive; Custer "carried on a mild flirtation with one of Spotted Tail's daughters," Buffalo Bill recalled, "and it was noticed also that the Duke Alexis paid considerable attention to another handsome redskin maiden."[24]

The next day, the Indians showed off their hunting methods, using the bow and arrow instead of firearms. Alexis, who had run into such difficulty taking down a buffalo with a pistol, was skeptical that bow hunting could amount to much. Custer took two Brulé bucks aside and told them to go find a buffalo, run it into camp, and demonstrate the lethality of the bow. Within an hour they returned, chasing a buffalo, whooping and yelling. They drove the animal into the camp where an eighteen-year-old Brulé named Two Lance "swiftly circled to her left and with bow full drawn drove his arrow into the body behind the shoulder. The animal fell, pierced through the heart." Two Lance then removed the bloody arrow and presented it to Custer, who handed it to the duke. Alexis was so impressed that he gave Two Lance a twenty-dollar gold piece and also purchased his bow and quiver of arrows as souvenirs.

The hunting party set out, the air colder and the snow deeper than the day before. Hundreds more Indians had arrived for the hunt, and Buffalo Bill recalled the "picturesque assemblage" of the "magnificent savage allies, in all the rainbow brilliancy of their native garb and fantastic adornment, mingled with the flower of the veteran cavalry of 'Uncle Sam.'" He said the "brilliant array of famed officers, and the gorgeously accoutred foreign officials, admirals and generals, and a detachment of the flower of our army, made a pageant so spirited as to linger in memory as a scene in every respect unique beyond compare up to date, and one well-nigh impossible in the future to duplicate."[25]

The royal party rode through a wide, winding canyon. Custer, in the lead, spotted the bison and gave a signal by riding in a circle, Indian style. Alexis rode up, and George pulled out his revolver.

"Are you ready, Duke?" he asked.

Alexis "drew off his glove, grasped his pistol, and with a wave of his imperial hand replied, 'All ready, now, General.'"[26]

They charged the animals, who broke. Alexis pursued a cow that had nimbly gained footing on the sloping side of the ravine and rode up the slope heedless of danger. The cow turned on the duke, but showing off his riding skill he expertly circled her and emptied the contents of his revolver, killing her. Her calf, which had been running along nearby, was also felled. The cow's head and tail were taken for trophies, while the calf was brought back to camp whole and eaten the next day for breakfast.

Meanwhile, several hundred Indians readied to dash on the scattering herd. They had stripped down for the hunt, "only a breech-clout around their loins, moccasins on their feet, no saddle, no bridle, the ponies with only a thin leather hackamore between their teeth," Buffalo Bill recalled. They were reducing weight so they could "ride like lightning." The chiefs lined up the riders "with the ponies foaming, prancing, and stamping their feet, impatient as their masters," and when the signal was given they were off in a cloud of dust.

"Thunder and lightning! What a tornado!" Bill wrote. "What a storm of horsemen, as, with impetuosity, these nomads dashed on their prey!" The scene became one of "an indescribable mix-up of flying arrows, accompanied with rifle shots, galloping horses, falling buffaloes, and fleet riding Indians on their wild ponies." Soon the prairie was strewn with fallen buffalo. "Calm and practical fellows were these Indians," Bill wrote. "Even the horses began quietly pasturing on the grasses, while the hunters proceeded to pull off the hide and cut out the tongues and favorite pieces of their native cattle, and preparing the meat in strips for preservation."[27] Later that day there was another feast to close the hunt.

The royal party then headed for Denver, accompanied by Custer, Sheridan, and the other American escorts. Alexis was eager to continue hunting, and when they got word of another large herd 130 miles east near Kit Carson, he was game for the challenge. Sheridan made arrangements to make the trip on cavalry horses, but he warned the duke that untrained mounts were unruly and skittish around the buffalo.

Chalkley M. Beeson, a twenty-four-year-old cowboy who accompanied the party on the hunt, described Custer then as "in the prime of life, a gallant figure with his flowing hair and his almost foppish military dress…. He was the ideal cavalryman, and the idol of the western army." Beeson loaned Custer an "almost unbroken" horse, and George proceeded to put the mount through its paces. Beeson said he had never seen a finer horseman. Custer "rode with the cavalry seat," he recalled, "but as easily and as gracefully as a born cowboy." George threw the reins on his neck and guided the horse "in a circle by the pressure of his knees, and drawing both his revolvers fired with either hand at a gallop with as much accuracy as though he were standing on the ground." Alexis, "who had seen the Cossacks of the Ukraine, declared it was the finest exhibition of horsemanship he had ever seen, and applauded every shot."[28]

After a long ride, scouts reported that the herd was just ahead, over a large rise. Custer gathered the hunters and gave tactical orders for the assault. "Boys, here's a chance for a great victory over that bunch of redskins the other side of the hill," he said. "Major B., you will take charge of the right flank, I will attend to the left. General Sheridan and the infantry will follow direct over the hill. Ready! Charge!"[29] The two columns of hunters galloped off around the hill and descended on the bison.

The abrupt appearance of the hunters spooked the herd, which began to stampede. As Sheridan had warned, the government-issue horses became increasingly agitated and unmanageable. Alexis's animal broke and ran out of control toward the rushing bison. Custer charged after the duke and angled Alexis's panicking horse away from the stampeding animals, regaining control by whip and spur. Other horses were spooked and ran about haphazardly, their riders unable to stop them. Some ran into a prairie dog town, unhorsing many riders. Bullets were flying, not always well aimed. Russian Count Bodisco, the charge d'affairs in Washington, fired a shot that went through Colonel Michael V. Sheridan's coat.

Meanwhile, Phil Sheridan and the rest of the party walked toward the crest of the hill to watch the hunt. Nearing the top, they saw several wounded buffalo coming toward them and readied their weapons to shoot. "Just then the whole crowd of hunters charged the hill from the opposite, shooting at the buffaloes," Chalkley Beeson recalled. Sheridan, directly in the line of fire, dropped to the ground and hugged the buffalo grass while bullets whistled by. "The bullets were dropping all around us," Beeson said. "I yelled to them to stop firing, but they were so excited that it looked for a little bit as though they would wipe out the entire command of 'infantry.'"[30]

When the chaos subsided, Sheridan leapt up and let out a string of curses at everyone available. "I think he was the maddest man I ever saw," Beeson recalled. "He didn't spare anybody in the bunch, not even Custer and the Grand Duke, and he included all their kinsfolk, direct and collateral. It was a liberal education in profanity to hear him."[31] But Alexis laughed off the incident and a diplomatic crisis was averted. The party returned with many cuts and bruises but no serious injuries.

Back at camp they found that the servants and camp followers had raided the Russian liquor trunk and were pleasantly inebriated. "Champagne bottles, liquor bottles, and every other kind of bottle littered the ground," Chalkley Beeson noted. "That battle-field showed more 'dead ones' than the hunting-ground did buffaloes." Then it was Custer's turn to begin cussing, and by Beeson's reckoning it even surpassed what the enraged Sheridan had let loose earlier in the day. "I cannot pay his efforts a higher compliment," the young cowboy wrote, "than to say that when Custer got through with that bunch they were pretty near sober, and that is cussing some."[32]

Alexis so enjoyed Custer's company that he asked him to accompany his party for the rest of their tour. They returned to Kansas, then headed east to Louisville, where Libbie joined the group. They toured Mammoth Cave, then headed south, enjoying the scenery and social life in the cities along the Mississippi. "Alexis is not concerned with the outside," Libbie wrote in her diary, "only with the pretty girls, with music, ... [with] his eternal cigarette and in joking with his suite and with the General."[33] Alexis and his party ended their grand tour of the United States in New Orleans in March and boarded a ship for Russia. Alexis later wrote a memoir of his journey, expressing his gratitude to Custer and including a photo of them together in their hunting garb.[34] "The picture still lingers in my mind," Buffalo Bill recalled years later, "with young General Custer predominating the grand assemblage. He was the life and spirit, one might say, of the occasion."[35]

CHAPTER TWENTY-FIVE

BATTLE ON THE YELLOWSTONE

In the summer of 1873, Custer returned to the West as part of an engineering and surveying party to explore a route between Bismarck and Bozeman, up the Missouri and Yellowstone Rivers. The Northern Pacific, the planned second transcontinental railroad, was projected to lay 6,800 miles of track starting on the Great Lakes and terminating at Puget Sound. The effort was supposed to be financed through proceeds from a forty million–acre land grant authorized by Congress in 1864. Track laying only began in 1870, however, and after several false starts, the railroad began to make progress with the backing of famed financier Jay Cooke, whose investment house had made a fortune selling government bonds to underwrite the Union war effort.

Cooke energized the effort, and the railroad reached Fargo in the Dakota Territory by 1872. Nevertheless, there were still endemic managerial problems, terrain challenges, and periodic attacks by local

Indians. The railroad relied on Army escorts for its workers, and in the summer of 1873, ten companies of the 7th Cavalry under Custer joined a larger force of infantry to guard engineers and surveyors venturing deep into traditional Indian lands along the Yellowstone.[1]

The expedition set off on June 20, 1873, with 79 officers, 1,451 men, 353 civilians, and 7 scouts. Frederick Dent Grant, the president's son, went along as an observer. He was only three years out of West Point but had been frocked to the rank of lieutenant colonel to serve on Sheridan's staff. This caused some disquiet among Grant's critics—the *Chicago Tribune* called it "one of the most shocking instances of injustice and nepotism which has ever characterized the action of the President," since Fred had done little in his career since graduating close to the bottom of his West Point class.[2] But he and George got along well during the expedition, exchanging Academy stories, no doubt of the "goaty" variety.

The Yellowstone expedition also reunited Custer with an old friend and rival. One afternoon he was resting when he heard someone asking which was General Custer's tent.

"Halloo, old fellow!" Custer said. "I haven't heard that voice in thirteen years, but I know it. Come in and welcome!" In walked the chief engineer of the survey party, his former schoolmate, companion, and battlefield adversary, Thomas L. Rosser.

Rosser had been in Fitzhugh Lee's command at the close of the Civil War. He had commanded Confederate forces on the first day of the Battle of High Bridge a few days before Appomattox, the last engagement Lee's army would ever win. The morning of April 9, 1865, Rosser led a successful charge through Union lines to the Lynchburg Road, and he and his men were still outside the pocket when the surrender took place. Rosser was among those cavalrymen "who took a professional pride in getting around the enemy," Porter Alexander explained, "and could not resist the opportunity."[3]

There was some debate over whether the Confederate cavalry who had broken the noose around Appomattox were included in Lee's capitulation, and it was decided that only those in the immediate vicinity could be considered surrendered. Rosser stayed briefly in the field, then retired to his home near Hanover Courthouse. Weeks later, while en route from Richmond to Washington, Custer made a detour to pay Rosser a visit. He pulled up his command and sent a note to the door:

Dear Friend,

The house is surrounded. You can't get away. Come on out and surrender yourself.

Regards,

G.A.C.

After the war Rosser worked as a civil engineer on several railroads before being hired to head up the Northern Pacific project. "Fanny" and "Tex" renewed their friendship and spent many hours together reliving old memories. Captain Myles Moylan, whom Rosser had captured during the Civil War, also joined in the discussions. "We talk over our West Point times and discuss the battles of the war," George wrote Libbie. They lay under the fly of Custer's tent on a buffalo robe, and it "seemed like the times when we were cadets together, huddled on one blanket and discussing dreams of the future."[4]

Professor William F. Phelps, who was along on the expedition and spent time with Custer and Rosser, described George as "of medium height, slender, slightly stooping, sharp featured, with a penetrating eye, large nose and long, light, curly hair resting almost upon his shoulders. In manner he is quick and nervous but singularly frank, sprightly and agreeable. In conversation his voice is usually high keyed and his style gay and rollicking." Phelps said Custer was dressed in "light-blue army pants tucked into high cavalry boots coming nearly to the knees, ... with a dark blue round-about coat, unbuttoned and trimmed according to his rank, no vest, a blue flannel shirt, and collar turned upon a red necktie, and an immensely broad-brimmed black hat." Phelps had expected more spit and polish and said, "Custer presented to my mind at the time anything but the picture of the ideal soldier." But the "peculiarities of person, costume and manner were soon lost in the charm of the conversation and the exceeding interest of the occasion." Phelps was more impressed with the six-foot-two Rosser, whom he described as erect, bronzed, calm, quiet, deliberate, firm, and thoughtful. "He is emphatically a man of power, and one well calculated to exert a commanding influence over others in whatever relation he may be placed," Phelps wrote.[5]

Colonel David S. Stanley of the 22nd Infantry regiment led the Yellowstone expedition. Stanley was an 1852 West Point graduate and, like Custer, a wartime major general. Stanley fought in the West, and his heroism at the Battle of Franklin in 1864 would be recognized with the Medal of Honor in 1893. Lieutenant Charles W. Larned wrote that Stanley "seems to be very much liked and impressed me favorably when I met him. Large, handsome and dignified."[6]

But Stanley and Custer did not get along. Custer is a "cold blooded, untruthful and unprincipled man," Stanley wrote his wife. "He is universally despised by all the officers of his regiment excepting his relatives and one or two sycophants.... I will try, but am not sure I can avoid trouble with him."[7] Custer's view of Stanley was a mirror-image. "General Stanley is acting very badly, drinking, and I anticipate official trouble with him," George wrote Libbie. "I should greatly regret this, but I fear it cannot be avoided."[8]

Despite Stanley's fondness for whiskey, he did not want to risk having spirituous liquors available in the field and ordered Fred Grant to find all the alcohol stores and have them destroyed. "Not a drink was left in the camp an hour after the order was issued," the *Boston Globe* reported. "The infantry sutler lost six barrels and the cavalry sutler seven."[9] Or so the reporter thought. Custer noted that Fred Grant was "greatly mortified" by the order, which would have cost their sutler, Augustus Baliran, thousands of dollars. So while waiting for the wagons to reach them, Fred announced he was going to take a nap and that he hoped "the Sutler will have anything of the kind hidden before I come to inspect." Custer and other teetotaling officers helped conceal the barrels until Stanley had a change of heart and rescinded the order. "Never were temperate officers so well supplied with intoxicants," George observed.[10]

Stanley sought to keep Custer contained during the expedition and ordered him to stay back with Rosser and his engineers, advancing slowly while the infantry pushed forward to the Yellowstone. The rear was an unaccustomed position for Custer, and an illogical place for the more mobile cavalry, so he decided to push forward anyway. "Custer having been given a little tether must needs throw off Stanley's shackles altogether and start off with heels-in-the-air on his own hook," Larned noted in his diary.[11]

One day, rather than assisting the baggage train over the Muddy River, he pressed out into the van, sending a note to Stanley requesting rations and forage. "After a march of eleven miles with considerable delay on account of the heavy condition of the prairie from hard rains," Larned noted, "an orderly courier from Stanley overtook our 'flaxen haired' chieftain presenting him with a *billet doux* to the effect he should halt on the spot."[12] Stanley angrily told Custer not to act without orders again.

Custer "was just gradually assuming command," Stanley wrote, "and now he knows he has a commanding officer who will not tolerate his arrogance."[13] The incident became a national news story, exaggerated in the retelling. The *Dubuque Herald* reported that "the gallant Gen. Custer was, for some reason not present known, placed under arrest by Gen. Stanley while on the march through the wilderness. Custer marched in the rear one entire day. The event created much excitement."[14] The *Boston Globe* embellished the story, saying that "a stir was created on the Yellowstone expedition by the arrest of General Custer by General Stanley, I did not learn true cause of the arrest, but Custer marched in the rear of his command one whole day before he was released. Custer's men denounced the arrest as an act of tyranny, while Stanley's men sustained their commander."[15]

But relations between Custer and Stanley soon settled down. After the colonel asserted his authority and Custer assented, Stanley grew more conciliatory. He named a brook they discovered Custer's Creek as a gesture, and he also allowed Custer's cavalry to forge out ahead of the column on scouting missions, which George led personally. Stanley wrote that in the days following the incident, Custer "has behaved very well, since he agreed to do so, went ahead every day to look up road and select the best camps."[16] Custer was looking for more than just campsites, however; if there was action to be had, he would find that, too.

The railroad route ran close to Indian lands, if not right through them. Article XVI of the 1868 Treaty of Fort Laramie stipulated that "the country north of the North Platte river and east of the summits of the Big Horn Mountains shall be held and considered to be unceded Indian territory, and also stipulates and agrees that no white person or persons shall be permitted to settle upon or occupy any portion of the same; or without the consent of the Indians, first had and obtained, to pass through the same." It is unclear where the northern terminus of the unceded lands was—probably at the Yellowstone by Sioux reckoning. The unceded lands were understood to be places where Indians could hunt game if they wanted or needed to. But the area became a haven for dissenters who refused to settle on the reservation and who continued to practice the traditional ways of life. Around three thousand Sioux and four hundred Cheyenne settled in this area, the former led by the Hunkpapa chief Sitting Bull.

"The country was comparatively unknown to any but our Indian guides," a reporter wrote. It was hard and monotonous going, with "extensive swells and billows of land, rolling away to the infinite distance; the same broken, cheerless buttes rising barren and treeless," though areas close by the rivers were greener and dotted with copses of woods. "This was the supposed region of the buffalo and where he is the Indian may be found living upon him for subsistence, and either roaming openly in defiance or lurking in ambush." The previous year a surveying party was attacked by Sioux, Cheyenne, and Arapaho warriors at Pryor's Creek near Pompey's Pillar.[17] Bloody Knife, the half-Sioux, half-Arickaree scout, predicted that they would meet some opposition in the Tongue River area. Seasoned plainsman Charley Reynolds said, "Probably the first that we know of Indians around us will be when someone straggling behind the column is found with his hair gone."[18]

On August 4, Custer, with A and B troops under command of Myles Moylan, was scouting west of the main column at Honsinger Bluff, seven miles west of the juncture of the Tongue and Yellowstone Rivers. Tom Custer and James Calhoun were also along, and the group totaled around one hundred men. It was a hot, sunny day, the temperature over 95 degrees. The day was uneventful, and after finding a suitable camp for the column on the floodplain of the Yellowstone with plenty of wood, he and his men relaxed, eating, napping, fishing, and grazing their horses.

After noon, Custer's pickets spied six Indians approaching. He was napping under a tree and awoke to the shout of "Indians! Indians!" followed by gunfire.[19] Custer ordered his men to mount, and he, Calhoun, and an orderly immediately gave chase, with Tom Custer following with a platoon of horsemen. Moylan then began to come up with the rest. The Indians headed for a wooded area two miles west of where Custer had stopped. But they were not fleeing very vigorously, and George sensed a trick.

Custer stopped the pursuit, and the fleeing Indians paused. Then over 250 mounted warriors broke from the woods, charging toward the cavalrymen. Indian scouts had spotted Custer's men earlier in the morning, and Hunkpapa Sioux from Sitting Bull's encampment of four hundred to five hundred lodges, west near Locke Bluff, had gathered in the woods for battle. Among them were war leader Rain-in-the-Face, a contingent of Oglala Sioux, and some Miniconjou and Cheyenne. By some accounts, the Sioux were led by Crazy Horse.

Tom Custer formed a skirmish line and opened up on the charging as George and the other two raced back. This slowed the Indian advance, giving time for the command to set up a defense in the woods where they had been resting. The dismounted cavalrymen formed an arc along a former streambed and opened fire with the Indians at four hundred yards. The Indians stopped and began exchanging fire with the troopers, to little effect on either side.

The Indian ambush had failed, but they had come to fight, and they sought various ways to break Custer's defense. A group tried to sneak up the riverbank and into Custer's rear to stampede the horses but were detected and driven off. They set fire to the grass to raise a smoke screen to cover their movements, but this also failed. The battle became an exchange of potshots that wore on for hours. Custer hunkered down, waiting for the advancing column to respond to the sound of the fight.

Some miles downstream from the battlefield, veterinary surgeon Doctor John Holzenger and sutler Augustus Baliran were hunting for fossils. Two privates were nearby, John Ball and another named Brown, the latter of whom was napping. Scout Charley Reynolds rode up and warned them there were Indians in the area and they should make for safety. But the area was rich in fossils, so they kept up their hunt. A short time later, several Indians, part of a scouting party led by Rain-in-the-Face, jumped from hiding, dragged Doctor Holzenger from his horse, and shot him. They then killed Baliran and Ball. Brown, roused from sleep, saw what was happening and leapt on his horse bareback, tearing back toward the column.

Stanley had heard firing ahead, but a scout had seen buffalo tracks heading in that direction and told him he thought the ruckus was caused by a hunt. Then Stanley heard gunfire much closer, and shortly after Private Brown barreled into sight crying, "All down there are killed!" Stanley sent the rest of the cavalry forward.

Meanwhile, Custer was in a difficult situation. He had been fighting for three hours, and ammunition was beginning to run low. Each man carried one hundred rounds, and they had exhausted most of their supply. Custer did not even know if relief from Stanley was coming. The Indians maintained "a perfect skirmish line throughout," according to Lieutenant Larned, "evincing for them a very extraordinary control and discipline."[20]

But eventually the Indians' discipline began to break down. The reason became apparent to the cavalrymen as they noticed a huge dust cloud behind the hills to their right, evidence of the relief column. As four squadrons of cavalry galloped into view, it was, George said, "time to mount our steeds and force our enemies to seek safety in flight, or to battle on more even terms."[21] He ordered his men to mount, then without pause charged the Indians. The warriors broke and fled upriver.[22] By the time the relief column arrived, the battle was over. Custer had won the field and suffered only a few men wounded.

The survey continued, though the loss of the three men to Rain-in-the-Face's scouts encouraged tighter security. On August 8, the expedition came across the recently abandoned site of Sitting Bull's village, and Stanley ordered Custer and 450 men to give chase. They tracked the Indians swiftly up the north bank of the river, and two days later reached a point three miles below the mouth of the Bighorn where the Indians had crossed. Custer attempted to make the south bank but the Yellowstone was too deep and swift.

The next day, "the river had fallen considerably and preparations were being made to cross over," Edward S. Godfrey wrote, "when a number of shots were fired from the woods on the opposite bank, and soon after the Indians appeared in force."[23] At first light, friendly Indian scouts came "tumbling down the bluffs head over heels, screeching, 'Heap Indian come.'" Hundreds of warriors appeared along the bluffs above the south bank of the river, firing at the cavalrymen, who returned fire with enthusiasm. Second Lieutenant Charles Braden was seriously wounded repelling a rush from a group of Indians who closed to within thirty yards of his position. This back-and-forth went on for some time, and while Custer's men were occupied, three hundred Indians crossed the river above and below their position, a tactic Sitting Bull had used against the surveying party the previous year. The Indians rushed to the high bluffs six hundred yards to Custer's rear and began to open fire.

The 7th was caught in a crossfire. Custer had a horse shot out from under him—the eleventh of his career—and his orderly, Private John H. Tuttle of Company E, who had been boldly standing in the open showing off his considerable skill as a sharpshooter, was killed. But Custer had been in tougher scrapes than this. He pushed a picket line toward the Indians to his rear, then ordered a charge.

"George sat on his horse out in advance, calmly looking the Indians over," Thomas Rosser wrote of the scene, "full of suppressed excitement, but also with calculating judgment and strength of purpose in his face … I thought him then one of the finest specimens of a soldier I had ever seen."[24] The sudden charge broke the Indian position, and the cavalry pursued them for three miles. Meanwhile, the main column had come up. Stanley ordered artillery fire placed on the ridgeline where the

Indians had congregated across the river, "producing a wonderful scampering out of sight," he wrote.[25]

In the engagements on the Yellowstone, the Indians were armed with new, advanced weapons, and had adapted to them with fresh tactics. But Custer's takeaway was that disciplined and well-organized cavalrymen employing coordinated firepower could hold their own against, and even defeat, superior numbers of Indians. "The Indians were made up of different bands of Sioux, principally Uncpapas," Custer wrote in his after-action report, "the whole under command of 'Sitting Bull,' who participated in the second day's fight, and who for once has been taught a lesson he will not soon forget."[26] A newspaper reporter who witnessed the battle concurred, saying the fights "will have an excellent moral effect upon them and teach them a lesson of our summary management in case of their hostility."[27] Stanley was more circumspect. "The loss of the Indians in these two affairs was considerable," he wrote, but "they are not badly enough hurt to be humble."[28]

Reaching Pompey's Pillar soon after the August 11 battle, the column went north to the Musselshell River, down the valley to the Big Bend, then divided. The 7th Cavalry headed back to Fort Lincoln directly, and Stanley with the rest of the expedition went south, going via the Yellowstone. Custer and his men arrived a day before Stanley, who had taken the steamer *Josephine* while the rest of his column went overland. The unexpected and early arrival of the 7th Cavalry became a general topic of conversation. "How did he come?" "Marched of course." "But that isn't possible." "Nonsense, nothing is impossible with Custer." The *Bismarck Tribune* hailed Custer as "a man in whom sloth took no delight, and as an officer the hero of more rapid marches and harder fights than almost any other noted in history."[29]

The Yellowstone expedition lasted 95 days, made 77 encampments, and covered 935 miles. It surveyed previously unmapped areas and found a number of possible railroad routes. The 7th Cavalry engaged the Indians, and Custer won his battles. He also brought back some bob-tailed cats, porcupines, antelope horns, and petrified wood to send to the Central Park Zoo.

But on September 18, 1873, a week before the expedition ended, the Cooke and Company investment bank, which had underwritten the Northern Pacific, went bankrupt. Cooke's firm had gone into enormous debt, and the tight money policy of the Grant administration dried up the bond market, driving away potential investors. The Northern Pacific could not support its obligations, and even Cooke was not too big to fail. His downfall led to other banks, railroads, and businesses going bust, precipitating the Panic of 1873. The economic hard times lasted in the United States for six years, and the main line of the Northern Pacific was not completed until 1883.

A year later, scout Charley Reynolds attended an Indian war dance, where he learned from "some educated half breeds" that a young warrior named Rain-in-the-Face was bragging that he had killed two civilian members of the Yellowstone expedition with his bare hands. Reynolds got word to Custer, who ordered his brother Tom and a squadron of cavalry to "arrest the red braggart and bring him to Fort Lincoln."[30] Tom found Rain-in-the-Face at the Standing Rock Reservation on December 13, 1874, and took him in, with some difficulty. The warrior was held at the guardhouse at Fort Lincoln until April 1875, when he escaped. Rain-in-the-Face made his way back to his people, vowing to cut out Tom Custer's heart and eat it.

Herman Bencke, *The Last Battle of Gen. Custer.*

CHAPTER TWENTY-SIX

CUSTER'S GULCH

old!" In the late summer of 1874, newspapers across the country trumpeted the latest discovery in the Black Hills region of the Dakota Territory. The headline was irresistible. Gold fever gripped the country. A rush was on to the new El Dorado. And the man most responsible for this was George Custer. "The newspaper reports were enough to set the world crazy," the *Bismarck Tribune* wrote, "but those of Gen. Custer, confirming all others, settles the question—and seals the doom of the hostile Sioux."[1]

That summer Custer led an expedition into the hitherto unexplored Black Hills. The area had long been the subject of legend for whites and Indians alike. The Sioux considered the hills sacred—as did the Kiowa a hundred years earlier, before the Sioux ran them out. The hills were a good wintering spot, with ample game and firewood. And, said Philip Sheridan, there was "an Indian romance of a mountain of gold." He had heard this tale in the 1850s from Belgian Jesuit priest Pierre Jean De Smet. De Smet was the first Catholic missionary to visit the area and was instrumental in convincing some of the more warlike bands to attend the 1868 peace conference that ended Red Cloud's War. De Smet was known to the Indians as "Black Gown" and "The Great Medicine Man," and for his influence among the Sioux, he was dubbed "Friend of Sitting Bull."

The "mountain of gold" De Smet told of was in fact a formation of yellow mica, but that detail was less noted. Few whites had actually been to the Black Hills—exploratory missions in 1859 and 1861 had been turned back—and after the Treaty of Fort Laramie, the area was off-limits to any but the Indians. This inspired speculation and jealousy, the lure of the unknown coupled with resentment of "savages" who didn't know what to do with the fortune they were supposedly sitting on. Many scoffed that profitable development of the region was barred by "Sioux superstition." Periodic stories of wildcat prospectors being scalped fueled the belief that the Sioux had something to hide.

The Fort Laramie Treaty established the Great Sioux Reservation in present-day South Dakota, west of the Missouri River. This included most of the Black Hills except for a portion in Wyoming.[2] The treaty set apart the land "for the absolute and undisturbed use and occupation of the Indians" and prohibited anyone else except officers of the government on official business to "pass over, settle upon, or reside in the territory."

The Black Hills were not only sacred but militarily significant. "It is used as sort of a back-room to which they may escape after committing depredations," Custer said in an interview, "remaining in safety until quiet is again restored."[3] In 1873, Sheridan recommended establishing an Army post nearby, arguing the Indians "would never make war on our settlements as long as we could threaten their families and villages in this remote locality, abounding in game and all that goes to make

Indian life comfortable." The Custer expedition was sent "with this purely military object in view."[4]

In July 1874, Custer led a one-thousand-man expedition to the Black Hills seeking a site on which to build the post. The group included ten companies of the 7th Cavalry, five of which were commanded by George A. Forsyth of Sheridan's staff; two companies of infantry, commanded by Major L. H. Sanger; and a battery of three Gatling guns and one Rodman cannon, commanded by First Lieutenant Josiah Chance. There were also sixty Santee and Arickaree scouts, among them Bloody Knife and Bear's Ears, plus naturalists, mapmakers, geologists, prospectors, and one hundred wagons. Fred Grant was along again as an observer, as was Captain William Ludlow, chief engineer of the Department of Dakota. Ludlow was one of the cadets in the "fair fight" Custer had called for the day before graduation in 1861 that led to his arrest.

The two-month expedition covered 1,200 miles. The column marched west from Fort Lincoln near Bismarck through the northern section of the Black Hills, then swung through Montana and Wyoming, entering the southern part of the hills from the west. Some thought Custer was marching into trouble. The Cheyenne, Kiowa, and Comanche were raiding in Kansas, and there were rumors of thousands of Sioux braves also on the warpath. "The Indian Bureau has fed the Indians all winter and the ponies are fat," Sherman commented wryly, "so the savage warrior is in fine trim for the acquisition of fresh scalps and plunder."[5]

Some thought Custer's expedition would spark a general Indian war. "There is no earthly doubt that the Sioux will fight and are preparing for the conflict," the *New York World*'s correspondent wrote as the expedition set out.[6] "Fighting these red-skins will be no child's play," the *Chicago Journal* opined. "An army will be needed to save the little force now marching up the Missouri River before they enter the last and superstitiously-held rampart of the native American Indian." The paper believed that "before the summer is past it will not be surprising if we learn of hot work there between Gen. Custer and his 1,000 soldiers and Red Cloud with his 10,000 braves."[7]

Others thought Custer was more than able to handle himself, as he had been on the Yellowstone expedition the previous year. A newspaper reporting on a patrol against the Sioux that spring asserted that Custer's command "is good for ten times its number, and if he meets them, will probably follow them into their reservations, after giving them a severe thrashing."[8] Custer's acumen, as well as the three Gatling guns he was taking into the Black Hills, would give the cavalrymen a decided edge.

The threats grew as the expedition moved deeper into Indian territory. In August, Hunkpapa chief and war leader Four Horns, Sitting Bull's uncle, reportedly took to the field with thousands of braves, saying there was "no excuse for any of the Indians to remain at peace with the treacherous whites," and he would "intercept Custer if he lost half the braves of the nation."[9] Custer's scout, Bloody Knife, spoke to four Sioux braves who said "the whole Sioux Nation" was awaiting them. As the expedition drew to a close, there was rumor of a major battle with four thousand Sioux in which Custer lost forty men.

But in fact there was no war, no battle, and not even many shots fired in anger. The only deaths were two privates, one by disease and the other by accident. Custer's only face-to-face Indian encounter was when he and some scouts discovered the small village of Hunkpapa leader One Stab and boldly entered it, professing peace. Custer and the chief smoked a pipe, and all seemed well. But later One Stab tried to steal a rifle from one of Custer's scouts, and presently he and his village vanished.[10]

Another Sioux leader named Two Bears stampeded some government mules and sent word that Custer was "an old woman."[11] But Custer and a few men quickly rounded up the mules, and Two Bears took no further action. "The Sioux complain that they had other business cut out for the summer, an expedition of their own against the Crows," one paper archly reported, "and as they cannot attend to Custer's raid and the Crows at the same time, they proposed that the General should postpone his movement till next season."[12]

For the most part the Black Hills expedition was enjoyable, passing through beautiful country in agreeable weather. The rugged landscape was magnificent, but the whites were not as impressed with the Sioux holy sites. When an Indian guide named "Goose" brought Custer to a sacred Sioux cave—a hole a few feet deep in the side of a sandstone cliff—Custer countered that in the East there was "a cave that went 11 miles under the Earth, through which streams ran, and where the fish were blind." Goose responded with "a long and loud laugh of incredulity."[13]

The hunting was excellent, the best Custer had ever seen. He and Ludlow killed a grizzly, taking half a dozen shots to fell the eight-hundred-pound beast. "On receiving the final shot he cocked himself up on his hind legs," a reporter wrote, "and showing his huge teeth, grinned defiance; but like all who fight Custer, he was compelled to surrender." The reporter said the bear looked so fearsome he would "rather see old Sitting Bull" than another like it.[14] In addition to his kills, George brought back alive two badgers, four owls, an eagle, and a young jack rabbit for the Central Park Zoo.

The most important thing they brought back, however, was gold. Members of the expedition found small deposits at several locations. Custer sent a dispatch from the field noting the discovery but added that further study was needed. Yet even a hint of confirmation of the gold legends was enough for the newspapers.

"GOLD IN THE GRASS ROOTS AND IN EVERY PANFUL OF EARTH BELOW," screamed the *Bismarck Tribune* on August 26. "Anybody Can Find It—No Former Experience Required." The fact that miners would likely load up on supplies passing through Bismarck on their way to the alleged goldfields leant an aspect of civic duty to the *Tribune*'s cheerleading. But other papers quickly picked up the story of riches for the taking, which most people either already believed, or wanted to.

Colorful anecdotes spread that fueled the gold fever. A story circulated that a squaw came into Fort Lincoln with a gold nugget the size of a hen's egg, which she had simply picked up in the hills. A satirical piece attributed a tale to Chief Spotted Tail that goats grazing on Black Hills grass dropped dead from lumps of gold in their bellies. Hunkpapa senior chief Running Antelope reportedly faced off with Custer about the expedition, complaining that when white men saw how rich the land and its mineral wealth were, they would want to take it—which was true whether or not gold was actually there.

Custer added to the rising mania when the expedition returned. He said in an interview that press reports of the gold finds "are not exaggerated in the least; the prospects are even better than represented." He added that "the scientific gentlemen are satisfied that far richer discoveries will be made on further exploration. The miners also agree with this view of the case."[15]

But the "scientific gentlemen" were more circumspect. The expedition's chief geologist, Newton H. Winchell, was skeptical about the gold finds, and he and another geologist named Donaldson "assert that Custer does not know of his own knowledge that any color of gold was found in the Black Hills."[16] Fred Grant concurred with the skeptics. The reasoned consensus was that there was probably some gold in the area, but not enough to justify the hysteria. "And so after all that has been said about the Black Hills by Custer and his 'merrie' men, there is no gold there," the *Hamilton Examiner* concluded. "Prof. Winchell of Minnesota has knocked the wind out of that bag of gas."[17]

A story went around that the gold that was discovered had been planted. The previous year there had been a fraudulent gold find near

Sioux City, and an 1872 diamond hoax in Wyoming had swindled investors out of over $500,000.[18] Conspiracy theorists pointed to the beleaguered Northern Pacific Railroad, alleging it was trying to raise the value of its land grant to get out of bankruptcy. According to one paper, "The question with those who are instigating the movement into the Black Hills is not, 'Is there gold out there?' It is, 'Can we get a rush of men through our cities, over our railroads, and a rush of money in our pockets?'"[19] An anonymous writer who claimed to have been on the expedition cautioned people not to think there was gold enough to pay for the trouble of going there. "Of course the people already in the d—d country would like to induce as many more victims to come as possible;—ditto the railroad people." The writer alleged that "somehow or another, Gen. Custer seems to be in the ring interested in 'bulling' that country—I suppose from interested motives, of which I know nothing."[20]

Custer bridled at such personal attacks. The fact of gold in the Black Hills, he said, was "as certain as the law of gravity."[21] General Forsythe agreed with his assessment, saying the area was as rich as Colorado or Montana. The *Bismarck Tribune* lionized him: "All men not dead to the necessities of the hour, to the progress of the age, welcome the discoveries of Gen. Custer, and hail him, and the noble officers who have supported him as benefactors."[22] In the same edition, the paper offered a "magnificent Chromo-lithograph of this popular cavalry commander" with every two-dollar yearly subscription.

Sheridan wrote a widely reprinted communiqué to Sherman saying that while he suspected there might be some gold in the area, it was not in great quantities. He feared that gold fever in the Black Hills would lead inevitably to conflict as trespassers encountered young warriors seeking to protect their lands. "Many of the persons now crazy to go [to] the Black Hills never think of how they are to exist after they get there, or how they could return in case of failure," he wrote.[23] Sheridan deployed troops at key transit points to try to interdict prospectors and enforce Sioux rights under the 1868 treaty. "Not until the treaty rights of the Indians are extinguished by Congress," the *Boston Globe* noted sarcastically, "can the impatient gold-seekers enter into the happy valley discovered by Custer, except at their own peril."[24] The paper called the Custer expedition "entirely uncalled for and useless, beside being in direct contravention of treaty stipulations."[25]

The debate over whether gold existed, and in what amounts, was overcome by circumstances. Gold fever had taken hold as the Panic of 1873 deepened into a depression. "The country is now restless and full of men out of employment who will not be curbed," the *Bismarck Tribune* noted, "men who are infatuated with the idea of sudden wealth, and who will stake life, home and all they hold dear to reach this new Eldorado."[26]

"In vain have the cool-headed warned the adventurous youth of the land not to snap at the gilded bait," one newspaper observed. "A tale of gold has always been a potent spell and centuries of bitter experience have not been sufficient to teach people that hunting the yellow sham does not pay."[27] Miners and speculators flooded into the Black Hills, and outfitters founded a town that they named after Custer. There was also a Custer Peak, Custer Gap, and Custer Crossing, and gold was being sought in a valley called Custer's Gulch.[28] The military could not stop the influx, and the *Bismarck Tribune* said it "would require a larger army than it would take to guard the Rio Grande, were every Mexican determined to supply himself with American stock."[29]

By the spring of 1875, Custer's main preoccupation was finding ways to stem the gold rush he had helped start. In an interview in May 1875, he said the government was determined to "labor faithfully in protecting the Indians in their undoubted right, at present, to that portion of the Black Hills included in the treaty."[30] Custer thought it would be wise to vacate the Indians' treaty rights however possible, for example by purchasing the Black Hills. He said that the time had come when "it must be decided whether the dog-in-the-manger mode of the Indians will be tolerated."[31]

The *New York Herald* described Custer around this time as "tall, lithe, well-formed, with soft, light hair, a blonde moustache and a smooth face. A person unacquainted with him would little suspect that he is the terror of the bloodthirsty Sioux." They said his "keen blue eyes look straight into the eyes of the listener, and his courteous and sincere manner puts one at ease on first entering the room. When animated, his eyes flash and his nerves seem touched with fire."[32]

But for now the mission of the "terror of the bloodthirsty Sioux" was to keep miners out of the Black Hills. Some were removed by force; others were interdicted while heading into the area.[33] Custer warned that just because some prospectors made it to the area did not mean others would survive the trip, especially once the Indians decided to take matters into their own hands. "It is the height of folly for parties to imagine that [miners] can march across the Plains after the Indians are on the warpath," Custer cautioned. Whites trying to slip into the Black Hills would either be "killed outright" or, if they reached the area, would be "prevented from leaving their strongholds or places of concealment."[34]

"We have at once the declarations that the miners must stay away but that they will secure plenty of gold if they will come," a Pennsylvania paper wrote. "Bayonets and gold are respectively the repelling and inviting influences. Which will be the most potent remains to be seen."[35]

Another Black Hills survey was planned to settle the gold question, hopefully debunking the more outlandish claims of riches and stemming the tide of miners. Custer assumed he would lead the expedition; in May 1875 he told the press that he was departing Fort Lincoln June 1, and if there were large numbers of miners in the hills, "it will probably take the whole summer to drive them out and keep out the intruders."[36] But Custer had become too controversial, and instead the mission was given to Lieutenant Colonel Richard I. Dodge of the 23rd Infantry.[37]

Columbia University mining geologist Walter P. Jenney and Henry Newton of the Interior Department conducted rigorous surveys at various locations in the Black Hills. They were escorted by four hundred soldiers and shadowed by miners hoping to make immediate use of their findings. "The yield of gold thus far has been quite small and the reports of richness of the gravel bars are greatly exaggerated," Jenney said in an early report. "The prospects at present are not such as to warrant extended explorations in mining."[38]

Yet such was the intensity of the gold mania that even this pessimistic report was read as confirming that gold could be found. "Prof. Jenney reports to Indian Commissioner Smith that the yield of gold is not sufficient to make it pay well," one paper noted, "but the great body of miners, always waiting for an excitement, will not hesitate to go on and prospect for themselves, on the assurance that there is gold there at all." The paper noted that "assurance was early and deliberately given by General Custer and never taken back. Resting on his word alone, it has been sufficient to attract several thousand miners to the outskirts of the Black Hills."[39] The *Oakland Tribune* wrote that "nothing can now prevent the invasion of the new El Dorado by thousands of men who have been held back by the uncertainty of the reported wealth of the Black Hills."[40]

Since the government could not stop the invasion, it opened negotiations to purchase the land from the Sioux. The idea had been floated since the first reports of gold. Members of Congress, government experts, pundits, and advocates from all sides debated which lands should be sold, what price was fair, and how the money could be distributed to the Indians without falling into the hands of unscrupulous Indian agents, politicians, lawyers, thieves, and swindlers.

But while politicians and newspaper editors debated the finer details of implementing the Black Hills purchase, they overlooked one important fact: the Sioux had little interest in making a deal. As soon as the 1874 expedition returned, a group of chiefs, including Running

Antelope and Fire Heart of the Blackfoot Sioux, had an audience with Custer and "strongly protested against the violation of the treaty of 1868 by the white men going to the Black Hills."[41]

In May 1875, a Sioux delegation led by Spotted Tail, Red Cloud, Lone Horn, and an Oglala leader named Sitting Bull (sometimes called "the good Sitting Bull" to differentiate him from the more famous Hunkpapa leader) came to Washington to discuss a variety of issues, including the invasion of lands guaranteed them by treaty, the desecration of their holy places in the Black Hills, insufficient rations and annuities, and corruption in the Indian agencies. They met with President Grant, acting Secretary of the Interior Cowen, and Commissioner of Indian Affairs Smith, but received little in the way of assurances, especially regarding food. In fact, the government was subtly creating the food shortage as a means of leverage. This prompted Chief White Swan to observe sarcastically that "the worse an Indian behaves the more he gets."[42]

Commissioner Smith was mainly interested in settling the Black Hills question. Congress had authorized $25,000 to buy out the tribal hunting rights guaranteed under the Fort Laramie Treaty and also proposed to allocate funds to move the Sioux to much better lands elsewhere. But the chiefs would not bargain. "Look at me!" Red Cloud told one of Grant's emissaries. "I am no dog. I am a man. This is my ground, and I am sitting on it."[43] Spotted Tail told Smith that he wanted nothing to do with lands outside those he was born in, and "if it is such a good country, you ought to send the white men now in our country there, and let us alone."

The May meetings went nowhere. Episcopal Bishop William H. Hare of the Missionary District of Niobrara, which included the Sioux reservation, prophetically warned that "we should not be surprised if, insisting now upon buying with money what the Indian does not wish to sell, we drive him to frenzy, our covetousness ends in massacre, and we pay for the Indians' land less in money than in blood."[44] But the Grant administration and Congress were still eager to buy their way to a solution to the Black Hills problem.

In September 1875, a delegation was sent to Red Cloud Agency to reopen negotiations after reports that Spotted Tail might be willing to make a deal. Commissioners included General Terry, Senator William B. Allison of Iowa, and retired General Albert Gallatin Lawrence, among others. They were escorted by two companies of cavalry. Terry was very much in favor of fair play with the Indians and letting them stay unmolested in the Black Hills if they wanted. Custer said that "the Indians have no better friend than Gen. Terry. When I say friend, I mean a man that will see that they are justly dealt with."[45]

The delegation arrived to find a massive gathering of perhaps twenty thousand Indians, mostly Sioux, but also some Cheyenne and Arapaho. Any deal would require three-quarters of the adult male Sioux voting in favor for it to take effect, according to the Fort Laramie Treaty, and the mood among the assembled Indians was bitter. The chiefs, under pressure from their own people, at first snubbed the government delegation. But as the whites prepared to leave after a few days, Red Cloud, Spotted Tail, and other chiefs consented to talk, and the session opened.

The Brulé and Oglala leaders were willing to listen, but others actively opposed any negotiations. By this time Spotted Tail and Red Cloud were considered "peace chiefs" and had lost their authority over the more warlike factions, who looked to Sitting Bull for leadership. This is particularly ironic in the case of Red Cloud, who had successfully prosecuted a war against the whites. As the two delegations began the talks, thousands of armed, mounted Indians formed a crescent around the meeting tents. The two cavalry companies, led by Colonel Anson Mills and Captain James Egan, were deployed at the rear and flanks of the meeting area, and soon every cavalryman had a warrior with a loaded rifle behind him.

A few dozen warriors rode around whipping up excitement, while others were creeping closer in some nearby bushes. Then a Sioux warrior named Little Big Man, one of Crazy Horse's lieutenants, rode into the circle with a rifle and threatened to shoot any Indian leader who agreed to sell the Black Hills.

The situation was tense; the commissioners and their escort could well have been massacred, with a fair number of Indians also killed. Sitting Bull the Good said aside to a friend, "There will be trouble here, and I will kill the first Indian that tries a shot. You stand by and watch me."[46] But Oglala leader Young-Man-Afraid-of-His-Horses had planned for trouble. At a prearranged signal, one hundred of his men moved quickly between the hotheads and the commissioners, and three grabbed Little Big Man and led him away. This temporarily defused the crisis, and Spotted Tail suggested moving the negotiations to the relative safety of nearby Camp Robinson. At the reconvened meeting, Terry proffered the government's offer for the Black Hills: a leasing arrangement at $400,000 per year, or purchase for $6 million. But again the Indians were not interested, and the commissioners returned home.[47]

The Black Hills issue continued to simmer into the fall. Anger over the invasion of their sacred lands, along with insufficient supplies and mismanagement on the agencies, drove increasing numbers of Indians to join Sitting Bull's band living in the traditional manner in the unceded lands to the west of the Sioux reservation. With the Black Hills incursion out of control and winter approaching, the government began to discuss a military solution.

In late November, William E. Curtis of the *Chicago Inter-Ocean*, who had accompanied the Yellowstone expedition and was now Washington bureau chief for the paper, reported that planning was under way for a winter campaign against Sitting Bull. The purpose of the campaign was to "whip the hostiles into subjection for protection to whites, and the benefit of friendly Indians, and as winter is the only time to fight Indians successfully, preparations are being made accordingly."[48] The *Bismarck Tribune*, noting rumblings in favor of possible American intervention to support an anti-Spanish uprising that had broken out in Cuba, said that "the American people would prefer a war with Spain, but any kind of war will satisfy those panting for a fight, if it is nothing more than a winter campaign against poor old Sitting Bull, which seems to have fully been determined upon."[49]

War was indeed determined upon; all it needed was a pretext. On December 3, 1875, Secretary of the Interior Zachariah Chandler—who as senator from Michigan had invited Libbie on the boat trip to City Point, Virginia, in July 1864 to visit her Autie—ordered all Sioux to return to the reservation by the end of January, or be sent back by force. The sixty-day timeline was unrealistic given the poor state of communications with the renegade bands and the severity of the winter. Runners did not even set out from the agencies seeking Sitting Bull until the second week in January. Like the similar return order before Washita, Chandler's demarche was really intended to establish a rationale for military operations.

Sitting Bull's people were not going to return to the reservation, and the miners, then numbering around 1,200, were still seeking the elusive Black Hills gold.[50] William Courtenay, who traded with the Indians along the Yellowstone and was sometimes robbed by them, wrote in an open letter, "Will the Government never undertake the chastisement of Sitting Bull and his band of murderers, refugees and outlaws?" He said that Rain-in-the-Face, Blade Moon, and Low Dog were "a few of the Indian outcasts and ruffians" who compose this "camp of cut throats, who for years have indulged with impunity in rapine and murder, and laughed at the Government."[51]

"At the time we Oglalas had no thought that we would ever fight the whites," Chief Low Dog said. "Then I heard some people talking that the chief of the white men wanted the Indians to live where he ordered and do as he said, and he would feed and clothe them." The very idea of being dependent on the government offended Low Dog. "Why should I be kept as a humble man, when I am a brave warrior and on my own lands?" he said. "The game is mine, and the hills, and the valleys, and the white man has no right to say where I shall go, or what I shall do. If any white man tries to destroy what is mine, or take what is mine, or take my lands, I will take my gun, get on my horse, and go punish him."

Months later Senator William B. Allison, the Iowa Republican who had been at the failed September 1875 conference at Red Cloud Agency, pleaded with the Senate to reach an agreement with the Sioux in regard to the Black Hills. He cautioned that "unless some action be taken soon by Congress to treat with these Indians … a general Indian war would take place."[52] But by then the war was already upon them. "Gen. Custer intended to make a conquest of the new country and it is likely that he has succeeded," one editorialist wrote at the start of the gold rush. "Swarms of gold hunters are now collecting in the frontier towns, waiting for the spring break up, when they will invade the Black Hills. It is painful to contemplate the change which will be wrought in the peaceful country of the Sioux."[53]

CHAPTER TWENTY-SEVEN

GRANT'S REVENGE

On February 1, 1876, Secretary of the Interior Chandler informed Secretary of War Belknap that since Sitting Bull's followers had not come to the reservation, they were to be considered hostiles and "turned over to the War Department for such action on the part of the Army as you may deem proper under the circumstances."[1] He washed his hands of whatever might happen next. "This wasn't a fight instituted by the Army for glory going purposes, or anything of that kind," Captain Frederick Benteen wrote, "but rather, 'twas a little gentle disciplining which the Department of the Interior ... had promised would be given the Indians if they, the nomads of the tribe, declined to come in to agencies in the Spring."[2]

Sheridan envisioned three columns converging on the Indians somewhere east of the Bighorn Mountains. He intended to overcome the Indians' advantage in mobility by gradually reducing the area in which they could evade his forces and presenting them with increasingly poor options. If all went as planned, the Indians would either be forced into a battle they could not win, or surrender and return to the reservations under armed escort.

However, Sheridan's plan had several drawbacks. The columns would operate on exterior lines, separated by vast distances, making it difficult to communicate and coordinate movements. They would not know how many Indians they faced, or where they were. If one column made contact with the enemy, it would have to herd the Indians toward the other forces, not knowing exactly where those forces were, and hoping the Indians did not move in another, unexpected direction. Worst of all, the plan assumed the Indians would not do what any conventional military force would do in this situation: engage each column separately and defeat them in detail.

If the Indians did not know the war was coming, it was not for lack of press coverage. The *Bismarck Tribune*'s November 20 headline, "Winter Campaign against Sitting Bull," announced the coming conflict even before Chandler set his deadline. Operational details followed: a December report said that the Army "will carry on concerted movements from two sides, and if they once get an opportunity will make it very interesting for the warriors."[3] In February the *New York Times* ran a front-page story outlining most of the campaign plan, with Custer and Brigadier General George Crook moving from the east and south respectively, to "join their forces and attack Sitting Bull in the Powder River country, which is west of the Black Hills, and about one hundred and fifty miles east of the Big Horn Mountains." The article estimated Sitting Bull's force at six hundred to one thousand warriors.[4] Later reports bumped this number up to 1,500.[5] A Wisconsin paper predicted that soon they would hear "that Sitting Bull's convictions have undergone a radical change, and, if he survives the heroic treatment to which he will be subjected that he has concluded to abandon war, go into the agricultural business and raise corn and potatoes for a living."[6]

The first attempt was made in early spring. A column of eight hundred men set out in March under George Crook, Sheridan's roommate at West Point, who had been a Corps commander under him in the Civil War. Crook had fought successfully against the Apaches and was well regarded on the frontier. The Indians referred to him as Gray Fox.

Crook's force, ten companies of cavalry and two of infantry under Colonel Joseph J. Reynolds, were accompanied by a host of scouts, civilian drivers, and 85 wagons pulled by 892 mules. They moved slowly over icy trails and through snow storms, enduring bitter cold. Eventually they located an Indian village near the Powder River, which they thought was Crazy Horse's. In fact it was a Cheyenne band under Old Bear and Two Moons moving away from the more warlike groups because they did not want their people involved in whatever conflict was coming. They fought an inconclusive battle on March 17. Reynolds's men burned the village before leaving, and some of the teepees, packed with ammunition, exploded. The expedition achieved little, and Crook court-martialed Reynolds for leaving wounded men on the field.

Colonel John Gibbon—known to the Indians as "White Whiskers"—meanwhile left Fort Ellis in Montana in early April with six companies of the 7th Infantry and four troops of the 2nd Cavalry under Major J. S. Brisbin. They were to patrol the north bank of the Yellowstone River and intercept the Indians, whom Crook was supposed to be driving north. But the expected fleeing bands never materialized, and according to Lieutenant John F. McBlain, Gibbon's column "had used up all the rations it had taken with it, had drained all the Montana posts, and had contracted for meats and hard bread, long before there was any apparent movement in the south."[7]

A third column was supposed to have been led by Custer from Fort Lincoln around the same time but was delayed.[8] George had been summoned to Washington to participate in a political drama then unfolding that would culminate in the impeachment of the secretary of war.

Republicans had dominated in the 1866 midterm election, and after Ulysses S. Grant won the presidency in 1868, the GOP—then known as the Gallant Old Party—had firm control of the government. But economic hard times caused by the Panic of 1873, along with resurgent support for Democrats in the South as Reconstruction waned, turned the 1874 congressional election into a rout. Democrats picked up ninety seats in the House, taking control of the body with a 69-seat, 61 percent majority. State legislatures sent a net of nine new Democrats to the Senate, though they still only held twenty-eight of seventy-six seats. But controlling the House was enough. With their newly won subpoena power, Democratic committee chairs began a series of high-profile hearings taking aim at members of the Grant administration and striking at its chief vulnerability, corruption.

"As the end of the Presidential term approaches the influence of the incumbent wanes," an English observer wrote, "especially in such an official place-seeking society as that of the national capital. The motto in the scramble is— 'Every man for himself.'" The assault on the Grant administration had become "callous and reckless, ready to sacrifice anything for the power that bestows the place. The telegrams now daily reaching Europe from Washington show that the House Democratic majority is determined to crush the Executive."[9]

Grant was never the direct target of the investigations, but they touched those closest to him. A group found skimming taxes on whiskey shipped from St. Louis, dubbed the Whiskey Ring, was said to include Grant's trusted private secretary, Orville E. Babcock, who had served with him through the war. Grant remained loyal to his friend, but even though Babcock was found not guilty in his trial, he resigned under a cloud.[10] Grant's brother Orvil, with whom he was not close, was also implicated in wrongdoing.

Custer was called to testify before the House Committee on Expenditures in the War Department, in an investigation of Secretary of War William Worth Belknap. The committee chairman Hiester Clymer, Pennsylvania Democrat and Belknap's former roommate at Princeton, was looking into allegations of kickbacks, bribery, and other corruption in the government-controlled system of post traderships. Sutlers were traditionally appointed by officers in the various commands, but after 1870 the appointments were centralized in the office of the secretary of war and became a matter of political patronage. Suspicions were aroused by the lavish lifestyle Belknap maintained in Washington— far too expensive for a public servant earning $8,000 per year. Evidence had been uncovered that Belknap and his wife had accepted tens of thousands of dollars in return for rights to Army post traderships in Indian territory.

For a serving Army officer, stepping into this partisan struggle was highly impolitic. By 1876, however, Custer was more openly affiliated with the Democrats. He praised George McClellan in his Civil War memoirs then being serialized in *Galaxy*, abandoning his earlier caution. Many remembered his support for Andrew Johnson in 1866, and during the 1868 election, when Grant ran against former New York governor Horatio Seymour, the *New York Citizen* put Custer on a list of Democrat generals, along with McClellan and Winfield Scott Hancock.[11] In 1872, Custer attended a meeting in Louisville called the "Straight Out Democratic Convention," a group of dissident Democrats unhappy with the party endorsing Liberal Republican party nominee Horace Greeley for president. Custer was also known as a favorite of, and sometimes anonymous reporter for, the anti-Grant *New York Herald*.

By the time Custer was called to testify, the anti-Belknap campaign was already well under way. The House Committee on Military Affairs, chaired by Democrat Henry B. Banning of Ohio, had concluded its investigation, and Belknap resigned on March 2, 1876, the morning the committee report was read, in an attempt to limit the damage to the administration. However, the issue was too politically advantageous for the Democrats to let go, and after another round of hearings the House voted unanimously to impeach Belknap, even though he was no longer in office.[12]

Custer testified that it was a common belief in the Army that the secretary was in league with the corrupt traders at Army posts and in Indian reservations. He said that Robert C. Seip, the appointed post trader at Fort Abraham Lincoln, engaged in price gouging, and when officers went five miles off post to purchase items at reduced cost, Seip threatened to use his high-level connections to have them punished. Seip and Alvin C. Leighton were subcontractors for retired Brigadier General John M. Hedrick and Washington attorney and Belknap friend E. M. Rice, who between them received one-half to two-thirds of the trading post's profits. Custer said that "out of his profits of $15,000 [Seip] only received $2,500; he said he did not know, but he understood a portion of it went to the Secretary of War."[13] Seip in his testimony confirmed the legal business relationship with Hedrick and Rice, but had no knowledge of payments to Belknap.[14]

Hedrick testified with Custer sitting beside Clymer, prompting the congressman with questions.[15] Hedrick denied that there were any bribes paid for the tradership and claimed he had made no money on his investment. In a newspaper column, Hedrick pointed out that if Belknap was receiving illicit payments from the Fort Lincoln trading post, it was "somewhat remarkable" that he left Custer, a known enemy, in command there. He also said that policy provided for a board to be appointed at each Army post to oversee prices, so if there was price gouging, it was Custer's fault for not stopping it.[16]

Custer raised a number of other issues, such as traders putting advanced weapons and rum in the hands of the Indians for profit, grain being stolen from Army stores and resold, and Belknap allegedly seeking ways to have whiskey smuggled from Canada at reduced rates, implicitly hinting at a Whiskey Ring connection. He also said that a presidential proclamation of January 1875 extending the boundary of the Great Sioux Reservation to include the east bank of the Missouri enhanced the value of the official traderships "by making them a more perfect monopoly, by removing all opposition and rivalry" from private traders.[17]

Custer was asked why he had never previously reported the many abuses he alleged. He cited a March 1873 War Department order that "no officer should suggest or recommend any action by members of congress in regard to military affairs" and mandating that "all petitions on these subjects be forwarded through the General of the Army and the Secretary of War." In addition, any officer visiting Washington while Congress was in session was required to register with the adjutant general and explain why he was in the city, under whose authority, and how long he was staying. Custer said this order "closed the mouths of all army officers with regard to the abuses that existed on the frontier" since they knew if they sent a complaint to Congress through the secretary of war's office, the complaints "would be pigeon-holed and the officers would probably be pigeon-holed, too."[18]

Custer incensed Belknap, who called his testimony "a collection of falsehoods, mean insinuations, and gossipy lies."[19] There were rumors that

Belknap's allies would find a way to court-martial Custer. George A. Forsyth, normally friendly to Custer, said that "he has yet to meet a single officer of the army who approves of the action of either Custer or [General Alexander] McCook as to their testimony, which they declare to be nothing but hearsay, and made up largely of frontier gossip and stories."[20]

"Custer testified like one spurred by a grievance," one report observed.[21] And he did seem to be out to settle some old scores. He privately gave damning information to investigators on the Banning Committee against 7th Cavalry Major Lewis Merrill regarding an alleged bribe Merrill had taken in 1870 as a judge advocate to arrange quartermaster Samuel B. Lauffer's acquittal during a court-martial. Merrill was also being looked at for accepting a $21,400 reward from the governor of South Carolina for his efforts in apprehending and convicting members of the Ku Klux Klan. The reward was not illegal, but since Merrill was acting in an official capacity, some considered it unprofessional. Merrill responded angrily in the *Army Navy Journal*, and one paper called the covert bribery charge a "vile slander" from the "immaculate Custer."[22]

Custer ignored his critics and spent much of his time meeting with important people in office calls, at official functions, and at dinners and receptions. "I cannot tell you how overwhelmed I am with engagements," he wrote Libbie.[23] Senator Thomas F. Bayard of Delaware, a leading Democrat and potential presidential contender, held a dinner in Custer's honor attended by Clymer and other political luminaries, including some former Confederates with whom Custer had battled. New York Democratic congressman Robert Roosevelt, uncle to the future president Theodore Roosevelt, invited Custer to a dinner at the Manhattan Club—"*the* Democratic Club of New York," he gushed to Libbie, though noting his duties in Washington conflicted.[24]

People speculated that Custer was seeking a brigadier's star under a future Democrat president, or appointment as secretary of war. Helping expose Belknap's corruption would have made him an attractive candidate for that post, in addition to his record of service. Democrats quoted Custer's congressional testimony extensively in their 1876 national campaign briefing book, which supported their key anti-corruption theme.[25]

There is a popular belief that George Custer was seeking the Democratic presidential nomination. At the time he predicted "some western man and a civilian will most likely be the Democratic nominee," but "the thing is in such a mix it is hard to say."[26] One of Custer's Arikara scouts, Red Star, stated thirty years after Little Bighorn that Custer had told them during the Sioux campaign that "no matter how small a victory he could win, even though it were only against five tents of Dakotas, it would make him President, Great Father, and he must turn back as soon as he was victorious."[27]

Even if Custer said this, it is unlikely he was actually seeking the nomination.[28] One reason was timing; the Democratic Convention was set for June 27, and even had Custer hurried off to victory, he would not have had time to translate that success into a nomination. He would also have had to overcome New York governor Samuel J. Tilden, who had a strong enough political machine to win the nod after two ballots.[29] Speculation beyond Tilden focused on Governor Thomas A. Hendricks of Indiana, who had almost captured the nomination in 1868.[30] "I think Hendricks has the best show of any of them," Custer said in a March 1876 interview.[31]

If the Democrats had wanted a war hero, they already had one in Winfield Scott Hancock. Hancock was very active in Democratic politics and a presidential hopeful in 1868 and 1876, finally securing the nomination in 1880, but losing to James A. Garfield.[32] So far as military men went, Custer thought nominating General Sherman was a "Capital suggestion" and that he would "run like a steer."[33] Sherman, famously disgusted with politics, wasn't interested.

Custer's name did not come up in public discussions of candidates for the 1876 race. Perhaps a victorious Custer could have been a vice presidential pick that year, but nothing more. However if Custer, the young, dashing, articulate Northerner and war hero, had been nominated, and had taken all the states Tilden won in the hotly contested and controversial 1876 race against Ohio Republican governor Rutherford B. Hayes, as well as his adopted home state of Michigan, the Boy General would have become, at age thirty-seven, the youngest man elected to the nation's highest office—the Boy President.

But even Custer knew this was not going to happen. And not all Democrats were Custer fans. New York congressman Samuel S. "Sunset" Cox, a known wit among the members, gave a lively speech on the Indian question with Custer present (George had been granted the privilege of the floor during his visit), with pointed references to Washita. Afterward, he came over and said, "Well, Custer, I guess I have taken your scalp."

"Wait till I get you on the Plains," George replied dryly. "Then I will turn you over to those gentle friends of yours."[34]

After a few weeks in Washington, Custer faced an even chillier climate. According to his testimony, in September 1875 he refused a delivery of eight thousand bushels of corn at Fort Lincoln, which he believed had been stolen from the Indian Bureau. He claimed he reported this through channels to the War Department, but word came back signed by the secretary of war to accept the corn.[35] Custer told the committee that food supplies at the Standing Rock Agency had run out that winter, with rapacious merchants selling scarce grain at extortionate prices, forcing some Indians to eat their ponies.

But when Chairman Clymer asked for a copy of Custer's original report, it could not be located. "No report of that character can be found," the War Department reported, "nor is there any record of the receipt of such report, or of any directions to General Custer from the War Department or any of its bureaus respecting this subject."[36] Close review of his testimony showed that most of it was not verifiable.

"General Custer is losing something of his prestige before the investigating committee," the *New York Times* reported. "He is full of information as an egg is of meat, but somehow it is only hearsay and gossip, and no witnesses appear to corroborate it. If this sort of thing goes too far, the Democrats, if they should have control of the next Administration, may not, after all, make him a Brigadier General."[37]

Custer happily left Washington on April 20, stopping off at the Centennial Exposition in Philadelphia before continuing to New York. But on April 24, the Senate managers of the Belknap impeachment called him back. Custer was growing anxious. The Sioux campaign awaited, and he sensed he had overplayed his hand in Washington. Ironically, in an effort to be released, he admitted what most of his detractors had already pointed out, that his evidence was mostly hearsay.[38]

George wrote to Libbie that he was being "called on to do more than I desire.... I care not to abuse what influence I have."[39] He said he sought to "follow a moderate and prudent course, avoiding prominence."[40] But it is hard to see how he could have been any more in the spotlight.

Sherman then stepped in to help. There was no love lost between Sherman and Belknap. Belknap has "acted badly by me ever since he reached Washington," Sherman wrote to his brother, Senator John Sherman.[41] Belknap had systematically undermined Sherman's power as commanding general. Sherman actually moved his headquarters to St. Louis in 1874 to escape Washington and the "ornamental part of the army" and to be with "the real working army."[42] Sherman liked Custer and had no particular problem with his role in taking Belknap down. The general had taken Custer to meet the interim war secretary, Alonzo Taft (father of the future president William Howard Taft), when he came to Washington, and George wrote Libbie that Taft "received me with great cordiality."[43] Seeing Custer's difficulty Sherman requested Taft write a letter authorizing him to go back to Dakota to prepare for the Sioux campaign.

Unfortunately, Grant "was not pleased with General Custer, and ... he wanted the expedition started out from Fort Lincoln without him."[44] Custer had done much to antagonize Grant, and his testimony compounded Grant's embarrassment. Custer, who was habitually sensitive to the political winds, seemed to be "trying to brow-beat the President," as Belknap wrote his sister. "He *may* succeed. Anything seems possible nowadays."[45]

Custer's motives are unclear. During the war he had enjoyed a good relationship with Grant, and he was very solicitous of Fred Grant.[46] He may have resented that Grant had not stepped in to stop the 1867 court-martial and had not helped him achieve the rank and station he felt he deserved. Perhaps he also secretly resented that young Fred wore the same rank he did, with no wartime experience and little record of accomplishment.

Custer criticized Grant's Indian policy in *My Life on the Plains* and worked behind the scenes with Democratic-leaning papers to defame the administration. That Grant would seek to remind him who was commander in chief is hardly surprising. Custer should have considered himself lucky to still be wearing the uniform. S. L. A. Marshall wrote that in Custer's postwar career he "proved to be both erratic and intractable, a source of worry to his military superiors, so impulsive that his actions several times shocked and embarrassed the President.... The wonder is that he was not bounced out of the Army."[47]

On April 28 Sherman telegraphed Sheridan that Grant had instructed to "send some one else than General Custer in command of that force from Fort Abe Lincoln."[48] On April 29 Sheridan suggested General Alfred Howe Terry, which was approved. Custer was frantic when Sheridan shared this information with him. The Belknap impeachment managers had released him the same day, but Sherman advised Custer not to leave Washington until he could get an audience with the president the following Monday. Sherman then left for New York.

Custer had tried to see Grant two times before and been snubbed. He sought a third audience with Grant on May 1 and waited five hours at the White House. While he was waiting, Deputy Quartermaster General of the Army Rufus Ingalls, whom Custer had known in the war, happened by. After conferring with Grant, Ingalls informed Custer that Grant would not see him, and that he might as well leave. Ingalls probably meant that George should leave the White House, not leave town, but that is how Custer took it. He checked out at the War Department and hopped a train west.

George was in Chicago in a rail car readying to leave for St. Paul on May 4 when he was detained. "I am at this moment advised that General Custer started last night for St. Paul and Fort Abraham Lincoln," Sherman had wired Sheridan. "He was not justified in leaving without seeing the President and myself. Please intercept him and await further orders; meantime let the expedition proceed without him."⁴⁹ Sherman had been trying to help Custer, but now George had pushed matters too far. He was charged with having left Washington without reporting to Grant or Sherman—though the former refused to see him and the latter was in New York City. That same day the *New York World* published a lengthy editorial entitled "Grant's Revenge," castigating the president for an act of "miserable vengeance" against Custer. The article contained details that could only have come from Custer himself, and it hurt his relationship with Sherman and Taft by publicly implying they sided with Custer over Grant.

Custer reported to Sheridan, who dressed him down for getting involved with politics at the expense of his duties. Custer sent two contrite telegrams to Sherman but was simply told to report to Fort Lincoln, where he would remain while the expedition went forward. On

May 5, Grant recommended command of the 7th Cavalry during the expedition be given to Major Marcus Reno. "The Army," Sherman said, "possesses hundreds of officers who are as competent for the command of any expedition as General Custer."[50]

Custer's removal from the Sioux campaign was widely commented on. "Everybody that has any acquaintance with [Custer] will admit that a little 'set down' will do him no harm," the *Baltimore American* opined. "Gen. Grant is very unlike Custer in his method of doing things, but he knows how to administer an effective 'snub' in a quiet way."[51]

But the anti-Grant papers were less measured. "The removal of General Custer from his command by the President is a scandalous performance," the *Indiana Democrat* groused. Custer's testimony "was displeasing to the extortionate post traders in whose interest the President has been working; and Custer is removed to deter other officers from telling what they knew."[52]

Custer went to see General Terry in St. Paul for one final try. According to Colonel Robert Hughes, Terry's brother-in-law, Custer begged Terry on his knees for help. Terry was sympathetic; he liked Custer and respected his experience in operations against the Indians. Terry, a graduate of Yale Law School, helped Custer draft a persuasive appeal to Grant,

"I appeal to you as a soldier to spare me the humiliation of seeing my regiment march to meet the enemy and I not share its dangers," he wrote.[53] Sheridan made his case, saying Custer's early return from suspension in 1868 had worked out well. And Terry cleared up the matter of the disputed corn shipment, saying there was no record of Custer's complaint because he had never passed it along to the War Department and instead authorized delivery himself.

On May 8, Grant relented. He allowed Custer to lead the 7th Cavalry on the campaign, but Terry remained in overall command of the mission. The Democratic press pounced. "General Custer goes in disgrace, being permitted to fight only under punishment," observed the *New York Herald*. "This last bit of news shows weakness and apology on the part of the President, but it does not wipe out the stain with which he has covered himself."[54] But the pro-Grant press pushed back, particularly noting the fickleness of papers that used to hold Custer in low regard. "No officer in the United States army has received more abuse from the democratic newspapers than the brilliant and dashing Custer," the *Baltimore American* noted. "But now that the president has found it necessary to give him a gentle reminder that there are courtesies due to superior officers, which the bravest of the brave are not at liberty to neglect, these caustic critics have suddenly discovered that Custer is the most accomplished officer in the United States army [and] that he is the greatest Indian fighter on the continent."[55]

Some papers had it right. "Gen. Custer, although he is a very garrulous man, and talks too much for his own good, is a gallant officer, whose past record ought to have spared him the humiliation from which he has so narrowly escaped," the *Chicago Tribune* noted. "It should prove a warning to him, however, of the danger of being such a swift and willing witness in partisan investigations, especially when it eventuates that he has nothing to say of any value."[56]

Custer was elated. He again was given a chance to salvage his career and reputation and find redemption on the battlefield. After Custer learned of Grant's decision, he ran into Captain William Ludlow and told him excitedly that once the campaign was under way he would "cut loose" at the first opportunity.[57] He planned to go out among the Indians and find a battle he would be remembered for.

CHAPTER TWENTY-EIGHT

"DON'T BE GREEDY"

Early on May 17, 1876, the 7th Cavalry set off from their camp near Fort Lincoln with close to 1,000 men, 1,700 animals, and 200 wagons, in a column stretching two miles. Mists lay low in the cool, early-morning darkness, and the cavalrymen had the illusion of "riding in the sky."[1]

The command passed the fort to cheers from the whites and wailing from the resident Indians, their traditional sendoff to warriors. The band struck up "Garryowen"; Tom Custer waved his hand toward the column and called to someone at the fort, "A single company of that can lick the whole Sioux nation!" He was perhaps unknowingly paraphrasing Fetterman's boast before he and his command were wiped out.[2]

George Custer was his usual flamboyant self, wearing his frontier garb, his hair cropped short. Reporter Mark Kellogg wrote: "Gen. George A. Custer, dressed in a dashing suit of buckskin, is prominent everywhere.

Here, there, flitting to and fro. In his quick eager way, taking in every-thing connected with his command, as well as generally, with the keen, incisive manner for which he is so well known. The General is full of perfect readiness for a fray with the hostile red devils, and woe to the body of scalp-lifters that comes within reach of himself and brave com-panions in arms."

The campaign was very much a family affair; Tom was there, of course, and brother-in-law James Calhoun. Along for the adventure was Custer's eighteen-year-old nephew, Armstrong "Autie" Reed, listed offi-cially as a herder but really just out for the summer with his uncle. Boston Custer was there too, as a "guide." Nevin Custer said that they had "gone back with [George] after his last visit home, just to see the country and be along with him as leader of the expedition."

Libbie accompanied the column for a day before riding back to the fort, and the couple had an emotional leave-taking. In light of later events, some took this as a premonition, but it was not unusual for them. While he was in Washington, George showed some of Libbie's love-laden letters to a woman who said, "Your sweetheart sent them. Never your wife."

"Both are one," George replied.

"What?" she said. "How long have you been married?"

"Twelve years."

"And haven't gotten over that?"

"No," George said. "And never shall."[3]

The Sioux campaign was relaunched with an almost identical plan to the one partially implemented weeks earlier.[4] Again it was a three-pronged operation. Crook was to move north from Fort Fetterman with 1,350 men, the largest of the three columns. Gibbon with five hundred men from the 2nd Cavalry and 7th Infantry would move east down the

Yellowstone River from Fort Ellis, and Terry would move west from Fort Lincoln with over nine hundred men, predominately the 7th Cavalry, under Custer, and including a small unit with three Gatling guns. Supply points were set along the Yellowstone where the steamers *Far West* and *Josephine* would periodically meet them. Libbie declined an invitation to accompany the ships to meet the column.

While the campaign plan was little changed, the facts on the ground had been in flux since Secretary Chandler's December 1875 ultimatum. It was no longer winter, and all the relative advantages the Army enjoyed in the colder months were lost. With the approach of summer, and the accompanying warmer weather, abundant grass, and better hunting, there were significantly more Indians in the area of operations. Besides, four months had passed since the January deadline to return to the reservations, with no dire consequences. If the Indians ever took Sheridan's threats seriously, they didn't now.

Meanwhile, the rationale for the campaign had been overcome by events. The Black Hills were not turning out to be the El Dorado that rumors and reporters had promised. Around the time Crook and Gibbon launched the first, failed Sioux expedition, a prospector named George Drake wrote to the *Kansas City Times*, "Tell the people in the States that the people who have a means of making a living had better remain there."[5] A reporter from the *Times* spoke to miners in the area, and while opinions on the prospects ranged from enthusiasm to disgust, most concluded there was not gold enough to justify the rush. He called this a "secret [that] has been jealously and closely guarded by those interested in mining claims and town property in Custer."[6] With interest waning, land values in Custer City had collapsed; lots that had sold for five hundred dollars dropped to two dollars. "As far as mining went," a reporter concluded, "Custer City was a delusion."[7]

James A. Tomlinson wrote to friends in Chicago, "I wish I was home. The Black Hills is a fraud of the first water. Be kind enough to advise any and all my friends to keep out of this corridor of hell, as nothing has really been found here to warrant them coming. There is more suffering than gold here. Oh God! how cold and hungry I am."[8] The *New York Times* reported that "the only lively business in the region is that of whiskey selling." The paper alleged that there was a "systematic attempt to mislead" and the entire story of gold was a "monstrous delusion." Miners were grossing an average fifty-five dollars per month, and "men who are willing to live on starvation diet in the wilderness, and in daily terror of death by violence, for that income, are crazy."[9] The *Times* called the notion of gold in the Black Hills "the champion swindle of the Centennial year."[10]

Some blamed Custer, accusing him of boosterism at best, and at worst collusion in fraud. But there was no evidence he ever profited personally from the gold rush, and the *Bismarck Tribune* mounted a vociferous and exaggerated defense. If Custer was guilty, the paper said, he was "guilty of causing at least fifty thousand people to get rich out of the ground the noble red man has no use for" and "opening the richest and most extensive gold fields the world ever knew."[11] It was an improbable claim, but history bore it out. In September 1874, Custer said that he was "satisfied that a rich mining region will be found in the northeastern portion of the Hills."[12] A year and a half later, four miners discovered the Homestake deposit fifty-six miles north of Custer City. Homestake became the largest and deepest gold mine in North America, and by the time it closed in 2002 it had produced over 2.7 million pounds of gold.

The Sioux expedition went forward regardless of the changing circumstances. Terry moved west on May 17; Crook set off from Fort Fetterman on May 29; and Gibbon's column, which had set off in April, was already camped along the Yellowstone.

The campaign attracted a lot of press attention. Sherman had sent word to Terry to "advise Custer to be prudent, and not to take along any newspapermen who always work mischief."[13] But Terry disobeyed Sherman's guidance and granted permission for a reporter from the *Bismarck Tribune* to come along. Mark Kellogg, a *Tribune* reporter and Associated Press stringer, went in place of editor Clement Lounsberry, who was nursing his ailing wife. Kellogg's reports were also carried in the *New York Herald*, where Custer had arranged to send his own anonymous reports. As one paper unkindly put it, "Gen. Custer is troubled with a personal vanity which makes him overly anxious to see his name in the papers."[14]

Terry's column moved west in search of the foe, said to be nearby and in large numbers. The country got progressively more difficult as they proceeded. Rains slowed the advance, muddy tracks hampering the wagons. Custer personally led some scouts, but they found only old Indian camps. Private Peter Thompson of C Company said that Custer's rushing ahead of the column "would have seemed strange to us had it not been almost a daily occurrence. It seemed that the man was so full of nervous energy that it was impossible for him to move along patiently." Custer's thoroughbred mounts outpaced the government-issued horses, and he also had his dogs along "for hunting purposes and many a chase he and his brother had when on this march."[15]

Boston Custer wrote to his mother that George, Tom, and he, with Lieutenant William Cooke, Second Lieutenant Winfield Scott Edgerly, and some soldiers and Indian guides, raced ahead of the column to the Powder River on June 7, seeking a passable route over the badlands, with sharp cliffs, sagebrush, and cactus. They were, he claimed, "the first white men to visit the river at this place." They got so far out in advance they had to stop, but the column caught up that night. Boston hoped the campaign would be a success, "and if Armstrong could have his way I think it would be," but other officers with limited experience and "having an exalted opinion of themselves, feel that their advice would be valuable in the field."[16]

Days passed with no signs of the enemy. "All stories about large bodies of Indians being here are the merest bosh," Custer wrote.[17] But as long as the Indians did not want to be found, the lumbering column would never find them. And elsewhere they were making their presence known.

On June 16 Crook's column reached the headwaters of the Rosebud River. He received a message from Sitting Bull via Crazy Horse saying, "Come so far, but no farther; cross the river at your peril."[18] Crook crossed, and the next day battle was joined. Crazy Horse struck first. The Indians mounted a series of massed frontal attacks on Crook's men, a rarity on the Plains, and wholly unlike the tactics of the Apaches Crook was used to fighting, who conducted ambushes with small bands.

"Come on Dakotas," Crazy Horse said, leading his warriors into the fray, "it's a good day to die!" But there was bravery evidenced on both sides, and when Colonel "Fighting Guy" Henry of the 3rd Cavalry was shot through both cheeks and partially blinded, he shrugged off the wound saying, "It's nothing. For this are we soldiers."[19]

They fought across the valley for six hours until, as one Indian participant put it, "we got tired and we were hungry, so we went home." Crook had suffered only fifty casualties and held the battlefield. He could have given chase, or resumed his march north down the Rosebud. But he had expended much of his ammunition, and rather than waiting for his train to come to him, he pulled back fifty miles to Goose Creek where his wagons were waiting. There, inexplicably, Crook sat until August.

Crook felt he had won the battle on the Rosebud, and perhaps he did by most measures. But he squandered his victory by not continuing north toward the other two converging columns. From the Indians' perspective, Crook won nothing. The whites approached; they were warned to stop; they kept on coming; there was a fight; then the whites went back the way they came. If anything, Crazy Horse could be justified in assuming the victory had been all on his side.

Crook also made no move to communicate directly with Terry or Gibbon to inform them of the Rosebud battle, or his unilateral decision to bow out of the campaign. This significant lapse in judgment compromised the entire expedition. His column represented about half the strength of the overall force, and Terry and Gibbon assumed Crook was still in the field and maneuvering according to plan. If a detached war party of Sioux and Cheyenne could push back Crook's men, the entire band of warriors from the combined nations could easily deal with the others—especially a flying column under Custer.

Libbie wrote to George of news reports of a "small skirmish" between Crook and the Indians. "They call it a *fight*," she wrote. "The Indians were very bold. They don't seem afraid of anything." But Custer did not receive the letter. Terry complained that he heard nothing from Crook and "if I could hear I would be able to form plans for the future more intelligently."[20] But by then Crook was out of action, waiting for reinforcements, and hunting and fishing in the Bighorn Mountains.[21] He sent word of the Rosebud battle to Sheridan in Chicago, but the dispatch did not reach Terry until a week after the battle at Little Bighorn. S. L. A. Marshall concluded, "The whole operation proceeded as if, instead of hunting Indians, the Army was seeking a memorable catastrophe."[22]

Once Terry's force reached the Powder River, they headed downstream to the supply point on the Yellowstone to find Gibbon. They still had not located the Indians. Crow scouts believed that the band would be found in the "big bend" of the Little Bighorn, then 120 miles distant. To try to get some grasp of where the enemy was, and perhaps where Crook had gotten to, Terry sent a scouting expedition up the Powder River under Major Marcus Reno on June 10.

Reno was a taciturn officer whom the Arikara scouts called Man With Dark Face. He entered West Point with the Class of 1855, but due to a series of washouts and reinstatements graduated two years late.[23] Like Custer, he was often caught breaking the rules, and over his six years he racked up 1,031 demerits, far outpacing Autie's 726. But Reno had six years to work on his total against Custer's four, and he averaged 171.8 per year versus George's 181.5.

Reno served in the Civil War as the commander of the 12th Pennsylvania Cavalry and rose to the rank of brevet brigadier general. He was one of three majors in the 7th Cavalry, and the only one present on the campaign. He had never fought in an Indian battle and never before served directly under Custer, since this was the first time all the companies of the regiment had gone on campaign. And Reno had definitely gotten off on the wrong foot with his commander. Weeks earlier when Custer was fighting for his command and career, Reno had lobbied to be named commander in his stead, and Grant concurred.

Reno scouted about sixty miles up the Powder River, then turned west. He found evidence of an encampment near the Tongue River, and even clearer signs along the Rosebud. Meanwhile, the rest of the command marched to the mouth of the Tongue River to meet the *Far West*, then proceeded to the Rosebud, linking up with Reno along the way on the nineteenth. His scout had gone farther and taken longer than expected, and Terry chastised him for exceeding his orders. But Reno brought back valuable information. He had run across the remains of huge campsites with evidence of around four hundred campfires, and a trail leading toward the Little Bighorn valley. Reno estimated around eight hundred enemy, though Terry assumed the number was closer to prior reports of 1,500. Custer, who had opposed the scout from the beginning, criticized Reno's "failure to follow up the trails [which] has imperiled our plans by giving the village an intimation of our presence."[24]

Terry's force arrived at the mouth of the Rosebud on June 21, meeting Gibbon with a battalion of troops, the rest encamped upstream. The two commanders and Custer held a meeting aboard the steamer *Far West* to plan their next steps. They came up with a plan for a two-pronged operation. Custer would leave June 22 and take the 7th Cavalry south up to the headwaters of the Rosebud, turn west to the upper reaches of the Little Bighorn valley, and move north downstream. Gibbon and Terry would meanwhile move to the mouth of the Bighorn and head upriver to the Little Bighorn. The idea was to catch the Indians in a pincer movement, assuming that the enemy was where they thought they were and that the timing worked. Terry wrote Sheridan that he hoped at least "one of the two columns will find the Indians."[25] Trooper McBlain believed "the plan would have worked admirably had both its parts been conducted as the commander had a right to expect they would be."

Custer was the wild card. Terry had wanted him to come on the expedition because of his knowledge of the area, his experience fighting Indians, and his tactical intuition. But Custer on the hunt was hard to restrain, and Terry complicated things by giving him a written order that allowed ample room for interpretation. "It is of course impossible to give you definite instructions as to your movements," Terry wrote. "Even were it otherwise, the Officer in Command has too much confidence in your zeal, energy and skill to give you directions which might hamper your freedom of action when you have got into touch with the enemy." He then gave Custer very definite instructions on his expected movements, but the damage was done. George assumed that Terry would let Custer be Custer.

Later that evening General Terry went back to Custer's tent to reinforce his intention that he should use his discretion if he encountered the Indians.

"Custer, I do not know what to say for the last," Terry said.

"Say what you want to say," George replied.

"Use your own judgment, and do what you think best if you strike the trail," Terry said. "And whatever you do, Custer, hold on to your wounded."[26]

Afterward, Custer emerged from his tent and saw Lieutenant Cooke and Lieutenant Edgerly sitting on a log smoking. "General, won't we step high if we do get those fellows!" Edgerly said.

"Won't we!" George replied. But he said it depended on the junior officers. "We are going to have a hard ride, for I intend to catch those Indians even if we have to follow them to their agencies."[27]

Boston Custer wrote to his mother that he was "feeling first-rate" and they would set off the next day. He said Armstrong was going "with the full hope and belief of overhauling [the Indians]—which I think he probably will, with a little hard riding. They will be much entertained."[28] He hoped to bring back one or two Indian ponies "with a buffalo robe for Nev."

Back at Fort Lincoln on the morning of the twenty-second, Libbie wrote, "My own darling—I dreamed of you as I knew I should…. Oh Autie how I feel about your going away so long without our hearing…. Your safety is ever in my mind. My thoughts, my dreams, my prayers, are all for you. God bless and keep my darling."[29]

That same morning, George wrote to Libbie about the freedom of action he believed Terry had given him on his "scout," quoting only the relevant portion of the order. "Do not be anxious about me," he wrote. "You would be surprised how closely I obey your instructions about keeping with the column. I hope to have a good report to send you by the next mail." He signed off, "Your devoted boy Autie."[30]

At noon the 7th Cavalry passed in review before Terry, Gibbon, and Custer as it made its way out of camp, heading for the Rosebud. The Indian scouts rode after, singing the traditional death songs that preceded a battle. They did so at George's request; as scout Red Star noted approvingly, "Custer had a heart like an Indian."[31]

Custer left to join his command. "God bless you!" Terry shouted after him.

"Now Custer, don't be greedy!" Gibbon added. "Wait for us!"

"No," George replied. "I won't."[32]

CHAPTER TWENTY-NINE

A RIDGE TOO FAR

A ccounts of conflicts have been questioned since Cain slew Abel, but few battles have been as minutely analyzed as the Battle of the Little Bighorn. "The incidents of a battle are so numerous and changing," Custer once wrote, "that the entire field may be regarded as an immense series of animated kaleidoscopes, the number of which is only limited by the number of observers, no two of the latter obtaining exactly the same view, and no individual probably obtaining the same view twice." He noted that "marked and sometimes apparently irreconcilable discrepancies occur in the recorded testimony of those who were prominent actors in the same event."[1]

The Battle of Little Bighorn especially is a topic that raises passionate arguments—and no clear answers. It has inspired more people to spend more time getting into more arguments over more facets than almost any battle in American history, save maybe Gettysburg, where Custer also fought. While the final truth of Little Bighorn remains elusive, the fact that people keep trying to uncover it, or become ardently convinced that they have, says more about Custer and his story than anything regarding the battle itself.

The force Custer led up the Rosebud included 31 officers, 566 men, 40-odd scouts, and around a dozen others. He left the available Gatling guns behind, in the interests of mobility, and refused the services of four companies of Gibbon's cavalry. Custer "thought his regiment strong enough to cope with any body of hostiles that might be out," Lieutenant McBlain said.[2] Terry also made him leave behind his brass band.

Custer set the pace hard from the start, seeking to overtake Sitting Bull's village as he had Stone Forehead's Cheyenne in 1869. On the second day, they came across some Sioux burial platforms that the scouts threw down, spilling corpses wrapped in buffalo skins. More important, they found the site of a major village. The encampment was huge; Lieutenant Edward S. Godfrey said that "one would naturally suppose these were the successive camping-places of the same village, when, in fact, they were the continuous camps of several bands." At the center was a thirty-five-foot pole, around which were piled buffalo heads, evidence of a ceremonial sun dance. In the remains of a sweat lodge, the soldiers found pictures traced in sand that looked like a battle. Here Sitting Bull, in an induced trance, had seen soldiers falling upside down into the Sioux camp, later interpreted as a premonition of the approaching battle.

They picked up a trail beyond the village, which continued upriver, and followed it into the late afternoon, to a point where it turned west up Davis Creek. The troops camped while scouts followed the trail into the hills. White Man Runs Him, Goes Ahead, and Hairy Moccasin reported back that the trail led over the Wolf Mountains to the Little Bighorn valley, where they assumed was a village.

Custer was at a critical decision point. He knew that Terry had expected him to go further up the Rosebud before crossing over to the Little Bighorn. But he was faced with a fresh trail, and closely tracking the foe was critical in Indian warfare. If he continued south, the village might have moved on by the time he came back down the other valley, and the trail might have gone cold.

George was troubled. Godfrey observed that Custer was subdued on the march, not his usual energetic self. "There was an indefinable something that was *not* Custer," he recalled.[3] After several hours' rest, Custer ordered the regiment to keep up the pursuit. At midnight they began the ascent into the hills. They rode six more miles that night and made camp at two in the morning.

On July 25 the scouts set out before sunrise, heading for a promontory on the high ground between the valleys known as the Crow's Nest. "The scouts came in and reported a large village in our front—the General was highly pleased to hear it," trooper Pat Coleman noted in his diary.[4] Coleman said this was the critical period; the old Custer had reemerged. "From the hour we left the Rosebud … his old-time restless energy had returned, and he seemed to think of nothing but to reach and strike the Indians." The pursuit was on in earnest. Custer's blood was up. "Every man [felt] that the next twenty-four hours would deside [*sic*] the fate of a good manney [*sic*] men and sure enough it did."[5]

Custer ordered the regiment to move forward cautiously, concealing the movement, while he rushed ahead to the Crow's Nest to have a look for himself. The village was fifteen miles distant but detectable from smoke rising from the valley and the sizeable pony herd that looked like "worms crawling in the grass."

"We scouts thought there were too many Indians for Custer to fight," White Man Runs Him recalled. "There were camps and camps and camps…. I would say there were between four thousand and five thousand warriors, maybe more, I do not know. It was the biggest Indian camp I have ever seen." Another scout mentioned that there were probably more braves than they could handle in two or three days. "One day, perhaps," George replied. The joke was lost on Bloody Knife, who signed to Custer, "You and I are both going home today by a road we do not know."

By 10:30 the regiment had moved up, concealed in a ravine. Custer's plan at that point was to attack early in the morning of July 26, using the rolling terrain along the route to mask his movements, and then spring on the village at dawn. He hoped that by then Terry's column would be moving in from the north, and the village would be trapped. Godfrey said on the twenty-fifth Custer wanted "ample time for the country to be studied, to locate the village, and to make plans for the attack on the 26th."[6]

But the attack plan hinged on their ability to take the Indians by surprise, and Custer soon received reports his troops had been spotted. On the night of June 24, a load of hard tack fell off a pack mule, and the next morning Sergeant William A. Curtis was sent with a team to find it. They came across some Indians breaking open the boxes, who rode off as the soldiers approached. The Indians later watched from high ground as they left. Some scouts reported other Indian sightings close to the camp.

Custer believed he had lost the element of surprise. He called his officers and said they would attack that day. As Godfrey wrote, "Our discovery made it imperative to act at once, as delay would allow the village to scatter and escape."[7] As the column readied to move, Custer said to Dr. H. R. Porter, one of his surgeons, "Porter, there is a large camp of Indians ahead, and we are going to have a great killing."[8]

In fact, the Indians in the large village had not seen Custer. The hard-tack looters had been from a separate band. Some Indian scouts from the village had reported to their chiefs that there were soldiers in the area, but not in great numbers. One Indian who saw a cloud of dust being kicked up by Custer's approaching column assumed it was from a herd of buffalo. No whites had ever attacked a full gathering of Indians in the middle of the day or afternoon, so when the morning passed peacefully the Indians relaxed. Furthermore, their village was so large they never thought the whites would do something as useless and foolish as attack them. If anyone was surprised that day, it was the Indians.

"Custer was mounted on his sorrel horse and it being a very hot day he was in his shirt sleeves," Private Peter Thompson recalled, "his buckskin pants tucked into his boots; his buckskin shirt fastened to the rear of his saddle; and a broad brimmed cream colored hat on his head, the brim of which was turned up on the right side and fastened by a small hook and eye to its crown. This gave him opportunity to sight his rifle while riding. His rifle lay horizontally in front of him; when riding he leaned slightly forward." He was flying the personal standard Libbie had made him; the regimental banner was left furled in the pack. The 7th Cavalry may have been on the march, but this was Custer's battle.

Custer divided his command into three battalions. Marcus Reno and Frederick Benteen each led three troops, Custer led five, and B Troop under Captain Thomas M. McDougall guarded the mule train.[9] Presumably he planned to strike the village from multiple points, the tactic he used to good effect at Washita. Custer and Reno advanced down Reno Creek toward the river, and Benteen was sent to the left to approach the river farther south. After patrolling a few miles in that direction and seeing no Indians ahead, Benteen angled back toward Reno Creek. It was "rather a senseless order," Benteen recalled, "carried out, I would have been twenty miles away."[10] According to Lieutenant Edgerly in Benteen's command, however, Custer may not have known exactly where the southern terminus of the village was, and Benteen's men were ordered "to go over to the left and charge the Indians as soon as we saw them."[11]

This supports the idea that the plan was to hit the village in three places, but there is no written order that details Custer's attack plan.

Around 2:00 p.m. the battalions on Reno Creek came across a lone teepee about five miles from the village. In it was the body of Old She Bear, a warrior killed fighting Crook on the Rosebud. The scouts lit the teepee afire, a characteristic act of contempt, which drew attention to their advance. Around that time Reno's chief of scouts, Lieutenant Luther R. Hare, and Custer's lead scout, Fred Gerard, reported Indians fleeing toward the river.

"Here are your Indians, General, running like devils!" Gerard shouted. Private Thomas O'Neill, looking at the village, recalled, "We could see the Indians, they looked very much like an ants nest that was disturbed running this way and that, and about a thousand of them in sight."[12]

Custer probably believed the Indians were preparing to take what they could from their encampment and quickly depart, perhaps mounting a hasty defense to slow his advance. But he misestimated his foe; the Indians wanted to fight. Custer did not know they had met and turned back Crook. Since Custer was coming from roughly the same direction, the Indians probably concluded it was a smaller group from the same force. And if they beat them once they could beat them again.

Custer divided his force and ordered Reno to pursue the fleeing Indians toward the river, cross it, then charge into the village, where he would be "supported by the whole outfit." The Indian scouts would meanwhile secure or run off the pony herd.

A half hour later, the column rode up over a ridge overlooking the river and the village, approximately three miles distant. "It is a lovely place," Pat Coleman wrote. "The valley is 1½ miles broad and four miles long, the river winding like a snake and dotted with Islands thickly studded with timber, the water clear as christal [sic] as it comes rushing from the Mountains." Cottonwood trees and underbrush hugged the banks, and the surrounding hills were covered with long grass.

The village stretched over four and a half miles along the river. The six tribal circles included bands of Teton Sioux: Hunkpapa, Sans Arcs, Miniconjou, Oglala, Blackfoot, Two Kettle, and Brulé. The Yankton and Santee Sioux were there, along with 120 Cheyenne lodges. The Hunkpapa circle was closest, at the southern tip of the village; the Cheyenne at the northern end.

Reno's troops galloped into the valley in columns of twos around 3:00 p.m. Resistance was light at first, and the Indians seemed to be scattering. "Thirty days' furlough to the man who gets the first scalp!" shouted Lieutenant Charles A. Varnum.[13]

Myles Keogh and Lieutenant William W. Cooke had ridden with Reno to the ford to get a sense of things and quickly estimate how the plan would unfold. During the advance, Cooke had told Reno that scout Fred Gerard reported the Indian village "three miles ahead and moving. The General directs you to take your three companies and drive everything before you. Colonel Benteen will be on your left and will have the same instructions."[14]

Keogh and Cooke then returned to Custer's battalion, which had peeled off onto the ridgeline. As Reno neared the village, he set up a dismounted skirmish line with the right flank anchored on a wooded section of dry riverbed. This was not part of the plan. Custer clearly had expected Reno to charge into the village mounted. Some say Custer waved his hat as he moved along the high ground, encouraging Reno or maybe urging him to keep moving. The story of the wave, like many details about the battle, is disputed. But if true it was the last Reno saw of Custer.[15]

Reno explained he thought he was "being drawn into some trap, as they would certainly fight harder and especially as we were nearing their village which was still standing." Also he "could not see Custer or any other support, and at the time the very earth seemed to grow Indians."[16]

The Indians did not expect the attack. "The soldiers charged so quickly [the Sioux council] could not talk," Chief Red Horse recalled. "We came out of the council lodge and talked in all directions. The Sioux mount horses, take guns, and go fight the soldiers. Women and children mount horses and go, meaning to get out of the way."

Crazy Horse led a growing number of Indians toward Reno's line on foot and horseback. Reno's men were firing on the village, with little effect at first. "It seemed to me that we were not within range," trooper Thomas O'Neill said, "as all our bullets fell short, and though the Indians were firing at us I did not see anyone hit."[17] Cheyenne leader Two Moons, watching from a distance, recalled the chaos of the mêlée. "I saw the white soldiers fighting in a line. Indians covered the flat. They began to drive the soldiers all mixed up—Sioux, then soldiers, then more Sioux, and all shooting. The air was full of smoke and dust."[18]

Indians moved on Reno's left, and some got close enough to engage hand-to-hand. Reno pulled back and pivoted counterclockwise 90 degrees, into a wooded bend in the river with his back to the water. It was a better position to deal with the growing threat he faced, but it was defensive; Reno was no longer able to press on the village. Fighting continued for another quarter hour, with Indians creeping through the underbrush up to Reno's position. The horses had been led back into the brush and were in danger of being taken, so an order was given to get to them, causing some confusion on the firing line. "I was fighting odds of at least five to one," Reno explained. "My only hope was to get out of the wood, where I would soon have been surrounded, and gain some higher ground."[19]

"Reno ordered his men to mount and 'charge'—he called it—to the rear," Dr. Porter recalled.[20] As Reno was giving the order to withdraw, Bloody Knife, Custer's favorite scout, took a bullet to the head, showering Reno with blood and brains. Reno panicked and bolted out of the timber, riding hard a mile upriver and crossing. Some followed, at least those who had noticed what was going on.

"Don't leave the line men!" Lieutenant Varnum called out. "There are enough of you here to whip the whole Sioux nation!"[21]

"What is this—a *retreat*?" Lieutenant Benjamin "Benny" Hodgson said as men bolted by him.

"It looks most damnably like a *rout*," another lieutenant replied. Hodgson rode for the river but was shot from his mount as he went down the bank. "For God's sake," he implored a passing trooper, "take me to the river!" He grabbed a stirrup and was dragged across, but Hodgson was shot again and killed as he staggered up the opposite bank.[22] Two Moons likened the sight of the men barreling over the riverbank and into the water to "buffalo fleeing." Some troopers took cover in the woods; others concealed themselves in folds in the steep riverbank. Some would survive, others not. But Reno's attack was over. By 4:00 p.m. he was digging in to a hilltop defensive position as Indians finished off whatever members of his battalion they could find. Reno had lost three officers and twenty-nine enlisted men killed, with seven wounded.[23]

Meanwhile, Custer had moved north along Sharpshooter Ridge and was unaware of how Reno's attack was developing. His exact route is unknown, but he was probably east of the crest, concealing his movement but also not allowing him to see Reno's lack of progress. When he topped the ridge and saw the extent of the village, Custer was exultant.

"We've caught them napping," he said to John Martin, a.k.a. Giovanni Martini, an Italian immigrant and Custer's orderly and trumpeter. He turned to his officers downslope behind him, waved his hat, and shouted, "Hurrah boys, we've got them!"

"There were no bucks to be seen," Martin recalled, "all we could see was some squaws and children playing and a few dogs and ponies. The General seemed both surprised and glad, and said the Indians must be in their tents, asleep."[24] Reno's men had yet to open fire, and most of the village was not yet on alert.

Sergeant Daniel Kanipe of Tom Custer's Company C said, "At the sight of the camp the boys began to cheer. Some horses became so excited that some riders were unable to hold them in ranks, and the last words I heard Custer say were, 'Hold your horses in boys, there are plenty of them down there for all of us.'"[25] According to Martin, Custer told the men they would go down, make a crossing, and capture the village. "The whole command then pulled off their hats and cheered," he said. "And the consensus of opinion seemed to be among the officers that if this could be done the Indians would have to surrender when they would return, in order not to fire upon their women and children."[26]

Custer sent Sergeant Kanipe back to urge Captain McDougall to bring up the pack train. A short time later, around 3:30 p.m., Cooke handed Martin a note Custer had dictated. "Trumpeter," Custer said, "go back on our trail and see if you can discover Benteen and give him this message. If you see no danger come back to us, but if you find Indians in your way stay with Benteen and return with him and when you get back to us report."[27] Martin set off south. Along the way he passed Boston Custer, coming up from the pack train.

"Where's the General?" Boston said.

"Right behind that next ridge you'll find him," he replied. Boston rode off, the sound of gunfire already audible to the north.[28] Lieutenant Edgerly, with Benteen's troop, also saw Boston pass by. "He gave me a cheery salutation as he passed," Edgerly recalled, "and then with a smile on his face, rode to his death."[29]

Custer and his men rode down a ravine called Cedar Coulee, which joined Medicine Tail Coulee, ending at a ford leading into the north end of the village near the Sans Arc and Northern Cheyenne lodges. At some point in this movement he released his scouts, White Man Runs Him, Goes Ahead, Hairy Moccasin, and Curley. According to the traditional account, Custer sent E and F Companies under Captain George Yates down to the ford, while he with C, I, and L Companies withdrew to the heights and headed north along Nye-Cartwright Ridge. Stories differ on whether Custer also went to the ford with Yates. Some say he was killed there. It might have been characteristic of Custer to charge down to the ford, but on the other hand he might have been planning a bolder move further on. John Martin says the whole command went down to the river.

Some Indians were already moving toward the ravine, and Yates repelled them with fire near the ford before heading back up to join the rest of the command at around 4:15 p.m. They rode northeast up Deep Coulee, meeting Calhoun with L Company on the high ground. Myles Keogh was on the slope behind him with I Troop, and Henry M. Harrington with C Company fronting a ravine to Calhoun's right. Yates and Smith took F and E Troops north one thousand yards to a prominence now known as Last Stand Hill.

The Last Stand came about by circumstance. By this time Indians, probably Crazy Horse's mounted Sioux and some Cheyenne, had gotten in front of the column. Custer's forward movement was blocked and the planned attack had failed, so he went from column to line and fought the battle he had. It was not the first time Custer was in a tough spot far from help. After all, he had made it through Trevilian Station and Brandy Station during the Bristoe Campaign. Custer might have moved north trying to locate Terry's column. He had ordered Benteen to join him, and if Custer knew that Reno had pulled back he might have hoped his battalion would come, too. But if he sent an order to Reno to come up, it never arrived.

Perhaps Custer felt that if he could consolidate the regiment, they could either hold off the enemy until Terry arrived, or fight their way north toward the approaching forces. Had Custer's battalion commanders reacted quickly to shifting circumstances, if they had his dash or intuition, had everything worked perfectly, even at this point there might have been a chance to come out of it alive. But as the Indians closed around him, and he looked vainly north for Terry and Gibbon, or south for Reno and Benteen, George may have realized that he had gone a ridge too far.

CHAPTER THIRTY

"HE WILL NEVER FIGHT ANYMORE"

No one can say for certain when George Custer died during the battle, or where. The Indian survivors of the action at what they called Greasy Grass Creek gave conflicting accounts, conditioned by time, memory, and the fog of battle.[1] Some said his soldiers fought bravely. "I never before nor since saw men so brave and fearless as those white warriors," Ogalala Chief Low Dog later recalled.[2] Others said they were cowardly. "[Custer's] soldiers became foolish, many throwing away their guns and raising their hands, saying, 'Sioux, pity us; take us prisoners,'" Red Horse said. "None were left alive for even a few minutes." Sitting Bull gave various unreliable accounts, in one version engaging in lengthy negotiations with Custer via letters exchanged in the days before the battle, and during the fight claiming the Great Spirit struck down many soldiers and their horses with lightning.[3] An old trapper who had known Custer and spoken to the

Sioux after the battle concluded, "I do not believe there is a man living, red or white, who knows how Custer died."[4]

A sense of the final scene on Battle Ridge may ironically have been captured by Frederick Benteen's imagined description of the end of Major Elliott and his men at Washita:

> Who can describe the feeling of that brave band, as with anxious beating hearts, they strained their yearning eyes in the direction whence help should come? What must have been the despair that, when all hopes of succor died out, nerved their stout arms to do and die? Round and round rush the red fiends, smaller and smaller shrinks the circle, but the aim of that devoted, gallant knot of heroes is steadier than ever, and the death howl of the murderous redskin is more frequent. But on they come in masses grim, with glittering lance and one long, loud, exulting whoop, as if the gates of hell had opened and loosed the whole infernal host. A well-directed volley from their trusty carbines makes some of the miscreants reel and fall, but their death-rattles are drowned in the greater din. Soon every voice in that little band is still as death.[5]

Custer made the best of his defense. Edward J. McClernand, who was with Gibbon's command, believed "the position [Custer took] was the best obtainable; the line he established on the ridge, running from this position towards the river, showed more care taken in deploying and placing the men than, in my opinion, was shown on any other part of the field."[6] General Nelson A. Miles, who conducted a detailed survey of the battle site in 1878 accompanied by twenty-five prominent Sioux and Cheyenne warriors who fought there, concluded that "no man of military knowledge in riding over this field now, and examining the position that Custer quickly took upon that crest commanding the valley, could fail to recognize the military ability of that commander; and those graves remain as monuments to the fortitude of men who stood their ground."[7]

"This is a good day to die, follow me!" Low Dog said as his braves galloped toward Custer's men.[8] The soldiers faced an improvised assault as each band arrived on different parts of the field. Sioux and Cheyenne warriors crossed downriver and came up a ravine, striking from the north and east, against F and I Companies (Yates and Keogh). E Company (Smith) faced a direct attack up from the river led by Cheyenne leader Lame White Man, who was later killed by friendly fire. Hunkpapa Chief Gall and Two Moons with his Cheyenne came up from the south, hitting C and L Companies (Harrington and Calhoun). Two Moons probably would not even have been there had his band not been turned back by Crook's attack on March 17. His profile later became well known; sculptor James Fraser chose him as one of the models for the obverse side of the famous Buffalo Nickel.

The Last Stand was not a close-in affair until the end. Some Indians used the terrain to conceal themselves, firing rifles and arrows from cover. Others rode about firing from horseback. Two Moons said his men made several charges on the troops on Calhoun Hill but were repulsed by heavy fire—perhaps the volleys the men on Reno Hill heard. "Then the shooting was quick, quick," he recalled. "Pop—pop—pop very fast. Some of the soldiers were down on their knees, some standing. Officers all in front. The smoke was like a great cloud, and everywhere the Sioux went the dust rose like smoke. We circled all around them—swirling like water round a stone. We shoot, we ride fast, we shoot again. Soldiers drop, and horses fall on them."[9]

"Among the bluffs there were numerous evidences of a desperate defense against overwhelming numbers," according to a contemporary newspaper account, "and indications of repeated defeats of attempts to reach the river or to break through the encircling savages."[10] Some say that part of the battle was over quickly—"about as long as it takes a hungry man to eat a meal," according to one Indian participant. Others say it lasted longer, but it could not have lasted more than an hour and a half.

Questions remain about how organized the defense was and how well each company fought. Contemporary battlefield archaeology suggests that the soldiers on Calhoun Hill mounted the more coherent defense, though one hundred years of souvenir hunting around Last Stand Hill probably removed a great deal of the spent cartridge evidence on that flank.[11] Gall and Two Moons said the southern flank broke first, though this may have been Calhoun pulling back in good order to assist Keogh. Custer wound up in the cluster of men on the north end of the field, but we don't know where he was or how he was managing his defense before the end. And many Indian accounts agree that Last Stand Hill was aptly named, since, as Lone Bear said, "There was a good stand made."[12]

Indians told Nelson Miles in 1878 that "the fight was kept up until all the troops were killed or disabled except about forty men on the extreme right of the line" who "as a last resort, suddenly rose and made a rush toward the timber skirting the bank of the Little Big Horn."[13] But none of them made it. Some troopers were found in ones and twos some distance from the defensive line, maybe slipping out through gaps in the heat of battle or galloping off on their horses before being hunted down and slain.

The Indians almost universally agreed after the battle that had the "squaw" Reno come down the ridge quickly to Custer's aid, they would have had trouble. Urgent action might have saved the day. "At a smart trot or gallop, as a cavalryman goes into action, fifteen minutes would have brought the whole command into the engagement," General Miles concluded after his study, "and the result might have been entirely different."[14] As Little Bighorn veteran William Taylor put it, "Reno proved incompetent and Benteen showed his indifference—I will not use the uglier words that have often been in my mind. Both failed Custer and he had to fight it out alone."

Benteen may have thought matters were somewhat in hand, at least at first. Sometime after 3:00 p.m., when he was five or six miles from the village, he encountered Sergeant Kanipe, who was on his mission from Custer to urge McDougall and the pack team up. As Kanipe rode off, he said to Benteen's men, "We've got 'em, boys, we've got 'em." Fifteen to twenty minutes later, Benteen received the now famous final message from Custer, borne by John Martin: "Benteen. Come on. Big village. Be quick. Bring packs. P[S] Bring pacs [*sic*]." Benteen had not seen any Indians, none in force anyway, and Martin told him that those in the village were "skedaddling." Benteen had a low opinion of Martin, "a thick headed, dull witted Italian, just about as much cut out for a cavalryman as he was for a King."[15] But Custer had said to be quick, and there was the sound of heavy gunfire in the distance. Captain Weir, a Custer favorite, counseled they ride hard to the sound of the guns. Benteen hesitated, so Weir and Company D rode off. Benteen then followed, not waiting for the pack train.

Benteen moved along the ridgeline and soon came across Reno's men struggling up the hill from the river, under fire. "I saw an immense number of Indians on the plain, mounted of course and charging down on some dismounted men of Reno's command," Benteen wrote his wife. "[T]he balance of R's command were mounted, and flying for dear life to the bluffs on the same side of river that I was. I then marched my 3 Co's. to them and a more delighted lot of folks you never saw."[16] Benteen's men helped drive off the Indians who, at the sight of reinforcements, broke off the attack. Some swung north to move toward the sounds of battle raging over four miles down the ridge.

"Where is Custer?" Benteen asked. Reno said he did not know. Custer and his men were miles away across rolling terrain, somewhere in the direction of the dust cloud raised by the hundreds if not thousands of Indians moving on his command from every side. Reno was immobilized; he had lost his nerve and his judgment. Some men wanted to get in the fight, saying, "Our command ought to be doing something or Custer would be after Reno with a sharp stick." They heard volley fire around 4:25 p.m., and someone said Custer was "giving it to them for all he is worth," but Godfrey probably correctly interpreted the unified fire as a distress signal.[17] Captain Weir and Reno argued sharply, then Weir took the initiative and moved his company north down the ridge, heading for Custer's position. But they had already lost precious time.

Weir rode about a mile and a half to the heights above Medicine Tail Coulee, about three miles from Calhoun Hill. Far off through the swirling dust, he saw horsemen riding and the distinctive swallowtail stars and stripes guidons of the 7th Cavalry.

"That is Custer over there!" he shouted, and ordered the company to make ready to ride to battle. A sergeant, standing next to Weir, stayed him.

"Here Captain," he said, "you had better take a look through the glasses." He handed Weir the binoculars. "I think those are Indians." On the distant ridge, mounted Indians rode in circles, waving the guidons, shooting down at the ground, dispatching the wounded.

Benteen had set off after Weir about twenty minutes later "with Guidons flying," as he wrote, "that Custer might see us." Instead he was spotted by an "immense body of Indians coming to attack us from both sides of the river."[18] Benteen and Weir hurried back to the hill they had come from, turning back Reno, who had finally followed about forty minutes after Benteen. The six companies formed a defensive ring with the horses and mules in the middle, the men digging in with their camp knives and tin cups. Warriors soon came riding and running over the hills in waves to finish off the soldiers.

"The Indians commenced to swarm around us like devils," Captain Francis M. Gibson of Benteen's battalion recalled, "thousands of them, all with modern rifles, while we were using old carbines, so we were immediately put on the defensive."[19] The men fought into the evening and through the night, holding off repeated Indian attacks. Indians crept so close they could throw rocks.

Reno was the senior officer present, but Benteen was in command, walking among the men, exhorting them to fight, and leading sallies outside the perimeter. "Benteen is one of the bravest men I ever saw in a fight," scout George Herendon recalled. "All the time he was going about through the bullets, encouraging the soldiers to stand up to their work and not let the Indians whip them; he went among the horses and pack mules and drove out the men who were skulking there, compelling them to go into the line and do their duty. He never sheltered his own person once during the battle, and I do not see how he escaped being killed."[20] By contrast, during the night Reno suggested that everyone who could should make a run for it on horses, and those wounded who could not ride be left behind.[21]

Some men left the line, not fleeing, but making the hazardous journey hundreds of yards to a bend in the river to fetch water. Twenty-four Medals of Honor were awarded for actions during the battle, and many citations simply read "Brought water for the wounded under a most galling fire." Private Peter Thompson of Company C, shot in the head and wounded on one such trip, made two more, "notwithstanding remonstrances of his sergeant." Otto Voit, a saddler with Company H, volunteered with three others to stand up in an exposed position and open fire on the enemy to divert attention from water teams making the trip in daylight.

And there were other acts of bravery, such as when Sergeant Richard P. Hanley of C Company took off after a stampeded mule loaded with critical ammunition and somehow brought it back under sustained fire lasting twenty minutes. Another trooper decided to send a message to the enemy; when a group rushed the line he "killed and scalped an Indian in plain view of the others," Dr. Porter recalled. "This frightened them, and they kept a safe distance away after that."[22]

"The sun was blazing hot" the next day, one Reno Hill defender recalled, "the dead horses were sickening, the air heavy with a hundred smells, the bullets thick, the men falling, and the bluffs for miles around black with the jubilant savages."[23] The fight continued until 1:00 p.m. the afternoon of June 26, when the Indians broke contact. "I did not want to kill any more men," Sitting Bull explained. "I did not like that kind of work. I only defended my camp. When we had killed enough, that was all that was necessary."[24] Chief Red Horse gave a more credible answer. "A Sioux man came and said many walking soldiers were coming near. The coming of the walking soldiers was the saving of the soldiers on the hill. Sioux can not fight the walking soldiers, being afraid of them, so the Sioux hurriedly left."[25]

The "walking soldiers" were Terry and Gibbon's column, approaching from the north. They had made good time on their march up the Yellowstone, covering the almost sixty miles from the Rosebud to the Bighorn in two days. But after crossing the river and heading south, the going got rough. "Those who participated in that march will not soon forget it," McBlain said, noting that Terry called it "one of the severest tests in the way of marching to which American soldiers had ever been put." But they doggedly pressed up the Bighorn seeking to close the trap on the Indians.

The first information they received about Custer's column was early on the morning of June 26, when Lieutenant James H. Bradley of the 7th Infantry and his scouts chased several Indians up the Little Bighorn valley. They eventually revealed themselves to be Crow scouts sent with Custer from Gibbon's command. They told an implausible tale of Custer's attacking the Indian village and then the "soldiers were shot down like buffalo." Terry and Gibbon dismissed this as "the imaginings of panic-stricken and cowardly Indians."[26]

As the column moved up the western bank of the Little Bighorn, they spotted a column of smoke ahead. Terry and Gibbon assumed that Custer had hit the Indian camp and was burning it. It seemed preferable to the story the Crow scouts told. Scouts set out to make contact with Custer but soon returned, reporting a large force of Indians to their front. But they were breaking up their encampment, readying to seek safety west in the Bighorn Mountains.

On the twenty-seventh, Lieutenant Bradley and some scouts cautiously made their way into the abandoned village site. The first sign they found of the fight was buckskin coats belonging to Lieutenants James G. Sturgis and James E. Porter, "blood-stained and with numerous bullet holes in each," McBlain wrote, and a glove belonging to Yates. Three burned human heads hung by a wire on one pole; on another was a man's heart. A white trapper named Ridgely allegedly being held hostage by the Indians at the time of the battle later told the tale of seeing cavalrymen taken prisoner and burned alive, though many today believe the story was a hoax. Two Moons and Little Knife told more credible stories of torturing prisoners.[27]

Then the first bodies turned up—Lieutenant Donald McIntosh and Charley Reynolds. "Tosh" McIntosh, a Canadian half-Indian, had been dragged from his mount during Reno's retreat. He was mutilated and unrecognizable but was identified by his brother-in-law, Lieutenant

Francis Marion Gibson in Reno's battalion, who noticed some sleeve buttons his sister had given her husband before leaving Fort Lincoln. There were also three lodges "filled with dead Indians, scaffolds here and there holding others, and evidences of hurried departure, [which] carried with them proofs that the killing was not altogether one-sided."[28]

The rest of the column began to arrive at ten that morning. They continued through the encampment site heading toward Reno Hill. Away to the left, Charles F. Roe noticed some dark objects scattered on the hillside across the river, which he assumed were dead buffalo.

Some of Reno's men who had hidden for two days in the woods at the south end of the village emerged as the column drew near. The rest of the survivors watched the column approach from the hilltop. "Can you imagine what a relief it was, and how grateful we felt when we saw these troops coming to succor us," Captain Francis M. Gibson wrote, "absolutely taking us right out of the jaws of death, and such a horrible death."[29] Some of the men on Reno Hill had supposed the relief column was led by Custer, who had abandoned them as he had Elliot at Washita, and was now returning. Others wondered aloud about Custer's impending court-martial for once again deserting his command.

But Terry met the survivors with tears in his eyes; he knew where Custer was. While Terry's troops had been examining the grisly discoveries in the abandoned Indian village, a scout rode up saying he had discovered a small group of dead soldiers further to the south. A second scout arrived telling of fifty dead troops. Then a third came in reporting two hundred corpses on the hill across the river. McBlain observed, "Now was the truth of the report brought us by the Crows made apparent."

Captain Gibson called the carnage on Battle Ridge "the most horrible sight my eyes ever rested on."[30] Charles F. Roe wrote his wife, "The battle field Kate was awful, awful—dead men & horses in all directions. Everyone of the bodies stripped, scalped and mutilated." In his diary he called it "the most terrible sight ever witnessed."

"It makes one heartsick to look over the battle ground and see the poor fellows," Lieutenant John Carland, Company B, 6th Infantry, with Gibbon's command wrote, "some of them with their entrails cut out, others with their eyes dug out and heart laid across their face. They even stooped to cut their pockets to get their money and watches."[31] Pat Coleman and some others went across the river to search for a member of their company and "could not recognize him. All of them were scalped and otherwise horably [*sic*] mutilated. Some had their heads cut off, others arms, one legs. [The Indians'] hatred extended even to the poor horses they cut and slashed them before they were dead.... Oh, what a slaughter. How manney [*sic*] homes are made desolate by the sad disaster."

Journalist Mark Kellogg's scalped, sun-bloated body was found near the river below Last Stand Hill and was identified by his boots. Nearby was a pouch with notes for the story he never wrote. He was the first AP reporter to die in battle. Kellogg's last dispatch to his editor read, "By the time this reaches you we would have met and fought the red devils, with what result remains to be seen. I go with Custer and will be at the death."

It was a family tragedy for the Custers; brothers George, Tom, and Boston were dead, along with Autie Reed, brother-in-law James Calhoun, and George's Scottish wolfhound, Tuck. Calhoun perished on the hill that bears his name. Boston Custer and Autie Reed died together near the foot of Last Stand Hill. Tom Custer was found severely mutilated near the hilltop. He could only be positively identified by a tattoo of liberty, the flag, and his initials, spotted by Lieutenant Edward S. Godfrey, who had served with him in the 21st Ohio in 1861.[32]

Hunkpapa Chief Rain-in-the-Face was said to have made good on his threat and cut Tom's heart out and paraded it through the Indian village on a pole. Henry Wadsworth Longfellow memorialized the event in verse, using poetic license to make it George Custer's heart that the chief "uplifted high in the air as a ghastly trophy, bore."[33] Rain-in-the-Face later described the event in bloody detail but recanted the story on his deathbed. He said he had simply taken credit for what he was being credited with.[34] In fact, Tom's heart was not cut out by anyone.

George Custer was found near Tom, naked and "as white and clean as a baby," according to Dr. Porter. He was wounded in his left breast and left temple. His body was propped at an angle formed by two of his men laying across each other, his arm across the top of them, the small of his back touching the ground, his head lying in his right hand as if in thought, smiling. "There he is, God damn him," Frederick Benteen said, standing over Custer's body, "he will never fight anymore."[35]

"Every one of them were scalped and otherwise mutilated but the General he lay with a smile on his face," Pat Coleman wrote. "The Indians eaven [sic] respected the great Chief." Low Dog explained that "the wise men and chiefs of our nation gave out to our people not to mutilate the dead white chief, for he was a brave warrior and died a brave man, and his remains should be respected."[36] But in general Indians did not desecrate corpses other than scalping or making signs like the Sioux death mark, a slash on the leg from the hip to the knee. Mutilation was most thorough and shocking when used to torture the living; scalping the dead was a means of preventing a fallen foe from entering the next life.

In any case, the Indians did not know who they had killed. "No warrior knew Custer in the fight," Hunkpapa chief Crow King stated. "We did not know him, dead or alive. When the fight was over the chiefs gave orders to look for the long-haired chief among the dead, but no chief with long hair could be found."[37] Low Dog concurred: "I did not see General Custer. I do not know who killed him."[38]

"I killed him," Rain-in-the-Face later claimed. "I made many holes in him. He once took my liberty; I took his life. I am glad I did."[39] But like the tale of Tom Custer's heart, he recanted this story too.

The timing, manner, and location of Custer's death have been open to endless speculation and mythmaking. Thirty-seven years after the battle, Custer's scout Curley—or someone claiming to be him—told a far-fetched tale of being present with the attacking force, which allegedly gave Crow scouts immunity, and seeing Custer in his final moments hacking down Sioux warriors with his saber. "You here, Curley?" Custer supposedly said. "We'll fight to the end!" A Sioux warrior then shot Custer in the chest, and Curley rushed forward and cradled his head as he died—so he said.[40] Another theory was that one of Custer's scouts shot him. Yet another has it that he committed suicide, or that all his men did, or they shot each other.[41] Robert Utley argues convincingly that stories of mass suicide on Last Stand Hill originated with Indians who came in to the agencies after the battle and did not want to be blamed.

Sitting Bull credited some deaths to lightning and to the troopers' own horses trampling them. But he maintained that Custer fought bravely to the end. The chief had not fought in the battle; his main contribution was encouraging warriors to fight bravely ("Sitting Bull was big medicine," Gall explained).[42] But he no doubt heard numerous accounts of the battle and gave his version a year afterward.

"It was said that up there where the last fight took place, where the last stand was made, the Long Hair stood like a sheaf of corn with all the ears fallen around him," Sitting Bull said. A few men still stood by him. "He killed a man when he fell," the old chief continued. "He laughed."

The interviewer sought to clarify: "You mean he cried out."

"No," Sitting Bull said, "he laughed; he had fired his last shot."

This was Custer in his final moment, as we might wish to remember him, expressing the sum of his existence: the gregarious goat of West Point, the mad demon of Civil War battlefields, laughing in the face of death, and ending his life with a smile.

Federic Remington, *A Suspended Equestrienne,* from Elizabeth B. Custer, *Tenting on the Plains* (New York: Charles L. Webster, 1893).

SO "JOYOUS" AND "RECKLESS OF IT ALL"

White stones, singly, in pairs, and in groups, stand scattered along Battle Ridge, marking where Custer and his men fell. They tell the story of the conclusion of the fight, but more particularly they speak to its importance. No other American battle has been so meticulously recorded and memorialized, every man honored with a marker on the spot where he met his end, the grisly scene frozen in time in clean, white marble.

Custer's luck had finally run out. Five of the twelve troops of his regiment were annihilated. Over 260 men of the 7th Cavalry and three civilians were killed or died of wounds, about 200 of them with Custer. Indian dead were probably half that number. Around fifty-five troops were wounded. According to tradition, the only known survivor from the 7th on Battle Ridge was Captain Keogh's wounded horse, Comanche, which was respectfully cared for by the regiment until it died in 1891.

It took days for word of the battle to get out. Terry and Gibbon were seven hundred miles from Bismarck. The quickest way back was by boat; the *Far West* had come up as far as the mouth of the Little Bighorn, but there was work to be done on the battlefield before the ship could cast off. The burial details began on June 28. George and Tom Custer were laid to rest side by side. Officers' graves were marked with slips of paper embedded in wooden disks or in spent cartridges, sealed with wax, and driven into the ground. The enlisted men, less well known outside their companies and harder to identify, were buried where they fell, in marked but nameless graves.[1]

The most seriously wounded were moved by litters the fifteen rough miles to the steamboat and packed aboard, accompanied by Dr. Porter, the sole surviving surgeon. The *Far West* finally departed on July 3, and the ship's captain, Grant Marsh, made the voyage to Bismarck in fifty-four hours, a remarkable feat given the uncertainties of navigating a mostly unfamiliar, uncharted river course. They arrived at the city at 11:00 p.m. on July 5. Captain Marsh, Dr. Porter, and Captain Edward W. Smith of Terry's staff went immediately to *Tribune* editor Clement Lounsberry to hand him the story of the century. The group hurried to the telegraph office at the Northern Pacific station, where telegraph operator J. M. Carnahan alerted the Fargo office to cut him through directly to St. Paul because "the Custers are all killed." Carnahan "took his seat at the keys and scarcely raised himself from chair for twenty-two hours," Dr. Porter recalled. "What he sent vibrating around the world is history."[2] Lounsberry meanwhile set type on a July 6 extra edition under the headline "MASSACRED." He worked from Terry's dispatch and the notes made by slain reporter Mark Kellogg.

Around 2:00 a.m., Captain Smith reported the news to Captain William S. McCaskey, who was in temporary command at Fort Lincoln. McCaskey assembled the officers and read them Terry's dispatch. It did not come as a complete surprise; there had been some excitement among

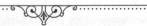

the Indians near the post for the last few days, and whispers of a battle, but no details. "The fearful depression that had hung over the fort for the last two days had its explanation then," Lieutenant G. L. Gurely noted.

There remained only to inform the spouses. The officers' wives had gathered in the Custers' parlor late the previous evening, nervous at the lack of hard news among the forbidding rumors. They attempted to sing hymns to calm themselves—someone started playing "Nearer, My God to Thee" on the piano, but Libbie cut her off, saying, "Not that one, dear." Instead they simply prayed and went to bed.

At 7:00 a.m. Captain McCaskey, Lieutenant Gurley, and post surgeon J. V. D. Middleton went next door to the back of the Custer quarters and told the maid Maria they wanted to talk to Mrs. Custer, Mrs. Calhoun, and Miss Reed. Libbie had not slept well that night; hearing footsteps she came out of her room in her housecoat, asking Lieutenant Gurley the reason for the early visit. He did not reply. The group gathered in the parlor, and McCaskey gave them the awful news.

"Imagine the grief of those women," Gurley recalled, "their sobs, their flood of tears, the grief that knew no consolation."[3] Maggie Calhoun, apparently not understanding, asked McCaskey, "Is there no message for me?" But the message was the same for all of them. After regaining her composure, Libbie, knowing there were more wives to be notified, asked for a wrap to accompany Captain McCaskey on that unhappy duty. "This battle wrecked the lives of twenty-six women at Fort Lincoln," Libbie wrote, "and orphaned children of officers and soldiers joined their cry to that of their bereaved mothers."[4]

The *Bismarck Tribune* had the most complete version of the massacre but did not get the scoop. On June 27, Terry wrote a preliminary account of events that he gave to a scout named Muggins Taylor, who

was to take it overland to Fort Ellis near Bozeman, where it could be wired out. The *Bozeman Times* ran an extra with the story July 3, but for some reason it was not sent out by telegraph. Meanwhile, Muggins had given an account to a reporter with the *Helena Herald*, and editor Andrew Jackson Fisk sent the news to the AP in Salt Lake City on July 5.[5]

Sheridan and Sherman dismissed this first report as a rumor. They generally distrusted the press, plus the scale of the massacre was implausible, and Custer had been falsely reported dead many times before. Official word, relayed by telegraph from Bismarck, through St. Paul and Chicago, reached Washington at 3:00 p.m. on July 6, eleven days after the first disastrous day of battle. Sherman received the confirmation during an interview in Philadelphia, where he was dismissing the stories of a massacre as speculation.

Nevin Custer was in Hastings, Ohio, headed back to Monroe when he got the news. "I didn't believe it at first," he said, "but I drove on home as fast as the team could travel and there I found Monroe all draped in mourning." Willard Glazier, formerly of the 2nd New York Cavalry, was riding west near Euclid, Ohio, on July 5 when he heard a rumor of the massacre. "The source of this information made it appear reliable," he wrote, "and yet comparatively few were disposed to believe it." Glazier said that "news was slow in reaching points east of the Mississippi and was then often unreliable," and that with respect to Custer, "people were wholly unprepared for the final result which was flashed across the country."[6]

The skepticism that greeted the first reports made the confirmation all the more shocking. Little Bighorn was compared to the massacre of over one hundred troops led by Major Francis L. Dade in Florida in 1835, or the 1862 uprising in Minnesota in which Santee Sioux under Little Crow killed 644 whites.[7] But the body count alone did not explain the stunned reaction. There had been more-deadly battles in recent

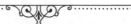

memory; the total casualties at Little Bighorn were small compared with many Civil War engagements. But that war had been over for more than a decade, and frontier battles with Indians were not supposed to end this way. And it was the first time that reports of Custer's death were true.

Custer's Last Stand launched a thousand debates, many of which continue to this day. A *New York Times* writer wisely predicted that "the affair will be made use of as an argument by those who insist upon transferring the Indian Bureau to the War Department, and also by those who oppose such legislation. It will be made an excuse for increasing the Army, and held up as a reason for cutting it down."[8] As with contemporary issues, the battle was viewed through many lenses, whether hindsight, political expediency, people with axes to grind, or those seeking to place blame. The battle became a national Rorschach test; people saw in it whatever they wanted, and still do.

For many, the massacre was a call for all-out war on the Indians. *Harper's Weekly* ran a cover illustration by Thomas Nast of a diplomat shaking hands with a warrior carrying a bloody club, the angry shade of Custer standing between them, mockingly titled "The New Alliance." Colonel William H. Rowan, a former rebel partisan ranger, offered the services of a regiment of ex-Confederates to avenge Custer's death "to let the world see that we of the 'Lost Cause' are not deficient in patriotism."[9] But not all former rebels concurred; a Tennessee paper asserted that given Custer's treatment of Mosby's men at Front Royal, he "deserved to be degraded by Grant, scalped by Sitting Bull, and hearted by Rain-in-the-Face."[10]

Buffalo Bill, who had already begun playing himself on stage shows in the East, had returned to the frontier during the Sioux expedition to scout with the 5th Cavalry. On July 17, 1876, the unit fought a skirmish with Northern Cheyenne braves at Warbonnet Creek in Nebraska. Cody galloped toward the Indians and shot the first brave who came into range. He leapt from his horse, tore off the Cheyenne's feathered head-dress, and scalped him. Cody raised the gory trophy aloft and said, "The first scalp for Custer!" Bill later learned that the man he had killed was named Yellow Hair.

The Sioux campaign continued into the spring of 1877, but in the end most of the Indians simply gave up and returned to the reservations. Sitting Bull, Gall, and Rain-in-the-Face fled to Canada. Crazy Horse surrendered, then was killed in captivity. There was no comparable Indian defeat to serve as a bookend to the Custer tragedy.

The Democratic press jumped on the election-year issue. A July 16 *New York Herald* editorial entitled "Who Slew Custer?" blamed President Grant both for seeking negotiations with the Indians and for the corruption in the agencies that Custer himself blamed for increasing tensions on the Plains. The pro-Tilden *New York World* suggested that if Custer had been in overall command of the expedition, it would have turned out differently, and that he died because of Grant's pettiness after Custer's testimony against Belknap.

"No military man ever charged Custer with conservatism, hesitation, excessive deference to the opinion of others, or unwillingness to 'go in and win,'" the pro-Republican *New York Times* countered.[11] Republicans blamed the Democrat-controlled House Appropriations Committee for refusing to fund outposts on the Yellowstone that would have enabled a more formidable force to take the field. Grant believed Custer bore sole responsibility, saying, "I regard Custer's Massacre as a sacrifice of troops, brought on by Custer himself, that was wholly unnecessary—wholly unnecessary."[12] But Nevin Custer said it was Grant's fault. "I didn't intend to say it, an' I won't say much," he observed many years later, "but I'll tell yuh this, if it hadn't been for U.S. Grant, George Custer would-a been alive today."

Those sympathetic to the Indians saw the tragedy as the inevitable and ironic outcome of the Black Hills gold rush that Custer helped encourage. The *New York Sun* blamed Custer's quest for fame. Custer meant "to fight alone, and alone win a great battle and harvest the glory of a victory which should put an end to Sioux warfare," the paper editorialized. "It was a great stake, gallantly but madly played for, and ruinously lost. The dashing cavalryman, charming gentleman, and accomplished scholar paid his life and the lives of his male relatives, and the lives of over three hundred of the best soldiers in the army, as the penalty for his rash ambition."[13]

Samuel D. Sturgis, whose son James died in the battle, concurred with this view and said Custer felt he needed to prove himself after being humiliated by President Grant. "What I especially deprecate is the manner in which some papers have sought to make a demigod out of Custer, and to erect a monument to Custer, and none to his soldiers," he said in an interview a few weeks after the massacre. "Custer was a brave man, but he was also a very selfish man. He was insanely ambitious for glory, and the phrase 'Custer's luck' affords a good clue to his ruling passion."[14] Sherman and Sheridan also thought the attack was ill-considered, though Sherman later told General Thomas L. Crittenden, whose son had also perished in the battle, "When Custer found himself in the presence of the Indians, he could do nothing but attack."[15]

George McClellan argued that Custer was not reckless but made a calculated risk based on years of experience in battle. "On that fatal day he simply repeated the tactics that he had so often successfully used against large bodies of Indians," McClellan wrote. But given his insufficient knowledge of the strength and morale of his opponents, as well as ignorance of the terrain on which the battle was fought, "he was suddenly surrounded by overwhelming masses of well-armed warriors, against whom the heroic efforts of his command wasted themselves in vain."[16]

Godfrey concurred, arguing that criticisms were based on hindsight and had Custer succeeded, "he would have been hailed as a genius and hero, and nothing ever would have been said about disobedience, rashness and blunders and court martial."[17]

Terry sought to dodge blame that might be cast in his direction by saying if Custer had followed orders, their columns would have met at the objective simultaneously, and the Indians would have been defeated. "The movements proposed for General Gibbon's column were carried out to the letter," Terry wrote, "and had the attack been deferred until it was up I cannot doubt that we should have been successful."[18] Custer would probably have argued that he was following his orders, since Terry told him to use his initiative. For his part Gibbon believed that speculation either way was pointless because "General Custer is dead and cannot tell his side of the story or of the motives which influenced his action."[19]

Some blamed Benteen for not responding more urgently to Custer's order to "come on" and "be quick." But most blamed Marcus Reno, either for not carrying the fight to the village as ordered, or for retreating across the river, or for not going to Custer's assistance when he could—or all three. Thomas Rosser wrote a widely reprinted letter to the *St. Paul Pioneer Press and Tribune* blaming Reno for deserting Custer, though this was only conjecture. Custer biographer Frederick Whittaker made a public case against Reno, implying he may have left George to die on purpose. Reno then demanded a court of inquiry to clear his name. The court met in 1879 and took testimony on the battle from many of the surviving participants. The proceeding found Reno not culpable for Custer's death, but that did not end the debate. Meanwhile, the hapless Reno was court-martialed twice for "conduct unbecoming an officer and a gentleman": first for attempting to take advantage of another officer's wife (1877) and then for drunkenness and lewd behavior directed at Colonel Sturgis's daughter (1879). He was found guilty both

times, suspended for the first offense, and discharged for the second. Reno died in 1889, and Libbie Custer successfully blocked his burial at Custer Battlefield National Cemetery, saying the honor did not befit the coward of the regiment.[20]

In 1877, on Sheridan's initiative, the bodies of most of the officers killed at Little Bighorn were exhumed for reburial.[21] Captains Tom Custer and Yates and Lieutenants Smith, McIntosh, and Calhoun were buried at Fort Leavenworth on August 3.[22] Lieutenant John J. Crittenden was not moved; his father General Crittenden argued that "there can be no fitter resting place for the true soldier than that spot which his blood has hallowed."[23] Boston Custer and Autie Reed were buried in the family plot in the Woodland Cemetery in Monroe, Michigan.

George Custer's body was packed in a wooden box, inspected at Fort Lincoln by post surgeon R. G. Read, and sealed. It was shipped to Poughkeepsie Cemetery in New York, just north of West Point, and placed in a vault to await burial. Eventually a rumor spread that the remains were not Custer's but a teamster's.[24] Frank Palmer of Company C, who had been part of the original burial detail, insisted this was impossible. And with the body came one of the Spanish spurs Custer had borrowed from Frank Huger after the Battle of Sailor's Creek a few days before Appomattox, which had originally belonged to Mexican president Santa Anna. Custer had neglected to return the spurs after the war, but Libbie gave the remaining one back to Huger.[25]

Custer's funeral took place on October 10, 1877. The coffin was draped in the same flag used in the funeral of Louis McLane Hamilton, killed at Washita, who was buried in Poughkeepsie. Thousands of people lined the streets of the town to watch the procession from the cemetery to the riverfront. Custer's remains were transported to West Point by the side-wheeled steamer *Mary Powell* and taken to the Cadet Chapel to lie in state. Custer's sword and hat were placed on the dais near a two-foot column of dried flowers, and a wreath encircling the words "Seventh

Cavalry" was at the foot. A festooned American flag was on the back wall above the head of the coffin, and a blue silk banner with gold letters that read "God and Our Native Land." The brief funeral service was conducted by post chaplain Dr. John Forsyth. Libbie, in black, was escorted by Superintendent Major General John Schofield. Emmanuel Custer was present, with Maggie Custer Calhoun and Nettie Smith. Lieutenant Braden, wounded on the Yellowstone in 1873, Custer classmate Stephen Lyford, who had served on his court-martial, and William Ludlow were among the pallbearers.

A draped caisson carried the coffin from the chapel to the cemetery. Libbie walked behind it, weeping, supported by General Schofield. A riderless horse followed, with the regalia of a major general, and backward-turned boots. Then came family and friends. The Corps of Cadets marched in their battalions, and the band played a dirge. Numerous Army and Navy officers, war veterans, and local militia units accompanied the procession, and thousands of people crowded the Plain and stood along the route.

They walked a half mile to a peaceful, shaded field on the escarpment above the Hudson River that had been a burial site since the time of the Revolution. Dr. Forsyth concluded the service by the graveside. George's remains were lowered into the earth; some dirt was sprinkled on top; and the Corps of Cadets fired three volleys in salute. The cadets honored George in another way he would have appreciated, adding a new verse to their traditional drinking song and informal hymn:

> In silence lift your glasses; a meteor flashes out.
> So swift to death brave Custer, amid the battle's shout.
> Death called—and crowned, he went to join the friends of long ago,
> To the land of Peace, where now he dwells with Benny Havens, Oh![26]

The Indian fighter, Boy General, and gallant goat of June 1861, had returned to West Point for his final rest.

Libbie Custer joined George there over half a century later. She died on April 6, 1933, two days short of her ninety-first birthday. She had never remarried but remained true to her Autie and his memory for the rest of her life. She had little means of support when George died, with no savings to speak of and a widow's pension of thirty dollars per month. She worked for the Society of Decorative Arts in New York City and over time developed her talents as a writer. She wrote three best-selling memoirs of her days with George, *Boots and Saddles*, *Tenting on the Plains*, and *Following the Guidon*, and also produced commentaries on art, culture, and public life. Libbie spent summers with other women writers and artists at the colony at Onteora Park in the Catskills, traveled the United States and the world, and lived comfortably to the end of her days.

Libbie tirelessly defended George and his image in the press and in public, writing detailed though idealized accounts of their life in the West and bluntly challenging the general's critics when they periodically appeared. She lobbied successfully to take down a statue of George by James Wilson McDonald that was erected on the Plain at West Point in 1879 without her approval or input. It was removed in 1884 and later disappeared under unusual circumstances.[27] An obelisk inscribed "George Armstrong Custer, Major General, U.S. Volunteers" was placed on the statue's decorative pedestal, and the monument currently stands at Custer's grave.

Libbie gave full support to the statue of George erected in Monroe in 1910 called *Sighting the Enemy*. It was by sculptor Edward Potter and portrays Custer at Gettysburg, on horseback, looking into the distance, during one of the key events of his life. It captures the same intense feeling that Rosser described in witnessing Custer about to charge on the

Yellowstone, the passion and anticipation of a battle to be joined. It was the General Custer that Libbie most wanted people to remember.

Libbie made public appearances at other commemorative events but skipped the fiftieth anniversary ceremony at the Little Bighorn battlefield in 1926. She never once visited the site of her Autie's death. She lived on Park Avenue late in life, a fixture in New York society, her spacious apartment a veritable museum of Custer artifacts. Libbie was buried alongside George at West Point, the band playing "Garryowen" as she was laid to rest.

By then George Custer might have been mostly forgotten, a soldier from times long past who had a brief moment of glory before his flame was extinguished. However, he was more famous than ever when Libbie died, and would remain so. Custer's Last Stand had taken on a symbolic role far greater than its military importance and was a vehicle for art, literature, history, strong emotion, and endless debate.

The tragic romance of Custer began early. *Galaxy* magazine, which had been serializing George's memoirs when he died, wrote, "Never was there a life more rounded, complete and symmetrical than that of George A. Custer, the favorite of fortune, the last cavalier." They said to him alone "was it given to join a romantic line of perfect success to a death of perfect heroism." They compared the cavalry at Little Bighorn to the Spartans at Thermopylæ and said it was Custer's fate "to die like Leonidas."[28] Novelist Frederick Whittaker rushed out *The Complete Life of General George A. Custer* in December 1876, a sensationalized biography that was criticized by some in the military establishment but became a popular hit.

George's admirer Walt Whitman wrote "A Death Sonnet for Custer," which appeared in the *New York Tribune* four days after news of the battle broke.[29] In this "trumpet note for heroes," he wrote,

Thou of sunny, flowing hair, in battle,
I erewhile saw, with erect head, pressing ever in
front, bearing a bright sword in thy hand,
Now ending well the splendid fever of thy deeds ...

Years later Whitman sat for an hour viewing John Mulvaney's wall-sized, twelve-foot-high mural, *Custer's Last Rally*, as he said, "completely absorb'd in the first view." Whitman cast the "painfully real, overwhelming" scene in terms of his thesis of the superiority of the American over the European, even in tragedy. The "muscular, tan-faced men, brought to bay under terrible circumstances," face "swarms upon swarms of savage Sioux, in their war-bonnets ... like a hurricane of demons." Custer "stands in the middle, with dilated eye and extended arm, aiming a huge cavalry pistol" as the men wring out "every cent of the pay before they sell their lives." Whitman said the scene was dreadful, "yet with an attraction and beauty that will remain in my memory."[30] A more-well-known depiction was Otto Becker's wholly imagined *Custer's Last Fight*, which was distributed as a promotional lithograph by the Anheuser-Busch brewing company and seen for years in bars and saloons across the country.

Articles, books, poems, and paintings such as these elevated the Custer legend in the decades after his death. Other works emerged that just as fiercely denigrated it. More than 135 years of these efforts have produced Custers for every taste and fancy, from the heroic to the demonic, from the sublime to the ridiculous.

"My every thought was ambitious," George wrote. "I desired to link my name with acts and men, and in such a manner as to be a mark of honor, not only to the present, but to future generations." Was this what he achieve? Custer wrote these words in the spring of 1867, shortly before the failed Hancock expedition and his court-martial. But the letter continued with a note of humility. "I find myself, at twenty-seven, with contentment and happiness bordering my path," he wrote. "My ambition has been turned into an entirely new channel. Where I was once eager to acquire worldly honors and distinctions, I am now content to try and modestly wear what I have, and feel grateful for them when they come, but my desire now is to make of myself a man worthy of the blessings heaped upon me."[31]

George Custer grew up a boy of modest means who asked little of the world but much of himself. He quickly achieved the greatness he sought, then spent the rest of his short life trying to live up to it, not always successfully. It was a very American life, self-created, boundary breaking, energetic, and with all his imperfections he never ceased to strive, create, and overcome. Custer lived on his own terms, and died on them.

"Life is worth living for—or it would be—if it abounded more in such types," wrote Charles Godfrey Leland, a folklorist, soldier, and scholar, after he visited George and Libbie at Fort Riley in 1869. "There was a bright and joyous chivalry in that man, and a noble refinement mingled with constant gaiety in the wife, such as I fear is passing from the earth." Leland said that he worried "there will come a time when such books [as Libbie's] will be the only evidences that there were ever such people—so fearless, so familiar with every form of danger, privation, and trial, and yet joyous and even reckless of it all."[32]

A NOTE ON SOURCES

Some of the primary sources used in *The Real Custer* are found in the United States Military Academy Special Collections. They include, *inter alia*, the George Armstrong Custer papers and papers of other graduates as cited, particularly documents in the files compiled by George W. Cullum for his *Biographical Register of the Officers and Graduates of the U.S. Military Academy* (3rd ed., 3 vols., 1891), also known as the "Cullum files"; the "x-files" of cadets who did not graduate; the Annual Reports of the USMA Association of Graduates; the 1952 *Register of Graduates and Former Cadets*; the *Register of Delinquencies, Staff Records, Post Orders, Special Orders*; and other sundry records. Other sources include records and documents from the National Archives in Washington, D.C., the Elizabeth Bacon Custer papers, and other collections as cited. All Custer letters are from the United States Military Academy Special Collections unless otherwise indicated.

Additional biographical details are from Francis Bernard Heitman, *Historical Register and Dictionary of the United States Army, from its Organization, September 29, 1789, to March 2, 1903*, Washington, DC: Government Printing Office (1903).

Civil War–era after action reports, correspondence and other such records are from *The War of the Rebellion: A Compilation of the Official Records of the Union and Confederate Armies* (Washington, DC: Government Printing Office, 1902), unless otherwise indicated.

Some of the secondary sources consulted are *The Custer Story: The Life and Intimate Letters of General George A. Custer and His Wife Elizabeth*, Marguerite Merington, ed. (New York: Devin-Adair, 1950); *The Civil War Memories of Elizabeth Bacon Custer: Reconstructed from Her Diaries and Notes*, Arlene Reynolds, ed. (Austin: University of Texas Press, 1994); Frederic F. Van de Water, *Glory-Hunter: A Life of General Custer* (New York: Bobbs-Merrill, 1934); D. A. Kinsley, *Favor the Bold* (New York: Holt, Rinehart and Winston, 1967–68); Jay Monaghan, *Custer: The Life of General George Armstrong Custer* (Boston: Little, Brown, 1959); Stephen E. Ambrose, *Crazy Horse and Custer: The Parallel Lives of Two American Warriors* (Garden City, NY: Doubleday, 1975); Louise K Barnett, *Touched by Fire: The Life, Death, and Mythic Afterlife of George Armstrong Custer* (New York: Henry Holt, 1996); James Welch, *Killing Custer* (New York: Penguin Books, 1995); and Thom Hatch, *The Custer Companion* (Mechanicsburg, PA: Stackpole Books, 2002). *The Real Custer* expands and is partly based on the account of Custer in the author's *Last in Their Class: Custer, Pickett and the Goats of West Point* (New York: Encounter Books, 2006).

Special thanks to Michael Donahue, chairman of the Art Department at Temple College and longest-serving seasonal park ranger at the Little Bighorn Battlefield National Monument, for his generous assistance and invaluable comments.

NOTES

INTRODUCTION

1. Frederick Whittaker, *A Complete Life of General George A. Custer* (Lincoln: University of Nebraska Press, 1993), first published in December 1876, 609–10. Whittaker is often faulted for not being accurate, to the point where, like Herodotus, historians avoid his work for fear of repeating a dubious tale.

2. Philip Quilibet (George Edward Pound), "Luck," *Galaxy*, October 1876, 555.

3. Data from Google Ngrams show a reader was over one hundred times more likely to see a reference to "George Custer" in a book in the year 2000 than in 1876, and the greatest growth in Custer references came after 1966.

4. Ronald Reagan, in a letter to Custer biographer David Humphreys Miller, June 21, 1984.

5. John McClelland Bulkley, *History of Monroe County Michigan*, vol. I (Chicago: The Lewis Publishing Company, 1913), 236–7.

CHAPTER 1

1. Warren Jenkins, *The Ohio Gazetteer and Traveler's Guide* (Columbus: Isaac N. Whiting, 1837), 334.

2.   Charles B. Wallace, *Custer's Ohio Boyhood* (Cadiz, OH: Harrison County Historical Society, 1993), 46. Emmanuel Henry Custer, born December 10, 1806, in Cresaptown, MD; died November 17, 1892, in Monroe, Michigan. On August 7, 1828, he married first Matilda Viers (March 4, 1804–July 18, 1835). Children: Hannah, Brice, William, and John A. He married his second wife, Mrs. Maria Ward Kirkpatrick (May 31, 1807–January 13, 1882), on February 23, 1836. Children: James, Samuel, George Armstrong, Nevin Johnson, Thomas Ward, Boston, and Margaret Emma.

3.   All Nevin Custer reminiscences from "Custer as His Brother Remembers Him," newspaper article, Topeka, Kansas, June 1910. Accessed from the Monroe County Library (MI).

4.   Louise Barnett, "Early Days," chapter 1 in *Touched by Fire: The Life, Death, and Mythic Afterlife of George Armstrong Custer* (New York: Henry Holt, 1996).

5.   Ibid.

6.   "Michigan's Tribute to General Custer," *Shreveport (LA) Caucasian*, May 31, 1910, 2. Whether he knew it or not, he was quoting lines attributed to Cherokee leader Tuskenehaw when his people were facing banishment on the Trail of Tears. "My voice is for war," he said. "I have killed all the whites I could find.... I, and all the brave warriors of my town, will die and be buried alongside of their fathers. Those who are afraid, like squaws, will let the white man come and drive them off. My voice is for war." "The West Fifty Years Hence," *Southern Literary Messenger* 4, 1838, 467.

7.   The Indians later massacred the American prisoners.

8.   John McClelland Bulkley, *History of Monroe County Michigan: A Narrative Account of Its Historical Progress, Its People, and Its Principal Interests*, vol. 1 (Chicago: The Lewis Publishing Company, 1913), 421–22.

9.   Ibid., 422.

10.   Ibid.

11.   Ibid., 233.

12.   "Custer as a Boy," *New York Times*, July 29, 1876, 2.

13.   Willard Glazier, *Ocean to Ocean on Horseback* (Philadelphia: Edgewood Publishing, 1899), 277–78. Glazier was a lieutenant in the 2nd New York Cavalry regiment before being captured and sent to Libby Prison in October 1863.

14. "Some Reminiscences of the Boyhood Days of General Custer and Bishop Simpson," *Belmont Chronicle (OH)*, March 4, 1880, 1.
15. Ibid.
16. Ibid.
17. Ibid.
18. Ibid.
19. GAC December 12, 1856.
20. Harrison County had also shifted districts as Ohio grew, being previously part of the Fifteenth, Nineteenth, and Eleventh Districts.
21. "Gen. Custer's Father," *Lafayette (LA) Gazette*, April 22, 1893, 1.
22. EBC in Arlene Reynolds, ed., *The Civil War Memories of Elizabeth Bacon Custer: Reconstructed from Her Diaries and Notes* (Austin: University of Texas Press, 1994), 9.
23. The Opposition party (1854–58) was one of the political parties that bridged the disintegration of the Whig party after the passage of the compromise Kansas-Nebraska Act in 1854 and the rise of the Republican party after 1856. The Oppositionists—the name referring to their opposition to the Democrats—controlled one hundred seats in the Thirty-fourth Congress, the largest party but lacking majority control. Bingham had been a lawyer in New Philadelphia, Ohio, and had served as district attorney for Tuscarawas County. He served eight nonconsecutive terms in Congress. Bingham was a special judge advocate during the trial of the Lincoln conspirators, helped manage the impeachment of Andrew Johnson, was principal author of the Fourteenth Amendment, and was U.S. minister to Japan, 1873–85.
24. "Gen. Custer's Father," 1.
25. "How Custer Went to West Point," *Hocking Sentinel (OH)*, August 16, 1900, 3.
26. "Some Reminiscences of the Boyhood Days of General Custer and Bishop Simpson," 1.

CHAPTER 2

1. EBC in Arlene Reynolds, ed., *The Civil War Memories of Elizabeth Bacon Custer: Reconstructed from Her Diaries and Notes* (Austin: University of Texas Press, 1994), 20.
2. James S. Robbins, *Last in Their Class: Custer, Pickett, and the Goats of West Point* (New York: Encounter Books, 2006), 1.

3.   GAC, August 7, 1857.

4.   Morris Schaff, *The Spirit of Old West Point, 1858–1862* (New York: Houghton, Mifflin, 1907), 86. Schaff knew Custer well at West Point and afterward, and his memoir of his cadet days is an important source on West Point in the years before and during the outbreak of the Civil War.

5.   See John Montgomery Wright, "West Point before the War," *Southern Bivouac*, June 1885, 13.

6.   Joseph Pearson Farley, *West Point in the Early Sixties: With Incidents of the War* (Troy, NY: Pafraets Book Company, 1902), 78.

7.   George Custer, "War Memoirs," *Galaxy*, April 1876, 450.

8.   GAC, January 27, 1858.

9.   GAC, June 30, 1858, from "Camp Jefferson Davis."

10.   Custer, "War Memoirs"; and GAC, December 13, 1859.

11.   Reverend J. William Jones, ed., "Generals in the Saddle," *Southern Historical Society Papers* 19, October 1891, 172.

12.   Marguerite Merington, ed., *The Custer Story: The Life and Intimate Letters of General George A. Custer and His Wife Elizabeth* (New York: Devin-Adair, 1950), 8.

13.   Wright, "West Point before the War," 18.

14.   GAC, December 13, 1859.

15.   McCrea letter, January 19, 1861.

16.   Custer letter, August 7, 1857.

17.   Quoted in W. Donal Horn, ed., *"Skinned": The Delinquency Record of Cadet George Armstrong Custer, U.S.M.A. Class of June 1861*, foreword by Blaine L. Beal (Short Hills, NJ: W. D. Horn, 1980), iii.

18.   Schaff, *The Spirit of Old West Point*, 194.

19.   McCrea letter, December 22, 1858.

20.   Memoir of George A. Woodruff, unpublished manuscript, USMA Archives, 24.

21.   Custer, West Point–era letter, date uncertain.

22.   Letter from T. Rowland written in 1860, reprinted in "Hazing at West Point," *Stevens Point Journal*, April 22, 1916.

23.   EBC in Reynolds, *The Civil War Memories of Elizabeth Bacon Custer*, 39.

24.   Custer, "War Memoirs," 454.

25.   Edward C. Boynton, *History of West Point, and Its Military Importance during the American Revolution: And the Origin and Progress of the United States*

Military Academy (New York: Van Nostrand, 1863), 279. Some have said that the demerits Custer was forgiven at the end of his first year were "Custer's luck," but in fact all cadets in his class were given the one-third reduction.

26. The one-third reduction explains Custer's comment about the 150-demerit limit. It was actually a one-hundred-demerit-per-semester limit, but plebes could go up another fifty since it would revert by one-third.

27. Custer, "War Memoirs," 452.

28. McCrea letter, September 23, 1860.

29. McCrea letter, January 19, 1861. McCrea offered helpfully that a better idea would have been to take the whole notebook and replace it later by bribing an employee at the hotel.

30. McCrea letter, February 10, 1861.

31. EBC in Reynolds, *The Civil War Memories of Elizabeth Bacon Custer*, 39.

32. Custer letter dated August 7, 1857.

33. "Affairs at West Point," *New York Times*, August 9, 1860.

34. "West Point and Newport," *New York Times*, September 11, 1860, 2.

35. "West Point," *New York Times*, September 13, 1860, 2.

36. R. W. Johnson, *A Soldier's Reminiscences in Peace and War* (Philadelphia: J.B. Lippincott, 1886), 25–27. Johnson graduated thirtieth of forty-three in his class and was a brevet major general in the Civil War.

37. Custer letter, August 7, 1857.

38. Custer letter, December 13, 1859.

39. Custer, "War Memoirs," 454.

40. Robbins, *Last in Their Class*, 21.

41. Edward K. Eckert and Nicholas J. Amato, eds., *Ten Years in the Saddle: The Memoir of William Woods Averell* (San Rafael, CA: Presidio Press, 1978), 38.

42. EBC in Reynolds, *The Civil War Memories of Elizabeth Bacon Custer*, 23.

CHAPTER 3

1. "The West Point Troubles," *New York Times*, October 21, 1871.

2. George Custer, "War Memoirs," *Galaxy*, April 1876, 449.

3. Quoted in George C. Strong, *Cadet Life at West Point* (Boston: T. O. H. P. Burnham, 1962), 297.

4. See Elizabeth D. J. Waugh, "Brothers at War," chapter 9 in *West Point* (New York: Macmillan, 1944).

5. Custer, "War Memoirs," 449.

6. John M. Parker III, "The Life of Francis Henry Parker, 1838–1897, A U.S. Army Ordinance Officer" (unpublished manuscript), USMA Archives, 32–33.

7. Custer, "War Memoirs," 449.

8. See Waugh, *West Point*, 115–16.

9. Custer, "War Memoirs," 449.

10. Jacob B. Rawles, "General Rawles Tells Stories of West Point's Famous Class of '61," *San Francisco Call*, March 20, 1910, 4.

11. Morris Schaff, *The Spirit of Old West Point, 1858–1862* (New York: Houghton, Mifflin, 1907), 145.

12. "The West Point Troubles."

13. Schaff, *The Spirit of Old West Point*, 147. Rodgers was an artillery officer during the first years of the Civil War and taught mathematics at West Point in 1864–65. He was a brigadier general and chief of artillery during the Spanish-American War.

14. Schaff, *The Spirit of Old West Point*, 144. Schaff believed that the Northern temperament, which withstood insults, tended to encourage the Southerners, who misconstrued taciturnity for lack of courage. "It took Gettysburg and the Wilderness and Chickamauga to prove them their fatal error," he wrote (see *The Spirit of Old West Point*, 83).

15. Lane resigned February 16, 1861, and became a Confederate artilleryman. He was in all the major battles in the East, serving under Pendleton at Gettysburg in the Sumter Artillery, Hill's Corps, Anderson's Division. He was probably at Appomattox as a lieutenant colonel.

16. Rawles, "General Rawles Tells Stories of West Point's Famous Class of '61," 4.

17. Ibid. Rawles confusingly says that Gibbes was present during this incident, but since he had graduated in July 1860, it was unlikely unless the straw poll was held before the 1860 graduation.

18. Schaff, *The Spirit of Old West Point*, 165. Lincoln was elected with just under 40 percent of the popular vote.

19. Schaff, *The Spirit of Old West Point*, 165.

20. Custer, "War Memoirs," 449.

21. McCrea letter, November 10, 1860.

22. William A. Elderkin letter, November 14, 1860, USMA Archives.

23. Custer, "War Memoirs," 449–50.

24. Letter from T Rowland dated November 11, 1860, in *Southern Atlantic Quarterly* 15, no. 1 (January 1916), 148.

25. Quoted in Peter S. Michie, *The Life and Letters of Emory Upton, Colonel of the Fourth Regiment of Artillery, and Brevet Major-General, U.S. Army* (New York: D. Appleton, 1885), 28.

26. *Janesville (WI) Gazette*, December 3, 1860, 1.

27. Edward C. Boynton, *History of West Point, and Its Military Importance during the American Revolution: And the Origin and Progress of the United States Military Academy* (New York: Van Nostrand, 1863), 281.

28. Custer, "War Memoirs," 451.

29. Rowland letter, December 27, 1860.

30. Custer, "War Memoirs," 450.

31. Rowland letter, December 27, 1860.

32. Custer, "War Memoirs," 450.

33. After the war, Young was a congressman, minister to Guatemala, and consul-general to Russia.

34. Schaff, *The Spirit of Old West Point*, 149.

35. Lynwood M. Holland, *Pierce M. B. Young: The Warwick of the South* (Athens: University of Georgia Press, 1964), 27.

36. Custer, "War Memoirs," 451.

37. Wiley C. Howard, *Sketch of Cobb Legion Cavalry and Some Incidents and Scenes Remembered* (Atlanta, GA, 1901), 4–5.

38. Custer, "War Memoirs," 452.

39. Ibid. Ball commanded the 8th Alabama Cavalry regiment during the war, and afterward he became an inventor. Kelly, in November 1863, became the youngest general in the Confederacy, a counterpart to his friend Custer, who achieved the same distinction in the Union Army six months earlier. Kelly was killed in 1864 during a raid near Franklin, Tennessee.

40. Parker, *The Life of Francis Henry Parker*, letter of April 7, 1861, 45–46.

41. Presidential order quoted in Schaff, *The Spirit of Old West Point*, 201–2.

42. Quoted in Schaff, *The Spirit of Old West Point*, 204.

43. Ibid., 208.

44. Custer letter, April 10, 1861, USMA archives.

45. Parker, *The Life of Francis Henry Parker*, letter of April 7, 1861, 44.

46. Custer letter, April 10, 1861, USMA archives.

47. Custer, "War Memoirs," 453.

48. Rowland letter, April 14, 1861.

49. "Detention of West Point Cadets in Philadelphia," *New York Times,* May 9, 1861. See also letter by Lieutenant William Anthony Elderkin (USMA May 1861), May 8, 1861, USMA Archives.

50. *New York Times,* June 22, 1861. The Class of 1862 almost graduated early as well, but it was felt that there was nothing to be gained putting officers in the field who were little better trained than the militia officers already being commissioned in large numbers balanced against such a severe disruption of the Academy system.

51. Parker, *The Life of Francis Henry Parker,* letter of May 18, 1861, 47.

52. "The West Point Cadets," *New York Times,* June 22, 1861.

53. GAC letter to his sister, May 31, 1861.

54. Quoted in James S. Robbins, *Last in Their Class: Custer, Pickett, and the Goats of West Point* (New York: Encounter Books, 2006), x. The book remains the invaluable guide to the goats.

55. Boynton, *History of West,* 281.

56. Custer, "War Memoirs," 454. Of the 330 serving West Point graduates appointed from the Southern states, 168 joined the rebellion, and 162 remained loyal to the Union. See Ellsworth Eliot Jr., *West Point in the Confederacy* (New York: G.A. Baker, 1941).

57. Custer, "War Memoirs," 454.

58. Two of them, Frank A. Reynolds and George Owen Watts, graduated and then resigned. Clarence Derrick, who graduated fourth in the class, also resigned after graduation.

59. Custer, "War Memoirs," 455.

60. "Custer's Failure at West Point," *Hamilton Examiner,* July 30, 1874, 2.

61. Ibid.

62. Custer, "War Memoirs," 455.

63. Ibid.

64. Ibid.

65. EBC in Arlene Reynolds, ed., *The Civil War Memories of Elizabeth Bacon Custer: Reconstructed from Her Diaries and Notes* (Austin: University of Texas Press, 1994), 34.

66. Stephen Vincent Benét graduated third in the Class of 1849. He spent the Civil War at West Point as an instructor and testing experimental ordnance. In 1874 he became the chief of ordnance of the U.S. Army.

67. Custer, "War Memoirs," 455.

68. Ibid., 456.

69. Ibid.

70. Ibid.

71. Special Orders No. 187, July 15, 1861, 8–9. It is hard to understand Hazen's assessment of Custer's conduct, since he had been given fifty-two demerits in the twenty-three days between the end of term and the incident in question. It may have been a case of one immortal looking out for another.

72. Memoir of George A. Woodruff, unpublished manuscript, USMA Archives, 28.

73. GAC letter to his sister, May 31, 1861.

CHAPTER 4

1. EBC in Arlene Reynolds, ed., *The Civil War Memories of Elizabeth Bacon Custer: Reconstructed from Her Diaries and Notes* (Austin: University of Texas Press, 1994), 5. Of the eighty-nine graduates of the two classes of 1861, forty-three were present at Bull Run.

2. George A. Custer, "War Memoirs," *Galaxy*, April 1876, 456.

3. Ibid., 457.

4. Custer, "War Memoirs," September 1876, 19.

5. Custer, "War Memoirs," April 1876, 624.

6. Custer, "War Memoirs," May 1876, 629.

7. Ibid., 628.

8. Custer, "War Memoirs," May 1876, 631; and June 1876, 811.

9. Custer, "War Memoirs," May 1876, 624.

10. Marguerite Merington, ed., *The Custer Story: The Life and Intimate Letters of General George A. Custer and His Wife Elizabeth* (New York: Devin-Adair, 1950), 13.

11. Custer, "War Memoirs," June 1876, 814.

12. John McClelland Bulkley, *History of Monroe County Michigan: A Narrative Account of Its Historical Progress, Its People, and Its Principal Interests*, vol. 1 (Chicago: The Lewis Publishing Company, 1913), 234.

13. Custer, "War Memoirs," September 1876, 299.

14. Custer, "War Memoirs," November 1876, 685.

15. Ibid.

16. See the account in "The Fighting Begins," chapter 5 of Tom Carhart, *Sacred Ties: From West Point Brothers to Battlefield Rivals* (New York: Berkley Publishing Group, 2010).

17. Custer, "War Memoirs," November 1876, 685–86.

18. Ibid., 692.

19. Ibid., 693.

20. Ibid., 694.

21. Ibid.

22. Francois Joinville to Edward Everett, Wednesday, November 9, 1864, Lincoln Papers, Library of Congress. Joinville acted as chaperon for his two nephews, who were on McClellan's staff and later wrote a book about his experiences.

23. Reports of Brigadier General John G. Barnard, U.S. Army, chief engineer of operations from May 23, 1861, to August 15, 1862.

24. Custer, "War Memoirs," October 1876, 455.

25. See the account by M. A. Luce, "Custer's First Battle," *Overland Monthly and Out West Magazine*, vol. 21 (March 1898), 280–81. Luce participated in the engagement as a member of the 4th Michigan.

26. Report of Lieutenant Nicolas Bowen, topographical engineers, U.S. Army, May 23–24, 1862; and "Skirmishes at Ellison's Mill, New Bridge, and Mechanicsville, Va.," May 25, 1862.

27. Reports of Brigadier General John G. Barnard, U.S. Army, chief engineer of operations from May 23, 1861, to August 15, 1862.

28. McClellan to Stanton, May 24, 1862, 9 p.m.

29. Willard Glazier, *Ocean to Ocean on Horseback* (Philadelphia: Edgewood, 1899), 278.

CHAPTER 5

1. George Brinton McClellan and William Cowper Prime, *McClellan's Own Story* (New York: C. L. Webster, 1887), 365.

2. George A. Custer, "War Memoirs," *Galaxy*, June 1876, 813.

3. Reports of Colonel William W. Averell, Third Pennsylvania Cavalry, commanding First Cavalry Brigade, of skirmish at White Oak Swamp Bridge, August 5–6, 1862.

4. GAC in Reynolds, *The Civil War Memories of Elizabeth Bacon Custer*, 27–28.

5. D. S. Freeman, *Lee's Lieutenants*, vol. 1, *Manassas to Malvern Hill* (New York: Scribner's, 1942), 233.

6. From an account by Mrs. E. B. Washington reprinted in "Amenities of War," *Louisiana Democrat*, February 13, 1878.

7. EBC in Reynolds, *The Civil War Memories of Elizabeth Bacon Custer*, 28.

8. E. B. Washington's account in "Amenities of War." Washington was sent to Fort Delaware in June 1862 and was exchanged that September for First Lieutenant James S. Blair of the First Maryland Volunteers. He went back to Johnston's staff.

9. EBC in Reynolds, *The Civil War Memories of Elizabeth Bacon Custer*, 30.

10. Custer letter of May 15, 1862, in Marguerite Merington, *The Custer Story: The Life and Intimate Letters of General George A. Custer and His Wife Elizabeth* (New York: Devin-Adair, 1950), 30.

11. Cf. Morris Schaff, *The Spirit of Old West Point, 1858–1862* (New York: Houghton, Mifflin, 1907), 179–182. Schaff incorrectly gives the family name as Durfee. Schaff suggested that Lea should be buried next to Custer at West Point, "in memory of the love of two cadets whose West Point friendship the bitterness of war could not destroy" (183). Bassett Hall, the site of the wedding, is currently a museum at Colonial Williamsburg.

12. Merington, *The Custer Story*, 35.

13. Custer, "War Memoirs," June 1876, 812–13.

14. D. H. Strother, "Personal Recollections of the War by a Virginian," *Harper's New Monthly Magazine*, April 1868, 581. Entry of November 9, 1862.

15. Ibid., 577. Entry of November 1, 1862.

CHAPTER 6

1. John McClelland Bulkley, *History of Monroe County Michigan*, vol. I (Chicago: The Lewis Publishing Company, 1913), 219–20.

2. EBC in Arlene Reynolds, ed., *The Civil War Memories of Elizabeth Bacon Custer: Reconstructed from Her Diaries and Notes* (Austin: University of Texas Press, 1994), 4.

3. Ibid.

4. EBC to GAC, August 14, 1864, in Marguerite Merington, ed., *The Custer Story: The Life and Intimate Letters of General George A. Custer and His Wife Elizabeth* (New York: Devin-Adair, 1950), 47.

5. EBC in Reynolds, *The Civil War Memories of Elizabeth Bacon Custer*, 5.

6. Ibid.

7. Ibid., 5–6.

8.   Ibid., 24.

9.   George A. Custer, "War Memoirs," *Galaxy*, June 1876, 809.

10.   EBC in Reynolds, *The Civil War Memories of Elizabeth Bacon Custer*, 7.

11.   GAC, April 13, 1863.

12.   GAC to Christiancy, May 31, 1863.

13.   Samuel Harris, *Personal Reminiscences of Samuel Harris* (Chicago: The Rogerson Press, 1897), 17, 23–24.

14.   Report of Brig. Gen. Alfred Pleasonton, U. S. Army, commanding Cavalry Division, of operation September 4-17 (1862).

15.   GAC to Augusta, October 3, 1862.

16.   GAC to Christiancy, May 31, 1863.

17.   GAC, June 8, 1863.

18.   See the account in Paul D. Walker, *The Cavalry Battle that Saved the Union: Custer vs. Stuart at Gettysburg* (Gretna, LA: Pelican Publishing, 2002), 81–82.

19.   GAC to Lydia, May 27, 1863.

20.   Edward G. Longacre, *The Cavalry at Gettysburg* (London: Associated University Presses, 1986), 108.

21.   Pleasonton's report, June 15, 1863.

22.   Henry C. Meyer, *Civil War Experiences under Bayard, Gregg, Kilpatrick, Custer, Raulston and Newberry* (New York: The Knickerbocker Press, 1911), 33.

23.   Ibid., 34.

24.   Hall in Edward P. Tobie, *History of the First Maine Cavalry, 1861–1865* (Boston: Press of Emery and Hughes, 1887), 160.

25.   Howe transcript, Maine State Archives.

26.   Longacre, *The Cavalry at Gettysburg*, 108.

27.   Munford's official report on Aldie dated August 7, 1863.

28.   Meyer, *Civil War Experiences under Bayard, Gregg, Kilpatrick, Custer, Raulston and Newberry*, 49.

29.   For a discussion of Confederate strategic and campaign-level decisionmaking on the Gettysburg campaign, see James A. Kegel, *North with Lee and Jackson: The Lost Story of Gettysburg* (Mechanicsburg, PA: Stackpole Books, 1996).

30.   Alfred Pleasonton, "The Campaign of Gettysburg," in *The Annals of the Civil War Written by Leading Participants North and South*, Alexander Kelly McClure, ed., 452. The promotions were in Special Orders 175, June 28, 1863.

Of the three, Farnsworth was not a West Point graduate; he joined the Army after being expelled from the University of Michigan in 1857, after a student died falling out a window during campus revelry in which he had participated.

31.   Quoted in D. A. Kinsley, *Favor the Bold* (New York: Holt, Rinehart and Winston, 1967–68), 134.

CHAPTER 7

1.   See Edward G. Longacre, *Custer and His Wolverines: The Michigan Cavalry Brigade, 1861–1865* (Conshohocken, PA: Combined Publishing, 1997).

2.   Eric J. Wittenberg, ed., *One of Custer's Wolverines: The Civil War Letters of Brevet Brigadier General James H. Kidd, 6th Michigan Cavalry* (Kent, OH: Kent State University Press, 2000), 46.

3.   Colonel Theodore Lyman, *With Grant and Meade from the Wilderness to Appomattox*, George R. Agassiz, ed. (Lincoln: University of Nebraska Press, 1994), 17.

4.   Quoted in D. A. Kinsley, *Favor the Bold* (New York: Holt, Rinehart and Winston, 1967–68), 138.

5.   Letter from Major General Henry Heth of A. P. Hill's Corps, A. N. V., *Southern Historical Society Papers*, vol. 4, 151–60. This statement has its critics, particularly among the cavalry. See John S. Mosby, *Stuart's Cavalry in the Gettysburg Campaign* (New York: Moffat, Yard and Company, 1908). A more balanced account is by Edward G. Longacre, *The Cavalry at Gettysburg* (London: Associated University Presses, 1986).

6.   Henry C. Meyer, *Civil War Experiences under Bayard, Gregg, Kilpatrick, Custer, Raulston and Newberry* (New York: The Knickerbocker Press, 1911), 49–50.

7.   Thompson later commanded the 6th at Brandy Station in October 1863. He was discharged June 1, 1864, because of wounds received in action. Thompson was made brevet colonel on March 13, 1865, for gallant and meritorious services during the war.

8.   See Frank Moore, ed., *Rebellion Record: A Diary of American Events; Documents and Narratives*, vol. 7, 185–86. Note that some sources place Custer leading the charge, but others do not. But it would be uncharacteristic for Custer not to have helped lead the charge; he led every one he had the chance to, previously and afterward. Also Private Churchill's heroics were noted at

the time, which could not have taken place had Custer not been in the thick of the fight.

9.　　John B. Bachelder, *The Bachelder Papers: Gettysburg in Their Own Words*, vol. 2, David L. Ladd and Audrey J. Ladd, eds. (Dayton, OH: Morningside Books, 1994), 1219.

10.　　McIntosh was from a long line of American soldiers going back to the Revolution. His brother, James McQueen McIntosh, was a Confederate Brigadier General who had been killed at the Battle of Pea Ridge, Arkansas, March 7, 1862.

11.　　Samuel Harris, *Personal Reminiscences of Samuel Harris* (Chicago: The Rogerson Press, 1897), 31.

12.　　James H. Kidd, "Address of General James Kidd at the Dedication of Michigan Monuments Upon the Battlefield at Gettysburg, June 12, 1889," *Journal of the United States Cavalry Association* 4, 1891.

13.　　Wittenberg, 145.

14.　　*Bachelder Papers*, vol. 2, 1207.

15.　　Ibid., 1257.

16.　　Ibid., 1280.

17.　　Ibid.

18.　　Quoted in Meyer, 51.

19.　　Kidd, *Personal Recollections of a Cavalryman with Custer's Michigan Cavalry* (Ionia, MI: Sentinel, 1908), 153.

20.　　*Bachelder Papers*, vol. 2, 1266.

21.　　In Longacre, *Custer and His Wolverines*, 238.

22.　　Note that a report of the battle said to be Custer's that appears in Frederick Whittaker's *A Complete Life of General George A. Custer* says that the charge of the 1st Michigan Cavalry was led by Colonel Town, not Custer.

23.　　*Bachelder Papers*, vol. 2, 1282.

24.　　Harris, *Personal Reminiscences of Samuel Harris*, 35.

25.　　Ibid., 1267.

26.　　Wittenberg, *One of Custer's Wolverines*, 155.

27.　　*Bachelder Papers*, vol. 2, 1208.

28.　　Speech by Captain Henry C. Parsons, Company L, 1st Vermont Cavalry, July 3, 1913. Parsons had participated in the charge.

29.　　Kidd, in his 1889 address said, "Custer's brigade lost one officer and twenty-eight men killed, eleven officers and 112 men wounded, sixty-seven men missing; total loss, 219. Gregg's division lost one man killed, seven officers and nineteen men wounded, eight men missing; total, thirty-five. In other words, while Gregg's division, two brigades, lost thirty-five, Custer's single brigade suffered a loss of 219."

30. Stuart's official report, August 20, 1863.

31. Edward Porter Alexander, *Military Memoirs of a Confederate: A Critical Narrative* (New York: Charles Scribner's Sons, 1907), 433.

32. *Bachelder Papers*, vol. 2, 1075.

33. Quoted in Whittaker's *A Complete Life of General George A. Custer* (Lincoln: University of Nebraska Press, 1993), 149.

CHAPTER 8

1. James H. Kidd, *Personal Recollections of a Cavalryman with Custer's Michigan Cavalry* (Ionia, MI: Sentinel, 1908), 200.

2. Quoted in Marguerite Merington, ed., *The Custer Story: The Life and Intimate Letters of General George A. Custer and His Wife Elizabeth* (New York: Devin-Adair, 1950), 11.

3. For a discussion of the challenges of covering the war, see Harold Holzer and Craig L. Symonds, eds., *The New York Times Complete Civil War, 1861–1865* (New York: Black Dog and Leventhal Publishers, 2010), 8–19.

4. "From the Army of the Potomac," *New York Tribune*, August 4, 1863, 1. Note that the piece got Custer's age wrong.

5. *Janesville Daily Gazette*, September 9, 1863, 3.

6. Harris, *Personal Reminiscences of Samuel Harris*, 45–46.

7. "Saved from a Federal Prison," *Confederate Veteran*, May 1893.

8. One account has Custer on this charge, but the report from Colonel Davies contradicts that. It was probably confused with the charge of the 1st Vermont.

9. Willard Glazier, *Three Years in the Federal Cavalry* (New York: R. H. Ferguson, 1870), 277.

10. Colonel Theodore Lyman, *With Grant and Meade from the Wilderness to Appomattox*, George R. Agassiz, ed. (Lincoln: University of Nebraska Press, 1994), 17; Frank Moore, ed., *Rebellion Record: A Diary of American Events; Documents and Narratives*, vol. 7, document 169; and "The War in America," *East London Advertiser*, October 3, 1863, 6.

11. Merington, *The Custer Story*, 62.

12. Ibid., 64.

13. EBC in Arlene Reynolds, ed., *The Civil War Memories of Elizabeth Bacon Custer: Reconstructed from Her Diaries and Notes* (Austin: University of Texas Press, 1994), 6.

14. GAC to Nettie, October 7, 1863, in Merington, *The Custer Story*, 65.

15. GAC to Nettie, October 12, 1863, in ibid., 66.

16. Glazier, *Three Years in the Federal Cavalry*, 328–30.

17. Stuart's AAR dated February 14, 1864.

18. Glazier, *Three Years in the Federal Cavalry*, 328–30.

19. John Esten Cooke, *Wearing of the Gray: Being Personal Portraits, Scenes, and Adventures of War* (New York: e. B. Treat, 1867), 257–58.

20. *Milwaukee Semi-Weekly Wisconsin*, October 24, 1863.

21. Pleasonton to Humphreys, October 11, 1863, 8:30 p.m.

CHAPTER 9

1. James H. Kidd, *Personal Recollections of a Cavalryman with Custer's Michigan Cavalry* (Ionia, MI: Sentinel, 1908), 216.

2. From the *Richmond Sentinel*, reprinted in Frank Moore, ed., *Rebellion Record: A Diary of American Events; Documents and Narratives*, vol. 7, 549.

3. Lee's report of December 7, 1863.

4. Stuart's report, February 13, 1864; also D. H. Hill Jr., *Confederate Military History, A Library of Confederate States Military History*, vol. 4, *North Carolina*, Clement Anselm Evans, ed. (Atlanta: Confederate Publishing Company, 1899).

5. P. M. B. Young, "The West Point Boys: Another Interesting Paper about the Men at the Military School, and Something of Their Careers; General Young Tells More of the Boys of '61," *Atlanta Constitution*, March 19, 1893, 9.

6. From the *Richmond Sentinel*, reprinted in Moore, ed., *Rebellion Record*, 549.

7. Quoted in Hill Jr., *Confederate Military History*, vol. 4, *North Carolina*.

8. From the *Richmond Sentinel*, in Moore, ed., *Rebellion Record*, 549.

9. "The Buckland Races" (to the tune of "Dearest May"), *Alexandria Gazette*, May 2, 1891, 4.

10. GAC to Nettie, October 20, 1863, in Marguerite Merington, ed., *The Custer Story: The Life and Intimate Letters of General George A. Custer and His Wife Elizabeth* (New York: Devin-Adair, 1950), 68.

11. GAC to Nettie, October 1863, in ibid., 69.

12. "Army of the Potomac: The Cavalry Reconnaissance on Sunday. Brisk Artillery Firing All along the Lines. The Enemy Driven Out of Their Rifle Pits. Lee Believed to Have Moved His Main Force Back from the Rapidan. Two Divisions of Gen. Hill's Corps Gone Southward. Dispatch to the Associated Press," *New York Times*, November 18, 1863.

13. Kidd, *Personal Recollections*, 129–30.

14. GAC to Nettie, October 9, 1863, in Merington, *The Custer Story*, 65.

15. GAC to Judge Bacon, October 1863, in ibid., 67.

16. GAC to Nettie, October 1863, in ibid., 70.

17. GAC to Nettie, October 27, 1863, in ibid.

18. In ibid., 72.

19. Libbie to GAC, December 27, 1863, in ibid., 75.

20. Libbie to GAC, October 1863, in ibid., 74.

21. Libbie to GAC, December 23, 1863, in ibid., 76.

22. Libbie to GAC, December 23, 1863, in ibid.

23. Libbie to GAC, December 27, 1863, in ibid., 75.

24. GAC to I. P. Christiancy, December 19, 1863.

25. Libbie to GAC, January 1864, in Merington, *The Custer Story*, 79.

26. GAC quoted by one of his officers in Arlene Reynolds, ed., *The Civil War Memories of Elizabeth Bacon Custer: Reconstructed from Her Diaries and Notes* (Austin: University of Texas Press, 1994), 8.

27. Nettie to GAC, January 1864, in Merington, *The Custer Story*, 78.

28. EBC in Reynolds, *The Civil War Memories of Elizabeth Bacon Custer*, 7.

29. Judge Bacon to his sister Charity, February 11, 1864, in Merington, *The Custer Story*, 81.

30. Rebecca Richmond to Mary Richmond, February 1864, in ibid., 81–82.

31. EBC to Judge Bacon, February 1864, in ibid., 84.

32. EBC to Judge Bacon, February 1864, in ibid.

33. EBC in Reynolds, *The Civil War Memories of Elizabeth Bacon Custer*, 35–36.

34. EBC in ibid., 44.

CHAPTER 10

1. EBC in Arlene Reynolds, ed., *The Civil War Memories of Elizabeth Bacon Custer: Reconstructed from Her Diaries and Notes* (Austin: University of Texas Press, 1994), 50.

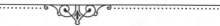

2. Quoted in D. A. Kinsley, *Favor the Bold* (New York: Holt, Rinehart and Winston, 1967–68), 139.

3. "From the Army of the Potomac," *New York Tribune*, August 4, 1863, 1.

4. Quoted in Shelby Foote, *The Civil War: A Narrative*, vol. 2, *Fredericksburg to Meridian* (New York: Knopf Doubleday Publishing Group, 1986), 572.

5. Lyman quoted in Eric J. Wittenberg, ed., *One of Custer's Wolverines: The Civil War Letters of Brevet Brigadier General James H. Kidd, 6th Michigan Cavalry* (Kent, OH: Kent State University Press, 2000), 45.

6. See Thomas Lowry, *The Story the Soldiers Won't Tell: Sex in the Civil War* (Mechanicsburg, PA: Stackpole Books, 1994), 154–55; and "Our Letter from Cairo," *Daily Alta California*, October 30, 1863, 1.

7. For general background on the raid see Duane P. Schultz, *The Dahlgren Affair: Terror and Conspiracy in the Civil War* (New York: W. W. Norton, 1998).

8. J. B. Stalb, "The 11th Pa. Cav.: The Time That It Did Not Go into Richmond," *National Tribune*, August 9, 1906.

9. John Adolphus Bernard Dahlgren, *Memoir of Ulric Dahlgren. By His Father, Rear-Admiral Dahlgren* (Philadelphia: J. B. Lippincott, 1872), 211. Letter dated February 26, 1864.

10. Quoted in Reynolds, *The Civil War Memories of Elizabeth Bacon Custer*, 50.

11. *The Soldier's Journal*, March 9, 1864, 28; and the *New York Tribune*, March 3, 1864.

12. *Memphis Daily Appeal*, March 11, 1864, 1, reprinted from the *New York Herald*.

13. *Dubuque Daily Democratic Herald*, March 3, 1864.

14. See the account in "The Cavalry Raid by Custer, Kilpatrick and Dahlgren," *Transactions of the Southern Historical Society*, 1 (1874), 155ff.

15. *The Soldier's Journal*, March 9, 1864, 28.

16. *Memphis Daily Appeal*, March 11, 1864, 1, reprinted from the *New York Herald*.

17. *Richmond Whig*, March 7, 1864, reprinted in the *New York Times*, March 12, 1864.

18. *Memphis Daily Appeal*, March 11, 1864, 1, reprinted from the *New York Herald*.

19. *Staunton Spectator*, March 8, 1864, 1.

20. March 1 report from the *World* summarized in the *Cleveland Morning Leader*, March 3, 1864, 1.

21. *Memphis Daily Appeal*, March 11, 1864, 1, reprinted from the *New York Herald*.

22. James H. Kidd, *Personal Recollections of a Cavalryman with Custer's Michigan Cavalry* (Ionia, MI: Sentinel, 1908), 247.

23. Ibid., 249.

24. "He Was There," *National Tribune*, May 31, 1894, 3.

25. Ibid.

26. *Staunton Spectator*, March 8, 1864, 1.

27. "He Was There," 3.

28. "Dahlgren's Raid," *National Tribune*, December 3, 1885, 1. J. W. Landern believed that "the hanging of that poor black man was a cruel and cowardly murder." He believed Robinson had misunderstood what Dahlgren intended, and said his "experience with the Southern blacks during the war proved to me they were truly loyal to us, and were ever ready and willing to peril their lives to aid a Union soldier." "He Was There," 3.

29. "Dahlgren's Raid," 1.

30. Ibid.

31. *Staunton Spectator*, March 8, 1864, 1.

32. Ibid.

33. Fitzhugh Lee to General S. Cooper, March 4, 1864.

34. Kilpatrick to Newhall, March 16, 1864.

35. EBC, March 28, 1864, in Marguerite Merington, ed., *The Custer Story: The Life and Intimate Letters of General George A. Custer and His Wife Elizabeth* (New York: Devin-Adair, 1950), 88.

36. "How Custer Went to West Point," *Hocking Sentinel* (Logan, OH), August 16, 1900, 3.

37. EBC, March 28, 1864 in Merington, *The Custer Story*, 89.

38. Quoted in Reynolds, *The Civil War Memories of Elizabeth Bacon Custer*, 52.

CHAPTER 11

1. EBC, March 28, 1864, Marguerite Merington, ed., *The Custer Story: The Life and Intimate Letters of General George A. Custer and His Wife Elizabeth* (New York: Devin-Adair, 1950), 87.

2. GAC to EBC, April 16, 1864, in ibid., 89.

3. David S. Stanley, *Personal Memoirs of Major-General D. S. Stanley, USA* (Cambridge: Harvard University Press, 1917), 18.

4. Wharton J. Green, *Recollections and Reflections* (Raleigh, NC: Edwards and Broughton Printing Company, 1906), 92–93.

5. James H. Kidd, *Personal Recollections of a Cavalryman with Custer's Michigan Cavalry* (Ionia, MI: Sentinel, 1908), 298–300.

6. John Hill Brinton, *Personal Memoirs of John H. Brinton, Major and Surgeon U.S.V., 1861–1865* (New York: Neale Publishing, 1914), 267.

7. Ibid., 239.

8. Grant to Halleck, May 11, 1864, 8:30 a.m.

9. Sheridan quoted in Merington, *The Custer Story*, 96.

10. "Sheridan's Grand Raid," *Morning Leader*, May 28, 1864.

11. Supplemental report of the Joint Committee on the Conduct of the War, in two volumes. Supplemental to Senate Report No. 142, 38th Congress, 2d session, 21.

12. Merington, *The Custer Story*, 98.

13. *American and Commercial Advertiser*, May 18, 1864, 1.

14. In W. C. King and W. Derby, eds., *Camp-Fire Sketches and Battle-Field Echoes of 61-5*, (Springfield, MA: King, Richardson, 1868), 250, 408–9.

15. GAC to EBC, May 14, 1864, in Merington, *The Custer Story*, 97.

16. See Jay Monaghan, "Custer's 'Last Stand'—Trevilian Station, 1864," in Paul Andrew Hutton, ed., *The Custer Reader* (Norman: University of Oklahoma Press, 2004), 53ff.

17. "A True Account of the Cavalry Battle at Trevillian's" *Edgefield (SC) Advertiser*, (reprinted from the *Richmond Sentinel*), July 13, 1864.

18. This was nearly identical to the circumstances for which Powhatan Clarke, the West Point goat of 1884, was awarded the Medal of Honor during the Geronimo Campaign.

19. GAC to EBC, June 21, 1864.

20. "The Last Great Cavalry Raid," *Nashville Daily Union*, June 25, 1864, 1.

21. Torbert's report of July 4, 1864.

22. "A True Account of the Cavalry Battle at Trevillian's."

23. Supplemental report of the Joint Committee on the Conduct of the War, in two volumes. Supplemental to Senate Report No. 142, 38th Congress, 2d session, 26.

24. Ibid.

25. Ulysses S. Grant, *Personal Memoirs of U. S. Grant* (New York: Charles L. Webster, 1885), 458–59.

26. GAC to EBC, June 21, 1864.

27. See Merington, *The Custer Story*, 123.

28. EBC to GAC in ibid., 102.

29. EBC to her parents, May 1, 1864, in ibid., 94.

30. EBC in Arlene Reynolds, ed., *The Civil War Memories of Elizabeth Bacon Custer: Reconstructed from Her Diaries and Notes* (Austin: University of Texas Press, 1994), 7.

31. GAC to EBC, May 1, 1864 in Merington, *The Custer Story*, 95.

32. Bingham in ibid., 109.

33. EBC to her parents, June 1864, in ibid., 108–9.

34. EBC to her parents, July 4, 1864, in ibid., 113.

35. EBC to her parents, April 1864 in ibid., 90.

36. Quoted in Reynolds, *The Civil War Memories of Elizabeth Bacon Custer*, 98.

37. From Caroline Dana Howe, "Young Custer's Bride," reprinted in ibid., 173–75.

CHAPTER 12

1. *London Guardian*, October 26, 1864, 1027.

2. Grant to Halleck, July 14, 1864.

3. *New York Daily Tribune*, August 22, 1864, 6.

4. Ibid.

5. Sheridan to Halleck, August 17, 1864.

6. *New York Daily Tribune*, August 22, 1864, 6.

7. In Marguerite Merington, ed., *The Custer Story: The Life and Intimate Letters of General George A. Custer and His Wife Elizabeth* (New York: Devin-Adair, 1950), 115.

8. *Sunbury (PA) American*, September 24, 1864, 2.

9. Charles Alfred Humphreys, *Field, Camp, Hospital and Prison in the Civil War, 1863–1865* (Boston: George H. Ellis, 1918), 160.

10. Quoted in Roger U. Delauter and Brandon H. Beck, *The Third Battle of Winchester* (Lynchburg, VA: H. E. Howard, 1997), 64.

11. *Indianapolis Daily State Sentinel*, September 23, 1864, 1.

12. Torbert's report, November 1864.

13. Merritt in his report of October 5, 1864.

14. *Sunbury (PA) American*, September 24, 1864, 2.

15. Wilson became Sherman's chief of cavalry for the Military Division of the Mississippi.

16. GAC to EBC May 16, 1864, in Merington, *The Custer Story*, 97.

17. Quoted in ibid., 121.

18. *London Guardian*, October 26, 1864, 1027.

19. Custer to Dana, September 30, 1864.

20. *London Guardian*, October 26, 1864, 1027.

21. Sheridan to Grant, October 7, 1864, 9 p.m.

22. *Philadelphia Evening Telegraph*, October 12, 1864, 1.

23. Dana letter of November 14, 1864, in John Harrison Wilson, *The Life of Charles Henry Dana* (New York: Harper and Brothers, 1907), 348.

24. Diary of Captain Robert E. Park, Twelfth Alabama regiment, entry of November 4–7, 1864, in Reverend J. William Jones, ed., *Southern Historical Society Papers*, vol. 2., 175.

25. On Rosser's brigade, see William N. McDonald, *A History of the Laurel Brigade* (Baltimore: Kate S. McDonald, 1907).

26. Philip Henry Sheridan, *Personal Memoirs of P. H. Sheridan*, vol. 1 (New York: Charles L. Webster, 1888), 56.

27. Ibid.

28. Custer report of October 13, 1864. See also the *New York Herald* report reprinted in *Philadelphia Evening Telegraph*, October 12, 1864, 1.

29. James H. Kidd, *Personal Recollections of a Cavalryman with Custer's Michigan Cavalry* (Ionia, MI: Sentinel, 1908), 316–17.

30. Frederick Whittaker, *A Complete Life of General George A. Custer* (Lincoln: University of Nebraska Press, 1993), 258. Some say Whittaker invented this event, but there is a sketch of it by Alfred R. Waud in the collection of the Library of Congress, mislabeled as a salute to Ramseur, not Rosser.

31. Custer report of October 13, 1864.

32. *Daily Ohio Statesman*, October 15, 1864, 3.

33. General T. T. Munford, "Reminiscences of Cavalry Operations," *Southern Historical Society Papers*, Reverend J. William Jones, ed., vol. 13, 134.

34. Custer report of October 13, 1864.

35. Early to R. E. Lee, October 9, 1864.

36. *New York Times*, July 9, 1876, 1.

CHAPTER 13

1. *New York Herald* report, reprinted in *Philadelphia Evening Telegraph*, October 12, 1864, 1.

2. William N. McDonald, *A History of the Laurel Brigade* (Baltimore: Kate S. McDonald, 1907), 308–9.

3. George Perkins, *Three Years a Soldier: The Diary and Newspaper Correspondence of Private George Perkins, Sixth New York Independent Battery, 1861–1864*, Richard N. Griffin, ed. (Knoxville: University of Tennessee Press, 2006), 293.

4. *New York Herald* report, quoted in the *Richmond Daily Dispatch*, October 24, 1864.

5. Custer report of October 22, 1864.

6. Supplemental report of the Joint Committee on the Conduct of the War, in two volumes. Supplemental to Senate Report No. 142, 38th Congress, 2d session, 44.

7. Colonel Whitaker quoted by Chaplain Humphreys, 176.

8. Report by Lieutenant Colonel John W. Bennett, 1st Vermont Cavalry, November 14, 1864.

9. *Washington DC Evening Star*, October 22, 1864, 1.

10. Report by Lieutenant Colonel John W. Bennett,.

11. George Quintus Peyton, *Stonewall Jackson's Foot Cavalry: Company A, 13th Virginia Infantry* (Shippensburg, PA: Burd Street Press, 2001), 130.

12. Papers of the Military Historical Society of Massachusetts, *The Shenandoah Campaigns of 1862 and 1864 and the Appomattox Campaign, 1865*, vol. 6 (Boston: The Military Historical Society of Massachusetts, 1907), 139.

13. *Washington DC Evening Star*, October 24, 1864, 2.

14. See Gary W. Gallagher, *Stephen Dodson Ramseur: Lee's Gallant General* (Chapel Hill: University of North Carolina Press, 1985).

15. Morris Schaff, *The Spirit of Old West Point, 1858–1862* (New York: Houghton, Mifflin, 1907), 56.

16. Ibid., 56–57. See also Gallagher, *Stephen Dodson Ramseur*, 26–27.

17. John Truesdale, *The Blue Coats, How They Lived, Fought and Died for the Union* (Philadelphia: Jones Brothers,1867), 180–81.

18. Lincoln to Sheridan, October 22, 1864.

19. Custer General Order of October 21, 1864.

20. Arlene Reynolds, ed., *The Civil War Memories of Elizabeth Bacon Custer: Reconstructed from Her Diaries and Notes* (Austin: University of Texas Press, 1994), 105.

21. News report quoted in Marguerite Merington, ed., *The Custer Story: The Life and Intimate Letters of General George A. Custer and His Wife Elizabeth* (New York: Devin-Adair, 1950), 126.

22. *Washington DC Evening Star*, October 24, 1864, 2.

23. "Sheridan's Victory," *New York Times*, October 27, 1864, 2.

24. GAC to EBC in Merington, *The Custer Story*, 119.

25. *The Raftsman's Journal*, October 19, 1864, 1.

26. Reynolds, *The Civil War Memories of Elizabeth Bacon Custer*, 74.

27. G. A. Custer, "War Memoirs," *Galaxy*, June 1876, 813.

28. GAC to Judge Bacon, January 1864, in Merington, *The Custer Story*, 80.

29. "Sheridan's Victory," *New York Times*, October 27, 1864, 2.

30. George A. Custer to Emanuel Custer, October 16, 1864.

CHAPTER 14

1. John W. Munson, *Reminiscences of a Mosby Guerrilla* (New York: Moffat, Yard, 1906), 146. For a general discussion of this issue, see Robert Russell Mackey, *The Uncivil War: Irregular Warfare in the Upper South, 1861–1865* (Norman: University of Oklahoma Press, 2004); and James Joseph Williamson, *Mosby's Rangers: A Record of the Operations of the Forty-Third Battalion of Virginia Cavalry from Its Organization to the Surrender*, 2nd ed. (New York: Sturgis and Walton, 1909).

2. "An Hour With Mosby," *Richmond Daily Dispatch*, December 1, 1864, 1.

3. EBC to her parents, May 1, 1864, in Marguerite Merington, ed., *The Custer Story: The Life and Intimate Letters of General George A. Custer and His Wife Elizabeth* (New York: Devin-Adair, 1950), 94.

4. Custer to Pleasonton, July 18, 1863.

5. Pleasonton to Humphreys, August 2, 1863.

6. Sheridan to Halleck, October 27, 1864.

7. E. A. Paul, "Operations of Our Cavalry: The Michigan Cavalry Brigade," *New York Times*, August 6, 1863.

8. J. H. Taylor to Major John M. Waite, August 28, 1864.

9. *Staunton Spectator*, August 25, 1863, 1.

10. Philip Henry Sheridan, *Personal Memoirs of P. H. Sheridan*, vol. 2 (New York: Charles L. Webster, 1888), 51.

11. Sheridan to Grant, October 7, 1864, 9:00 p.m.; and Sheridan, *Personal Memoirs*.

12. Sheridan, *Personal Memoirs*, vol. 2, 52.

13. Report in the *New York Times*, August 25, 1864.

14. Williamson, *Mosby's Rangers*, 215.

15. Ibid., 214–15.

16. Munson, *Reminiscences of a Mosby Guerrilla*, 147. In addition to the passion of the moment, there was a general order among Confederate troops that no quarter was to be given to soldiers found burning homes.

17. Grant to Sheridan, August 16, 1864.

18. Sheridan to Grant, August 17, 1864.

19. Mosby to Robert E. Lee, October 29, 1864.

20. "Hanging of Mosby's Men in 1864," 'B.' in Warrenton Virginia, February, 1896, *Southern Historical Society Papers* 24, J. William Jones, ed., 108–9. See also Jay W. Simson, *Custer and the Front Royal Executions Of 1864* (Jefferson, NC: McFarland, 2009). Jay Simson argues that Custer was not involved in the actual executions but was in the vicinity and stood out because of his distinctive appearance, so newspaper accounts placed the blame on him. Simson makes the case that Brigadier General Alfred Torbert ordered the hangings and was most responsible for them. The Confederates, however, still blamed Custer.

21. "Hanging of Mosby's Men in 1864," 108–9.

22. John H. Alexander, *Mosby's Men* (New York: The Neale Publishing Company, 1907), 141.

23. "Hanging of Mosby's Men in 1864," 108–9.

24. Ibid.

25. John W. Munson, *Reminiscences of a Mosby Guerrilla* (New York: Moffat, Yard, 1906), 149.

26. Mosby to Robert E. Lee, October 29, 1864.

27. Robert E. Lee to Office of the Secretary of War, November 3, 1864; H. L. Clay to Robert E. Lee, November 19, 1864.

28. This account follows Williamson, *Mosby's Rangers*, 288ff, and "An Hour with Mosby," *Richmond Daily Dispatch*, December 1, 1864.

29. Alexander, *Mosby's Men*, 143–44

30. Quoted in Williamson, *Mosby's Rangers*, 452ff.

31. Report of finding the bodies by O. Edwards to Lieutenant Colonel C. Kingsbury, November 7, 1864.

32. Ibid.

33. Mosby to Sheridan, November 11, 1864.

34. Williamson, *Mosby's Rangers*, 317.

35. Sheridan to Halleck, November 26, 1864.

36. Forsyth to Merritt, November 27, 1864.

37. Walt Whitman, "A Glimpse of War's Hell Scenes," *Specimen Days*, in *The Portable Walt Whitman*, 550.

CHAPTER 15

1. George Perkins, *Three Years a Soldier: The Diary and Newspaper Correspondence of Private George Perkins, Sixth New York Independent Battery, 1861–1864*, Richard N. Griffin, ed. (Knoxville: University of Tennessee Press, 2006), 300.

2. *Philadelphia Evening Telegraph*, November 25, 1864, 1.

3. Sheridan to Grant, December 20, 1864, 10:30 a.m.

4. *New York Tribune* report, reprinted as "Cavalry Fight in the Valley—Amusing Scenes," in the *Richmond Daily Dispatch*, December 30, 1864.

5. Ibid.

6. Sheridan to Rawlins, December 24, 1864; R. E. Lee to Seddon, December 23, 1864.

7. Grant to Sheridan, February 20, 1865, 1:00 p.m.

8. Sheridan report, March 2, 1865.

9. Jubal A. Early, *A Memoir of the Last Year of the War of Independence, in the Confederate States of America* (Toronto: Lovell and Gibson, 1866), 132.

10. *New York Herald*, March 10, 1865.

11. Sheridan report, March 2, 1865.

12. Supplemental report of the Joint Committee on the Conduct of the War, in two volumes. Supplemental to Senate Report No. 142, 38th Congress, 2d session, 53.

13. Early, 133.

14. "The Yankees in Charlottesville," *Richmond Daily Dispatch*, March 15, 1865.

15.   EBC in Arlene Reynolds, ed., *The Civil War Memories of Elizabeth Bacon Custer: Reconstructed from Her Diaries and Notes* (Austin: University of Texas Press, 1994), 33.

16.   Ibid.

17.   *Richmond Daily Dispatch*, March 24, 1865, and the *Knoxville Whig*, December 20, 1865.

CHAPTER 16

1.   For general reference, see Chris M. Calkins, *The Appomattox Campaign, March 29–April 9, 1865* (Conshohocken, PA: Combined Books, 1997).

2.   Frederick Cushman Newhall, *With Sheridan in the Final Campaign against Lee*, Eric J. Wittenberg, ed. (Baton Rouge: Louisiana State University Press, 2002), 36.

3.   *Daily Ohio Statesman* (Columbus), April 04, 1865, 3.

4.   Capeheart received the Medal of Honor for saving the life of a drowning soldier during the Valley campaign. His brother Major Charles E. Capehart also received the award for a separate action.

5.   Henry Edwin Tremain, *Last Hours of Sheridan's Cavalry: A Reprint of War Memoranda* (New York: Bonnel, Silver and Bowers, 1904), 53.

6.   Ibid., 54.

7.   Charles Alfred Humphreys, *Field, Camp, Hospital and Prison in the Civil War, 1863–1865* (Boston: George H. Ellis, 1918), 238.

8.   Ibid., 241.

9.   Ibid., 242.

10.   Sheridan to Warren, April 1, 1865, 4:40 a.m.

11.   Fitzhugh Lee, *General Lee: A Biography of Robert E. Lee* (New York: D. Appleton, 1894), 376.

12.   George Pickett, *The Heart of a Soldier: Intimate Wartime Letters from General George E. Pickett, CSA, to His Wife*, La Salle Corbell Pickett, ed. (New York: Seth Moyle, 1913), 171.

13.   *New York World* report quoted in "The Fall of Richmond," *Supplement to the Guardian* (UK), April 19, 1865, 1. The report described Five Forks as "a magnificent strategic point. Five good roads meet in the edge of a dry, high, well-watered forest, three of them radiating to the railway, and their tributaries unlocking all the country."

14.   Newhall, *With Sheridan in the Final Campaign against Lee*, 48–49.

15. Details on the Warren incident are in Bruce Catton, "Sheridan at Five Forks," *Journal of Southern History*, August 1955, 305–15.

16. George E. Farmer to his father, April 14, 1865, Gilder Lehrman Collection: GLC00808.01

17. Quoted in Richard Wheeler, *Witness to Appomattox* (New York: HarperCollins, 1991), 75.

18. Pickett, *The Heart of a Soldier*, 173–74.

19. "Sheridan's Ride," *Indiana (PA) Democrat*, March 4, 1875, 1.

20. *New York World* report, quoted in "The Fall of Richmond," *Supplement to the Guardian* (UK), April 19, 1865, 1.

21. Pickett, *The Heart of a Soldier*, 173–74.

CHAPTER 17

1. Frederick Cushman Newhall, *With Sheridan in the Final Campaign against Lee*, Eric J. Wittenberg, ed. (Baton Rouge: Louisiana State University Press, 2002), 114.

2. Robert Stiles, *Four Years under Marse Robert* (Washington, D.C.: Neale Publishing, 1904), 326–27.

3. John Brown Gordon, *Reminiscences of the Civil War* (New York: Charles Scribner's Sons, 1904), 423–24.

4. The actual name of the stream is Sayler's Creek, but most contemporary sources refer to it as "Sailor's Creek," which will be used throughout.

5. George Pickett, *The Heart of a Soldier: Intimate Wartime Letters from General George E. Pickett, CSA, to His Wife*, La Salle Corbell Pickett, ed. (New York: Seth Moyle, 1913), 177.

6. In Lydia Minturn Post, ed., *Soldiers' Letters, from Camps, Battle-Field and Prison* (Washington: U.S. Sanitary Commission, 1865), 463–64.

7. Charles Alfred Humphreys, *Field, Camp, Hospital and Prison in the Civil War, 1863–1865* (Boston: George H. Ellis, 1918), 268–70.

8. *Burlington Free Press*, April 21, 1865, 2.

9. Custer in *The Custer Story*, 150–51.

10. Capehart to EBC, quoted in Elizabeth B. Custer, "A Beau Sabreur," in *Uncle Sam's Medal of Honor*, Theophilus F. Rodenbough, ed. (New York: G. P. Putnam's Son, 1886), 227.

11. Quoted in Jay Monaghan, *Custer: The Life of General George Armstrong Custer* (Boston: Little, Brown, 1959), 238.

12. In Arlene Reynolds, ed., *The Civil War Memories of Elizabeth Bacon Custer: Reconstructed from Her Diaries and Notes* (Austin: University of Texas Press, 1994), 138.

13. Two sailors also were given this distinction, coxswain John Cooper, and boatswain's mate Patrick Mullen.

14. In Reynolds, *The Civil War Memories of Elizabeth Bacon Custer*, 138.

15. *Cleveland Morning Leader*, April 11, 1865, 1.

16. Stiles, *Four Years under Marse Robert*, 333.

17. Walter Harrison, *Pickett's Men: A Fragment of War History* (New York: D. Van Nostrand, 1870), 157.

18. Kershaw in Merington, *The Custer Story*, 153.

19. *Burlington Free Press*, April 21, 1865, 2.

20. Quoted in E. P. Alexander, "Lee at Appomattox," in *Battles and Leaders of the Civil War*, vol. 5, Peter Cozzens, ed. (Champaign: University of Illinois Press, 2002), 641.

21. Eppa Hunton, *Autobiography of Eppa Hunton* (Richmond: The William Byrd Press, 1933), 124.

22. Ibid.

23. Sheridan to Grant, April 6, 1865.

24. Papers of the Military Historical Society of Massachusetts, vol. 6, *The Shenandoah Campaigns of 1862 and 1864 and the Appomattox Campaign, 1865* (Boston: The Military Historical Society of Massachusetts, 1907), 447.

25. Morris Schaff quoted in Reynolds, *The Civil War Memories of Elizabeth Bacon Custer*, 144.

26. Ulysses S. Grant, *Personal Memoirs of U. S. Grant* (New York: Charles L. Webster, 1885), 551.

27. Frederick Cushman Newhall, *With Sheridan in the Final Campaign against Lee*, Eric J. Wittenberg, ed. (Baton Rouge: Louisiana State University Press, 2002), 107.

28. Augustus Woodbury, *The Second Rhode Island Regiment: A Narrative of Military Operations in Which the Regiment Was Engaged from the Beginning to the End of the War for the Union* (Providence: Valpey, Angell, 1875), 354.

29. Frances Andrews Tenney, *War Diary of Luman Harris Tenney, 1861–1865* (Cleveland: Evangelical Publishing House, 1914), 156.

30. Sheridan to Grant, April 8, 1865, 9:40 p.m.

31. Supplemental report of the Joint Committee on the Conduct of the War, in two volumes. Supplemental to Senate Report No. 142, 38th Congress, 2d session, 66.

32. Sheridan to Grant, April 8, 1865, 9:20 p.m. See also Philip H. Sheridan, "The Last Days of the Rebellion," *North American Review*, September 1888, 275.

33. Morris Schaff, *The Sunset of the Confederacy* (Boston: John W. Luce, 1912), 209. They were about two hundred miles from Tennessee at the time.

34. Reynolds, *The Civil War Memories of Elizabeth Bacon Custer*, 143.

35. Humphreys, *Field, Camp, Hospital and Prison in the Civil War*, 284.

36. Tenney, *War Diary of Luman Harris Tenney, 1861–1865*, 156.

37. "Captured at Appomattox," *Maine Bugle*, January 1896, 274.

38. *Danville Register*, October 17, 1905.

39. Quoted in Schaff, *The Sunset of the Confederacy*, 225.

40. Charles A. Phelps, *Life and Public Services of Ulysses S. Grant* (Boston: Lee and Shepard Publishers, 1872), 290.

41. E. G. Marsh in *Soldiers' Letters, from Camps, Battle-Field and Prison*, Lydia Minturn Post, ed. (Washington, D.C.: U.S. Sanitary Commission, 1865).

42. These and many of the following details come from Lee's artillery chief Edward Porter Alexander, in "Lee at Appomattox: Personal Recollections of the Break-Up of the Confederacy," *Century Magazine*, April 1902, 921–31; Alexander, *Military Memoirs of a Confederate: A Critical Narrative* (New York: Charles Scribner's Sons, 1907), chapter 23 passim; as well as other sources cited.

43. There are several versions of this encounter. Some say it was Custer's chief of staff, Colonel Edward Whitaker, who met with Longstreet, but Longstreet in his memoir says otherwise. Whitaker had met with Gordon shortly before Custer arrived and was asked to locate Sheridan, who was riding to Appomattox Court House. See also John Brown Gordon, *Reminiscences of the Civil War* (New York: Charles Scribner's Sons, 1904); and the letter by E. G. Marsh, 15th NY Cavalry, in *Soldiers' Letters, from Camps, Battle-Field and Prison*. Alexander in his *Military Memoirs of a Confederate* says Longstreet rebuffed Custer "very roughly, far more so than appears in Longstreet's account of the interview" (608). William Miller Owen, from whom some of these quotes are taken, was an eyewitness. See his *In Camp and Battle with the Washington Artillery* (Boston: Ticknor and Company, 1885), 384–85.

44. Tenney, *War Diary of Luman Harris Tenney, 1861–1865*, 159.

45. Humphreys, *Field, Camp, Hospital and Prison in the Civil War,* 289.

46. Horace Porter, *Campaigning with Grant* (New York: The Century Company, 1906), 486.

47. Quoted in Schaff, *The Sunset of the Confederacy,* 169–71. With Babcock were Captain William McKee Dunn for the Union, Confederate Lieutenant Colonel Charles Marshal as aide to Lee, and rebel Private Joshua O. Johns.

48. Quoted in ibid., 169–71.

49. In Walter Clark, ed., *Histories of the Several Regiments and Battalions from North Carolina in the Great War 1861–'65,* vol. 2 (Goldsboro, NC: Nash Brothers), 578.

50. Porter, *Campaigning with Grant,* 486.

51. *New York Times,* April 20, 1865, 2. The entire Mclean House disappeared eventually. In 1891 M. T. Dunlap bought the house for $10,000 with a view toward putting it on display at the Chicago World's Fair, or on the Mall in Washington. The house was disassembled and put into crates. But financing for the venture fell through, and over time the contents of the crates were taken by souvenir hunters. When the National Park Service acquired the property in 1948, only the foundations were left. See Dorothea Andrews, "'Surrender House' Will Stand Again," *Washington Post,* January 4, 1948, M17.

52. Richard Miller Devens, *The Pictorial Book of Anecdotes and Incidents of the War of the Rebellion,* (Hartford: Hartford Publishing, 1967), 348.

53. Reynolds, *The Civil War Memories of Elizabeth Bacon Custer,* 152–53.

54. Custer promised the flag to Libbie. "With the verdancy of youth," she later wrote, "I really expected to see a veritable flag, though I don't know that I went so far as to hint that gallant men carried one around ready for emergencies. When I found myself in possession of a large honey-comb towel the poetry departed out of my anticipations." "Surrender Relics," *Washington Post,* April 1, 1905, 14.

CHAPTER 18

1. Alexander in Peter Cozzens, ed., *Battles and Leaders of the Civil War,* vol. 5 (Champaign: University of Illinois Press, 2002), 651.

2. GAC, April 9, 1865, Appomattox Court House.

3. Chamberlain, *The Passing of the Armies,* 250.

4. Quoted in Richard Wheeler, *Witness to Appomattox* (New York: HarperCollins, 1991), 233.

5. Longstreet in *New York Times,* July 24, 1885.

6. Quoted in Arlene Reynolds, ed., *The Civil War Memories of Elizabeth Bacon Custer: Reconstructed from Her Diaries and Notes* (Austin: University of Texas Press, 1994), 143.

7. Ibid., 146.

8. Ibid., 150.

9. Ibid.

10. Nettie died in 1868 of heart disease shortly after giving birth to a son, Jacob Humphrey Greene.

11. *New York Times,* April 20, 1865, 2.

12. *The Diary of Horatio Nelson Taft, 1861–1865*, vol. 3, *January 1, 1864–May 30, 1865*, entry of May 24, 1865, Library of Congress, Manuscript Collection.

13. Joshua Lawrence Chamberlain, *The Passing of the Armies: The Last Campaign of the Armies* (New York: G. P. Putnam's Sons, 1915), 331.

14. Ibid., 328.

15. "Review of the Armies," *New York Times,* May 24, 1865, 1.

16. Whitman in *Specimen Days*, journal entry for May 21, 1865.

17. *The Diary of Horatio Nelson Taft, 1861–1865*, entry of May 24, 1865.

18. "Sherman on the Grand Review," *New York Times*, July 4, 1890, 1. The competitive Sherman saw to it that his troops were well drilled and prepared for the review. The eastern and western armies contested on more than the parade route. Assistant Secretary of War Charles Henry Dana wrote, "Sherman's troops are now all camped just outside of Washington north of the Potomac, it having been found advisable to separate them from the Army of the Potomac, whose camps are all on the south side of the river. A good many fights have occurred between the private soldiers of the two armies. I have heard of one or two men who have been killed, and one or two who have been seriously wounded. Sherman's men are also pretty troublesome to the farmers and other quiet people where they are." In John Harrison Wilson, *The Life of Charles Henry Dana* (New York: Harper and Brothers, 1907), 366.

19. H. M. Gallaher. "The Great Review," *Burlington Iowa Hawkeye*, June 5, 1865.

20. *Cleveland Daily Leader*, June 1, 1865.

21. Horace Porter, *Campaigning with Grant* (New York: The Century Company, 1906), 507.

22. Rev. H. M. Gallaher. "The Great Review," *Burlington Iowa Hawkeye*, June 5, 1865.

23. *Cleveland Daily Leader*, June 1, 1865.

24. *Marysville (OH) Tribune*, May 31, 1865, 1.

25. Ibid.; and "A Historic Promenade," *New York Times*, February 7, 1881, 1. President Johnson was late to the event and did not witness Custer's "charge."

26. "The Nonsense of War Stories," *Washington National Republican*, March 18, 1881.

27. *Washington National Republican*, March 21, 1881.

28. GAC quoted in Reynolds, *The Civil War Memories of Elizabeth Bacon Custer*, 160.

29. "An Incident of the Great Review," *New York Times*, July 10, 1876, 2.

30. Quoted in Jay Monaghan, *Custer: The Life of General George Armstrong Custer* (Boston: Little, Brown, 1959), 251.

31. *Cleveland Daily Leader*, June 1, 1865.

CHAPTER 19

1. Sheridan to Granger, June 10, 1865.

2. Grant to Sheridan, June 3, 1865.

3. Sheridan to Grant, July 1, 1865.

4. Supplemental report of the Joint Committee on the Conduct of the War, in two volumes. Supplemental to Senate Report No. 142, 38th Congress, 2d session, 73.

5. "Custer's Cruelty," special to the *Chicago Times*, February 3, 1886, reprinted in Charles H. Lothrop, *History of the First Regiment Iowa Cavalry* (Iowa: Beers & Eaton, 1890), 277.

6. M. Quad. [Charles Bertrand Lewis], "Army Letter," *Indiana True Republican*, July 13, 1865, 1.

7. Quoted in Elizabeth B. Custer, *Tenting on the Plains or General Custer in Kansas and Texas* (New York: Charles L. Webster, 1887), 62–63.

8. Custer statement to Major George Lee, AAG, Military Division of the Gulf, October 26, 1865

9. E. Custer, *Tenting on the Plains*, 69.

10. Sheridan to M. G. Rawlins, June 29, 1865. Sheridan had appointed Merritt chief of cavalry in the southwest, and technically commanded both columns.

11. Forsyth endorsement to Custer statement of October 26, 1865.

12. Custer statement to Major George Lee, AAG, Military Division of the Gulf, October 26, 1865.

13. Forsyth endorsement to Custer statement of October 26, 1865.

14. Custer statement to Major George Lee, AAG, Military Division of the Gulf, October 26, 1865.

15. Forsyth endorsement to Custer statement of October 26, 1865.

16. E. Custer, *Tenting on the Plains*, 66.

17. For an extremely biased account of the Lancaster case, see Antoinette Barnum Ferris and Michael Griffin, *A Soldier's Souvenir, or, the Terrible Experiences of Lieutenant L. L. Lancaster, of the Second Wisconsin Cavalry: A Martyr to the Cause of Truth and Justice, Compromising Short Biographical Sketches* (Eau Claire, WI: Pauly Bros., 1896).

18. "Custer's Cruelty," 278–79. See also the more credible account of the surgeon of the Second Wisconsin, 280.

19. Lothrop, *History of the First Regiment Iowa Cavalry*, 227–28.

20. Ibid., 218.

21. E. Custer, *Tenting on the Plains*, 75.

22. "Custer's Cruelty," 278.

23. Lothrop, *History of the First Regiment Iowa Cavalry*, 229

24. Ibid., 223.

25. E. Custer, *Tenting on the Plains*, 83.

26. Ibid., 86.

27. *Army and Navy Journal*, April 8, 1880, 708. Sheridan later explained to a group of Texans that he made the remark after returning from an expedition to the Rio Grande "sick, tired, dusty, and mad," and was annoyed at a journalist who asked him how he liked Texas.

28. E. Custer, *Tenting on the Plains*, 79–80.

29. Lothrop, *History of the First Regiment Iowa Cavalry*, 280.

30. Ibid., 290.

31. Ibid., 271.

32. "A Soldier's Opinion of Gen. Custer," *White Cloud Kansas Chief*, October 18, 1866, 1.

33. "Custer's Cruelty," 279.

34. Quoted in *History of the First Regiment Iowa Cavalry*, 219.

35. Custer statement to Major George Lee, AAG, Military Division of the Gulf, October 26, 1865.

36. Army of the Ohio, General Field Orders #11, August 31, 1863.

37. Quoted in *History of the First Regiment Iowa Cavalry*, 232.

38. Ibid., 290.

39. "Condition of Texas," *New York Times*, March 5, 1866.

40. Forsyth endorsement to Custer statement of October 26, 1865.

41. E. Custer, *Tenting on the Plains*, 122–23.

42. Quoted in *History of the First Regiment Iowa Cavalry*, 272. "Bohoy" was a slang term implying a certain rascality.

43. E. Custer, *Tenting on the Plains*, 154.

44. Ibid.

45. Lothrop, *History of the First Regiment Iowa Cavalry*, 238.

46. Ibid., 240.

47. E. Custer, *Tenting on the Plains*, 157.

48. Lothrop, *History of the First Regiment Iowa Cavalry*, 241.

49. Ibid., 241.

50. E. Custer, *Tenting on the Plains*, 157.

51. Among others, they met former Monroe resident Colonel Groome, a hero of the disastrous 1813 Battle of Frenchtown, who had resettled in Texas.

52. E. Custer, *Tenting on the Plains*, 153.

53. *Southern Intelligencer* (Austin), February 8, 1866, 3.

54. Lothrop, *History of the First Regiment Iowa Cavalry*, 233.

55. "2nd Cavalry," in *A History of the Troops Furnished by the State of Iowa to the Volunteer Armies of the Union Which Conquered the Great Southern Rebellion of 1861* (New York: J. B. Lippincott, 1866).

56. Custer's name was one on a list of about fifty or so confirmed, including his old rival Judson Kilpatrick.

57. E. Custer, *Tenting on the Plains*, 72.

58. M. Quad [Charles Bertrand Lewis], "Army Letter," 1.

CHAPTER 20

1. Elizabeth B. Custer, *Tenting on the Plains or General Custer in Kansas and Texas* (New York: Charles L. Webster, 1887), 196.

2.   Marguerite Merington, ed., *The Custer Story: The Life and Intimate Letters of General George A. Custer and His Wife Elizabeth* (New York: Devin-Adair, 1950), 162.

3.   E. Custer, *Tenting on the Plains*, 195.

4.   GAC to EBC, March 18, 1866, in Merington, *The Custer Story*, 179.

5.   E. Custer, *Tenting on the Plains*, 195.

6.   Ibid., 198.

7.   EBC to Mrs. Sabin, May 1866, in Merington, *The Custer Story*, 182.

8.   Ibid., 183.

9.   Data below are from Mark G. Grandstaff, "Preserving the 'Habits and Usages of War': William Tecumseh Sherman, Professional Reform, and the U.S. Army Officer Corps, 1865–1881, Revisited," in *Journal of Military History*, July 1998, 521–45.

10. E. Custer, *Following the Guidon*, 282.

11. EBC in Arlene Reynolds, ed., *The Civil War Memories of Elizabeth Bacon Custer: Reconstructed from Her Diaries and Notes* (Austin: University of Texas Press, 1994), 49.

12. Quoted in GAC to EBC, March 12, 1866, in Merington, *The Custer Story*, 177.

13. Merritt was promoted to command the 5th Cavalry on July 1, 1876.

14. For Averell's brevetting to general ranks, see *Journal of the Executive Proceedings of the Senate of the United States*, vol. 14, part 2, 980, 982. Averell was reappointed to the Army by an act of Congress dated August 1, 1888, at the rank of captain. But Averell was by this time independently wealthy and sought the reappointment so he could serve as the assistant inspector general of the Soldier's Home in Bath, New York, and look after the welfare of the veterans who lived there.

15. "Letter from General Custer," *Freemont (OH) Journal*, March 2, 1866.

16. *House Reports*, 39 Cong., 1 Sess., No. 30, Pt. 4, 72–78 (Ser. 1273).

17. Custer to Andrew Johnson, August 13, 1866.

18. George A. Custer, "The Philadelphia Convention," *New York Times*, August 22, 1866.

19. *The Anderson (SC) Intelligencer*, August 30, 1866, 1.

20. *Marshall (MI) Democratic Expounder*, August 16, 1866, 1.

21. Custer letter quoted in *Washington (DC) National Republican*, August 27, 1866, 2.

22. *Columbia (SC) Daily Phoenix*, August 22, 1866, 3.
23. GAC to J. M. Howard, January 19, 1864, in Gilder Lehrman Collection #GLC09024; and "Maj-Gen Custer on the Punishment of the Rebel Leaders," *New York Times*, May 7, 1865, 2.
24. *Detroit Free Press* editorial quoted in *Hillsdale Standard*, September 11, 1866.
25. Custer, "The Philadelphia Convention."
26. Custer letter quoted in *Washington (DC) National Republican*, August 27, 1866, 2.
27. *Burlington Hawkeye*, August 31, 1866.
28. *Dubuque Herald*, September 29, 1866.
29. Gideon Welles, *Diary of Gideon Welles, Secretary of the Navy under Lincoln and Johnson, with an Introduction by John T. Morse, Jr.* (New York: Houghton Mifflin, 1911), 589.
30. "A. Johnson at Indianapolis," *Burlington Daily Hawkeye*, September 13, 2, and "The President's Tour," *New York Times*, September 14, 1866, 5.
31. John Y. Simon, ed., *Papers of Ulysses S. Grant*, vol. 16 (Carbondale: Southern Illinois University Press, 1988), 547.
32. Quoted in Garry Boulard, *The Swing around the Circle* (iUniverse, 2008), 160.
33. *Toledo Blade*, September 26, 1866.
34. Noted in *Burlington Hawkeye*, September 4, 1866.
35. "Amphitheatrum Johnsonianum," July 30, 1866.
36. Quoted in Boulard, *The Swing Around the Circle*, 163.
37. "Kicked by Political Friends," *Hillsdale Standard*, October 9, 1866.
38. *Papers of Andrew Johnson*, vol. 11, 314. Barns was something of a Judas himself. He later made common cause with the Radical Republicans to have himself appointed U.S. pension agent in Detroit.
39. "The Long Haired Custer," *Dubuque Herald*, November 1, 1866.
40. Petroleum V. Nasby (David Ross Locke), *Ekkoes from Kentucky* (Boston: Lee and Shepard Publishers, 1888), 100.
41. "Nasby's Last," *The (St. Alban's) Vermont Daily Gazette*, November 17, 1866.

CHAPTER 21

1. EBC to Rebecca Richmond, December 6, 1866, in "Mrs. General Custer at Fort Riley, 1866," Minnie Dubbs Millbrook, ed., *Kansas Historical Quarterly* 40, no. 1, Spring 1974, 63–71.

2.　Quoted in *Rutland Daily Globe*, April 21, 1876, 2. Maginnis served in the 11th Vermont Infantry regiment in the Civil War and later was a U.S. congressional delegate from the Montana Territory. He never actually fought Indians.

3.　Gibbon in Sarf, 53.

4.　"Gen. George A. Custer," *New York Times,* December 31, 1867.

5.　See generally, Edward M. Coffman, "Army Life on the Frontier 1865–1898," *Military Affairs,* Winter 1956, 193–201; and Major E. A. Garlington, "The Seventh Regiment of Cavalry: The Army of the United States" in *Historical Sketches of Staff and Line with Portraits of Generals-in-Chief,* Theo F. Rodenbough and William L. Haskin, eds. (New York: Maynard, Merrill, 1896), 251–52.

6.　"The Regular Army—Wanted, A Man," *Burlington Hawkeye,* September 24, 1868.

7.　Elizabeth B. Custer, *Tenting on the Plains or General Custer in Kansas and Texas* (New York: Charles L. Webster, 1887), 397.

8.　Robert M. Utley, *Frontier Regulars* (New York: Macmillan, 1973), 23.

9.　Theodore R. Davis, "A Summer on the Plains," *Harper's New Monthly Magazine,* February 1868, 298. Interestingly, Davis notes that there was no desertion among the black "Buffalo Soldier" regiments (305).

10.　In Stephen E. Ambrose, *Crazy Horse and Custer: The Parallel Lives of Two American Warriors* (Garden City, NY: Doubleday, 1975), 270.

11.　Pope to Sherman, August 25, 1865.

12.　"Condition of Texas," *New York Times,* March 5, 1866.

13.　Albert and Jennie Barnitz, *Life in Custer's Cavalry: Diaries and Letters of Albert and Jennie Barnitz, 1867–1868,* Robert M. Utley, ed. (New Haven: Yale University Press, 1977), 52–53.

14.　Kenneth M. LaMaster, *Forth Leavenworth* (Chicago: Arcadia Publishing, 2010), 40.

15.　For a useful narrative on the Fetterman massacre, see S. L. A. Marshall, *Cimsoned Prairie* (Cambridge, MA: Da Capo Press, 1972), 48–73.

16.　Pope to Col. T. S. Bowers, June 3, 1865.

17.　G. M. Dodge to Pope, August 2, 1865.

18.　"Reported Massacre by Indians," *Philadelphia Evening Telegraph,* December 27, 1866, 4.

19. GAC to EBC, May 2, 1867, in Marguerite Merington, ed., *The Custer Story: The Life and Intimate Letters of General George A. Custer and His Wife Elizabeth* (New York: Devin-Adair, 1950), 199.

20. *Anglo American Times*, May 18, 1867, 10.

21. *Anglo American Times*, May 25, 1867, 5.

22. Davis, "A Summer on the Plains," 295.

23. Barnitz and Barnitz, *Life in Custer's Cavalry*, 34.

24. GAC to EBC, May 2, 1867, in Merington, *The Custer Story*, 199.

25. *Bedford (IA) Southwest*, May 4, 1867.

26. GAC to EBC, May 2, 1867, in Merington, *The Custer Story*, 199.

27. Davis, "A Summer on the Plains," 298.

28. Barnitz and Barnitz, *Life in Custer's Cavalry*, 44.

29. Barnitz in Evan S. Connell, *Son of a Morning Star: Custer and Little Bighorn* (New York: North Point Press, 1984), 168.

30. Quoted in Utley, *Cavalier in Buckskin: George Armstrong Custer and the Western Military Frontier* (Norman: University of Oklahma Press, 1991), 50.

31. Barnitz and Barnitz, *Life in Custer's Cavalry*, 51.

32. Davis, "A Summer on the Plains," 298.

33. GAC in Merington, *The Custer Story*, 205.

34. GAC in ibid., 206.

35. Davis, "A Summer on the Plains," 301.

36. W. T. Sherman to John Sherman, in *The Sherman Letters*, Rachel Sherman Thorndike, ed. (New York: Charles Scribner's Sons, 1894), 289.

37. E. Custer, *My Life on the Plains*, 40.

38. Account in the *Boston Daily Globe*, April 15, 1873, p. 4.

39. *Philadelphia Evening Telegraph*, July 8, 1867, 1; Davis, "A Summer on the Plains," 303.

40. *New York Tribune*, July 01, 1867, 4.

41. *Anglo American Times*, July 20, 1867, 7.

42. *St. Cloud Journal*, July 18, 1867, 2.

43. *Philadelphia Evening Telegraph*, July 24, 1867, 8.

44. *Philadelphia Evening Telegraph*, July 22, 1867, 8.

45. E. Custer, *Tenting on the Plains*, 699, 702.

46. Parsons left the service in 1870 to become an Episcopal Minister. He died in 1878 in Memphis during a Yellow Fever epidemic after ministering to the dying and is recognized by the church as one of the "Martyrs of Memphis."

47. See General Court Martial of General George Armstrong Custer, 1867. Records of the Office of the Judge Advocate General (Army), Record Group 153, Publication Number T1103; National Archives, Washington.

48. "Gen. Hancock and the Indians," *Burlington Weekly Free Press*, September 6, 1867, 2.

49. GAC, September 26, 1867, USMA Special Collections.

50. "Soldiers have been sentenced to be branded, as well as marked, with D, both for desertion and for drunkenness. The mark has commonly been placed on the hip, but sentences to be branded on the check and on the forehead have been adjudged. Other markings imposed by our courts have been H D for Habitual drunkard, M for mutineer, W for worthlessness, C for cowardice, I for insubordination, R for robbery, T for thief. Sometimes also entire words were required to be marked as 'Deserter,' 'Habitual Drunkard,' 'Mutineer,' or 'Swindler.' The branding was done with a hot iron; the marking with India ink or gunpowder, usually pricked into the skin or tattooed." See Colonel William Winthrop, *Military Law and Precedents*, 2nd ed. (Washington: Government Printing Office, 1920), chapter 20, section 6.

51. "The Defence of Gen. Custer," *New York Times,* December 28, 1867, 1.

52. GAC, September 26, 1867, USMA Special Collections.

53. EBC to Rebecca Richmond, November 20, 1867, in Merington, *The Custer Story*, 214.

CHAPTER 22

1. GAC, December 2, 1867, USMA Special Collections.

2. Quoted in Shirley A. Leckie, *Elizabeth Bacon Custer and the Making of a Myth* (Norman: University of Oklahoma Press, 1993), 105.

3. Editorial from the *Adrian Michigan Times*, quoted in the *Defiance (OH) Democrat*, December 28, 1867.

4. GAC, December 2, 1867, USMA Special Collections.

5. See Minnie Dubbs Millbrook, "Rebecca Visits Kansas and the Custers: The Diary of Rebecca Richmond," *Kansas Historical Quarterly*, Winter 1976, 366–402.

6. Ibid.

7. *Harrisonburg Rockingham Register and Advertiser*, January 23, 1868, 3.

8. Trial coverage in "Gen. Custer Accused of Murder," *Fairfield Herald* (SC), January 29, 1868, 2.

9. Harney built a reputation as a fierce Indian fighter in the Second Seminole War and on the Plains. But he was an honest and fair man, and after his death in 1889 the Sioux bestowed on Harney the name "Man-Who-Always-Kept-His-Word."

10. "The New Indian War on the Plains," *Philadelphia Evening Telegraph*, August 29, 1868, 4.

11. Theodore R. Davis, "A Summer on the Plains," *Harper's New Monthly Magazine*, February 1868, 298.

12. "Letter from a Female Captive among the Indians," *Fremont (OH) Weekly Journal*, January 8, 1869, 1.

13. Theodore R. Davis, "A Summer on the Plains," *Harper's New Monthly Magazine*, February 1868, 307.

14. D. A. Kinsley, *Favor the Bold* (New York: Holt, Rinehart and Winston, 1967–68), 78.

15. In some respects it was similar to special operations successfully conducted during the Second Seminole War.

16. Forsyth's account of the fight is in his memoir, *Thrilling Days in Army Life* (New York: Harper Brothers, 1900).

17. Addison Erwin Sheldon, *History and Stories of Nebraska* (Chicago: University Publishing, 1914), 135.

18. Dodge to Pope, August 2, 1865.

19. Theodore R. Davis, "A Summer on the Plains," *Harper's New Monthly Magazine*, February 1868, 293–94.

20. Philip Henry Sheridan, *Personal Memoirs of P. H. Sheridan*, vol. 2 (New York: Charles L. Webster, 1888), 307, 297–98.

21. W. T. Sherman to Grenville M. Dodge, September 24, 1868, quoted in Robert G. Athearn, *William Tecumseh Sherman and the Settlement of the West* (Norman: University of Oklahoma Press, 1956), 224.

22. Robert Utley, *Cavalier in Buckskin: George Armstrong Custer and the Western Military Frontier* (Norman: University of Oklahma Press, 1991), 61.

23. GAC letter, October 8, [1868], USMA Special Collections.

24. Sherman to Hazen, September 26, 1868.

25. Sherman to General W. A. Nichols, October 9, 1868.

26. Quoted in Vincent Coyler, "Notes among the Indians II," *Putnam's Monthly Magazine of American Literature, Science and Art*, October 1869, 474–81.

27. Hazen to Sherman, November 22, 1868.

28. Keim's account of the events, based on his newspaper dispatches and follow-up research, was first published in 1870. DeBenneville Randolph Keim, *Sheridan's Troopers on the Borders: A Winter Campaign on the Plains* (Philadelphia: David McKay, 1885).

29. Ibid., 103.

30. *Anglo-American Times*, December 5, 1868, 78.

31. Albert and Jennie Barnitz, *Life in Custer's Cavalry: Diaries and Letters of Albert and Jennie Barnitz, 1867–1868*, Robert M. Utley, ed. (New Haven: Yale University Press, 1977), 215–16.

32. Keim, *Sheridan's Troopers on the Borders*, 113

33. Meder to Godfrey, November 27, 1927, Godfrey Papers, USMA Special Collections.

34. Custer AAR to Sheridan, November 28, 1868.

35. Sheridan, *Personal Memoirs of P. H. Sheridan*, vol. 2, 315.

36. See Vincent Colyer, "Shall the Red-Men be Exterminated?" *Putnam's Magazine*, September 1869, 372.

37. Frank W. Blackmar. ed., *Kansas: A Cyclopedia of State History, Embracing Events, Institutions, Industries, Counties, Cities, Towns, Prominent Persons, etc.*, vol. 2 (Chicago: Standard Pub., 1912), 177.

38. Elliott in Evan S. Connell, *Son of a Morning Star: Custer and Little Bighorn* (New York: North Point Press, 1984), 195.

39. Letter by Frederick Benteen to William J. De Gresse, December 22, 1868, reprinted in the *New York Times*, February 14, 1869, originally appearing (unsigned) in the *St. Louis Democrat*.

40. "Indian Relics," *New York Times*, June 13, 1869.

41. Letter by Frederick Benteen to William J. De Gresse, December 22, 1868, reprinted in the *New York Times* February 14, 1869, originally appearing (unsigned) in the *St. Louis Democrat*.

42. Meder to Godfrey, November 27, 1927, Godfrey Papers, USMA Special Collections.

43. Letter by Frederick Benteen to William J. De Gresse, December 22, 1868, reprinted in the *New York Times*, February 14, 1869, originally appearing (unsigned) in the *St. Louis Democrat*.

44. "Indian Treatment of Whites," *Vermont Daily Transcript*, January 9, 1869, 2.

45. *Memphis Daily Appeal*, January 4, 1869, 1.

46. "The End of the Indian War and 'Ring,'" *New York Times,* December 22, 1868, 6; and "Sheridan's Winter Campaign," *New York Times,* December 4, 1868, 4.

47. Sheridan, *Personal Memoirs of P. H. Sheridan,* vol. 2, 318.

48. *Anglo American Times,* February 13, 1869, 14.

49. "The Indians. Col. Wyncoop's Letter Resigning His Agency," *New York Times,* December 19, 1868, 3. Note that Wynkoop believed that any excesses on the campaign would be committed by Indian scouts and militia units, not by U.S. Army troops.

50. *Anglo American Times,* February 13, 1869, 14.

51. Nelson Appleton Miles, *Personal Recollections and Observations of General Nelson A. Miles* (Chicago: Werner,1896), 150.

52. Quoted in the *Anglo American Times,* April 26, 1873, 10.

53. Sheridan denied saying this, though witnesses claim he did. But Sheridan did not originate the expression. In May 1868, on the floor of Congress, Montana delegate James M. Cavanaugh said, "I like an Indian better dead than living. I have never in my life seen a good Indian—and I have seen thousands—except when I have seen a dead Indian." *The Congressional Globe: Containing the Debates and Proceedings of the Second Session, Fortieth Congress* (Washington: Office of the Congressional Globe, 1868), 2638. See also *Ohio Statesman,* June 4, 1868, 1.

54. GAC to EBC, January 1869, in Marguerite Merington, ed., *The Custer Story: The Life and Intimate Letters of General George A. Custer and His Wife Elizabeth* (New York: Devin-Adair, 1950), 224.

55. *Newport Daily News,* March 18, 1869.

56. *New York Times,* March 21, 1869.

57. See March 21, 1869, dispatch in the *Grand Traverse Herald,* April 15, 1869.

58. *Galveston Flakes Daily Bulletin,* April 8, 1869, 1.

59. *My Life on the Plains,* 241.

60. Custer's report in the *Galveston Flakes Daily Bulletin,* April 8, 1869, 1.

61. See report in "Official Report of General Custer's Late Campaign—Rescue of the Two Female Captives," *New York Herald,* April 3, 1869, 3. A detailed though dramatized account of these events is in Charles J. Brill, *Conquest of the Southern Plains* (Oklahoma City: Golden Saga Publishers, 1938), chapters 10 and 11.

CHAPTER 23

1. George Armstrong Custer, *My Life on the Plains. Or, Personal Experiences with Indians* (New York: Sheldon and Company, 1874), 20.
2. *Anglo-American Times,* July 23, 1870, 11.
3. Custer, *My Life on the Plains,* 37–39.
4. Quoted in Shirley A. Leckie, *Elizabeth Bacon Custer and the Making of a Myth* (Norman: University of Oklahoma Press, 1993), 122.
5. EBC to GAC, July 1873, in Marguerite Merington, ed., *The Custer Story: The Life and Intimate Letters of General George A. Custer and His Wife Elizabeth* (New York: Devin-Adair, 1950), 250.
6. Godfrey to Roe, February 28, 1918, Godfrey papers, USMA Special Collections. Godfrey continued, "I feel indignant over such lies and I've got to explode a little to get it out of my system, and this time you are the goat!"
7. GAC to EBC, 1871, in Merington, *The Custer Story,* 235.
8. Toledo Commercial report reprinted as "How the Generals Kissed," *Hagerstown (MD) Mail,* October 31, 1873, 1.
9. *Frank Leslie's Illustrated Newspaper* 37, no. 945 (November 8, 1873), 140.
10. Oral History Interview with Keith Wilson Jr., March 8, 1989, by Niel M. Johnson, Harry S. Truman Library, Independence, Missouri, 20–21.
11. Custer, *My Life on the Plains,* 191.
12. For details, see Richard G. Hardorff, ed., *Washita Memories: Eyewitness Views of Custer's Attack on Black Kettle's Village* (Norman: University of Oklahoma Press, 2006), 231–32.
13. See Jeffry D. Wert, *Custer* (New York: Simon and Schuster, 1997), 33–35 and 287–88.
14. GAC to EBC, February 13, 1869, Gilder Lehrman Collection #GLC06179.
15. Robert Utley, *Cavalier in Buckskin: George Armstrong Custer and the Western Military Frontier* (Norman: University of Oklahma Press, 1991), 46.
16. Larned quoted in George Frederick Howe, "Expedition to the Yellowstone River in 1873: Letters of a Young Cavalry Officer," *Mississippi Valley Historical Review,* December 1952, 523. Larned's description of Custer's orders is reminiscent of the reaction of officers and civilians at the Rumsfeld-era Pentagon to the ubiquitous directives known as "snowflakes."
17. Ibid., 524.
18. Manuscript in Godfey Papers, USMA Special Collections.

19. Interview with Sturgis, originally printed in *the Chicago Tribune*, reprinted in the *Army and Navy Journal*, July 29, 1876.

20. Benteen's disappointed Confederate father said he wished his son would die with the war's first bullet, and that ideally it would be fired by a family member.

21. Benteen letter to Theodore W. Goldin.

22. Comment by Robert M. Utley in *Life in Custer's Cavalry*, Robert M. Utley, ed. (New Haven: Yale University Press, 1977), 251.

23. Custer, *My Life on the Plains*, 21.

24. Ibid., 17.

25. Ibid.

26. Custer, *My Life on the Plains. Or, Personal Experiences with Indians*, 12, 16.

27. Reprinted in "General Custer on the Sioux Indian Problem," *Worthington (MN) Advance*, June 4, 1875, 1.

28. Custer, *My Life on the Plains*, 21.

29. Reprinted in "General Custer on the Sioux Indian Problem," 1.

30. Ibid.

31. Custer, *My Life on the Plains*, 17.

32. Ibid., 18.

CHAPTER 24

1. Alexis de Tocqueville had prophesied forty years earlier that the United States and Russia seemed "called by some secret desire of Providence one day to hold in its hands the destinies of half the world." Alexis de Tocqueville, *Democracy in America*, J. P. Mayer, ed., vol. 1, 413.

2. *His Imperial Highness the Grand Duke Alexis in the United States of America during the Winter of 1871–72* (Cambridge: Riverside Press, 1872), 47. Reports such as this led to rumors in Moscow that the Grand Duke had married a Russian woman in America against the tsar's wishes.

3. For Custer's time in Kentucky, see Theodore J. Crackle, "Custer's Kentucky: General George Armstrong Custer and Elizabethtown, Kentucky, 1871–1873," *Filson Club History Quarterly* 49 (April 1974): 144–55.

4. *Wichita Eagle*, April 6, 1876.

5. "On Receiving an Eagle's Quill from Lake Superior," *Poems of John Greenleaf Whittier* (Boston: James R. Osgood and Company, 1878), 141.

6. Randolph B. Marcy, *The Prairie Traveler: A Handbook for Overland Expeditions* (New York: Harper and Brothers, 1859), 234.

7. Letter of June 28, 1973, in David S. Stanley, *Personal Memoirs of Major-General D.S. Stanley, USA* (Cambridge: Harvard University Press, 1917), 239.

8. *The Petroleum Centre (PA) Daily Record*, August 5, 1872, 2.

9. Dodge, *The Hunting Grounds of the Great West*, 133.

10. Ibid., 131.

11. Ibid., 143.

12. Frank A. Root and William Elsey Connelley, *The Overland Stage to California* (Topeka: Crane, 1901), 33.

13. EBC to Rebecca Richmond, December 6, 1866, in "Mrs. General Custer at Fort Riley, 1866," Minnie Dubbs Millbrook, ed., *Kansas Historical Quarterly* 40, no. 1, Spring 1974, 63–71.

14. Ibid., note number 35.

15. *Philadelphia Evening Telegraph*, December 22, 1866, 2.

16. See Minnie Dubbs Millbrook, "Big Game Hunting with the Custers, 1869–1870," *Kansas Historical Quarterly*, Winter 1975, 429.

17. *His Imperial Highness the Grand Duke Alexis in the United States of America during the Winter of 1871-72*, 161. This book is based on stories published in the *New York Herald*. See also the account in "A Famous Buffalo Hunt," *Omaha Sunday Bee*, November 29, 1908.

18. *His Imperial Highness the Grand Duke Alexis in the United States of America during the Winter of 1871-72*, 157.

19. Quoted in W. L. Holloway, *Wild Life on the Plains and the Horrors of Indian Warfare* (St. Louis: Excelsior Publishing, 1891) 342.

20. *His Imperial Highness the Grand Duke Alexis in the United States of America during the Winter of 1871-72*, 161.

21. Buffalo Bill quoted in Holloway, *Wild Life on the Plains and the Horrors of Indian Warfare*, 343–44.

22. "The Imperial Buffalo Hunter," *New York Herald*, January 16, 1872, 7.

23. "A Rare Old Beast," *Leavenworth Weekly Times*, January 18, 1872, 1.

24. Quoted in Holloway, *Wild Life on the Plains and the Horrors of Indian Warfare*, 342.

25.   Buffalo Bill, *True Tales of the Plains* (New York: Cupples and Leon, 1908), 172–73.

26.   *New York Herald*, January 16, 1872, 7.

27.   Buffalo Bill, *True Tales of the Plains*, 174–75.

28.   "A Royal Buffalo Hunt," *Transactions of the Kansas State Historical Society*, vol. 10, *1907-1908*, George W. Martin, ed. (Topeka: State Printing Office, 1908), 576–77.

29.   Ibid., 577.

30.   Ibid.

31.   Ibid., 578.

32.   Ibid., 579.

33.   EBC diary entry of February 5, 1873, in Merington, *The Custer Story*, 247.

34.   "A Grand-Duke's Book on America," *Appleton's Journal*, Jaunary 10, 1874, 55.

35.   Buffalo Bill, *True Tales of the Plains*, 175–76.

CHAPTER 25

1.   For the official report, see D. S. Stanley, *Yellowstone Expedition of 1873* (Washington: Government Printing Office, 1874).

2.   "An Outrage," *Chicago Tribune*, March 23, 1873.

3.   E. P. Alexander, "Lee at Appomattox," in *Battles and Leaders of the Civil War*, vol. 5, Peter Cozzens, ed. (Champaign: University of Illinois Press, 2002), 927.

4.   Quoted in Stephen E. Ambrose, *Crazy Horse and Custer: The Parallel Lives of Two American Warriors* (Garden City, NY: Doubleday, 1975), 360.

5.   "Custer and Rosser," *Bismarck Weekly Tribune*, December 15, 1875, 3. See also Professor Phelps's short biography of Custer in "Notes on the Yellowstone XIII," *National Teacher's Monthly*, November 1875, 16–19.

6.   Larned in George Frederick Howe, "Expedition to the Yellowstone River in 1873: Letters of a Young Cavalry Officer," *Mississippi Valley Historical Review*, December 1952, 526.

7.   Letter of June 28, 1873, in David S. Stanley, *Personal Memoirs of Major-General D. S. Stanley, USA* (Cambridge: Harvard University Press, 1917), 239.

8. GAC to EBC, June 1873, in Marguerite Merington, ed., *The Custer Story: The Life and Intimate Letters of General George A. Custer and His Wife Elizabeth* (New York: Devin-Adair, 1950), 251–52.

9. *Boston Daily Globe*, August 19, 1873, 1. The article noted "the officers take Jamaica ginger as a substitute, while the men prefer pain killer."

10. GAC to EBC, June 1873, in Merington, *The Custer Story*, 252.

11. Larned diary, June 29, 1873, USMA Archives.

12. Ibid.

13. Stanley, *Personal Memoirs of Major-General D. S. Stanley*, 240.

14. *Dubuque Herald*, August 10, 1873, 1.

15. *Boston Daily Globe*, August 19, 1873, 1.

16. Stanley, *ersonal Memoirs of Major-General D. S. Stanley*, 241.

17. See M. John Lubetkin, *Jay Cooke's Gamble: The Northern Pacific Railroad, the Sioux, and the Panic of 1873* (Norman: University of Oklahoma Press, 2006), 135ff.

18. "The Yellowstone Country," *Boston Daily Globe*, October 16, 1873.

19. For Custer's account, see George A. Custer, "Battling with the Sioux on the Yellowstone," *Galaxy*, July 1876, 91–102.

20. Larned in Howe, "Expedition to the Yellowstone River in 1873," 532.

21. Custer, "Battling with the Sioux on the Yellowstone," 102.

22. "The Yellowstone Expedition," *Ohio Democrat*, August 29, 1873.

23. Manuscript in Godfrey Papers, USMA Special Collections.

24. Rosser to EBC, in Merington, *The Custer Story*, 261.

25. Stanley's official report, 6. See also an account of the battle in the *Janesville (WI) Gazette*, August 25, 1873, 1.

26. Custer AAR August 15, 1873, reprinted in *Boots and Saddles*. Also see Major E. A. Garlington, "The Seventh Regiment of Cavalry: The Army of the United States" in *Historical Sketches of Staff and Line with Portraits of Generals-in-Chief*, Theo F. Rodenbough and William L. Haskin, eds. (New York: Maynard, Merrill, 1896), 256–57.

27. "The Yellowstone Country," *Boston Daily Globe*, October 16, 1873.

28. Stanley's dispatch in *Daily New Mexican*, September 11, 1873.

29. "Home Again," *Bismarck Tribune*, September 24, 1873, 1.

30. Joseph Henry Taylor, *Sketches of Frontier and Indian Life on the Upper Missouri and Great Plains* (Bismarck: J. H. Taylor, 1897), 159.

CHAPTER 26

1. "Black Hills," *Bismarck Tribune*, August 26, 1874, 1.
2. The Army also agreed to close three forts along the Powder River, abandoning the Bozeman Trail. See Charles Francis Roe, "Custer's Last Battle," a monograph published by the National Highways Association, New York City (1927), 1.
3. "Custer Interviewed," *Bismarck Tribune*, September 2, 1874, 1.
4. Sheridan to Sherman, March 25, 1875. Reprinted in the *Indianapolis Journal*, March 27, 1875, 1.
5. Sherman quoted in the *Anglo-American Times*, June 25, 1874, 12.
6. Reprinted as "Gen. Custer's Military Expedition to the Black Hills," *Ohio Democrat*, August 21, 1874, 1.
7. Reprinted as "Custer's Anabasis," *Troy (IL) Weekly Bulletin*, July 23, 1874.
8. "Indians! Why Custer Follows the Red Man's Track," *Bismarck Tribune*, June 3, 1874, 1.
9. "Expedition Rumors," *The Bismarck Tribune*, August 19, 1874, 1.
10. "El Dorado," *Bismarck Tribune*, August 19, 1874, 1–2; and Forsythe's account in "Scenes and Incidents of the Black Hills Expedition," *Ohio Democrat*, September 18, 1874, 1.
11. "Custer's Raid to the Black Hills," *Anglo-American Times*, July 11, 1874, 6.
12. Ibid.
13. "Custer's Expedition to the Black Hills," *Anglo-American Times*, August 22, 1874, 10.
14. "Custer's Gulch," *Bismarck Tribune*, August 26, 1874, 2.
15. "Custer Interviewed," *Bismarck Tribune*, September 2, 1874, 1.
16. "Custer's Counsel," *Burlington Hawkeye*, September 12, 1874, 1.
17. *Hamilton Examiner*, September 24, 1874, 2.
18. On Sioux City, see "Black Hills," *Cambridge City (IN) Tribune*, March 25, 1875, 1.
19. Ibid.
20. "Black Hills," *Palo Alto (IA) Pilot*, April 1, 1875, 1.
21. "The Black Hills," *Burlington Hawkeye*, September 3, 1874, 3.
22. "Black Hills," *Bismarck Tribune*, August 26, 1874, 1.
23. Sheridan's letter was reprinted in "The Black Hills," *New York Times*, March 27, 1875, 2.
24. "Sheridan's Order," *Boston Daily Globe*, September 7, 1874, 4.

25. "Another Raid on the Red Man," *Boston Daily Globe*, October 23, 1874, 4.

26. "Black Hills," *Bismarck Tribune*, 1.

27. *Fort Wayne Daily Sentinel*, March 13, 1875.

28. After 1908, the whole area became part of Custer National Forest.

29. "Custer's Gulch," *Bismarck Tribune*, August 26, 1874, 2.

30. Reprinted in "General Custer on the Sioux Indian Problem," *Worthington (MN) Advance*, June 4, 1875, 1.

31. "The Black Hills," *Burlington Hawkeye*, September 3, 1874, 3.

32. Quoted in the *Anglo-American Times*, June 12, 1875.

33. See John D. McDermott, "The Military Problem and the Black Hills, 1874–1875," *South Dakota History*, Fall/Winter 2001, 188–210.

34. Quoted in the *Anglo-American Times*, June 12, 1875.

35. *Shenango Valley Argus*, August 14, 1875.

36. *Janesville Gazette*, May 22, 1875, 1.

37. See Watson Parker, *Gold in the Black Hills* (Pierre: South Dakota State Historical Society Press, 2003). Other notables on the mission were Calamity Jane Cannary and Moses Milner, a.k.a. California Joe.

38. *Oakland Daily Evening Tribune*, June 24, 1875.

39. *Sterling Gazette*, June 30, 1875.

40. *Oakland Daily Evening Tribune*, June 24, 1875.

41. "The Indians Protest," *Burlington Hawkeye*, September 12, 1874, 1.

42. "Another Indian Talk," *Washington Evening Star*, May 21, 1875, 1.

43. Ulysses S. Grant, *The Papers of Ulysses S. Grant: 1875*, John Y. Simon, ed. (Carbondale: Southern Illinois University Press, 2003), 122.

44. Quoted in John S. Gray, *Centennial Campaign: The Sioux War of 1876* (Norman: University of Oklahoma Press, 1988), 19.

45. Reprinted in "General Custer on the Sioux Indian Problem," *Worthington (MN) Advance*, June 4, 1875, 1.

46. "Senator Allison's Party: How Near They Came to Being Scalped," *Cedar Falls Gazette*, October 15, 1875, 1.

47. See Joseph Agonito, *Lakota Portraits: Lives of the Legendary Plains People* (Guilford, CT: Globe Pequote Press, 2011), 74; "The Indians: Heap Bad Indian Break Up Council," *Burlington (IA) Hawkeye*, September 28, 1875, 1; and "The Great Indian Council," *Washington Evening Star*, September 27, 1875, 1.

48. The Chicago Inter Ocean report was noted in "Winter Campaign Against Sitting Bull," *Bismarck Tribune*, November 20, 1875, 1.

49. *Bismarck Tribune*, November 20, 1875, 4.

50. "The Black Hills Country," *New York Times*, January 25, 1876, 1.

51. "Sitting Bull," *Bismarck Tribune*, January 19, 1876, 2.

52. *New York Sun*, June 4, 1876, 5.

53. *Fort Wayne Daily Sentinel*, March 13, 1875.

CHAPTER 27

1. Senate Executive Document no. 81, volume 1664, July 13, 1876.

2. F. W. Benteen, "An Account of the Little Big Horn Campaign," typescript copy, USMA Archives, 11.

3. "Prospective Trouble on the Frontier," *Burlington Daily Hawkeye*, December 23, 1875, 3. The article incorrectly reported that the two prongs would launch from Fort Lincoln and Fort Bufort.

4. "An Indian War Anticipated," *New York Times*, February 21, 1876, 1.

5. *Burlington Hawkeye*, March 1, 1876, 1.

6. *Janesville (WI) Gazette*, March 2, 1876, 1.

7. John F. McBlain, "With Gibbon on the Sioux Campaign of 1876," *Journal of the United States Cavalry Association*, June 1896, 139–48.

8. In an interview with the *St. Paul Dispatch*, General Terry was very open about this military movement. "Gen. Custer, with another strong and well provided force, will set out from Ft. Lincoln, for a co-operative movement, but it would be impossible for him to leave at the date fixed," he said. Reprinted in the *Palo Alto (IA) Reporter*, March 11, 1876, 1.

9. "The Position at Washington," *Anglo-American Times*, March 10, 1876, 9.

10. See Timothy Rives, "Grant, Babcock and the Whiskey Ring," *Prologue*, Fall 2000.

11. Reprinted in the *Anglo-American Times*, September 19, 1868, 11. The pro-Grant *Philadelphia Evening Telegraph* remarked that Custer and other Democratic-leaning former generals were found "in close company with ... Lee, and Beauregard, and Hampton, and Forrest, and almost every man of high or low repute who wore the uniform of grey." *Philadelphia Evening Telegraph*, September 11, 1868, 4.

12. The Senate voted 35 to 25 to convict, failing to achieve the necessary two-thirds majority.

13.   "Custer on the Stand," *Indiana Democrat*, April 4, 1876, 1.

14.   *Congressional Series of United States Public Documents*, volume 1715 (Washington: Government Printing Office, 1876), 570.

15.   "General Hedrick," *Burlington Daily Hawkeye*, April 20, 1876, 2.

16.   Ibid.

17.   *Congressional Series of United States Public Documents*, 12.

18.   "What General Custer Knows of Affairs on the Frontier," *Burlington Hawkeye*, April 5, 1876, 1.

19.   "General Custer's Testimony," *Burlington Daily Hawkeye*, April 18, 1876, 4.

20.   Ibid. Alexander McDowell McCook, USMA 1852, was a wartime volunteer and brevet major general who after the war served mainly in Texas, and at the time of the Belknap impeachment was a staff colonel and aide-de-camp to General Sherman.

21.   "Notes from the Capital," *New York Times*, April 7, 1876, 1.

22.   "Custer Contradicted by Merrill," *New York Times*, April 5, 1876, 1; and "A Slander Refuted," *Washington National Republican*, April 5, 1876, 1.

23.   GAC to EBC, April 8, 1876, in Marguerite Merington, ed., *The Custer Story: The Life and Intimate Letters of General George A. Custer and His Wife Elizabeth* (New York: Devin-Adair, 1950), 283.

24.   Ibid., 284.

25.   See *The Campaign Text Book: Why the People Want a Change; The Republican Party Reviewed, Its Sins of Commission and Omission* (New York: Democratic Party National Committee, 1876), 316–19. In the 1884 race, the Democrats presented Custer's father to a massive pre-election rally in Michigan to invoke the spirit and memory of the state's favorite son. *New York Times*, October 30, 1884, 2.

26.   "Lively Interview with Gen. Custer," *Bismarck Tribune*, March 8, 1876, 4.

27.   Orin G. Libby, ed., *The Arikara Narrative of Custer's Campaign and the Battle of the Little Bighorn* (Norman: University of Oklahoma Press, 1998), 58–59.

28.   A more detailed analysis of the question of Custer running for president is presented in the author's *Last in Their Class: Custer, Pickett, and the Goats of West Point* (New York: Encounter Books, 2006).

29.   For information and data on the elections cited, see Robert A. Diamond, ed., *Congressional Quarterly's Guide to US Elections* (Washington, D.C.: Congressional Quarterly, 1975). In 1872 the Democrats endorsed Horace Greeley,

the candidate of the liberal faction of the divided Republican party. But even with his party split, Grant won reelection with 55.6 percent of the vote, a 3 percent increase over his 1868 total.

30. See for example, "Tilden Out of the Contest," *New York Times*, June 23, 1876, 1.

31. "Lively Interview with Gen. Custer," 4.

32. For Hancock's political career, see generally David M. Jordan, *Winfield Scott Hancock: A Soldier's Life* (Bloomington: Indiana University Press, 1988), chapters 24 and 26.

33. "Lively Interview with Gen. Custer," 4.

34. GAC to EBC, April 8, 1876, in Merington, *The Custer Story*, 284.

35. See generally, "Rascalities of the Army Traders," *New York Times*, March 30, 1876, 1.

36. "A Report Which Gen. Custer Claims to Have Made Is Nowhere to Be Found," *New York Times*, April 19, 1876, 1.

37. "Gen. Custer and Gen. Merrill," *New York Times*, April 19, 1876, 1.

38. "Gen. Custer's Testimony," *New York Times*, May 5, 1876, 1.

39. GAC to EBC, April 1876, in Merington, *The Custer Story*, 289.

40. GAC to EBC, April 28, 1876, in ibid., 292.

41. W. T. Sherman to John Sherman, November 17, 1875.

42. W. T. Sherman to John Sherman, October 23, 1874.

43. GAC to EBC, April 1, 1876, in Merington, *The Custer Story*, 281. Grant went through three secretaries of war after Belknap: George M. Robeson, who was secretary of the navy, acted as war secretary *ad interim*, March 2–6, 1876; Alphonso Taft, March 8–May 22; and James D. Cameron after May 22.

44. Sherman in *The Papers of Ulysses S. Grant: 1876*, John Y. Simon, ed. (Carbondale: Southern Illinois University Press, 2003), 72.

45. Belknap in *The Papers of Ulysses S. Grant*, 60.

46. "Marriage of Lieut. Grant," *New York Times*, October 21, 1874, 8.

47. S. L. A. Marshall, *Cimsoned Prairie* (Cambridge, MA: Da Capo Press, 1972), 103.

48. Sherman in *The Papers of Ulysses S. Grant: 1876*, 71.

49. Robert Utley, *Cavalier in Buckskin: George Armstrong Custer and the Western Military Frontier* (Norman: University of Oklahoma Press, 1991), 162.

50. *New York Times*, May 6, 1876, 5.

51. Reprinted as "Custer's Grievance," *Burlington Hawkeye*, June 1, 1876, 1.
52. *Indiana (PA) Democrat*, May 4, 1876, 2.
53. Custer quoted in Sarf, 65.
54. *New York Herald*, quoted in the *Fitchburg Daily Sentinel*, May 12, 1876, 4.
55. Reprinted as "Custer's Grievance," *Burlington Hawkeye*, June 1, 1876, 1.
56. Quoted in L. G. Walker, *Dr. Henry R. Porter: The Surgeon Who Survived Little Bighorn* (Jefferson, NC: McFarland, 2008), 45.
57. Quoted in Utley, *Cavalier in Bucksin*, 163.

CHAPTER 28

1. Marguerite Merington, ed., *The Custer Story: The Life and Intimate Letters of General George A. Custer and His Wife Elizabeth* (New York: Devin-Adair, 1950), 296.
2. Tom Custer, quoted in ibid., 296.
3. GAC to EBC, April 17, 1876, in ibid., 290.
4. For information on the Sioux Campaign generally, see John S. Gray, *Centennial Campaign: The Sioux War of 1876* (Norman: University of Oklahoma Press, 1976); Wayne Michael Sarf, *The Little Bighorn Campaign, March–September 1876* (Conshohocken, PA: Combined Books, 1993); and Robert M. Utley, *Custer and the Great Controversy* (Lincoln: University of Nebraska Press, 1998); as well as other works cited below.
5. *Palo Alto (IA) Reporter*, March 11, 1876, 1.
6. Reprinted as "The Black Hills," *Titusville (PA) Herald*, March 28, 1876, 1.
7. Leander P. Richardson, "A Trip to the Black Hills," *Scribner's Monthly*, April 1877, 754. Richardson visited the area a month after the Little Bighorn battle.
8. *Nebraska Advertiser*, May 4, 1876.
9. Reprinted as "The Black Hills Gold Fraud," *Tiffin (OH) Tribune*, April 13, 1876, 1.
10. See for example, "A Vain Search for Gold," *New York Times*, April 30, 1876, 10.
11. *Bismarck Weekly Tribune*, February 23, 1876, 3.
12. "Custer Interviewed," *Bismarck Tribune*, September 2, 1874, 1.
13. Quoted in Evan S. Connell, *Son of a Morning Star: Custer and Little Bighorn* (New York: North Point Press, 1984), 106.
14. "Gen. Custer," *St. Cloud Journal*, May 11, 1876.

15. Peter Thompson, *Peter Thompson's Narrative of the Little Bighorn Campaign, 1876: A Critical Analysis of an Eyewitness Account of the Custer Debacle*, Daniel O. Magnussen, ed. (Glendale: A. H. Clark, 1974), 59.

16. Boston Custer to his mother, June 8, 1876, in Merington, *The Custer Story*, 300–1.

17. Custer quoted in Sarf, *he Little Bighorn Campaign*, 135.

18. In S. L. A. Marshall, *Cimsoned Prairie* (Cambridge, MA: Da Capo Press, 1972), 127. Also see J. W. Vaughn, *With Crook at the Rosebud* (Mechanicsburg, PA: Stackpole Books, 1994).

19. In Marshall, *Cimsoned Prairie*, 129. Henry barely survived the wound and continued his distinguished career, being awarded a Medal of Honor in 1893 for his heroism at Cold Harbor in 1864, rising to the rank of brigadier general and serving as military governor of Puerto Rico in 1898.

20. Terry quoted in Marshall, *Cimsoned Prairie*, 118–19.

21. See Anson Mills, *My Story* (Washington, D.C.: Byron S. Adams, 1918), 450.

22. Marshall, *Cimsoned Prairie*, 122.

23. Reno was a good friend of West Point washout and painter James McNeill Whisler, and joked with him that if Whisler made a career of the Army, no one would have ever heard of his mother.

24. GAC to EBC June 1876, in Merington, *The Custer Story*, 305.

25. Quoted in Gray, *Centennial Campaign*, 140.

26. Eyewitness conversation as related in Nelson Appleton Miles, *Personal Recollections and Observations of General Nelson A. Miles* (Chicago: The Werner Company, 1896), 204–5.

27. Edward C. Bailly, "Echoes from Custer's Last Fight: Accounts by an Officer Survivor Never Before Published," *Military Affairs*, Winter 1953, 176. See also Edgerly in Merington, T*he Custer Story*, 309.

28. Boston Custer to his mother, June 21, 1876, in Merington, *The Custer Story*, 306.

29. EBC to GAC, June 22, 1876, in ibid., 307.

30. GAC to EBC, June 22, 1876.

31. Quoted in Gray, *Centennial Campaign*, 151.

32. A. Ward, "The Little Bighorn," *American Heritage*, April 1992; Sarf, *The Little Bighorn Campaign*, 160; F. W. Benteen, "An Account of the Little Big Horn Campaign," typescript copy, USMA Archives, 1.

CHAPTER 29

1. Custer, "War Memoirs," *Galaxy*, March 1876, 319–20.

2. John F. McBlain, "With Gibbon on the Sioux Campaign of 1876," *Journal of the United States Cavalry Association*, June 1896.

3. Godfrey quoted in Wayne Michael Sarf, *The Little Bighorn Campaign, March–September 1876* (Conshohocken, PA: Combined Books, 1993), 175.

4. Diary of Troop Pat Coleman, USMA Archives.

5. Ibid.

6. Godfrey quoted in Marguerite Merington, ed., *The Custer Story: The Life and Intimate Letters of General George A. Custer and His Wife Elizabeth* (New York: Devin-Adair, 1950), 313. Godfrey later challenged the idea that June 26 was the predetermined date for the columns to meet. He said that if Custer had followed Terry's order to the letter, he would have been hard pressed to get back that far north by the twenty-sixth. He also pointed out that they had taken fifteen days' rations, of which they used less than a week's worth. Godfrey to Roe, February 28, 1918, Godfrey papers, USMA Special Collections.

7. Godfrey in ibid., 315.

8. "Custer's Last Fight," *St. Paul Globe*, April 26, 1897, 6. Custer wanted Porter to ride with his command group, but Chief Surgeon Dr. George Edwin Lord refused, thus saving Porter's life and sacrificing his own.

9. Marcus Reno led A, G, and M troops; Frederick Benteen led D, H, and K troops; Custer had C, E, F, I, and L troops; and B troop guarded the mule train.

10. Benteen quoted in S. L. A. Marshall, *Cimsoned Prairie* (Cambridge, MA: Da Capo Press, 1972), 138.

11. Edgerly in Edward C. Bailly, "Echoes from Custer's Last Fight: Accounts by an Officer Survivor Never Before Published," *Military Affairs*, Winter 1953, 173.

12. Letter to General Edward S. Godfrey, August 17, 1908, USMA Archives. O'Neill was Lieutenant McIntosh's cook. He later was a sergeant. He died in 1914 and is buried in Arlington National Cemetery.

13. "Sergeant John M. Ryan," *Hardin Tribune*, June 22, 1923. Ryan was first sergeant for Company M.

14. See testimony of Sergeant Edward Davern, F Company, 7th Cavalry, in *The Official Record of a Court of Inquiry Convened at Chicago, Illinois, January 13, 1879, by the President of the United States upon the Request of Major Marcus*

A. Reno, 7th U.S. Cavalry, to Investigate His Conduct at the Battle of the Little Big Horn, June 25–26, 1876 (Pacific Pallisades, CA: W. A. Graham, 1951), 286.

15. Custer historian Michael Donahue has done numerous site tests of the "hat waving" theory and concluded that the distances make the story impossible to believe. He points out that the story did not come from Reno but others. Correspondence with the author, April 3, 2014.

16. Reno in Merington, *The Custer Story*, 318.

17. Letter to General Edward S. Godfrey, August 17, 1908, USMA Archives.

18. "Account of Battle at Little Bighorn, by Two Moon," History Resource Center (Farmington Hills, MI: Gale Group) document number BT2352000951.

19. Reno quoted in Joseph Henry Taylor, *Sketches of Frontier and Indian Life on the Upper Missouri and Great Plains* (Bismarck: J. H. Taylor, 1897), 164.

20. "Custer's Last Fight," *St. Paul Globe*, April 26, 1897, 6.

21. Letter to General Edward S. Godfrey, August 17, 1908, USMA Archives.

22. Charles Francis Roe, "Custer's Last Battle," a monograph published by the National Highways Association, New York City (1927), 9.

23. Reno quoted in Taylor, *Sketches of Frontier and Indian Life on the Upper Missouri and Great Plains*, 164.

24. From an interview with W. A. Graham in 1922., published in "Come On! Be Quick! Bring Packs!," *Cavalry Jounral*, July 1923, and reprinted in W. A. Graham, *The Custer Myth: A Source Book for Custeriana* (Harrisburg: Stackpole, 1953), 287–94.

25. Kanipe in Sarf, 212.

26. John Martin, interview with Walter Mason Camp, October 24, 1908, Camp MSS, field notes, John Martin, folder 3, Lilly Library, Indiana University.

27. Ibid.

28. In Sarf, 213–14.

29. Edgerly in Sarf, 216.

CHAPTER 30

1. See generally, Richard G. Hardorff, ed., *Lakota Recollections of the Custer Fight* (Lincoln: University of Nebraska Press, 1991).

2. "The Custer Fight," *New York Times*, August 10, 1881, 2, from the Fort Yates correspondent of the *Cincinnati Commercial*.

3. "The Death of Gen. Custer: Sitting Bull Tells the Story of the Fight," *New York Times*, May 7, 1881, 3.

4.   "Another Story of Gen. Custer's Death," *New York Times,* January 7, 1883, 5, reprinted from the *Mile City (MT) Journal.*

5.   Letter by Frederick Benteen to William J. De Gresse, December 22, 1868, reprinted in the *New York Times* February 14, 1869, originally appearing (unsigned) in the *St. Louis Democrat.* A thorough attempt at reconstruction is in John S. Gray, *Custer's Last Campaign: Mitch Boyer and the Little Bighorn Reconsidered* (Lincoln: University of Nebraska Press, 1991).

6.   E. J. McClernand, "The Fight on Custer Hill," in Charles Francis Roe, "Custer's Last Battle," a monograph published by the National Highways Association, New York City (1927), 38. McClernand received the Medal of Honor for bravery at Bear Paw Mountain during the Nez Perce War a year after the Custer battle.

7.   Nelson Appleton Miles, *Personal Recollections and Observations of General Nelson A. Miles* (Chicago: The Werner Company, 1896), 290.

8.   Ibid.

9.   "Account of Battle at Little Bighorn, by Two Moon," History Resource Center, Farmington Hills, MI: Gale Group, Document Number BT2352000951.

10.   "The Story Told," *Worthington (MN) Advance,* July 20, 1876, 1.

11.   See Richard Allan Fox Jr., *Archaeology, History, and Custer's Last Battle: The Little Big Horn Reexamined* (Norman: University of Oklahoma Press, 1993).

12.   Hardorff, *Lakota Recollections of the Custer Fight,* 162.

13.   Miles, *Personal Recollections and Observations of General Nelson A. Miles,* 288–89.

14.   Ibid., 290.

15.   F. W. Benteen, "An Account of the Little Big Horn Campaign," typescript copy, USMA Archives, 9.

16.   W. A. Graham, "The Lost Is Found: Custer's Last Message Comes to Life," *Cavalry Journal,* July–August 1942, reprinted in W. A. Graham, *The Custer Myth: A Source Book for Custeriana* (Harrisburg: Stackpole, 1953), 296–300.

17.   Godfrey in Marguerite Merington, ed., *The Custer Story: The Life and Intimate Letters of General George A. Custer and His Wife Elizabeth* (New York: Devin-Adair, 1950), 318–19.

18.   Graham, "The Lost Is Found," in Graham, *The Custer Myth.*

19.   Gibson in Merington, *The Custer Story,* 316.

20.   Herndon quoted in Frances Fuller Victor, *Eleven Years in the Rocky Mountains and Life on the Frontier,* Part 2 (Hartford: Columbian Book, 1877), 51.

21. Godfrey to Roe, February 28, 1918, Godfrey papers, USMA Special Collections. Granted, Godfrey heard this secondhand from Benteen.

22. "Custer's Last Fight," *St. Paul Globe*, April 26, 1897, 6.

23. Ibid.

24. "A Talk With Sitting Bull," *New York Times*, August 7, 1881, 2.

25. The stand on Reno Hill compares favorably to the Battle of Rorke's Drift in the Zulu War, which would take place three years later.

26. John F. McBlain, "With Gibbon on the Sioux Campaign of 1876," *Journal of the United States Cavalry Association*, June 1896.

27. "The Custer Massacre," *Nebraska Advertiser*, September 21, 1876, 1.

28. McBlain, "With Gibbon on the Sioux Campaign of 1876." See also the press account reprinted in Major Sir Rose Lambart Price, *The Two Americas: An Account of Sport and Travel* (Philadelphia: J. B. Lippincott, 1877), Appendix C.

29. Gibson in Merington, *The Custer Story*, 317.

30. Ibid.

31. "General Custer's Last Moments," *Bristol (VA) News*, July 25, 1876, 1.

32. For detailed information on the locations of the bodies on the field, see Douglas D. Scott, P. Willey, Melissa A. Connor, *They Died With Custer: Soldiers' Bones from the Battle of the Little Bighorn* (Norman: University of Oklahoma Press, 1998).

33. H. W. Longfellow, "The Revenge of Rain-in-the-Face," *West Point Tic Tacs* (New York: H. Lee, 1878), 113–14.

34. See Charles A. Eastman, "Rain-in-the-Face: The Story of a Sioux Warrior," *Outlook*, October 27, 1906, 507–12.

35. Benteen quoted in Evan S. Connell, *Son of a Morning Star: Custer and Little Bighorn* (New York: North Point Press, 1984), 78.

36. "The Custer Fight," *New York Times*, August 10, 1881, 2, from the Fort Yates correspondent of the *Cincinnati Commercial*. Other accounts say that Custer had an arrow through his penis and a slash on his left thigh that may not have been visible to eyewitnesses who say that his body was not desecrated.

37. Ibid.

38. Ibid.

39. "Gen. Custer's Murderer," *New York Times*, February 12, 1881, 1.

40. "Survivor Tells of Custer Fight," *Washington Herald*, September 21, 1913, 7. Among other problems with the story: Custer was not carrying a saber that

day, nor was anyone else; "Curley" says the moment he described is portrayed in one of the famous Custer paintings, probably Otto Becker's wholly imagined *Custer's Last Fight*, which was distributed as a promotional lithograph by the Anheuser-Busch brewing company, and in which he is fighting with saber raised; and "Curley" said he was sometimes known as Bloody Knife, who was another person entirely and killed at Little Bighorn.

41.   Thomas B. Marquis, *Keep the Last Bullet for Yourself* (New York: Reference Publications, 1976).

42.   "Custer's Slayer," *Washington National Republican*, July 22, 1881, 1; and "Custer's Last Fight," *St. Paul Globe*, April 26, 1897, 6. In later accounts Sitting Bull claimed to have personally led warriors against both Reno's first attack and Custer.

CONCLUSION

1.   "General Custer's Burial," *New York Times*, September 13, 1878. See also Douglas D. Scott, P. Willey, and Melissa A. Connor, *They Died with Custer: Soldiers' Bones from the Battle of the Little Bighorn* (Norman: University of Oklahoma Press, 1999).

2.   "Custer's Last Fight," in *St. Paul Globe*, April 26, 1897, 6. See also Marguerite Merington, ed., *The Custer Story: The Life and Intimate Letters of General George A. Custer and His Wife Elizabeth* (New York: Devin-Adair, 1950), 320–21.

3.   "Custer's Last Fight," in *St. Paul Globe*, April 26, 1897, 6. Also Merington, *The Custer Story*, 321–23.

4.   Elizabeth Custer, *Boots and Saddles* (New York: Harper and Brothers, 1913), 255.

5.   "Montana Papers Got Scoop: Tribune Not First to Print News," *Bismarck Tribune*, July 6, 1976.

6.   Glazier, 229, 275.

7.   "The Causes and Consequences," *New York Times*, July 7, 1876, 1.

8.   "What Is Thought in Washington," *New York Times*, July 8, 1876, 1.

9.   "Another Ex-Confederate Offers to Avenge," *Bristol (VA) News*, July 25, 1876, 1.

10.   *Briston (TN) News*, August 15, 1876, 2.

11.   "Politics Run Mad," *New York Times*, July 8, 1876, 4.

12.   Grant quoted in Utley, 44.

13. Ibid.

14. Interview with Sturgis, originally printed in the *Chicago Tribune*, reprinted in the *Army and Navy Journal*, July 29, 1876. See also Sturgis in "Gen. Custer's Death," *New York Times*, July 17, 1876, 5; "Gen. Custer's Death," *New York Times*, July 18, 1876, 5; and "Sturgis on Custer," *New York Times*, July 21, 1876, 8.

15. Crittenden letter quoted in James B. Fry, "Comments by General Fry on the Custer Battle," *The Century*, January 1892, 387, fn 2.

16. George McClellan, *McClellan's Own Story: The War for the Union, the Soldiers Who Fought It, The Civilians Who Directed It, and His Relations to Them* (New York: Webster Publishers, 1886), 365.

17. Godfrey to Roe, February 28, 1918, USMA Archives.

18. Terry's communiqués were reprinted in the *New York Times*, July 7, 1876, 1.

19. Quoted in Charles Francis Roe, "Custer's Last Battle," a monograph published by the National Highways Association, New York City (1927), 34.

20. In 1967, the Army Board of Corrections reversed the decision of the court-martial, and Reno was reburied with honors at the Custer Battlefield National Cemetery.

21. See John S. Gray, "Nightmares to Daydreams," *By Valor and Arms, Journal of American Military History* 1 (Summer 1975), 30–39, for information on parties visiting the battlefield.

22. "Officers Who Died with Custer," *New York Times*, August 4, 1877, 5. Lieutenant McIntosh was later transferred to Arlington National Cemetery.

23. Quoted in *New York Times*, May 21, 1877, 1. Crittenden's remains were left buried where he fell until 1931, when they were relocated to the National Cemetery. His isolated gravesite was not being properly cared for, though the family was at first told it was because of a plan to relocate a road.

24. See "Gen. Custer's Remains," *New York Times*, September 1, 1878.

25. The spur is in the possession of the Virginia Historical Society. By coincidence, Santa Anna died in Mexico City four days before Custer, at age eighty-two, impoverished and forgotten.

26. Benny Havens died May 27, 1877, at ninety years.

27. The full story of the enduring mystery of the Custer statue is in *Last in Their Class*, 405–8.

28. "General George A. Custer," *Galaxy*, September 1876, 363.

29. "A Death-Sonnet for Custer," *New York Daily Tribune*, July 10, 1876, 5.

30. Walt Whitman, "Custer's Last Rally," *Specimen Days*. See also Robert Taft, "The Pictorial Record of the Old West. IV. Custer's Last Stand. John Mulvany, Cassilly Adams, and Otto Becker," *Kansas Historical Quarterly*, November 1946, 361–90.

31. Quoted in "Mrs. Custer's Army Life," *Atlantic Monthly*, September, 1888, 426.

32. Charles Godfrey Leland, *Memoirs* (New York: D. Appleton and Company, 1893), 333.

INDEX